# Paul's Faith and the Power of the Gospel

A Structural Introduction to the Pauline Letters

# Paul's Faith and the Power of the Gospel

DANIEL PATTE

FORTRESS PRESS    PHILADELPHIA

**Library of Congress Cataloging in Publication Data**
Patte, Daniel.
   Paul's faith and the power of the Gospel.

   Bibliography: p.
   Includes index.
   1. Bible. N.T. Epistles of Paul—Theology. 2. Paul, the Apostle, Saint.    I. Title.
   BS2650.2.P37          227'.06          82-7416
   ISBN 0–8006–1682–0                      AACR2

9605E82   Printed in the United States of America   1–1682

*A Franz J. Leenhardt, pour son 80<sup>ème</sup> anniversaire*
*et à Gabriel Vahanian*

# Contents

# Preface

THE FORM and the content of this book might at first seem to be at odds with each other. While it is an "introduction" to Paul written for students and for those without previous training in biblical studies, this work also attempts to make a contribution to scholarly research on Paul.

This book guides the readers through each of Paul's letters and thus provides an introduction to each letter; and yet a theme is developed as the discussion moves from one letter to another. The reading of each letter contributes to a progressive elucidation of the main characteristics of Paul's faith.

The readers might be surprised that this introduction proposes a *structural* reading of Paul's letters. The term "structural" evokes complicated and abstract figures, technical vocabulary—often termed "jargon"—and a disinterest in historical questions, but I have included only a few simple figures and have limited the technical vocabulary to a few terms (semantic universe, convictional pattern, homologation, dialogic level, warranting level) with which the readers will quickly become familiar. Structuralist terminology and theoretical models have been "translated" and expressed in readily understandable metaphors or parables. Finally, this structural reading takes into account—and indeed is based upon—results of historical, literary, and textual studies of Paul's letters.

In short, this book is both an introduction to Paul's letters and an introduction to structural reading; but it aims at contributing to the scholarly research on Paul in that it systematically explores neglected dimensions of his letters. Thus, far from being at odds with each other, the form and the content of this book are closely intertwined. Its presentation, format, and style have been dictated by its specific goal.

## AN INTRODUCTORY STYLE

The introductory style of this book is the direct consequence of its aim to elucidate the main characteristics of Paul's faith. When one studies the characteristics of a phenomenon, the hope is that the phenomenon might be compared and contrasted with similar phenomena. As a result of our study, one should be in a position to compare Paul's faith with other types of faith. The question is then, For whom is this book written? Who might want to compare Paul's faith with other types of faith? Biblical scholars might want to compare it with other types of biblical faith, but such a study might also interest people who are not specialists in biblical studies. For instance, students of world religions might wish to compare Paul's faith with the types of faith which characterize Eastern religions. Divinity school students might wish to compare the faith of Paul with that of major figures in church history or in the history of Judaism. And seminarians, together with pastors and lay people, might want to compare Paul's faith with the faith which characterizes contemporary Christian communities.

These considerations led me to write in an introductory style so that the book might be used in college and seminary-level classes as well as in nonacademic circles. Footnotes address issues that biblical scholars and graduate students might wish to pursue.

## A STRUCTURAL INTRODUCTION

The decision to write in an introductory mode presented me with a challenge, since I intended to use an approach which, so far, had remained very technical; as is explained in Chapter 1, a study of Paul's faith (rather than his theology) demands a structural approach.

My first attempt to write such a book (in 1972–73) was inadequate because of a weakness in methodology. A simplified structural methodology can be sound only if it is developed on the basis of a complete theory concerning how meaning is produced in and by discourse. Therefore, while gathering material for this book, I took time to study semiotic and structuralist theories and then to develop a detailed method of structural exegesis, first for the study of narrative texts (Daniel Patte, *What Is Structural Exegesis?* [Philadelphia: Fortress Press, 1976]; and Daniel Patte and Aline Patte, *Structural Exegesis: From Theory to Prac-*

*tice* [Philadelphia: Fortress Press, 1978]) and then for the study of didactic texts, such as Paul's letters (*Aspects of a Semiotics of Didactic Discourse: Analysis of I Thessalonians* [Urbino, Italy: Center for Semiotic Studies, 1980]). Only after this long methodological excursus was I in a position to develop simplified structural approaches which could produce sound exegetical results and which a reader could easily follow and use without prior acquaintance with semiotic and structural research. The simplified structural approaches applied in this book are rigorous enough for describing the *main* characteristics of an author's faith, even though scholars will want to verify the conclusions of such readings with the help of more refined tools.

In preparation for this book, I made detailed analyses of various Pauline texts by using the more technical methodology. These studies have not been included in this book, since they were used merely to test the validity of the simplified approaches.

## A PRESENTATION FOLLOWING THE DISCOVERY PROCESS

Using the simplified structural approaches, I chose to write this book as a presentation of the discovery process so as to invite the readers to participate in it. Had I presented the results of this research in a more systematic and shorter treatment, the conclusions would have appeared arbitrary and the readers would not have been invited to pursue this reading of Paul.

Since a person's faith can be viewed as characterized by a specific *system* of convictions (see Chapter 1), our task is to reconstruct this system on the basis of the elements discovered in the letters. In following the discovery process, our study is somewhat similar to the task of reconstructing a jigsaw puzzle without the help of a picture of the landscape it represents. At first, one can put together the pieces at the edge of the puzzle; they can be easily recognized because of their distinctive shape. Once this is done, one can begin to guess what kind of landscape is represented. Then, one discovers that some of the remaining pieces fit together. A tree, a house, an animal appear. But one does not yet know their respective places in the overall picture. If one perseveres, however, one discovers where they belong. Similarly, at first (Chapter 2), we shall identify broad features of Paul's system of convictions (of his faith). This will not allow us to reach definite conclusions, but it will raise specific questions which will lead us to consider aspects of Pharisaic Judaism, Paul's former religion (Chapter 3), and other features of Paul's letters. Discovering how these features are interrelated (Chapters 4 and 5) will lead us to raise other questions. Only as we reach the point where everything begins to fit together (Chapters 6 and 7) will the full implications of earlier observations appear. Chapter 7 (on Romans) presents the overall picture of Paul's system of convictions, and this is where the conclusions of our research can be found. The last chapter (Chapter 8) tests these conclusions by checking to see if they apply to other texts (1 and 2 Corinthians) and studies Paul's view of the church and of ethics in light of his basic system of convictions.

I chose this mode of presentation because it forms an argument which progressively provides the basis for my conclusions and because it helps the readers to become successively acquainted with the several structural approaches needed in this kind of study. Thus this book truly remains at the introductory level; it is an introduction to several kinds of structural readings.

## AN INTRODUCTION TO EACH LETTER

A structural reading aimed at elucidating the main characteristics of Paul's faith needs as its starting point an understanding of (a) the overall arguments of the letters, (b) the historical setting of the texts (so as to make sense of its many references to that setting), and (c) the nature of the texts, so it must avail itself of certain results of historical, literary, and textual studies. Therefore, our discussion of each letter begins with a presentation of results of historical, literary, and textual studies, that is, with a brief review of the issues traditionally treated in an "Introduction to the New Testament." Then each letter is submitted to one (or a few) specific structural reading(s) so as to elucidate various characteristics of Paul's faith.

Using this procedure, we can simultaneously introduce Paul's letters, introduce different and complementary structural approaches, and show the main characteristics of Paul's faith.

As a consequence of this procedure, however, our conclusions remain tentative and incomplete. All the structural readings (and not merely one of them) should be applied to each letter. For our purpose, these limitations are themselves an asset; the readers are invited to pursue their own readings of Paul's letters in order to verify, modify, or complement our conclusions. In this way, this "Structural Introduction to the Pauline Letters" will also serve as an invitation to read his letters.

## A STRUCTURAL INTRODUCTION TO PAUL

This book is also introductory in the sense that it does not presuppose knowledge of the extensive scholarly literature devoted to Paul's letters. In short, I have chosen to study Paul's *faith*. As is explained in Chapter 1 and further discussed in Chapters 2 and 6, Paul's faith should not be confused with his theology. Faith and theology are closely interrelated, but they involve very different kinds of "logic." This distinction has long been perceived (thanks to research in the history of religions) and has influenced Pauline studies from Wrede to E. P. Sanders and J. Christiaan Beker. Yet we had to wait for semiotic and structuralist research to develop a method of delineating the distinction between faith (the mythical logic of the "savage mind," to use Levi-Strauss's phrase) and theology (the logic of the rational mind), and also the perception of their interrelation in a discourse (theology and faith are interrelated as narrative syntax and semantics are), which are clear enough to be the basis for a systematic study of an author's faith.

In order to study systematically the main characteristics of Paul's faith, I had to raise specific structural questions which are different from those raised by most of the extensive scholarly literature on Paul's letters. Consequently, the readings of Paul's letters presented in this book cannot be in a constant dialogue with the many scholarly studies which endeavor to elucidate their theological dimensions. An argument concerning Paul's faith cannot be directly informed by, and compared point by point with, an argument concerning Paul's theology. These arguments deal with different issues, or approach the same issues from quite different perspectives. Thus, they must be allowed to unfold themselves independently of each other, before being compared with each other as entire arguments. In other words, the comparison of our structural readings of Paul's letters with the various "theologies of Paul," such as those of Baur, Beker, Bornkamm, Bultmann, Davies, Käsemann, Munck, Sanders, Schoeps, Schweitzer, Whiteley, and Wrede (to name only a few), would have to be carried out at the end of this book. Yet this would be an *appendix* as long as the book itself and would presuppose a knowledge of these works, and so it does not have a place in an "Introduction to the Pauline Letters." I envision such a discussion in a future publication.

Some short comparisons with other studies of Paul's letters are nevertheless helpful in order to show the points of convergence and divergence between our structural reading and other readings. I chose to discuss, primarily in the footnotes, some aspects of a few commentaries readily available in English, in order to highlight certain points or to take note of certain textual difficulties.

These remarks should help readers understand the main features of this book:

- It is an introduction to Paul, presenting each of his letters by dealing briefly with the usual introductory issues.
- It is an introduction to a structural approach aimed at elucidating the main characteristics of an author's faith; it presents several kinds of structural readings in succession.
- It is aimed at elucidating the main characteristics of Paul's faith and dealing with a neglected dimension of these letters.
- Because of the nature of this book, we will not be able to discuss in detail the interrelations of our conclusions with the results of studies focused on Paul's theology.

## A SYSTEMATIC STUDY OF PAUL'S FAITH

Allow me to emphasize once more that faith and theology are not directly comparable. Faith as characterized by a system of convictions should be distinguished from theology. If this distinction is not maintained, certain of our observations and conclusions will seem to be nonsense. For instance, our study will lead us to conclude that Christ and the kerygma are not at the center of Paul's *faith* (as system of convictions), but I do not deny that Christ and the kerygma are the very center of Paul's *theology*. This distinction between faith and theology will also be helpful in our study (see Chapters 6 and 7). Many passages in which Paul seems to contradict himself suddenly become clear when this distinction is kept in mind. And, as we shall see, Paul's use of central concepts, such as justification/righteousness, are greatly clarified when one understands that they function at two levels of Paul's discourse: the convictional level (the level of faith) and the theological level.

Another benefit of this structural approach is that it opens up the possibility of a hermeneutic. This elucidation of the main characteristics of Paul's faith compels the readers to compare their own faith to that of the Apostle to the Gentiles (even though our study does not deal with contemporary issues and remains purely descriptive). In such a confrontation our faith does not measure up to that of Paul. But what a challenge! For me at least, such a structural reading of Paul not only opens the possibility of a hermeneutic, but compels me to carry it through. It is hoped that patient structural exegeses (those presented in this book, as well as more detailed exegeses) will in some measure guarantee the validity of this hermeneutic.

This presentation of the main characteristics of Paul's faith will also challenge the understandings of Paul commonly held in scholarly circles. Nothing less than Paul's views of what was achieved by Christ's death and resurrection, of the church, and consequently of his authority as apostle are at stake, as becomes clear in Chapters 7 and 8. I have long resisted—or I should say, repressed—the conclusions toward which all my analyses were pointing. It is as if these structural readings have lifted a veil—often perceived by scholars such as Krister Stendahl—which was obscuring from the consciousness of the West (for how long? the church historians will have to say) a challenging and central aspect of the faith of the Apostle to the Gentiles. New Testament scholars will need to evaluate these conclusions. In so doing, they will need to assess critically my use of the structural methodology in the form of simplified approaches, and also to evaluate the structural methodology itself. But for the first time they will be able to carry out their assessment on the basis of substantial exegetical results.

### Acknowledgments

This book is dedicated to Franz J. Leenhardt, who at the University of Geneva taught me never to be satisfied with an exegesis which does not open the possibility of a hermeneutic; who patiently led my first vacillating exegetical steps; and from whom I learned so much about Paul's letters. His 1962 lectures on Romans 4 were, in fact, the starting point of a long pilgrimage which led to the writing of this book.

This book is also dedicated to Gabriel Vahanian, who honors me by his friendship—a constant source of encouragement in my work—and who, through his theological research, strives to prolong in our contemporary culture the difficult road proposed by Paul. His theology—

which simultaneously affirms the contemporary culture and takes an iconoclastic stance against it, emphasizes the present and points to the utopia—reminds me of Paul's own views.

This book bears the marks of the *Sitz im Leben* in which it was elaborated, the community of New Testament scholars of the graduate program at Vanderbilt University. Paul Aspan, John Jones, Robin Mattison, Edward McMahon, Gary Phillips, Karl Plank, Pamela Thimmes, Larry Vigen, and Larry Welborn have each contributed to the final form of this book through their comments, corrections, and criticisms of either a part of the manuscript or its entirety. Special thanks are due to John Darr, who has helped me improve greatly the English style of this work by patiently correcting it and reading it aloud with me. In the process he has also contributed to the content of this book through his suggestions and probing questions. His presentation of the chronologies of Paul, a valuable review of the main scholarly opinions on this complex topic, appears as the Appendix. My colleagues Professor Peter Haas (Jewish Studies) and Professor Volney Gay (Psychology of Religion) have kindly reviewed Chapter 3 and a part of Chapter 7, respectively. The Rev. Lewis Wilkins, Professor W. D. Davies (Duke University), my colleague Professor Gerd Lüdemann (New Testament), and John A. Hollar of Fortress Press have taken the time to do a close reading of the entire manuscript. Their numerous and quite different suggestions and questions have been invaluable in helping me strive to insure that this book will, on the one hand, serve the needs of the church (by the clarity of its style, its metaphors, and parables) and, on the other hand, comply with the demands of the more rigorous New Testament scholars (by accuracy of each detail of the exegesis). I attempted to satisfy all these critics, but this does not mean that I succeeded. I alone must assume the responsibility for the content of this work.

The preparation of this book has been facilitated by the knowledge that even a very difficult ("crassoté!") rough draft would be transcribed into an accurate manuscript. I therefore wish to express my gratitude to Barbara Gay, Pat Mundy, and mainly Josée Byers (who has typed the bulk of the text) for their diligent and devoted work in preparing this manuscript.

The writing of such a book demands time. Such time for research and writing in various locations was given to me by the University Research Council of Vanderbilt University in the form of grants that I gratefully acknowledge. But time for writing was also given to me by my wife, Aline, and our children, Murielle, David, and Chantal, who constantly encouraged me by their support and by their willingness to sacrifice the time I should have spent with them.

DANIEL PATTE
Vanderbilt University

# Abbreviations

| | |
|---|---|
| AB | Anchor Bible |
| *AJS* | *American Journal of Semiotics* |
| BNTC | Black's New Testament Commentaries (=HNTC) |
| *BJRL* | *Bulletin of the John Rylands University Library of Manchester* |
| *Bull.* | *Bulletin du Groupe de Recherches Sémio-Linguistiques (EHESS) Institut de la Langue Française (CNRS)* |
| *CC* | *The Christian Century* |
| CNT | Commentaire du Nouveau Testament |
| *ET* | *Expository Times* |
| GBS | Guides to Biblical Scholarship |
| *HTR* | *Harvard Theological Review* |
| Hermeneia | Hermeneia—A Critical and Historical Commentary on the Bible |
| HNTC | Harper's New Testament Commentaries (=BNTC) |
| ICC | The International Critical Commentary |
| *IDB* | *The Interpreter's Dictionary of the Bible.* 4 vols. Edited by George A. Buttrick and Keith Crim. Nashville: Abingdon Press, 1962. |
| *IDBS* | *The Interpreter's Dictionary of the Bible, Supplementary Volume.* Edited by Keith Crim et al. Nashville: Abingdon Press, 1976. |
| *JAAR* | *Journal of the American Academy of Religion* |
| *JBC* | *The Jerome Biblical Commentary.* Edited by Raymond E. Brown et al. Englewood Cliffs, N.J.: Prentice-Hall, 1968. |
| *JBL* | *Journal of Biblical Literature* |

| | |
|---|---|
| *JQR* | *Jewish Quarterly Review* |
| *LB* | *Linguistica Biblica* |
| LCL | Loeb Classical Library |
| NCBC | New Century Bible Commentary |
| NICNT | New International Commentary on the New Testament |
| PTMS | Pittsburgh Theological Monograph Series |
| *NTS* | *New Testament Studies* |
| *RSR* | *Religious Studies Review* |
| *RQ* | *Revue de Qumran* |
| *SB* | *Sémiotique et Bible* |
| SBL | Society of Biblical Literature |
| SBLDS | Society of Biblical Literature Dissertation Series |
| SBLSBT | Society of Biblical Literature Sources for Biblical Study |
| SBT | Studies in Biblical Theology |
| *Semeia* | *Semeia: An Experimental Journal for Biblical Criticism* |
| SNTSMS | Society for New Testament Studies Monograph Series |

# 1

---

# An Invitation to Rediscover
# Paul's Faith

AN INTRODUCTION to the Pauline letters. I take the subtitle of this book literally. This is an invitation to read Paul's letters, not the scholarly literature on Paul. I do not deny the validity of introductions aiming at reviewing the results of the research on Paul and their usefulness for those who want to pursue advanced studies of the New Testament. Indeed, I will suggest readings in scholarly works which are useful for a better understanding of one or another aspect of Paul's letters. But one should not forget that the goal of this scholarly literature is to help us read *Paul*. An introduction to Paul, although based on scholarly research, should not betray this goal.

So as to be an invitation to read Paul, my discourse needs to communicate the fascinating character of his letters and also to show how to read them responsibly. For this purpose I focus my presentation of Paul on what is for me a constant source of amazement: the faith of the Apostle to the Gentiles. This is a faith about which he can boast and which drives him both to proclaim the Gospel in the most adverse situations and to rebuke anyone (including Peter) who in his view distorts the Gospel. At the same time, it is a faith which makes Paul into the humble servant who has been "crucified with Christ" and who bends over backward to be the loving brother of sinners, Gentiles, Jews, and "weaker brethren." My hope is that a presentation with this focus will help the readers to become as fascinated as I am with Paul, so that they might want to read these letters over and over again.

In order to discover and appreciate what characterizes Paul's faith, we need to read his letters in a disciplined fashion. Because his faith structures his way of thinking and thus his way of writing, as well as his life and ministry, our reading will be primarily structural. It would be more accurate to speak of several readings, since we will elucidate characteristics of Paul's faith through a series of readings pursuing various questions. Historical questions will prepare the way for structural readings, which will be our main concern because they lead to an understanding of Paul's faith. Thus the subtitle of this book is "A Structural Introduction to the Pauline Letters."

Each of these readings will be presented as an example for the reader's own reading of any of Paul's letters. *This is an introduction to reading Paul.* Scholars will want to go beyond these readings by proceeding to detailed studies of the texts with the help of more refined methods. Despite their relative simplicity, however, the readings here proposed allow us to come to conclusions well grounded in Paul's texts. For this reason I will not attempt to give all the answers. To begin with, I do not have them and cannot pretend to understand everything about Paul's faith. More important, to do so would mislead the readers into thinking that they do not need to read Paul's letters beyond our present reading. I would then have failed in my effort to invite them to read Paul! This is why in this *introduction* I will be concerned primarily with formulating questions which should be raised for a proper understanding of Paul. I will propose interpretations of various passages in terms of each of these questions, but the results should be viewed as tentative conclusions which need further verification. Each conclusion should be thought of as a new question, that is, could this be a valid description of Paul's view? In other words, although I will provide adequate grounding for each of my proposals, they should still be viewed as invitations to read further into Paul's letters.

## ON READING PAUL'S LETTERS

This book is thus an invitation to a reading of Paul's letters aimed at elucidating the main characteristics of Paul's faith. But what happens when we read? What kind of reading is necessary for elucidating the characteristics of a phenomenon? To be more specific, what kind of reading is necessary for understanding what characterizes the author's faith? We need to address these issues before proceeding to our reading of Paul's letters.

## Reading as Seeing Dimly in the Mirror of
## Our Pre-Understandings

Reading is somewhat like a dialogue. Either implicitly or explicitly, the readers address questions to the text and the text gives the answers—or, we should say, the readers ask questions for which they find answers in the text. No reading is innocent. While it is not necessarily premeditated, it is nevertheless "pre-motivated." If we are willing to read these letters, it is because we expect to find in them something of interest to us. Even before beginning to read them, we have a pre-understanding of what we will find in these texts.[1] In our present human condition, we have no other choice but to see the text dimly in the mirror (1 Cor. 13:12) of our pre-understandings.

Paul's teaching helps us understand our situation as readers. Anticipating our discussion of 1 and 2 Corinthians, we can note that this situation is not desperate. Certainly, seeing in a mirror (in this passage a "dark" mirror, such as a polished piece of bronze which provides only an uneven reflection) is seeing a deformed image which can be misinterpreted. Reading with pre-understandings, we run the risk of misreading. But even this is seeing, and despite the deformed image, we are able to recognize it, if only approximately. It is not the total and immediate communication that we might wish for, but it is communication.

Actually, pre-understandings play a positive and necessary role. Without them no fruitful reading would take place. If we were not looking forward with anticipation for something in the text we would not read it, or we would be so bored while doing it that we would read "in vain" (to use one of Paul's favorite phrases). If I am eager to read Paul's letters and to invite others to read them with me, it is because, according to my pre-understanding, these texts deal with issues which I cannot ignore and provide answers which are particularly relevant. And this is the case whether or not I am always conscious of this pre-understanding.

Furthermore, having a pre-understanding of a text, that is, coming to the text with a question, does not in itself engender a misreading, provided that the question is legitimate, that the text, because of its nature, can truly be expected to have an answer for it. The problem is that any pre-understanding, even the most fanciful one, can motivate us to read a text. It is thus essential to verify that our pre-understandings—our questions—are legitimate. To this end we need to be aware of the type of questions we bring with us to the text, so that we can be in a position to ascertain whether or not the text can be expected to provide answers for them. Otherwise we will run the risk of subconsciously looking for answers to questions that the text cannot address and "finding" these answers by projecting them on the text. In this case no dialogue with the text takes place. We have enclosed ourselves in the circle of our own knowledge, which often leads to a misreading of texts. The conflicting interpretations of the Bible which surround us should be constant reminders of this danger: all of them cannot be valid.

Paul helps us understand the reason for these misreadings. In the text mentioned above, he emphasizes that "we see in a mirror dimly" and not "face to face," so as to rebuke "enthusiasts" who are "puffed up with knowledge" (cf. 1 Cor. 8:1–3) and boast about their knowledge. In Paul's view, this attitude which leads them to misunderstand the Gospel and to be trapped in their human wisdom results from their conviction that they see "face to face," perfectly. In fact, they deny their present human condition and its limitations. They pretend (and indeed convince themselves) that they do not see in a dark mirror even though they actually do so. Similarly, we risk entrapment in these circular misreadings whenever we pretend not to have pre-understandings. Enthusiastic readers who believe that they can understand the biblical text perfectly are tragically caught up in such misreadings, as are more cautious readers who, during the process of reading, lose track of their pre-understandings. The latter is easy to do, especially when one pursues several questions at the same time. In order to avoid such misreadings, we must strive whenever possible to be aware of our pre-understandings throughout our reading.

Two strategies will help us to do so. On the one hand, we shall formulate our questions as explicitly and as precisely as possible. On the other hand, we shall consciously focus our reading on one (or a very few) question(s) at a time. In this way, throughout the reading, we will remain as aware of our questions/pre-understandings as possible and, at least to a certain extent, will prevent the subconscious introduction of new questions. This means that we will have to perform several readings of a given text, rather than a single one following several questions. But in so doing we shall limit the possibilities of misreading. This does not mean that our readings will be perfect, however. We will need to keep in mind that our readings are like "seeing dimly in a mirror." Our readings provide only for somewhat approximate perceptions of Paul's teachings and views.

A variety of questions can legitimately be addressed to any given text, and therefore many valid types of reading are possible. For instance, it is legitimate to read Paul's letters so as to elucidate his views on certain ethical and philosophical issues, insofar as these texts deal with such issues.[2] Similarly, a philologist or linguist might want to study Paul's complex terminology, to show the specific way in which he uses it in comparison with the ways it is used in other texts;[3] it is clear that Paul uses certain Jewish and Hellenistic terms in his own way. A text critic might read these letters to study the textual problems they involve.[4] Indeed, these ancient letters reached us in the form of a number of manuscripts which are more or less dependable and differ on many points of detail. A literary critic might want to examine Paul's style and the literary genre of his writings,[5] since Paul's letters include rhetorical and stylistic devices, as well as "quotations" belonging to other kinds of literature (e.g., hymns). Historical readings of these letters are also possible; one can raise questions concerning the chronology of Paul's life,[6] the dates of the letters, their historical settings, the community life and the institutions of early Christianity, the theological conflicts which took place at that time, and so on. These questions address concerns about the development of early Christianity in a complex religious and cultural setting. Questions concerning Paul's theology (his Christology, his eschatology, his doctrine about the righteousness of God, his anthropology, etc.) can also be legitimately raised.[7] Even though they should not be viewed as proposing a systematic theology, these letters include many theological statements and are witnesses to the progressive development of Paul's theological thinking. Religious readings (such as devotional readings or study of the religious dimensions of the texts) are also possible, since it is clear that these texts express religious views.

These and many other approaches to the text are potentially valid, provided that the specific questions they bring to the texts are defined in such a way that the texts truly have answers for them. Because of our limitations, however, we can responsibly perform only a few readings, which are best done one at a time. We must therefore select some of them, or even one specific type of reading (as we often do spontaneously). This is not to deny the validity of other types of reading. Actually we will often have to call upon the results of other readings, because all of them are necessarily interrelated, since they elucidate different dimensions of the meaning of the same texts. Thus we shall not ignore the long and rich history of interpretations of Paul's letters. Nevertheless, I have chosen to focus on a specific set of questions concerning the religious dimensions of these letters.

## A Descriptive Reading

The primary goal of our reading of Paul's letters is to elucidate what *characterizes* Paul's faith. This implies that our reading will be aimed at providing a *description* of Paul's faith so that it might be compared and contrasted with other types of faith. Therefore it will be a scholarly study, a study attempting to be "objective" and "scientific" in the limited senses that these words have in literary studies (by contrast with their meanings in the physical sciences).

The question then is: how does one show what characterizes a text? That is, how does one show what distinguishes a given text from other texts? The answer is: through comparison. It follows that a descriptive reading with this goal cannot consider a text in isolation. The text must be read together with other texts with which it will be compared, or at least it must be read in such a way that this comparison might be possible. This demands specific attitudes toward the text.

First, such a comparative reading cannot allow itself to follow the text, nor can it allow itself to be absorbed by the text. The reader must look at the text from a distance, to be in a position to see other texts at the same time. In this sense such a reading can be said to be objective; the text is viewed as an object to be compared with other texts-objects.

Second, this comparative reading must be such that its results might be readily compared with the results of a similar reading of other texts. For this purpose, it is necessary to read a particular text in terms of categories which transcend both its specific features and those of the other texts with which it will be compared. This principle is actually quite simple, as the following example shows. One of the characteristics of Paul's writings is that they are letters, but we cannot fully apprehend what is so characteristic about that fact as long as we do not compare Paul's writings with other texts in terms of the broader category "literary genre." Assuming that we know exactly what a literary genre is, we are then in a position to determine the specificity of the literary genre used by Paul. For instance, the letter genre used by Paul may be contrasted with the literary genres of the Gospels, of sermons, or of other letters.

Note the steps involved in this comparative reading. A first step is the introduction of a category which transcends both Paul's letters and other texts. In our study we shall use the category "faith." A second step is the precise definition of this category, so that we will know what set of questions is to be addressed to the text. The third step is a descriptive reading which involves the elucidation of the specific way in which the phenomenon defined by the category is manifested in a text. At this point we will be in a position to compare the results of these readings and to show what characterizes Paul's writings at that level. Such a comparative reading is legitimate only insofar as the chosen category and the questions which guide the reading correspond to features actually present in the text.

My primary concern will be to provide a partial descriptive reading that the readers are invited to pursue. The comparisons will be limited to that of Paul's faith with Jewish types of faith as expressed in early Jewish literature. But if our description of Paul's faith is properly done, the comparison with other kinds of faiths, whether of Paul's time or of our own time, will become possible.

## Studying the Characteristics of Paul's Faith

First, we need to define as precisely as possible the category which will dominate our reading: the author's faith. How can the phenomenon called "faith" or "believing" be defined? What is the place and role of an author's faith in his or her writings? In other words, how is the author's faith manifested in a text? Can we even speak of faith as something which belongs to an author?

I choose to focus our reading on *Paul's faith* because, in my view, faith is the most central and fundamental dimension of a religion. Many things in a religion can change, but as long as faith remains unchanged, that religion endures. Theological formulations and doctrines, symbols and rituals, individual life styles, and community organizations can eventually be changed without affecting the "identity" of a religion as long as its faith remains the same. Conversely, even if most of the theological formulations and doctrines, symbols and rituals, life styles and organizations remain unchanged, when faith changes, the religion has lost its original identity. It is then another religion.

But how can one pretend to describe a faith? Is not faith a personal, indeed, intimate part of the believers' experience, even though shared with a community of believers? Is not faith a mysterious reality which moves the depths of the believers' being? Is not faith a fleeting happening which transforms darkness into light? Is not faith something unutterable, best perceived in silence? And when the believers themselves want to speak about their faith, are they not forced to speak about it indirectly, in symbols and images?

All this is true. The Gospel according to John expresses this mysterious reality of faith in striking terms: "The wind blows where it wills, and you hear the sound of it, but you do not know whence it comes or whither it goes; so it is with every one who is born of the Spirit" (John 3:8). Faith as such cannot be described. Yet the image of the wind suggests that it is nevertheless possible to describe what *characterizes* a faith. While we cannot directly perceive the wind, we can say much about it by considering its effects. By observing the clouds, the smoke of a chimney, the branches of a tree, we can tell its direction. From its effects on our skin, we can tell if it is cold or warm. With the help of the proper instruments, we can even tell its exact speed. So it is with faith. We can observe its effects or functions. We readily recognize, at least approximately, the types of faith that people hold by observing their behavior. The believers' faith affects their daily life if they are true believers. It affects their behavior in all the concrete situations in which they find themselves, but also the way they speak and, most important for our present purpose, the way they write.

This last statement might appear to be too strong. In our secular culture we are accustomed to seeing people "practicing their faith" on Sunday morning or on the Sabbath, and behaving the rest of the time exactly like those who do not practice a religion. Their "faith" affects only a part of their lives. I wrote "faith" between quotation marks because, in such cases, what we call (and indeed what they call) their faith is not actually their faith. If faith is a mysterious reality which moves the depths of the believers' beings, it cannot but affect their entire lives. I would even go further and say that whether or not someone is religious (i.e., practices a religion), one has a faith (possibly a secular faith, which would then be designated in nonreligious terms) which makes its imprint on everything one does. To put it in biblical terms, the question is not to know whether or not one is led by a spirit, but rather to discern by which spirit this person is led. Therefore, we conclude that we can study only the effects of a faith or its functions. On this basis the characteristics of a faith need to be established. Thus our definition of "faith" can be only a functional definition.

If at the present time we can undertake a systematic reading of Paul's letters aimed at describing what characterizes his faith, it is because appropriate instruments have been devised for that purpose. I am referring to the so-called "structural methods" of textual analysis. During the last two decades, a new field of research, semiotics, was developed, with the aim of better understanding the phenomenon of human communication in all its aspects. One branch of semiotic research made considerable progress toward the understanding of how discourse (oral or written, narrative or logical) functions. A. J. Greimas's work[8] is especially helpful in that it allows us to perceive the role (effect) of faith in a discourse (although Greimas does not use the term "faith"). On this basis, methods of analysis have been developed for a very precise study of what we have termed the effects of a faith upon an author's discourse.[9] These methodological tools are too sophisticated for our present purpose. They would demand a minute analysis of Paul's letters, and we would be lost in a mass of details which would hide the broader characteristics of Paul's faith. This is why I here use a relatively broad structural approach, a simplified method of reading which is derived from these more sophisticated methods. This approach will allow us to reach results which are sound, although they need to be verified through a more detailed analysis. This is another reason why my "conclusions" should be viewed as questions rather than definitive results.

Before proceeding with such readings, we need to define as clearly as possible the phenomenon we want to study. The semiotic and structural theoretical research helps us understand what faith is and how an author's faith is manifested in his or her writings.

## FUNDAMENTAL QUESTIONS FOR OUR READING OF PAUL'S LETTERS

Our reading of Paul's letters will be aimed at elucidating what characterizes his faith. In order to do that, we need to reflect upon the nature of faith as a general phenomenon. People have faith. They believe.

What does this mean? We shall proceed by successive approximations, first formulating broad questions, then the more refined questions.

### Believing and Knowing: Convictions and Ideas

Having faith and believing are, together with knowing and thinking, cognitive activities.[10] But we sense a profound difference between them. Believing entails having knowledge, but it also includes a type of knowing so peculiar that we need to make a clear distinction between believing and knowing. At first glance, the process through which we come to believe and that through which we come to know appear to be different. We associate the one with a church or synagogue setting and the other with a school setting.

This first observation is reinforced when we read Paul, especially 1 Cor. 13:8–13. In this passage Paul opposes "faith," "hope," and "love," which abide, to "prophecies," "tongues," and "knowledge," which will pass away because they are imperfect. Thus, for Paul, faith is not knowledge. Without here attempting to discuss the specific view of faith held by Paul, we can nevertheless note that he does not oppose faith and knowledge in terms of their content or subject matter. He closely associates knowledge with prophecies (cf. 1 Cor. 13:9–11). It is a religious knowledge, a knowledge received through revelations with both present and future aspects, and it is furthermore associated with ecstatic experiences, such as speaking in tongues. Faith, through its association with hope, is closely connected with expectations for the future. Note also that it is linked to a certain type of behavior, love.

Although we need to be cautious in our use of this text of Paul (due to the technical nature of the term "knowledge"), the opposition between faith and knowledge that the text suggests corresponds to a distinction that we can recognize in our own experience, even if Paul did not have the same situation in mind. One can know everything about a religion without believing in that religion. A scholar can eventually have a better knowledge of a religion than some of its adherents and yet not share their faith. Thus we conclude that believing and knowing do not owe their dissimilarity to their subject matter. They are different types of cognitive activities which can have the same subject matter. Therefore it appears that the difference between believing and knowing must be found in the ways they function.

Two other concepts, *conviction* and *idea*, will help us progress toward

a definition of faith. Conviction is closely associated with faith and believing, while idea is associated with knowledge and thinking. A clear
understanding of the difference between conviction and idea and of the
way they function, whether in religious or secular situations, will dis-
close the nature of faith, its role, and its place in an author's writings.
For indeed, *faith is nothing other than holding to a system of convictions or, better, being held by a system of convictions.*

A conviction and an idea can have the same subject matter, for instance, the view that God exists. Believers have a certain conviction
about the existence of God, but this view can also be a doctrine, an idea
that believers and nonbelievers alike may discuss and even hold as valid.
The difference between conviction and idea appears when we note the
ways in which this view is held to be true in each case.

For the believers, it is obvious that God exists. They are convinced
this is true. No philosophical or theological argument is necessary to
demonstrate it, and an argument demonstrating that God does not exist
does not affect their conviction, if it actually is a conviction. This observation is consistent with the etymological meaning of the term according
to which a conviction "imposes itself upon the believer as a self-evident
truth," as C. Loew[11] puts it. For the believers, God exists because they
"know" he exists. A conviction is a self-evident truth.

By contrast, the truth of an idea depends upon a demonstration. Thus
one can hold the idea that God exists, if one is satisfied with the validity
of a given philosophical or theological argument. But if the argument is
shown not to be valid, or is simply forgotten, the idea is no longer
viewed as true. Furthermore, the truth of an idea can be relative. It can
be "approximately," "possibly," or "certainly" true according to the relative validity of the argument upon which it is based. By contrast, a
conviction is "true" without any qualification.

### A FIRST SET OF QUESTIONS

Elucidating the characteristics of Paul's faith we are compelled to ask:
What did the Apostle to the Gentiles view as self-evident? What did he
take for granted and as absolutely true? Raising these questions will
involve us in an unusual attitude vis-à-vis the text. Normally when we
read we are concerned to take note of the ideas established by the text's
argument. This is quite proper, because Paul's letters, containing arguments, are meant to communicate ideas to the readers, for instance,

ideas concerning the proper theological stance or the proper Christian life. However, we need to focus our attention on something other than these ideas, namely, on the convictions that he also expresses in these letters. Because convictions are self-evident and because they cannot be demonstrated by an argument, they remain in the background of a discourse. A better understanding of the difference between convictions and ideas will help us formulate more precise questions to guide our reading.

## The Motivating Power of Convictions

The difference between ideas and convictions appears most clearly when we consider our relationship to them. We can manipulate ideas. They are building blocks for various types of discourses. We may string them together in a logical order to form a new argument. In this way we generate new ideas. We have power over ideas, but they have merely an indirect power upon us.

By contrast, convictions have direct power over us.[12] To begin with, they impose themselves upon us. We do not generate them, or at least we do not do so by means of logical arguments. At any rate, they are perceived as having their origin outside of us. They transcend us. Traditionally, believers have viewed convictions as revealed, as having their origin in the divine (a view which is consistent in that they are perceived as absolutely true). But those who consider themselves nonbelievers (e.g., agnostics or atheists) also have convictions. Even though they do not claim for them a divine origin, they attribute their convictions to a transcendent reality, for example, to Science or to the Scholarly Consensus.

Besides their power to impose themselves upon us, convictions also have power over us, that is, they cause us to act in certain ways. As we well know, convictions can drive believers to the most eccentric behavior. They readily suffer persecution and even martyrdom for their convictions, as many have through the centuries. Their convictions may drive them to give all their belongings to the poor and to go on perilous missionary journeys to convert the heathen, but they may also drive them to wage ruthless religious wars against those who do not share their faith. Without necessarily engendering such extreme behavior, convictions are constantly shaping the believers' lives in all their aspects. Convictions motivate, orient, and thus structure all the believers' activities, their behavior, their way of thinking, their way of speaking or writing.

By contrast, ideas alone, even the better ideas, are largely powerless to motivate us. Ideas do cause us to do various things and may also have power over us. But it is not the same power that convictions exert upon us, for the power of ideas derives from convictions.

Convictions and ideas have different and complementary roles in causing us to act. When people do something it is because the subjects of the action have been empowered to do so in two ways. First, their *will* to act in certain ways has been established.[13] This action is perceived either as desirable (i.e., as something which is interesting and even fascinating to do) or as something that one has to do because of its high value. In either of its forms, the will to act is established by the convictions held by the subjects.

But willing to do something is not sufficient to carry out a given action. *One also needs to know how to do it.*[14] Ideas establish this knowledge. A logical reasoning (a hierarchically organized string of ideas) establishes how to do it. Ideas determine the specific kinds of actions that the subjects need to perform in order to reach what their convictions have established as a meaningful purpose.

It appears that the meaningfulness of an argument and thus of its individual ideas depends upon convictions. It would not make sense to "plot" how to carry out an action if one was convinced that this action is meaningless or an evil to be avoided. It is a conviction which, on the one hand, *guarantees the validity of the argument* (the conviction guarantees the validity of the premises on the basis of which the argument can unfold logically) and, on the other hand, *establishes the will* to carry out what is prescribed by the argument.

### A SECOND SET OF QUESTIONS

These remarks suggest that in order to discover what is self-evident for Paul, that is, the convictions which characterize his faith, we will need to raise the following questions about each letter: What is Paul's motivation for writing it? What establishes his will to write as he does? In order to address these questions, we will need to focus our attention primarily on the overall argument of a letter, rather than considering in detail its various parts. But to do so, we need to acquire a more refined understanding of the way in which an author's faith is manifested in a discourse.

## Convictions Undergirding a Discourse

We have suggested that the validity and the meaningfulness of an idea depend upon its being involved in a logical argument, a hierarchically organized string of ideas. But such an argument can be so organized only if there is a principle of organization, that is, an anchor point, a certitude, a self-evident truth, or, better, a series of such anchor points, a system of convictions. Thus we can already suggest that a system of convictions—a faith—is what provides the principle of organization of an argument and that, therefore, it is not directly apparent. Because of its function, it *undergirds* the argument. It is manifested *in the way* in which the argument is shaped or structured, that is, *in the way* in which ideas are interrelated. And it might be added that this is true whatever the ideas involved might be.

Because of the close interaction between ideas and convictions, the same convictions may undergird arguments about very different subject matter. For instance, a specific conviction about the Christians' relation to Christ can be manifested in quite different arguments (as Paul does in his various letters), but the same ideas can be used in arguments undergirded by different systems of convictions. As the Gospel according to Matthew (7:21) expresses it, "Not every one who says to me, 'Lord, Lord,' shall enter the kingdom," that is, not everyone who says "Lord, Lord" has the true type of faith. Two arguments can speak about Christ as Lord, about the kingdom, and so on, and still be undergirded by different convictions.

### HOW CONVICTIONS STRUCTURE BEHAVIOR

Since convictions structure an argument and orient it in such a way that it expresses a knowledge which is ultimately useful in reaching what is desirable (as defined by the convictions), a convenient starting point for assessing the type of convictions held by a speaker is to consider how he or she behaves. The behavior of people shows most directly what is important for them (what they actually view as desirable); it might be difficult to perceive it in their discourses, especially when they are incomplete, as is often the case, or when they are voluntarily or involuntarily deceitful (e.g., hypocritical speech). In the Gospel according to Matthew, for instance, we find a warning against false prophets (Matt. 7:15–20). Their discourses are deceitful; they sound like true prophets and yet preach a false faith! Thus the question is: How should one recognize the false prophets? "You will know them by their fruits." In their behavior you can recognize what truly motivates them, that is, their convictions. Thus you can distinguish who among the various prophets has the true faith and who does not. This is a convenient starting point for investigating the convictions which in more subtle ways also undergird their discourses.

Paul also expresses that the believers' behavior manifests their convictions. In Gal. 5:22–23 he speaks of the fruit of the Spirit (love, joy, peace . . .). Being "led by the Spirit" (Gal. 5:18) is nothing more than having the convictions given by the Spirit. As we have already noted, convictions are perceived by the believers as revealed by God, here by his Spirit. These convictions from the Spirit have (or should have) power over the believers, who should be led by the Spirit and should "walk according to the Spirit," rather than carry out "the desires of the flesh" (Gal. 5:16). Following the "desires of the flesh" is following other convictions (see Chapter 2). Walking according to the Spirit is the same as submitting to the desires of the Spirit rather than to the desires of the flesh (Gal. 5:17). This leads the believers to bear the fruit of the Spirit rather than the fruit (works) of the flesh. Thus, without saying it directly, Paul implies that one can discern whether or not someone is inspired by God's Spirit (i.e., whether or not someone has the convictions or desires given by the Spirit) by considering that person's behavior.

Can we be more specific and ask what in a person's behavior manifests the convictions? What is the fruit of the Spirit? "Love, joy, peace, patience, kindness, goodness, faithfulness, gentleness, self-control" (Gal. 5:22–23). Here Paul does not list any specific activity, such as "giving money to the poor," but rather broad types of behavior. For instance, love can be expressed in many different actions and attitudes according to the circumstances, and yet in each of these actions or attitudes one can recognize love. Clearly the observer does not see the feeling "love," but rather a certain *pattern* of behavior which manifests it.

This observation illustrates a general principle: the effect of faith is that it imposes upon a believer's behavior a certain *pattern*, not that it dictates specific actions. Therefore, in order to recognize what characterizes someone's faith, we need to identify the characteristic patterns (or structures) of that person's behavior. This confirms our earlier suggestion that a system of convictions structures and undergirds an argument. We had also noted that the content of the argument (the ideas) is almost irrelevant for an understanding of the nature and role of convictions. This is confirmed when we note that it is not the "content" of the behavior which makes it "fruit of the Spirit." As Paul expresses it elsewhere (1 Cor. 13:3), giving away all that one has, and even giving one's body to be burned, are actions which can be performed without love, despite their apparent "love content." It is the form, the pattern, the structure of a behavior which manifest the person's faith. [15]

### HOW CONVICTIONS STRUCTURE PAUL'S LETTERS

We cannot study Paul's behavior to discern what characterizes his faith. We are not in a position to observe his behavior. We have only his letters, written discourses. They do include information about his life (his Jewish life, his conversion, his ministry as Apostle to the Gentiles, his interaction with the rest of the church, etc.). But these passages cannot be taken as if they were an observation of his complete behavior, the patterns of which we could then study. Paul tells his readers about this or that aspect of his experience in the context of arguments. His descriptions of his own behavior are thus shaped by their place in these arguments. At the very least, he chose to mention certain aspects of his experience and to omit others for the sake of the arguments. Consequently, despite the value and usefulness of the information he gives us, on the basis of these passages we cannot truly perceive the "shape" of his complete behavior. The historical conclusions proposed by various scholars are nothing but reconstructions, even with the use of rigorous historical methods. It is better to study the original sources, such as Paul's discourses, to elucidate his faith patterns. This is not to say that we will not take into consideration what Paul says about himself. These passages do manifest his convictions, but they do so in the same way as any other part of his letters. The way in which he retells his own story is shaped by his convictions.

For similar reasons, we cannot take into account the presentation of Paul's ministry in the Book of Acts. [16] Despite the historical information which it contains, and which needs to be taken into account for a historical reconstruction of Paul's life, this account is primarily Luke's discourse shaped by Luke's convictions. If we were to study it, we would elucidate what characterizes Luke's faith rather than Paul's faith, and there is no guarantee that the two are identical.

For our study of what characterizes Paul's faith, the only data available are his letters and the ways in which his arguments are organized. These manifest what has power to motivate him, that is, his convictions or, using his vocabulary, the Spirit which leads him. Consequently, there is no point in discussing a method which would allow us to study systematically how people's behavior manifests their convictions. Rather, we need to find out how we should read a text so as to discern the convictions which undergird it. So we will consider briefly the various ways in which convictions shape an argument. It is especially helpful to note that besides the convictions which establish what is desirable or prescribed (the good) and thus what is to be avoided or forbidden (the evil), there are also convictions which establish what is real (for Paul, for instance, the existence of God) and what is illusory (for Paul, that an idol has a real existence [1 Cor. 8:4]).

### HOW CONVICTIONS ESTABLISH WHAT IS
### DESIRABLE AND GOOD

We have noted that an argument can formulate ideas of what is desirable only if there is already something which is established as self-evidently good and desirable,[17] that is, if one already has a conviction about what one wants to do or be. Obviously this entails other convictions about what is evil and thus to be avoided (convictions about what one does not want to do or be). On the basis of these convictions, the argument can formulate a series of other things to be avoided. Similarly, and beyond our example, it is only if one has convictions about what is *prescribed* (or forbidden), that is, about things which one has to do (or which one should not do), that the argument can formulate other things which are prescribed or forbidden.[18] This also involves convictions about who (or what) has the authority to prescribe or to forbid on the basis of which the argument can formulate who or what else has this type of authority.

Only if arguments and individual ideas are based on such convictions can they be convincing, that is, be viewed as proposing or establishing courses of action which the subjects will perceive as proper and good. In saying this, I presuppose that any idea or any argument *ultimately* aims at causing us to do something, which might only be a very remote goal, as in the case of abstract philosophical arguments or of purely theoretical research. But even in such cases, it is hoped that the arguments being unfolded will provide the knowledge necessary to do the good that one wants to do, and to avoid the evil that one does not want to do or should not do.[19] Thus, abstract ideas and arguments themselves are convincing (compelling) only if they are perceived as properly based upon convictions which establish for the subjects the good which is desirable and/or prescribed.

### HOW CONVICTIONS ESTABLISH WHAT IS REAL

Ideas and arguments based upon this first type of conviction can be convincing, but this is not enough to insure that they will be convincing. Another type of conviction is also necessary. Arguments must be logical. Ideas are valid only if they are the results of logical arguments. To be logical, an argument must follow certain rules which govern the way in which a given statement (an idea about something) can legitimately be related to another statement (an idea about something else) so as progressively to form a hierarchically organized string of ideas, that is, an argument. But as we well know, two arguments, each with impeccable logic (i.e., strictly following the rules of logic), can be contradictory. They might be contradictory because they are based upon different convictions about what is desirable and/or prescribed. But this also happens when the arguments are in agreement on a point; we suspect that other convictions are at work. Indeed, the logical truth of an argument is based upon convictions about the reality[20] of the situation under discussion. These convictions are nothing other than particular perceptions of the relations between the things (concrete objects or abstractions) which are dealt with in the statements.

Consider the following example:

> Hence, as to the eating of food offered to idols, we know that "an idol has no real existence," and that "there is no God but one." For although there may be so-called gods in heaven or on earth—as indeed there are many "gods" and many "lords"—yet for us there is one God, the Father, from whom are all things and for whom we exist, and one Lord, Jesus Christ, through whom are all things and through whom we exist. However, not all possess this knowledge. But some, through being hitherto accustomed to idols, eat food as really offered to an idol; and their conscience, being weak, is defiled. Food will not commend us to God. We are no worse off if we do not

eat, and no better off if we do. Only take care lest this liberty of yours somehow become a stumbling block to the weak. (1 Cor. 8:4–9)

In this text Paul argues against the Corinthian enthusiasts. Their reasoning can be summarized as follows: "We know that an idol has no real existence. Therefore, food offered to idols is not really offered to another god and thus one cannot be defiled by eating it. We are free to eat it." Paul's argument is quite different: "Indeed, we know that an idol has no real existence, but there are believers who, although they have converted to the Gospel and the One God, do not have this knowledge and still perceive this food as really offered to an idol. In effect, while the idols have no real existence their power over weaker believers is a reality which needs to be taken into account. And thus it is better not to eat food offered to idols."

The logic of both arguments is clear, but they are based on two perceptions of the reality of the situation. On the one hand, idols have no real existence and thus have no power over Christian believers. On the other hand, idols have no real existence but nevertheless have a real power over the weaker believers. The perception of the *reality* of the situation and of the *necessary* relations in these perceptions of reality manifest convictions which undergird the logical arguments.

These observations can be shown to be valid for the logical development of any argument. It is always based upon convictions about *what is real* and about what is illusory (what seems to be but is not). Furthermore, this perception of reality involves convictions about what is *necessary* and what cannot possibly be. Different logical arguments can presuppose different convictions about what is real and about how "things" are necessarily related to each other.

But is not "what is real" the same for everybody? Of course, in a general sense it is. For instance, the reality of the human body is something that everyone can acknowledge, but it is perceived quite differently by different people. In our view the physicians know the true reality of the human body. Yet through the centuries this perception changed dramatically, as Michel Foucault has shown in his study of medicine during the last two centuries in the Western world.[21] And Western and Chinese physicians have quite different views of the reality of the body. Of course, we are convinced that the scientific view of the human body held by Western physicians expresses its true reality. To us it is self-evident, because we hold the conviction that Western science is conducted according to principles which guarantee a true knowledge of reality.

An argument is thus structured by two types of convictions: (1) the convictions which establish what is desirable or prescribed (the good) and what is to be avoided or forbidden (the evil); and (2) the convictions which establish what is real and thus necessary, as well as what is illusory and thus what cannot possibly be.

## A THIRD SET OF QUESTIONS

It now appears that the self-evident truths which motivate an author's writing are actually the two types of convictions we just described. Our reading should therefore be guided by questions concerning those convictions. What in this text is posited by Paul as real or as illusory? What relations are posited as necessary because of the reality of the situation? What relations are posited as impossible because they contradict the same reality? What is posited as good and desirable? What is posited as evil and to be avoided? What is posited as prescribed? What is posited as forbidden? Who has the authority to prescribe and who does not?

Note that the answers to these questions will provide us with only a *list* of convictions. These answers are helpful in elucidating what characterizes Paul's faith. Convictions are the stuff out of which faith is made, but such a list of convictions would not explain two striking features of faith. First, it would not explain the effect of faith upon a discourse. One should keep in mind that faith structures the believers' discourses as well as their behavior. We can suggest that convictions have this power because they are themselves organized so as to form a system. Second, it should now be clear that a faith can be manifested in a behavior or a discourse even when only a few of the believers' convictions are themselves manifested (as in the case of the false prophets whose faith can be recognized in their behavior). This suggests that what is truly characteristic of a faith is not the number of convictions or even the specific kind of convictions they involve, but rather the way in which the convictions are organized to form a system.

This is what we now need to understand by considering the implications of the fact that the convictions have to be viewed as forming a system, and that a part of a system of convictions can manifest a believer's faith as a whole.

## Faith as Convictional Pattern

SYSTEM OF CONVICTIONS AS
SEMANTIC UNIVERSE

In order to understand how a system of convictions is organized, we begin by noting how the convictions which establish what is good and those which establish what is real are interrelated. It is easy to perceive that these two types of convictions have complementary functions—two steps of a single process. Only after the establishment of what is real can what is desirable in turn be established. The convictions first establish what belongs to the realm of the real, by allowing the believers to sort out the mass of data provided by human experience in order to distinguish in it the real from the illusory. Then the convictions distinguish what is good from what is evil in the realm of the real.

Thus the believers' faith is characterized by a specific system of convictions which can be termed a *semantic universe.*[22] In this phrase, the term "universe" signifies that a system of convictions establishes a realm of reality in which the various elements of human experience are interrelated in a necessary way. The term "semantic" signifies that each element of this universe is perceived as having a specific value by comparison with the values of the other elements. An element can have the value good or evil as well as any value in between.

We may then say that having faith is living *in* one's system of convictions since it forms a semantic universe. Paul speaks of a life *"in* Christ" and *"in* the Spirit." We will need to examine whether or not this means a life in a semantic universe characterized by convictions about both the reality of and the high value of Christ and the Spirit. At any rate, the believers' convictional system constitutes the milieu in which they live.

In Chapter 2 we will discuss how a believer lives in a system of convictions. Here we simply note that a semantic universe is like the air we breathe. It surrounds us, and we take it so much for granted that most of the time we are not even aware that we constantly breathe it. Similarly, believers take for granted the semantic universe established by their faith. Most of the time they are not aware that their semantic universe keeps them alive by providing purpose and meaning for their lives, that is, by establishing the meaningful context in which it will be possible for them to find their identities. They are merely aware that this or that activity is fascinating, interesting, or worth pursuing, without being fully conscious of the origin of these feelings. They also act spontaneously in certain ways with the assurance that it is correct behavior, or organize their discourses (including their written discourses) because "it sounds right," because "it makes sense." They are not aware of the convictions which brought them to perceive the value and meaningfulness of these actions and which led them to choose these actions rather than others or those forms of argument rather than others. But whenever their semantic universe and therefore their faith is threatened, violent reactions are the immediate responses. Their life is threatened. Then one can observe emotional (panic-like) reactions, passionate pleas, and in extreme cases, persecutions of and even war against those who threaten the faith.

Faith is a mysterious reality because it surrounds us with a semantic universe. We cannot speak or think about our faith (our convictions) directly, because it provides the context for all discourse and thought, including discourse and thought about faith. And thus our discourses about our faith cannot but be tautological. God exists because I know he exists. It is self-evident. And thus we can only bear witness to our faith. Our discourses, whatever their subject matter, bear witness to our faith in that they take place in the semantic universe established by our faith.

### THE CHARACTERISTIC PATTERN OF A
### SEMANTIC UNIVERSE

The question then is: how does a discourse bear witness to its author's faith? Any given discourse (as well as any given aspect of somebody's life) *cannot* manifest the entire semantic universe which includes by definition all aspects of human experience (be they concrete or cognitive). A given discourse has a topic, a subject matter, which necessarily deals only with a small part of such a semantic universe. And yet it manifests the author's faith as a whole.

Another analogy might be helpful here. The semantic universe can be compared to the physical, natural universe. The natural world is a whole which holds together what might appear to be many disparate elements. The unifying factor is that all the elements of the physical world obey the same fundamental natural laws. The same laws are at work in a grain of sand, in a drop of water, in living cells, as well as in planets and in complex creatures. In fact, certain scientists strive to express these fundamental laws in a single abstract formula, that is, as a single fundamental law. For our purpose, it is enough to note that this single fundamental law would express how various elements of the physical world are interrelated. The natural phenomena are quite different from each other because they involve elements of various sizes and of various degrees of complexity. If the scientists are right, however, any natural phenomenon is nothing other than a specific manifestation of this fundamental law which can be expressed in "secondary" natural laws characterizing a given type of natural phenomenon. I called these other natural laws "secondary" because they are nothing else than the manifestations, in specific cases, of the fundamental law.

The same is true in the case of a semantic universe. In its entirety it is organized according to a certain fundamental law which characterizes a given faith. This law establishes the convictional pattern according to which all the elements of the semantic universe are interrelated. Whatever part of the semantic universe happens to be under consideration, it manifests this fundamental law, this same pattern. When various specific instances are considered, the relations will at first seem to be different because they deal with various aspects of human experience. However, by comparing those relations, one soon discovers that they are peculiar manifestations of the same convictional pattern.[23]

We can now understand how a discourse—such as any of Paul's arguments—bears witness to its author's faith. Whatever its specific topic, that discourse is organized according to the fundamental convictional pattern which characterizes the author's faith. It is undergirded by a limited number of convictions organized according to the pattern which characterizes the author's specific system of convictions.

## RELIGIOUS AND NONRELIGIOUS CONVICTIONS

Leaving aside the analogy of the physical universe and its (hypothetical) fundamental law, consider further how a system of convictions is organized. We commonly acknowledge that it is organized hierarchically; we view certain convictions as more basic or central than others. This is implied in the legitimate distinction that we make between "religious" and "nonreligious." Often we use the term "religious" to designate basic parts of the system of convictions in which the fundamental convictional pattern is *established*. Similarly, we use the term "nonreligious" to designate secondary parts of this system in which this convictional pattern is *applied* or duplicated. The semantic universe can thus be viewed as ever-expanding, framing every new situation and new experience according to the pattern of its core (the religious core).

This phenomenon reflects the process through which a semantic universe is established and constantly reasserted. The convictional pattern which characterizes a faith is first established around the elements of human experience which pose the most difficult existential problems for an understanding of the meaningfulness of human experience. For instance, what is the meaning and purpose of life since it ends up in death? For certain religions this is the fundamental problem. But now if in a system of convictions life is related to a God (e.g., if it is a gift of God the Creator), and death to eternal life (another gift of God the Creator), then life is no longer an absurdity ending in the nothingness of death. Note that these convictions involve a certain perception of the reality of life and death. In the above example, death is not actually perceived as really being the "end of life," but is somewhat illusory. These convictions also involve a perception of the respective value of life and death. In our example, since death is linked with eternal life, it is no longer an absolute evil, and consequently life is no longer an absolute good to be preserved at all cost. Such relations between life and death, perceived differently in various religions, are the central theme of many religious discourses (e.g., sermons) and religious rituals (such as funeral services and, in Christianity, the Lord's Supper and baptism). But the pattern thus established will also be found in the believers' secular discourses and activities. The elements of human experience which are associated (even though quite remotely) with life or death are interrelated in the same way as life and death are interrelated according to the believers' faith.

In other religions the central issue is that concerning the relationship of the human community to nature or other crucial problems posed by human existence, such as injustice and violence in a society. The convictional resolution of these problems establishes the fundamental convictional pattern in terms of which the entire semantic universe is organized.

Convictions about life and death and about nature and culture[24] are usually part of the cluster of fundamental convictions which establish the characteristic convictional pattern of a faith, even though we most often designate a faith by making reference to only one distinctive conviction which is a part of this cluster. Thus we speak of a Christ-centered faith, of a Scripture-centered faith, or of an eschatological faith (focused on a conviction about the end of time). But these designations are only approximations. The truly characteristic feature of a faith is the pattern formed by the interrelation of convictions in a cluster. In fact, as we shall see, the convictions are defined by their interrelations. Therefore, for instance, we will need to speak of different types of Christ-centered faith. Several faiths have a conviction about Christ in their clusters of fundamental convictions, but in each this conviction has a different place and role, and consequently the conviction about Christ is defined in a different way each time.

Thus a faith first posits a cluster of basic convictions which resolve an existential problem or, more positively, establish the meaningfulness of an essential aspect of human experience, what is real and illusory, good or evil in it. In this way, a pattern of relations among a series of elements of human experience (which includes the divine in most religions) is established. Then this pattern is applied to the rest of human experience. A meaningful and purposeful life can be envisioned only if the rest of human experience is (or at least can potentially be) perceived according to this pattern. Thus our entire semantic universe is structured by this pattern. But if one's daily life does not corroborate it, the validity of this pattern—that is, how it defines what is real and good—cannot be maintained. The believers lose their faith, and their entire semantic universe progressively crumbles. As long as such people do not have a new system of convictions, they find themselves faced with a meaningless life.

In a religion, the network of basic convictions is again and again "re-presented" to the believers so that they might be in a position to apply this convictional pattern to all the aspects of their experience, including new situations and new ideas, even though they might involve matters which are far removed from the "religious" subject matter. This is why we can say that a system of convictions is ever-expanding and that, whatever its subject matter, any set of convictions manifests what characterizes a given faith, a specific convictional pattern.

## A FOURTH SET OF QUESTIONS

It follows that in order to elucidate the characteristics of Paul's faith, we need to raise the question: what is the convictional pattern which undergirds his arguments? In order to address this multifold question, our reading needs to identify the convictions which undergird each letter or argument and then to study their interrelations. Whatever might be their subject matter (e.g., Christ, the church, or concrete situations), convictions are opposed in pairs as real is opposed to illusory or as good is opposed to evil. But they are also correlated with each other. For instance, we have suggested that a conviction about life could be correlated to a conviction about God the Creator. We therefore need to demonstrate how convictions form a cluster characterized by a certain pattern of relations. In each specific text of Paul's letters, we will find a specific cluster of convictions. In certain passages, it concerns "theological" subjects (e.g., God, the "world," Christ, sinners, grace, the works of the Law). In other passages, it concerns the daily life of the Christian communities (e.g., money, food, family matters, political issues). At first, these clusters will seem quite different from each other, but a closer examination will show similarities in the pattern which characterize each cluster. In this way we will see the characteristics of Paul's faith, that is, his distinctive way of interrelating the various elements of human experience. We shall see, for instance, that the relation Paul perceives between God and human beings has a pattern similar to the relation he sees between the Christian communities and the Jewish and Hellenistic cultures, and similar to the relation among the Christian believers in their community life.

Thus, our reading will constantly raise questions concerning *relations* among sections of Paul's letters, rather than asking what these units mean in and of themselves. These relations manifest what characterizes Paul's faith and also define his convictions.

The four sets of questions we have formulated throughout this chapter demand that we adopt a specific attitude toward Paul's letters so that we can elucidate the characteristics of his faith:

1. Our reading needs to be focused upon what is self-evident for Paul, that is, not upon what Paul wanted to say (his ideas) but rather upon what he took for granted.

2. Our reading needs to be focused upon what motivated Paul to develop his argument as he did. This necessitates a careful study of how the entire argument of a letter unfolds. So we will begin by attempting to understand an argument as a whole. On this basis specific concepts, phrases, or parts of the argument will then be investigated. This approach is to be contrasted with other ap-

proaches which begin by studying the discrete elements of Paul's writings and then seek to understand the overall argument on this basis. The overall information (set of ideas) of a text might be viewed as the sum of its parts, but convictions can be understood only as parts interrelated in a whole (a system manifested by the entire argument).

3. Our reading will try to show what the author posits as real, illusory, good, evil, and so on. For this purpose, we will need to show upon what Paul focuses his attention. What, in his letters, is posited as guaranteeing the validity of his arguments? For this we will need to investigate the relative weight, importance, and role given to various parts of the arguments.

4. Finally, our reading will be focused upon "relations," so that the convictional pattern characteristic of Paul's faith can be established. This also entails the elucidation of what could be called the convictional logic (by contrast to the argumentative logic) at work in a discourse (see Chapter 2).

Such are the general features of our attempt to elucidate Paul's type of faith. More specific questions, prompted by the varied character of Paul's letters, will be addressed in our discussion of given texts, but these remarks should suggest the kind of reading we will perform. We will be reading Paul in this unusual way because we want to consider an aspect of Paul's letters which is most often neglected. Our reading will enable us to show what characterizes Paul's faith in a way that it can be compared and contrasted with other types of faith, so that changing our reading habits will have been worthwhile.

## OUR READING OF THE PAULINE CORPUS

The letters in the Pauline corpus have different subject matter. Each addresses a specific situation as it relates to a given community (or person, in the case of the letter to Philemon). They exhibit different stages of theological reflection, showing the development of Paul's thought during his ministry. But we can assume that they manifest the same faith, that is, the same convictional pattern, provided that during the period in which he wrote these letters Paul did not "convert" from one type of faith to another.

When we acknowledge the power of a system of convictions and that in a conversion a semantic universe crumbles (a dramatic experience whether it is sudden or progressive) before another one can take its place, we must conclude on the basis of our reading that Paul's faith did not change in the period during which he wrote his letters. Throughout this period he saw himself as "apostle to the Gentiles." He had certainly "grown in" that faith. Now we understand what this means. Growing in a faith means that one expands his or her semantic universe so that a larger part of experience is viewed in terms of the convictional pattern of one's faith. Therefore we can surmise that all of Paul's letters manifest the same type of faith—assuming, of course, that they were indeed written by him.

New Testament scholars have raised questions concerning whether or not Paul authored several of the letters attributed to him in the New Testament. For various reasons, some quite convincing, others more debatable, it has been claimed that Ephesians, Colossians, 2 Thessalonians, 1 and 2 Timothy, and Titus were written by Paul's disciples in his name rather than by Paul himself. On the other hand, that Paul authored Romans, 1 and 2 Corinthians, Galatians, Philippians, 1 Thessalonians, and Philemon is universally unquestioned. One should consult the standard handbooks on such introductory questions.[25] We shall devote our entire study to these seven letters, leaving aside the letters whose authorship is debated.

Our reading of the Pauline corpus will be devoted to the seven letters, which we now list in the order in which they will be studied: Galatians, 1 Thessalonians, Philippians, Philemon, Romans, and 1 and 2 Corinthians. Furthermore, our study will focus upon Paul's own discourse. This means that we shall not study the traditions that Paul uses in his letters (such as the hymn in Phil. 2:6–11 or the tradition he quotes in 1 Cor. 15:3–7) in and of themselves. Our goal is not to elucidate the systems of convictions expressed in these traditions before Paul used them. In his letters these traditions are fully integrated into Paul's own discourse and in the process reinterpreted so as to participate in expressing his own system of convictions together with the rest of his discourse. We aim to show how Paul interrelates these traditions with the other elements of his discourse. Our study will benefit from the numerous studies devoted to elucidating the original meaning of these traditions and other historical studies of Paul's letters, but the questions we will pursue are different from those raised by many of these previous studies.

Similarly, our goal is not to follow the development of Paul's thought and missionary activity, but rather to elucidate the system of convictions (and its specific convictional pattern) that provided the framework within which his thought and activity could meaningfully unfold. Therefore, our study of Paul's letters need not follow their chronological order, which at any rate is difficult to establish with precision, as shown by the diversity of views held by scholars (see "Appendix: Chronologies of Paul"). Our study will involve a series of readings focused on specific questions which will allow us to elucidate progressively Paul's system of convictions and its pattern. This means that we shall successively consider various "clusters of convictions"—central themes found in specific parts of the letters—the examination of which will allow us to apprehend how Paul's faith holds together his various perceptions of human nature, of society and culture, of the world and history, of other religions and their relationship to the gospel, as well as his view of the church and the Christian life in relation to God, to Christ Jesus, to the Spirit, and to Scripture.

Each of these themes may be found in almost any one of the letters, yet a given letter often expresses one theme more directly than others. Our study of each letter will therefore include, after an examination of its overall argument, a more detailed discussion of one or several of its main themes. To avoid repetition, we will not study the same theme (themes) in each letter. Rather, we will incorporate in our discussion of a given letter references to the expression of this theme in other letters. A reading focused on a specific theme will deal only with that part of the letter in which it is expressed. We shall read the letters in the order which makes it easier to understand these themes and therefore what characterizes Paul's faith.

## SUGGESTIONS FOR FURTHER READING

The understanding of faith as system of convictions (in contrast to ideas) is based upon structural and semiotic research on human communication. Because this research has in the last few years reached the point where an overall theory concerning the characteristics of human communication could be formulated, we were in a position to envision approaches for the study of the system of convictions undergirding a text.

D. Patte, *What Is Structural Exegesis?* discusses (1) the importance of introducing structural methodologies as a complement to historical methodologies so as to insure that biblical exegesis leads to hermeneutic and (2) some of the main features of structural methodologies. D. and A. Patte, *Structural Exegesis: From Theory to Practice* discusses more specifically how these methods can be used for studying systems of convictions (semantic universe) and describes with an application the detailed structural method which needs to be used for this purpose.

The simplified approaches we shall use have been elaborated on the basis of the method presented in *Structural Exegesis: From Theory to Practice* and the new elements provided by the comprehensive theory proposed in A. J. Greimas and J. Courtés, *Semiotics and Language: An Analytical Dictionary*. For a brief overview of the theory, see D. Patte, "Greimas' Model for the Generative Trajectory of Meaning in Discourses," *AJS* 3 (1982): 59–78.

Semiotic and structural methodologies are the result of diversified interdisciplinary research which began with V. Propp's work on Russian folk tales in the 1920s. For an overview of the development of structural methodologies as applied to the study of texts, see R. Scholes, *Structuralism in Literature: An Introduction*; T. Hawkes, *Structuralism and Semiotics*; and M. Corti, *An Introduction to Literary Semiotics*. Yet it should be noted that these books reflect the "state of the art" before complete theories were proposed by U. Eco, *A Theory of Semiotics* (1976), and by Greimas and Courtés, *Semiotics and Language* (1978).

For the development of the application of structural methodologies to biblical studies, see *Semeia: An Experimental Journal for Biblical Criticism*, especially volumes 2, 6, 10, and 18 (vol. 6 is devoted entirely to translations by W. G. Doty of central essays by Erhardt Güttgemanns). For the use of structural methodologies at the Centre pour l'Analyse du Discours Religieux (Lyon, France), see J. Calloud, *Structural Analysis of the Narrative*, and The Entrevernes Group, *Signs and Parables: Semiotics and Gospel Texts*.

The complete theoretical explanation of the view of faith presented in this chapter can be found in D. Patte, "The Interface of Semiotics and Faith: Greimas's Semiotics Revisited in Light of the Phenomenon of Religion," *Recherches Semiotiques/Semiotic Inquiry* 2, no. 2 (1982).

# 2

---

# Galatians: For Freedom Christ
# Has Set Us Free

GALATIANS IS an ideal starting point for our study of Paul's faith because it manifests most of his central convictions according to which the Gospel means freedom for believers. In addition its polemical character brings to the surface the system of convictions which normally undergirds a discourse. In this relatively short letter Paul is led to express what is most characteristic of his faith in order to defend his Gospel against certain opponents. Our reading of this letter will allow us to formulate hypotheses concerning the characteristics of Paul's faith which we will need to verify and complement through our reading of Paul's other letters. In other words, our study of Galatians will produce not definitive results but *questions*, which will guide our reading of the other letters.

First, we will reflect upon the ways in which our modern convictions could mislead us as we read this letter. Next, in a *first reading*, we will consider the letter in a historical perspective in order to achieve a general understanding of its overall argument. Then, in a *second reading*, a structural reading, we will seek to determine in a preliminary, tentative way the role of Paul's system of convictions in this argument. In a *third reading* we will formulate a series of hypotheses concerning various elements of Paul's system of convictions: those convictions which allow him to conclude, on the one hand, that "there is neither Jew nor Greek" and, on the other hand, that "for freedom Christ has set us free." We shall then verify these hypotheses in a preliminary way through additional readings of parts of the letter and through an examination of the relations among the Gospel, Judaism, and Hellenistic religions as expressed in this letter. In a *fourth reading* we will make a preliminary assessment of the convictions presupposed (and expressed) by such phrases as "justification through faith" and "justification through the works of the Law." Finally, on the basis of these evaluations, we will be able to discern what needs to be elucidated in our reading of the other letters.

## GALATIANS AND THE MODERN READER

Before delving into Galatians, a warning is necessary. We will find ourselves attracted by Paul's arguments and convictions because they often are closely related to some of the basic convictions of our Western culture. Even though they might have been prompted by the influence of the biblical teachings, our convictions are not necessarily the same as Paul's. Thus we will be tempted to project upon the text our own convictions and consequently to misinterpret his letter. This is a constant problem which we can never entirely escape. Yet it might be well to note some of the points where our modern views seem to converge with, and diverge from, Paul's views.

Freedom is strongly emphasized in the letter to the Galatians: "For freedom Christ has set us free; stand fast therefore, and do not submit again to a yoke of slavery" (Gal. 5:1); "You were called to freedom" (Gal. 5:13). In brief, "the Gospel means freedom."[1] For us also, freedom is an important value. But are we thinking about the same freedom? We shall attempt to understand Paul's concept of freedom by determining with what other concepts it is associated or contrasted in the letters. Our own understanding of freedom can be recognized from the following phrases which show, at least in a superficial way, the types of things with which we associate it: freedom of the individual; freedom of speech; freedom of religion; political freedom. We should also note that we speak of freedom as a right, that is, as something we have from birth, as something which is an intrinsic part of our human nature. For us, the lack of freedom (in whatever situation) means that we have been deprived of *our* freedom, of *our* (human) right. These remarks are made only as a hint that Paul might have a quite different view of freedom and that when we find such a key term we should not assume that we understand it. In fact, according to our methodology, we should assume that we do *not* understand it. We should consider the term "freedom" as a largely unknown term, as the x in an algebra problem. Our task is to find out what $x$ stands for by considering what is associated or contrasted with it, that is, by examining its place in the structure of Paul's system of convictions. In order to elucidate convictions, we need to study their interrelations.

The task will be complicated because the term "freedom" is associated in various ways with other key terms, which will also have to be considered as unknowns. For instance, Paul associates freedom with the Law. Thus a large part of Paul's argument in Galatians is aimed at showing that the Gospel means freedom from the Law. Such a phrase is closely related to some of our modern views. We would spontaneously identify it with our own rejection of legalism. For us, legalism is a wrong religious attitude because it involves a form of religion which is superficial, artificial, and thus hypocritical in that it ignores personal religious experience. We will need to find out if this is what Paul meant by considering the term "Law" as an unknown and by studying what is associated with it. We will proceed in a similar manner with many other terms and concepts.

Successive readings of Galatians will lead us to apprehend some of the characteristics of Paul's faith manifested in this letter. We must consider all the key terms used in this text of another age as unknown (as in an algebra problem which would begin by a formula including a string of unknown terms: $a$, $b$, $c$, $x$, $y$, $z$). The readings will allow us progressively to ascertain the meaning of these key terms, first by considering how certain terms are defined (at least in part) by their referring to something outside the text. This would correspond to an algebra problem formulated in this way: "in the specific case under consideration $a$, $b$, $c$ have the following values, $a = 4$, $b = 2$, $c = 9$." Other readings will examine how the rest of the terms are defined through their interrelations in the text. This would correspond to determining the value of $x$, $y$, and $z$ through the study of how these terms are interrelated with $a$, $b$, and $c$. Of course, my reference to a simple algebra problem should not be taken literally. It is just an analogy. A major difference is that in Paul each term has several dimensions to its meaning. We will focus on only the key terms, those terms which are most helpful for understanding what characterizes Paul's faith as a system of convictions. Yet the analogy can be carried one step further. We shall be using a "formula" through which all these unknown terms are interrelated. This "formula" is the set of rules which governs human communication, and more precisely here, the way in which humans organize meaningful discourses. These rules are technically known as semiotic structures, to which we have alluded in Chapter 1. As we proceed, we shall take into account a few of these rules which are particularly helpful in understanding the text under study. They will be explained in concrete terms at the appropriate time.

Our first goal is to acquire a general understanding of what Paul talks about and therefore of his argument. At this stage we will not have any understanding of what characterizes Paul's faith. Several other readings, focused on the ways in which his argument is organized, will be necessary for this latter purpose. In light of Chapter 1, it should now be clear why we need to determine the place and role of key terms and concepts in the system of convictions viewed as a network of relations. We should also be aware that the organization of this system is not confused with the organization of ideas (including theological and moral ideas) into arguments such as those found in many passages of Paul's letters where he attempts to demonstrate a point or a series of points. Convictions are not demonstrated truths. Therefore, in order to find out how Paul's key terms and concepts express *his* faith, we also need to discover how his system of convictions is organized. In this letter Paul facilitates our task. His argument is frequently broken up and becomes apparently illogical, because he is so upset with the Galatians' attitude. Rather than following the logic of his argument, Paul follows, at these points, the "logic" of his system of convictions which emerges on the surface of the text. Far from being incoherent, Paul's discourse, comparable to that of an attorney defending a cause in a court of law, is a passionate and powerful plea in which everything is aimed at convincing (that is, at changing the convictions of) his addressees.[2] This is what we will demonstrate through our additional readings of the text.

## FIRST READING: HISTORICAL CONTEXT

The first reading is aimed at (a) identifying some central elements of the letter, which because they refer to specific persons and situations can be understood in terms of the historical context in which the letter was written, and (b) understanding, on this basis, the general argument of the letter.[3]

This letter is written by Paul the apostle. Paul's authorship is accepted in contemporary scholarship. He addresses the churches of Galatia, that is, the churches in a region of Asia Minor called Galatia. We are not certain of the exact region to which Paul refers. This name was used to designate both a province of the Roman Empire (which extended into the south of Asia Minor) and the territory occupied by the Galatian people (in central Asia Minor). Scholars tend to favor the latter location, but it is impossible to prove that this was where these churches were located.[4]

At any rate, the Galatians (a people which moved into Asia Minor several centuries earlier) were by Paul's time thoroughly Hellenized—at least in the towns. In other words, they were fully integrated in the Hellenistic culture. This was no longer the classical Greek culture of the great philosophers; rather, it was a syncretistic culture in which Greek traditions had been blended with the local traditions and customs as well as with traditions originating in Eastern regions such as Mesopotamia and Egypt. Greek philosophy played a role, but only in a popularized form, the teaching of the philosophers of the gate influenced by the Stoics and the Cynics (a teaching focused on ethics).[5] At that time in such Hellenistic regions a diversity of cults and religions coexisted in a climate of relative tolerance. This benevolent religious pluralism can be understood when one is aware that these religions were, despite significant differences, cosmological religions (i.e., religions perceiving as divine the cosmic order manifested in the cycle of nature or in the cycles of the sun, moon, and stars) and that the individual experience of the believer was particularly valued. This latter trend occurred in the "mystery cults," in which the initiation of the individual believer to the secret teaching of the cult played a central role. As a result of these two factors (and other sociological factors), these religions were open to influences from each other and often became syncretistic.[6] Because of the value given to individual religious experience, noncosmological religions could also be tolerated. Such was the case with Judaism. But we cannot tell if there were Jewish communities in Galatia, although recently discovered inscriptions in central Asia Minor would suggest this (if it is actually the location of the churches to which Paul wrote). In any event, the letter does not presuppose that the Galatians were Jews before their conversion.[7] On the contrary, it makes it clear that, from Paul's perspective, they were pagans worshiping "beings that by nature are no gods" (Gal. 4:8), which they called "elemental spirits of the universe" (i.e., of the *cosmos*; 4:3). From these polemical statements we can deduce that the Galatians were involved in one or another cosmological religion. We may also assume that the Galatians were relatively well educated, because Paul expected them to follow the sophisticated argument of his letter.

The occasion of the letter is clear. Paul established these churches by preaching a "Gospel free from the Law" (we will have to understand what this phrase means). Then he departed to continue his missionary work elsewhere. After an unknown length of time, other missionaries came to Galatia preaching "another gospel" and demanding that the Galatian Christians be circumcised and follow the Law. These were Paul's opponents.

Who were these opponents? The primary evidence we have is found in the letter, in the allusions to the teaching of these opponents contained in Paul's arguments against it. Although scholars have various theories, the majority believe that these opponents were Judaizers, Christians of Jewish origin who demanded that all Christians, including those of Hellenistic origin, follow the Law and thus, in effect, become Jews as well as Christians.[8] For Paul, this type of teaching was in contradiction to the Gospel.

In Gal. 1:11—2:14, we find a long biographical statement through which Paul intends to demonstrate in a general way the validity of his teaching—a Gospel without the Law for the Gentiles. From this passage we learn much about Paul's life and the early church. He was a devoted Jew (more precisely, a Pharisee, as is expressed in Phil. 3:5–6) who persecuted the church. After his conversion, he began his ministry without consulting the leaders of the church in Judea. He nevertheless claims that he was approved by them (Gal. 1:23–24).

The description of the meeting in Jerusalem (cf. Acts 11:30; 15; 18:22)—often called the Apostolic Council[9]—shows that the conflict over Paul's teaching had begun much earlier than the time of the letter. Even though he decided to go to Jerusalem "by revelation," the meeting was certainly called by the leaders of the church in Jerusalem: "I went up by revelation; and I laid before them . . . the gospel which I preach among the Gentiles, lest somehow I should be running or had run in vain" (Gal. 2:2). The purpose of the meeting was to examine the validity of Paul's Gospel, which did not demand that the Gentile (non-Jew) convert be circumcised and follow the Law. It is a fundamental issue which could have divided the early church into two separate churches. Despite the objections of "false brethren" (possibly related to the "circumcision party" [Gal. 2:12], which might have been behind Paul's opponents in Galatia), the "pillars," that is, James, Peter (Cephas), and John, decided to recognize both forms of the Gospel as valid. An agreement was thus reached concerning the division of the missionary work. James, Peter, and John would preach to the Jews a Gospel with the Law. Paul and Barnabas would preach to the Gentiles a Gospel without the Law. In addition, the Gentile churches would provide financial support for the Jerusalem church (called the "poor," although we do not know whether they were poor because of harsh economic situations, persecutions, or special religious vows). This collection, in which the Galatians participated (1 Cor. 16:1), was important for Paul because it was a visible sign of the unity of the church in spite of the two forms of the Gospel. It was also a tangible reminder that the Jerusalem church had recognized the validity of the Gospel without the Law.

The description of the incident at Antioch (Gal. 2:11–14), the confrontation between Peter and Paul, shows the fragility of the relationship between the two groups. The Gentile Christians and the Jewish Christians could not share any table fellowship (and thus could not celebrate the Lord's Supper together, since it involved an actual meal) because the Gentile Christians did not observe the laws of purity and the dietary laws followed by the Jewish Christians. At first, the fact that Peter shared meals with the Gentile Christians might have looked like a breakthrough toward unity. But when "men from James" arrived, he withdrew, and Barnabas with him. The result was that Paul stood isolated. Even Barnabas who was supposed to preach the Gospel without the Law to the Gentiles had given up! What was the outcome of this incident? We do not know. Yet we can guess that if Peter had conceded his point, Paul would have mentioned it. Apparently the lasting result of this confrontation, which seems to have been well known in the early church,[10] was that Paul and Barnabas separated (Acts 15:36–39, without mentioning the incident at Antioch, describes another dispute between Paul and Barnabas during that period which led to their separation). Paul was now the only missionary of Jewish origin proclaiming the Gospel without the Law to the Gentiles.

The rest of the letter does not provide many other direct pieces of information about the historical situation. From Gal. 3:2–5 we learn that the manifestation of the Spirit and miracles were a significant part of the Galatian churches' experience. Consequently Paul addresses them by saying "You who are spiritual" (6:1). In 3:27 it is mentioned that the Galatians were baptized. In 4:13 it is noted that Paul was sick when he first preached the Gospel to the Galatians, who nevertheless received him well.

The exhortations of Galatians 5 and 6 suggest that, besides the issue of the Law, the Galatians had other problems. It seems that despite their "spirituality" there was strife or at least tension among them. Thus Paul warns them, "If you bite and devour one another take heed that you are not consumed by one another" (Gal. 5:15; cf. also 5:26). Among them also were people "overtaken in trespass" (cf. 6:1) who, in one way or another, led an immoral life. This might have been one of the reasons which led them to welcome the teaching of the Judaizers. In such a situation, the Law would complement the Gospel by providing clear ethical guidelines and thus a basis for rebuking immoral people, while a Gospel without the Law would allow these people to say that in the Spirit they were totally free to act in whatever way they were moved.[11]

Finally, we know that Paul dictated his letter, rather than writing it himself, as he indicates in his own handwritten conclusion (Gal. 6:11–18). We have only indirect evidence concerning the date of this letter. Since Paul argues for a Gospel of freedom manifested in the experience of the Spirit, many scholars conclude that Galatians was written before 1 and 2 Corinthians, in which he confronts people who hold almost the same views as those expressed by Paul here. In the name of their spiritual experiences and of the freedom of the Gospel, some Corinthians adopted attitudes and beliefs that Paul had to rebuke vigorously. In the letter to the Romans, after the dispute with the Corinthians, he is much more cautious when he speaks about freedom and the Spirit. Other scholars, on the basis of a study of the references to the collection for the Jerusalem church, conclude that Galatians was written shortly after 1 and 2 Corinthians (see "Appendix: Chronologies of Paul").

We can now summarize the argument. Paul first states the problem: the Galatians are turning away from the Gospel he preached to them in order to adopt "another gospel," which he considers a perversion of the Gospel of Christ (Gal. 1:6–10). The first part of the argument is devoted to showing that his Gospel is from God—indeed, directly received from God through a revelation of Jesus Christ—and not transmitted to him by humans (Gal. 1:11–17). The validity of his first missionary activity was recognized by the churches in Judea (1:18–24). In brief, the Galatians should not turn away from a Gospel which has a divine origin and which is recognized as valid by the churches in Judea. The same argument is further developed in Gal. 2:1–14, which shows that James, Peter, and John have themselves recognized the validity of a gospel without the Law for the Gentiles, despite Peter's relapse at Antioch.

In the central passage of the letter (Gal. 2:15—5:12) we find the main argument. Its unfolding is difficult to follow at times, but its point is clear: as Christians of Hellenistic origin they should not follow the Law and receive circumcision, because that would be in contradiction to the Gospel, which signifies freedom from any yoke and thus from the Law. They are justified by faith, "for through the Spirit, by faith, we wait for the hope of righteousness" (5:5), and thus they should reject those who demand that they be circumcised and observe the Law.

The last part addressed another problem: What are the guidelines for a good Christian life without the Law? Paul answers: bearing the fruit of the Spirit, the first of which is love (Gal. 5:21–23; cf. also 5:13–14). This is another law, "the law of Christ" (6:2).

The handwritten conclusion comes back to the main issue. They should not follow the Law, "for neither circumcision counts for anything, nor uncircumcision, but a new creation" (Gal. 6:15). And he assumes that the problem is settled, or at least he does not want to hear about it anymore (6:17).

## SECOND READING: CONFLICTING SYSTEMS OF CONVICTIONS

We could have carried the preceding reading much further, showing in greater detail the unfolding of the argument in each paragraph. In this way we could have discussed Paul's *ideas* about various topics. But this is not our goal. We want to know what characterizes Paul's *faith* and thus how his system of convictions is organized. The question is then, How can we recognize his convictions in the text? We have suggested that convictions undergird a discourse and thus structure it. But how can we identify them in a first approximation? Since they are not ideas which fit neatly into a logical argument, the convictions are to be sought "in the cracks," in what is *odd* in the argument, in what does not contribute to the unfolding of the argument or even hinder it. Thus we need to read the text in a way in which we are not accustomed. Usually, when we read, we assume that the logical argument unfolds coherently, and thus we find a place in its logic for what might be odd. But we shall here let ourselves be puzzled by the text, focusing our attention on the strange reasonings, the apparent contradictions, the repetitions, and similar phenomena. Instead of "playing smart" (the text is not clear, but I understand what it means), we need to "play dumb" (I do not understand; it does not make sense; it does not add up). In this way we will identify places in the text where Paul presupposes something—and indeed presupposes his system of convictions, which is a system of *presupposed* values.

## An Emotional Letter

When one compares the introduction of Galatians with those of the other letters, one cannot but be struck by the difference in mood. Each of Paul's other letters (with the exception of 2 Corinthians) includes in its opening statements an expression of thankfulness, but in the introduction of the letter to the Galatians there is no thanksgiving for his addressees. There is nothing he can be thankful for, because in his view they have forsaken the faith. Instead of a thanksgiving, he writes, "I am astonished that you are so quickly deserting him who called you in the grace of Christ" (Gal. 1:6). This is not to say that the Galatians have no faith, but that their faith is no longer the true faith, because it is related to "another gospel" and no longer to the one they received from Paul.

Paul's letter to the Galatians is in large part devoted to a violent polemic against this "other gospel" which the Galatians have adopted, or at least are tempted to adopt. Two types of faith—two systems of convictions—are in radical conflict. Paul's tone and vocabulary show how crucial this issue is for him. He declares those who preach (or would preach) this other gospel *anathema*, accursed. In so doing he uses strong religious language or, more precisely, cultic, ritualistic language.[12] In effect, Paul invokes God's curse upon these people not only once but twice (Gal. 1:8, 9). Later in the letter he also says that the Galatians are "bewitched," that is, under a magic spell and therefore under some evil power which keeps them in bondage (3:1). Further on, he insists that "all who rely on works of the law," which include those who follow this "other gospel," are "under a curse" (3:10). This highly emotional language signals that for Paul something fundamental is at stake in this conflict of systems of convictions. It is worth noting that he emphasizes that he himself would be accursed, radically rejected by God, if he were to preach this other gospel (1:8), which is not actually the Gospel of Christ. In other words, were Paul to preach the other gospel he would lose his identity as "apostle . . . through Jesus Christ and God the Father" (1:1).

The preceding remarks about the emotional tone of this letter and about Paul's deep involvement in this conflict are not an attempt to analyze Paul's psychological state of mind. Rather, they suggest that the total person is involved whenever there are conflicting systems of convictions. The power that systems of convictions have over believers is in this letter openly manifested in the clash of the two systems of convictions and in the emotional response it triggers. Because of this clash, the text's system of convictions and its power (which normally undergird a discourse and its "logical," "rational" argument) emerge on the surface of the discourse in what we usually associate with emotional, "irrational" reactions. Yet I put the terms logical, rational, and irrational in quotation marks because systems of convictions have their own logic, their own organization which we call *convictional logic* so as to distinguish it from the rational logic of an argument—which we call *argumentative logic*.[13]

Argumentative logic proceeds by demonstrating a point with the help of a series of appropriate arguments showing the validity of this point; then on the basis of this first result, it moves to the demonstration of another point, and so on, up to the main conclusion. Convictional logic is quite different from argumentative logic, since it gives coherence to a system of values (or convictions) rather than to the unfolding of an argument. It is this convictional logic (that follows what we called a convictional pattern) which is manifested in the emotional responses we find in these first verses.

This letter is not merely describing conflicting systems of convictions. Through it Paul aims at convincing his readers to "convert" back to the true Gospel. This cannot be achieved by the use of argumentative logic, because it is not a matter of transmitting ideas but rather of transmitting self-evident truths, that is, convictions. Better, it is a matter of giving another coherence to the organization of the Galatians' convictions (for, as we shall see, the problem is not so much that they have wrong convictions but rather that in their new faith these convictions are wrongly interrelated). In order to achieve this goal, one needs to use special types of discourses. Certain kinds of narratives, such as Jesus' parables, have this function. But nonnarrative discourses in which the convictional logic is strongly emphasized, and which are therefore highly symbolic, poetic, or emotional in character, can also have this function. Thus we can already suggest that the expression of Paul's emotional response and the use of strong religious language (about curses and magical spells), besides being a description of his feelings, also play a role in communicating convictions to the addressees.[14]

In order to take into account the logic of Paul's system of convictions, we first need to identify the points where the unfolding of the discourse does not seem to be coherent (according to an argumentative logic) because there are repetitions that hinder the development of the argument, or strange kinds of reasonings, or open contradictions of itself, or highly metaphoric language. We shall see that this incoherence is also found in other letters when Paul speaks of the Law. By exploring what gives coherence to the letter's discourse, we will begin to see how a convictional logic functions and recognize important characteristics of Paul's system of convictions.

### Repetitions, Metaphoric Language, Strange Reasonings, Contradictions

The emotional tone of the first verses is shown by a series of repetitions. We have already noted the repetition of the cursing of Gal. 1:8, 9, but in these verses we find so many repetitions that the discourse does not seem to progress. For instance, we read, "Paul an apostle—not from men nor through man" (1:1); "Am I now seeking the favor of men . . . ? Or am I trying to please men? If I were still pleasing men . . ." (1:10); "the gospel which was preached by me is not man's gospel" (1:11); "I did not receive it from man" (1:12); "I did not confer with flesh and blood" (1:16). Any one of these statements would have been sufficient to convey the point that Paul did not receive his apostolate and his Gospel from humans. There are a series of corresponding statements affirming that his apostolate and his Gospel are from God and through Jesus Christ (1:1, 10, 12, 16). In the first verses we therefore find not the unfolding of a logical argument but a series of apparently juxtaposed statements making the same point over and over. Clearly Paul is upset because, as he understands it, the validity of his proclamation—his Gospel—and his authority as apostle (they are indissolubly linked one with the other) have been rejected by the Galatians. The weakness of the argumentative logic suggests that, in Paul's view, what is being rejected is not some ideas about the Gospel and his apostolate but convictions.

As he retells the story of his conversion and then of his interactions with the other apostles (Gal. 1:11—2:10), we find that the argument unfolds more coherently, supported by the ordered sequence of these events. Yet let us emphasize the content of the agreement reached at Jerusalem during the Apostolic Council. It affirmed two Gospels: a Gospel *without* the Law for the Gentiles (i.e., the Gospel preached by Paul and recognized by the other apostles) and the Gospel *with* the Law for the Jews, which Peter, James, and John preach and which Paul also sees as valid. The Jews are circumcised, but as the incident at Antioch suggests, they also continue to follow the Law—at least the dietary laws, but perhaps also many or all of the other laws—and Paul seems to accept this attitude since he subscribes to the agreement. Note that in the dispute at Antioch, Paul rebukes Peter not for eating kosher food with other Jewish Christians (i.e., for following the Law) but for changing his mind. When Peter stopped eating with the Gentiles, he gave the impression that he felt he had sinned by eating impure food, an attitude which led certain Gentile Christians (and even Barnabas) to think that they themselves should follow the Law.

While Paul seems to accept two forms of the Gospel, for him there is only *one* Gospel (Gal. 1:7). We have to let ourselves be puzzled by this. What is the logic which allows him to consider these two forms of the Gospel as one and the same? For Paul, the Jewish Christians could both follow the Law and be "not justified by works of the Law but through faith in Jesus Christ" (2:16). How did he reach this conclusion?[15] And why does he condemn so strongly a Gospel with the Law for the Gentiles? We shall see that it is because of the place of the Law in his system of convictions. In other words, in order to understand Paul's attitude toward Peter and his Gospel to the circumcised, we need to take into account Paul's presupposed convictional logic.

The end of Galatians 2 and the following chapters endeavor to show that the Gospel is the proclamation of justification through faith, not through works of the Law. While the argument of Gal. 2:14–21 unfolds logically, Paul uses highly metaphoric language to speak about his relation to the Law: "I through the law died to the law. . . . I have been crucified with Christ" (2:19–20). This suggests once more that the convictional logic is close to the surface. Note also that this metaphoric development is prompted by a discussion of the conflict between the convictional systems of the "circumcision party" (2:12), with which Peter temporarily or permanently associates himself, and of Paul.

At the beginning of Galatians 3 (vv. 1–5), we find an emotional tone comparable to that of the first chapter. "O foolish Galatians! Who has bewitched you . . . ?" (3:1); "Are you so foolish?" (3:3). In addition, the same theme is repeated over and over: "Did you receive the Spirit by works of the law, or by hearing with faith?" (3:2; cf. 3:3, 3:5). This once more suggests that the convictional logic has emerged on the surface of the text. It becomes clear that Paul is unhappy that the Galatians have turned away from his "Gospel without the Law" to adopt a "gospel with the Law."

The argument of Galatians 3 and 4 (the central argument of the letter) is basically a demonstration that one is justified through faith and not through works of the Law. In this passage, we detect a series of strange reasonings and apparent contradictions, breaks in the normal argumentative logic. The statement that "Scripture . . . preached the gospel beforehand to Abraham" (Gal. 3:8) is metaphoric (cf. the anthropomorphization of Scripture which "preaches") and involves an apparent anachronism: the Gospel (of Christ? cf. 1:7) is preached to Abraham. Furthermore, the use of biblical texts involves a peculiar reasoning allowing Paul, for instance, to conclude, from a biblical text about Abraham, that Gentiles are justified by faith (3:6–9) or, from another biblical text, that Christ was cursed (3:13). A similar reasoning is also found in 4:21–31, where Paul interprets the story of Abraham, Sarah, and Hagar. This peculiar kind of reasoning can fully be understood only if we recognize the role of the convictional logic in it (see also Chapter 6). That convictional logic plays an important role in the organization of this discourse is made obvious by the presence of what would be contradictions according to argumentative logic. In 3:7 and 3:29 it is affirmed that the believers are "sons" or "offspring" of Abraham, while in 3:16 it is argued that only one is "Abraham's offspring," Christ. It therefore seems that the "demonstration" that the believer is justified by faith is not the argumentative demonstration of an idea, but rather the establishment and communication of a conviction.

Similarly, when one tries to follow the argument in Galatians 4 it is often difficult to determine about whom he is speaking. After the example of the heir who is no better than a slave as long as he is a child, Paul writes, "So with us" (Gal. 4:3). "Us," "we," refers to Paul and his Galatians readers. Before converting to the Gospel, however, Paul was a Jew, while the Galatians believed in a Hellenistic cosmological religion. But then note how he speaks of this situation before conversion (when a "child," according to the preceding example): "When *we* were children, *we* were slaves to the elemental spirits of the universe" (i.e., as he explains later, slaves to "beings that by nature are no gods" [4:8], slaves to idols). Here the "we" is actually understood as a "you" designating the formerly pagan Galatians. But then the text moves on to say that Christ redeemed "those who were under the law" and then adds, "so that *we* might receive adoption as sons" (4:5). Here the "we" refers to those who were under the Law, that is, to the Christians of Jewish origin, including Paul. And yet, the "we" clearly includes the Galatians also. They are among those who received adoption as sons by being freed from the Law (even though they were in bondage to idols and not to the Law), as Paul makes clear by continuing his argument: "And because you are sons . . ." (4:6). We can understand why this discourse has such a fragmented argumentative logic when we consider its content and its goal. It aims at establishing the true identity of the Galatians—their convictions about themselves.

When we consider what Paul says about the Law, the argument is even more confusing. In it Paul contrasts Law and promise (see, e.g., Gal. 3:18), and then he goes on to say that the Law has no authority because "it was ordained by angels through an intermediary" (3:19). He then adds, "Now an intermediary implies more than one; but God is one" (3:20). This amounts to saying that the Law is not from God.[16] But Paul does not want to say this. He wants to affirm that the Law and the promise are not contradictory. Therefore he asks, "Is the law then against the promises of God?" (3:21). He answers his own question with a vigorous denial: "Certainly not! By no means! No, it cannot be!" In fact, throughout his arguments about the Law in Galatians and elsewhere (especially in Romans), Paul seems to pile up contradictions on top of contradictions.

For instance, in Romans 7, Paul has to deny vigorously what could be inferred from his discourse. "What then shall we say? That the law is sin? By no means!" (Rom. 7:7, using the same phrase as in Gal. 3:21). He needs to make this strong denial because he repeatedly asserts that the Law gives life to sin and brings about sin. For instance, we can read: "our sinful passions, aroused by the law" (Rom. 7:5); "If it had not been for the law, I should not have known sin" (7:7, where "knowing" has to be understood both as intellectual knowledge, i.e., recognizing sin, and as the concrete knowledge found in the Hebraic usage, the practice of sin); "sin, finding opportunity in the commandment" (7:8); "Apart from the law sin lies dead" (7:8); "when the commandment came, sin revived" (7:9). Is this not saying that the Law is sin? And yet at the same time Paul wants to affirm that "the law is holy, and the commandment is holy and just and good" (Rom. 7:12) and that "the law is spiritual" (Rom. 7:14). Paul clearly wants to maintain that the Law is holy, from God, and even that the Law should be fulfilled—"For the whole law is fulfilled in one word, 'You shall love your neighbor as yourself'" (Gal. 5:14). He also says that the Law should be read: "Do you not hear the law?"[17] (Gal. 4:21). But although Paul is constantly quoting the Law as authoritative Scripture, at times he does so in order to use the Law against itself. In Gal. 3:12 he quotes Lev. 18:5, "He who does them [the commandments] shall live by them," as a demonstration that "the law does not rest on faith."

Besides these apparent internal contradictions we also note how contradictory it is to affirm, on the one hand, the holiness, the spiritual character, of the Law and, on the other hand, to say, as Paul does in Gal. 3:21, that the Law cannot bestow life, and even in other texts that the Law actually brings about death: it bears "fruit for death" (Rom. 7:5), proves "to be death to me" (Rom. 7:10), and is the ally of sin bringing about death (Rom. 7:13; 1 Cor. 15:56). If the Law is holy and from God, it should bring life and salvation, not death.

By broadening the scope of our investigation to include all of Paul's letters, we could show many other apparently contradictory statements about the Law. But the above observations suggest that the issues concerning the relationship of Gospel and Law are indeed linked with Paul's central convictions.

## Systems of Convictions in Conflict

This preliminary reading shows that where the argumentative logic is broken up—that is, where we find redundancies, highly metaphoric language, peculiar reasonings, and apparent contradictions—Paul is in fact dealing with the interrelation (and often conflict) of certain systems of convictions. The main clash is between Paul's system of convictions (characterized by a Gospel without the Law) and the "heretic" Galatians' system of convictions (characterized by a Gospel with the Law).

Other systems of convictions are involved, however. First, there is the system of convictions of the other apostles, which is characterized by a Gospel *with* the Law *for the Jews* and by the recognition that the Gentiles may follow a Gospel without the Law. Paul considers this just as valid. By contrast, he has a highly negative view of the system of convictions of the "circumcision party" that we call the Judaizers, which is also characterized by a Gospel with the Law, but with the view that the Gentiles should themselves follow the Law (be circumcised). It is this latter system of convictions that the heretic Galatians have adopted or are tempted to adopt. We find allusions to two other systems of convictions: the one that Paul had before his conversion (i.e., the Pharisaic system of convictions) and the one that the Galatians had before their conversion (a Hellenistic system of convictions).

Six systems of convictions—six types of faith—are thus interrelated in this discourse. In fact, the main goal of this letter is to "convert" the heretic Galatians (or the potentially heretic Galatians) from one system of convictions (their heretic system to be identified with the Judaizers') to another one (Paul's system of convictions, which was also the Galatians' when they followed him). I use the verb "to convert" because conversion is what takes place when one passes from one faith to another, a faith that involves different fundamental convictions and thus a different convictional pattern. For Paul the Galatians' faith in the "other gospel" is radically different from the faith in the (only true) Gospel to which Paul wants them to return.

We find three types of "conversions" mentioned or alluded to in the text, and a fourth one that the letter hopes to achieve. All are conversions to the true Gospel, with one exception: the Galatians' conversion from the true Gospel to the "other gospel" (which is not really a Gospel, as Paul says in Gal. 1:7). That conversion is, in Paul's view, a reverse conversion, an apostasy; it is going back to something like their former Hellenistic religion: "How can you turn back again to the weak and beggarly elemental spirits, whose slaves you want to be once more?" (Gal. 4:9). That is why this third conversion is represented in Table 1 in a different way.

Table 1 outlines the parallelism of the various "conversions," with the

TABLE 1: CONVERSIONS ALLUDED TO IN GALATIANS

| | | | |
|---|---|---|---|
| 1a. Conversion of Paul | | *from* Pharisaism | *to* Gospel |
| 1b. Conversion of Peter and other Jews | | *from* Judaism | *to* Gospel with the Law |
| 2. Conversion of Galatians | | *from* a Hellenistic religion | *to* Gospel without the Law |
| 3. Conversion of (some) Galatians | *from* Gospel without the Law | *to* "another gospel" | |
| 4. Hoped-for conversion of Galatians | | *from* "another gospel" | *to* Gospel (without the Law) |

exception of the third, which stands out as a reverse conversion. Since each case represents the passage from one system of convictions to another, it can be read as a pair of opposed convictional systems. Thus, in the first case we find the opposition "Pharisaic system of convictions *versus* Gospel as a system of convictions." Similar oppositions are found in the other cases. Table 1 also suggests the correlations between the various systems and thus how a part of Paul's system of convictions is organized. A third reading will allow us to elucidate it in a more precise way.

## THIRD READING: THERE IS NEITHER JEW NOR GREEK

Our second reading of Galatians allowed us to see not only where and how the argumentative logic is disrupted in the first four chapters but also that the development of Paul's discourse is in part governed by his perception of a conflict among systems of convictions. This led us to see that his convictional logic plays an important role in the organization of his discourse. Through a third reading aimed at elucidating how the convictional logic functions in a part of the letter, we will be able to understand the coherence of a larger unit of Paul's discourse which leads to the conclusion "there is neither Jew nor Greek" (3:28; cf. also 6:15).

For this purpose we need to try to understand how Paul's convictional logic functions in this letter by constructing a tentative "model" of a part of Paul's system of convictions. "Model construction" (formulating a hypothesis) is an important step in structural readings. A few words concerning the characteristics of convictional logic will be enough to explain how we shall proceed. Then we will perform our third reading aimed at verifying in a general way the validity of our "model" (or hypothesis).

### The Organization of a System of Convictions

First, we need to note that a system of convictions can (and usually does) involve convictions about other systems of convictions. To avoid this confusing vocabulary, we can say that Paul's system of convictions involves convictions about the "religions" of the Pharisees, of Hellenistic people, and of those Galatians following another gospel, as well as convictions about their relationship to his own "religion" (his faith in the Gospel) and to the "religion" of other Christians (the faith of the Jewish Christians and of the Galatians before their relapse). Thus Paul has convictions about other systems of convictions and about their relationship to his.

We have also alluded to the relations which characterize the organization of a system of convictions. At this point we emphasize two of these relations: oppositions and homologations. First, the convictions are organized in pairs of opposed convictions. To put it simply, how could one say that something is "good" if one does not know what is "evil"? Thus a given conviction about something good or positive is necessarily opposed to a conviction about something else which is evil or negative. For instance, Paul the apostle opposes his conviction about the positive value of the Gospel to his conviction about the negative value of his former Pharisaism. A system of convictions is composed of a long series of such pairs of opposed convictions. However, we shall consider only the more important pairs of convictions, since these will be sufficient to show the convictional pattern which characterizes Paul's faith.

When this is understood, the concept of *homologation* does not present any difficulty. It means that in a system of convictions these pairs of opposed convictions are perceived as *equivalent* to each other.[18] To put it simply, all these pairs of opposed convictions are perceived as expressing the same opposition between a given view of the good and a given view of the evil. This is not denying that these pairs are different from one another, but that these differences are perceived as secondary in comparison to the fundamental identity which is found in them. Thus the pairs of opposed (systems of) convictions corresponding to the conversions of Paul, of the other apostles, and of the Galatians (converted by Paul the first time and, it is hoped, a second time through the letter) are perceived as equivalent to each other. This also means that all the positive (systems of) convictions are themselves perceived as equivalent to each other. The same is true of the negative (systems of) convictions. Let us tentatively represent in Table 2 the relations in that part of Paul's system of convictions which we have begun to discuss.

TABLE 2: THE INTERRELATIONS OF SYSTEMS OF
CONVICTIONS IN GALATIANS

| | | |
|---|---|---|
| Paul's Gospel (for the Gentiles) as a system of convictions | vs. | Pharisaic system of convictions |
| ‖‖ | | ‖‖ |
| Peter's Gospel (with the Law) as a system of convictions | vs. | Jewish (Pharisaic?) system of convictions |
| ‖‖ | | ‖‖ |
| The Galatians' Gospel (without the Law) as a system of convictions | vs. | Hellenistic religions as systems of convictions |
| ‖‖ | | ‖‖ |
| The Galatians' Gospel as a system of convictions (a Gospel without the Law to which they will, it is hoped, come back) | vs. | The "other gospel" as a system of convictions (a gospel with the Law)[19] |

NOTE: By convention we set the negative convictions in the right-hand column. The symbol ‖‖ represents a relation of equivalence between two homologable terms.

The relations represented in Table 2 show that various forms of the Gospel can be viewed as equivalent to each other. Thus the Gospel as the system of convictions of the converted Paul can be viewed as homologable to the Gospel of the other converted Jews and to the Gospel of the converted Gentile Galatians. In other words, these Gospels, despite their differences, would share with each other something so fundamental that all of them merit the title "Gospel." This might be why Paul could consider them one and the same Gospel. In view of Paul's insistence on freedom, we can expect that the positive value they share is that they involve "freedom" (from other systems of convictions, but also possibly in another sense).

Similarly, Paul's Pharisaic system of convictions (to which we can assimilate the Judaism of other apostles even though they might have followed another kind of Judaism before their conversion, since Paul does not make any distinction) would be correlated with, and thus homologable to, the Hellenistic system of convictions and also to the heretic system of convictions (the "other gospel"). These three systems, despite their differences, would share something fundamental with each other: all of them are non-Gospel, because each of them involves bondage. Indeed, Paul speaks of the Law of the Pharisaic system as a religious bondage ("we were confined under the law" [Gal. 3:23], "under a custodian" [3:25], and under "the curse of the law" [3:13]), of the Hellenistic religion of the Galatians as another bondage ("You were in bondage to beings that by nature are no gods" [4:8], that is, to idols which are also called "elemental spirits of the universe" [4:3, 9]), and of the Galatians' present beliefs in the "other gospel" as still another religious bondage (they are "bewitched," under a magic spell [3:1]; they want to be "slaves" once more [4:9]).

All these homologations suggested by Table 2 remain to be demonstrated by studying Paul's system of convictions as it is manifested in his discourse. But first we need to emphasize another implication of these relations of equivalence. According to convictional logic, one can substitute equivalent terms for each other. Thus, for instance, Paul can speak of his experience in terms of the Galatians' experience, since in his system of convictions Paul's and the Galatians' experiences have equivalent value. To be specific, he can speak of the passage from the Pharisaic faith to the Gospel while at the same time speaking of the passage from the Hellenistic faith to the Gospel,[20] and all this can take place more or less implicitly. To be even more specific, Paul can speak of the Pharisaic faith or even of one of its elements while speaking of the Hellenistic faith or of one of its elements, and vice versa. In fact, this is the same process we find in metaphors—when, for instance, the description of a rose is simultaneously the description of a beloved woman. The differences are that in a system of convictions many such metaphoric relations are at work at the same time and that, in most cases, they remain hidden in the discourse. These "metaphoric" relations are simply presupposed. In Galatians, as suggested, this convictional logic comes to the surface and thus directly gives coherence to a discourse which at several points appears incoherent according to argumentative logic. Keeping these remarks in mind, we will now be able to perceive the convictional coherence of a part of Paul's discourse.

### Freedom and Bondage (Gal. 1:3–5 and 4:1–10)

Let us first consider how Paul presents the Gospel in his opening statement:

> Grace to you and peace from God the Father and our Lord Jesus Christ, who gave himself for our sins to deliver us from the present evil age, according to the will of our God and Father; to whom be the glory for ever and ever. Amen. (Gal. 1:3–5)

Most noteworthy here is the description of what Christ accomplished: he "gave himself for our sins to deliver us from the present evil age." The vocabulary is surprising. It describes the effect of the Gospel both for those of Jewish origin (like Paul) and for those of Hellenistic origin (like the Galatians).

The first part of this formulation, "Christ gave himself for our sins," is comparable to what we find elsewhere in Paul's letters, for instance, in 1 Cor. 15:3, where we read: "Christ died for our sins in accordance with the scriptures." In the latter text "scriptures" obviously refers to the Old Testament, the Jewish Scripture. Anticipating our discussion of this text, we can note that the event "Christ crucified," which, taken by itself, is foolishness, nonsense (1 Cor. 1:18–25), and a stumbling block (Gal. 5:11), makes sense when considered in terms of the Jewish Scripture. Thus the earliest church could understand that "Christ died *for our sins*" by identifying him with, for instance, the suffering servant of Yahweh, who "was wounded for our transgressions," "was bruised for our iniquities" (Isa. 53:5), and "makes himself an offering for sin" according to "the will of the Lord" (Isa. 53:10). In 1 Cor. 15:3 Paul repeats this formulation which he received from the earliest church. The phrase Christ "gave himself for our sins," as well as the statement "according to the will of our God and Father," makes use of a Jewish vocabulary related to the vocabulary of the Old Testament. In other words, this is what the Gospel means for the Christians of Jewish origin like Paul.

The second part of this formulation, "to deliver us from the present evil age," introduces a quite different vocabulary. The Greek term translated by "age" is *aiōn*, which is a technical term. The "present age" is opposed to the "age to come" in Jewish Apocalypticism as an age dominated by the power of evil or, better, by evil powers which have cosmic dimensions. Only their defeat by divine intervention will bring about the "age to come," which is perceived as the age of a *new* Jerusalem, a *new* world or a "*new* creation" (a phrase Paul uses in Gal. 6:15). *Aiōn* is found in later Gnostic documents as a designation for evil cosmic powers and is also found in the context of Hellenistic syncretistic cults (such as the cult of Mithras).[21] In view of Paul's concern to show the correlation of the Jewish-Christian experience with that of the Galatians (see our discussion of Galatians 4, below), we need to assume that he expected his addressees to understand this term. While Paul may have found this concept in Jewish Apocalypticism, he certainly chose to use it in writing to the Galatians because it made sense in their Hellenistic religious experience; for them the *aiōn* was a "power" (since people needed to be delivered from it). Furthermore, we can say that *aiōn* designates a "cosmic power," since before their conversion the Galatians were involved in Hellenistic religions which can be ranged among the cosmological religions (as implied by the terminology of Gal. 4:3, 9). According to these somewhat diverse religions, the cosmic order (observed, e.g., in the regular cycles of the sun, the moon, the planets, or stars) was viewed as the absolute divine order. This fundamental conviction demanded that the believers view society and their individual lives as absolutely structured by this cosmic order, which manifested itself in what was perceived as cosmic powers of one kind or another. We can infer from 4:3 and 9 that the Galatians called them "elemental spirits of the universe" (or, in a more literal rendering, "elemental spirits of the *cosmos*"). Thus the believers in these cosmological religions perceived their fate as determined by these cosmic powers. This type of faith is similar to modern beliefs in astrology; for believers in the signs of the zodiac their horoscope is a "fate" that they cannot escape, even though knowing it allows them to make the best of it.

It appears, therefore, that the phrase "to deliver us from the present evil age" expresses what the Gospel means for the Galatians formerly involved in these Hellenistic cosmological religions. These religions were not perceived as evil by the Hellenistic believers (otherwise they would have abandoned them), but now, from the perspective of another system of convictions (i.e., after their conversion to the Gospel), the cosmic power is perceived as "evil" and as an unbearable bondage. For them the Gospel means deliverance from this bondage of the evil cosmic power.

Thus, already in this introductory statement, we find Paul expressing what the Gospel means both for him (and other Christians of Jewish origin) and for the Galatians (before their relapse). In the first phrase, Christ "gave himself for *our* sins," the plural first-person pronoun equates the Galatians to Paul, a Christian of Jewish origin. They also benefit from the reconciliation through Christ, according to which God is "not counting their trespasses against them" (2 Cor. 5:19), even though sin became a problem for them only in retrospect (because of the Law the Jews "knew" what trespasses were [Rom. 7:7], the Galatians did not). In the second phrase, "to deliver *us* from the present evil age"—which is posited here as a second (and main) stage of what is accomplished by Christ—the plural first-person pronoun equates Paul to the Galatians. This second case is even more significant for the understanding of the letter and of Paul's faith. According to Paul's convictional logic, the Pharisaic religion is like the Hellenistic religions. It involves an evil power which keeps the Jews in bondage, as the Hellenistic religions do. Thus the Jews also need to be delivered from this power. We can already suggest that this evil power which keeps the Jews in bondage is an idol, as it is in the case of the Hellenistic religions. This is certainly implied already here by the term *aiōn*, although it becomes explicit only later on when Paul writes in Gal. 4:8, "you were in bondage to beings that by nature are no gods." This is the very definition of an idol.

In Gal. 4:1–7 we find the same pattern. The original situations of Paul and the Galatians are perceived as equivalent to the extent that the two blend into one another.

I mean that the heir, as long as he is a child, is no better than a slave, though he is the owner of all the estate; but he is under guardians and trustees until the date set by the father. So with us; when we were children, we were slaves to the elemental spirits of the universe. But when the time had fully come, God sent forth his Son, born of woman, born under the law, to redeem those who were under the law, so that we might receive adoption as sons. And because you are sons, God has sent the Spirit of his Son into our hearts, crying, "Abba! Father!" So through God you are no longer a slave but a son, and if a son then an heir. (Gal. 4:1–7)

Here Paul brings into play a third situation, a fictional one in which a child under guardians and trustees "is no better than a slave, though he is the owner of all the estate." Such analogies establish on the surface of the text relations among equivalent situations even as does the convictional logic in the very texture of the discourse. This analogy of the child under guardians first establishes a relation with what precedes. Even though the vocabulary is different, the reader identifies it with the preceding description of the Jews under the Law: "the law was our custodian until Christ came" (Gal. 3:24). The relation of equivalence with the situation of the Galatians before their conversion is established in 4:3. They who are "slaves to the elemental spirits" are "children." We have already discussed how the plural first-person pronouns equate Paul (and his experience as a Pharisee under the Law) to the Galatians ("slaves to the elemental spirits") in 4:3, 5. These verses express more explicitly what we found in 1:3–5 about the equivalence that exists in Paul's system of convictions between Pharisaism and Hellenistic religions, emphasizing how the Gospel as the system of convictions of both Paul and the Galatians is opposed to their respective former religions. They are no longer slaves but sons (this is expressed in one way for the Jewish Christian in v. 5 and in another for the Galatians in v. 7). That is, they are now in a position to call God "Abba! Father!" (or "our Father," as is already said in 1:5).

From the perspective of the Gospel as a system of convictions, "there is neither Jew nor Greek" (3:28), because "in Christ Jesus you are all sons of God" (3:26), because all of you have "put on Christ" (3:27). Paul's discourse in Galatians makes it clear that the Gospel radically abolishes the difference between Jews and Greeks. From the perspective of the Gospel, Christians of Jewish origin and Christians of Hellenistic origin are "equivalent." But this was true before their conversion. Jews and Hellenistic idolaters are equivalent because they are all under custodians, under bondage, that is, slaves. They are all idolaters. This view is sheer nonsense for the Pharisees, who so completely devote themselves to the worship and service of the God who is One. Paul struggles with this issue elsewhere (Romans 9–11). Yes, there is a significant difference between Jews and Greeks, but beyond this difference, and in spite of it, from the perspective of the Gospel they are fundamentally in the same position. "There is neither Jew nor Greek."

With the following verses, Paul introduces a third situation (or a fourth one, if we count the analogy of the child under guardians) as equivalent to the others.

> Formerly, when you did not know God, you were in bondage to beings that by nature are no gods; but now that you have come to know God, or rather to be known by God, how can you turn back again to the weak and beggarly elemental spirits, whose slaves you want to be once more? You observe days, and months, and seasons, and years! (Gal. 4:8–10)

The Galatians' adoption of the "other gospel," which, as we saw, is a gospel with the Law, is now depicted by Paul as turning "back again to the weak and beggarly elemental spirits." That is, the "other gospel" is shown to be equivalent to their former cosmological religion. Thus again Paul can simultaneously speak of the two religions, and does so in verse 10. One would expect the description of the Jewish festivals (prescribed by the Law) when he describes the religious festivals they now observe, but he uses a vocabulary which is better interpreted as referring to cosmological festivals. The common characteristic which allows Paul to consider the "other gospel" and the Hellenistic religions as equivalent is once more that both are slavery (4:9) by contrast to the Gospel, which is freedom (5:1).

When one has perceived in these texts the homologations among the Jewish faith, the Hellenistic faith, and the faith in the "other gospel," and the homologations among the Gospel of the former Jews (the circumcised) and the Gospel of the former Hellenistic believers, one can surmise that Paul implies these homologations in other parts of his letter, although more discreetly. And we can now begin to see that these homologations are based upon the opposition between freedom and bondage, which appear to be a pair of fundamental convictions in Paul's system. These are religious freedom and religious bondage: freedom as sons in a special relation to God the Father; bondage as curse and magic spell. But, as we shall see, they also apply to other dimensions of human experience,[22] and especially to the realm of social interrelations: "there is neither slave nor free" (speaking of actual slaves working for free people) and "there is neither male nor female" (Gal. 3:28). Yet this freedom and this bondage first of all characterize types of faith (systems of convictions). The importance of these concepts is clear, but we need to ask, In what sense does the Gospel mean freedom? In what sense are the other faiths bondage? These questions touch at the central characteristics of Paul's faith. We need to consider them in detail, especially because in our culture it is difficult for us to conceive of religion as an enslaving power. Instead, we dismiss it as superstition, that is, as a wrong attitude which, we trust, some education will easily overcome.

## THE GOSPEL: A FREEING POWER?

Most modern Western people usually dismiss phrases like "who has bewitched you?" (Gal. 3:1) or "all who rely on works of the law are under a curse" (3:10). We do so in various ways. Some might say that Paul was still imbued with mythical (or mythological) thinking, that Paul was caught up in a "primitive" way of thinking and still believed in magic ("bewitched") and in the power of curses. Others might merely pretend to respect the authority of his letters by saying, "These are merely figures of speech." The fact is that most of us do not believe in the *power of religion*. We might believe in the power of our own religion (and thus, for instance, in the power of prayer), but even in this case we deny the power of other religions; with tricks or illusions, they pretend that they have power, but in fact they have no real power. We might even want to quote Paul on this point, "We know that 'an idol has no real existence'" (1 Cor. 8:4; cf. Gal. 4:8). But the context shows that Paul is very much concerned with the power that these nonexistent idols have upon the "weaker believers," and, as we shall see, in many places he acknowledges the power of idols (to which he gives various names).

We have already discussed in general terms the power of systems of convictions, but in order to progress in our study of Galatians and to understand in what sense the Gospel is freedom, in contrast to the other religions, which are bondage, we need a more concrete understanding of how this power works. For this purpose it is best to take a modern example.

A modern system of convictions at work—the choice is not easy. I will not take an example in the religious domain, because as mentioned above, at best, the readers would agree with it only if it happens to be dealing with their own specific religions. Noting that our culture is very committed to the welfare of the individual person (for instance, we object to the depersonalizing effect of technology), we can surmise that fundamental convictions of our contemporary view concern the establishment of one's personal identity (or the purpose and meaning of one's life). In this, our culture can be contrasted to other cultures which give priority to the meaning and purpose of society (such would be the case of an ideal communist culture) or of the world or cosmos (as was the case of the Mesopotamian culture, for instance). Thus, in our culture we can expect to find systems of convictions at work in personal relationships. Love, the romantic love of a couple, provides a good example of the way in which convictional systems have power. It should suffice to evoke briefly a love story.

## The Power of a System of Convictions[23]

A man and a woman love each other; in fact, they are on their honeymoon. We say, "They are *in* love." Taken literally, this means that they live inside their love, and this is indeed correct. Their love completely structures their lives, but it is not something that they have deliberately chosen (if they are truly in love). The man has not decided to love the woman after a careful, rational argument through which he would have systematically matched his interests, his views, his goals, his definition of feminine beauty, and so on (as the computers of certain marriage agencies do). Neither did the woman. They simply *fell* in love. For him it was self-evident that she was the woman of his life. For her it was self-evident that he was the man of her life. And, as we know, objective standards of beauty and matched interests are often not taken into account. To fall in love is to adopt convictions, or actually to adopt a limited system of convictions—or, better, to "be adopted" by it. It is to be caught under the power of convictions. Indeed, lovers may be "spellbound" (in some instances when meeting each other for the very first time). An examination of the vocabulary about romantic love would show the frequency of religious terms describing love as an ecstatic experience. Conversely, we could find the vocabulary about romantic love constantly used in religious texts and already in the Old Testament prophets. I want instead to emphasize the way in which love structures the couple's lives, for it is not manifested only in those intimate moments where they directly express their love for each other. These moments are the rituals in which their love-convictions are again and again reestablished and reinforced. Their entire life together is affected, permeated by their love. Because of it our lovers see everything in a new way. Anything which is favorable to their love or promotes it is beautiful and marvelous, whether it be an apartment which is ugly according to objective standards or a natural occurrence such as a destructive thunderstorm. And, of course, the beloved is beautiful. Indeed, they are happy, and everything which participates in their love is euphoric from their standpoint. By contrast, whatever hinders their love takes on negative connotations. They violently rebel and hate parents who oppose their love, even if earlier they dearly loved them. They readily abandon activities and possessions which before were of great value to them. Such is the case in the classic examples of lovers abandoning families or promising careers without hesitation. Even their work takes on a new meaning because of their love, if for no other reason than the money earned will be spent together. We should also note that the love life of our couple involves many duties and chores: cleaning the house, taking the garbage out, cooking, shopping. It involves a great limitation of their freedom: now they go everywhere together. This implies that one or the other has to give up what he or she would have liked to do. It involves waiting for each other. So their love often brings about many limitations, duties, chores, but they are happy to carry them out—for love's sake. They are in love, and what is happiness if not being in love? Without entering into a long discussion of happiness, we can say that our lovers are happy because their love gives them a feeling of wholeness. They feel good about themselves because all the discrete parts of their lives and experience are now fitting together. Their love integrates everything, holds everything together. They have meaning and purpose. They are no longer lost and searching for themselves. Their love gives them identities, true identities.

But if someone asks our lovers to explain what they mean by the phrase "I love you," which they use so often, they might answer by speaking in vague terms of certain deep feelings or by describing their love life. If this questioner persists and asks how each knows that the other loves him or her, the response might point to certain attitudes of the love partner. Our questioner might then respond, "How do you know these attitudes are not faked?" The answer to this will invariably be something like, "I simply know they are truly loving attitudes! I simply know that he/she loves me." Love cannot be demonstrated, cannot even be fully defined. It is self-evident or it is not love. It cannot be pinpointed as manifested in any particular aspect of their life, for their love is manifested in their entire life, or they are not truly in love. Even their love rituals which express their love with more intensity cannot become the only manifestation of their love without destroying it (and transforming it into a mere sex affair). Their love permeates everything or they are not truly in love. It is as a self-evident system of convictions (involving convictions about the value of all aspects of life centered around fundamental convictions concerning their relations) that love has the power to hold together the lovers' entire life, to establish their identity, and to impose upon them a heavy yoke (chores, duties, limitation of freedom) which they are happy to carry and which seems light to them.

This is how any system of convictions is bewitching, keeping the "believers" under its spell, a welcome spell for the believers (our lovers). But for those outside, and more specifically for those in conflicting systems of convictions (the parents of our rebellious lovers), this spell is an evil spell, a curse.

## Being under the Power of the Gospel and Freed by It

This example of a system of convictions at work helps us understand why Paul speaks as he does about the Galatians. From the standpoint of his own system of convictions, they are under an evil spell, under a curse, because by accepting another system of convictions, they forsook all they had gained from his sharing the (true) Gospel with them. In the same way that they had received the Gospel because a power intervened in their life (because they were inspired by the Spirit [Gal. 3:2–5]), so they must have accepted this other system of convictions because they were "inspired," but this time by an "evil spirit." Thus it is appropriate to say that they were bewitched (even as our lovers "fell" in love).

For Paul, the Gospel establishes the true meaning and purpose of life, his true identity which is somehow characterized by his relationship to God (by contrast to the lovers whose fundamental convictions are about their relationship to each other). As a preliminary hypothesis we can say that through his system of convictions, that is, through the Gospel of Christ, Paul (and other believers) is established in the right relationship with God (somewhat as the lovers are established in the right relationship to each other through their love—we will discuss the important difference between the two cases). This right relationship with God is what Paul expresses by terms like "righteousness" and "justification" (the same term in Greek) which, as we shall discuss in detail, are terms designating a relation (with God).

The equivalent of falling in love is, in Paul's case, the revelation of the Gospel (Gal. 1:12) or the revelation of Christ (1:16). Paul insists that this is something which *happened* to him. God revealed the Gospel and his Son to him. In the same way that the man and the woman mysteriously fell in love, and suddenly or progressively (according to the case) their relationship became totally different, so Paul mysteriously "fell in the Gospel" and suddenly his relationship with God was totally different. The Gospel of Christ has power over Paul, and now all of Paul's life is understood in terms of the Gospel; or, better, all the elements of his life and experience are now integrated and held together by the Gospel as a system of convictions in which Christ plays an important role (which we have yet to examine).

Paul acknowledges that the Gospel of Christ has power over him when he says, for instance, "I bear on my body the marks of Jesus" (Gal. 6:17; the word translated "marks" is a term which usually refers to the "branding" of slaves showing that they belong to a given master). This statement at the conclusion of the letter echoes his self-designation in 1:10 as "slave of Christ" (often translated "servant"). He also speaks of the believers as "those of Christ," a phrase which may express the power of the Gospel upon the believers (and thus it is often translated as "those who belong to Christ"; cf. RSV at 5:24) but also express another kind of relation to Christ. At any rate, it is clear that Paul is conscious that the system of convictions, "Gospel of Christ," has power over him and the believers. This power is further demonstrated by his violent reaction against the "other gospel," which he perceives as a threat to his own convictional system. The power that the Gospel has over him (providing him with true identity, meaning, and purpose) is manifested in his stern rebuke of the Galatians.

Being under the power of the Gospel, Paul rejects his former system of convictions, his Pharisaic faith. Speaking of his experience as a devoted Pharisee, he writes in Phil. 3:7, "Whatever gain I had, I counted as loss for the sake of Christ." In Galatians he expresses the same attitude by saying, "I died to the law" (Gal. 2:19; the Law is the central element of the Pharisaic convictional system). And thus he sees his former convictions about the Law as being a curse which kept him under its (magical) power and prevented him from assuming his true identity as a person in a specific relationship with God, which he calls "righteousness" and "faith." The Gospel of Christ establishes him in this new and true identity as apostle.

Thus we could say that the Gospel means freedom because it frees the believers from other systems of convictions which, by definition, are false and have evil power over people (since they are not the convictional systems of the believers) while, by definition, the Gospel is true (because it is the convictional system of the believers). The problem with this suggestion is that, on the one hand, any system of convictions gives to its adherents freedom from other such systems, and that, on the other hand, despite Paul's claim to the contrary, the Gospel would then be keeping people in bondage as much as any other system of convictions. Paul wants to affirm that the Gospel has power over him and the believers, but he also wants to insist that it is a liberating power and not an enslaving power.

Let me restate the problem with which we are confronted, because it is essential to our understanding of Paul. The apostle wants to claim that the Gospel is a unique system of convictions, a very special type of faith. It alone is true, it alone provides true identity, that is, the true relationship with God, true righteousness. Consequently, Paul claims that the Law—that is, a system of convictions centered around the Law (or Torah, or again Scripture)—cannot provide this true righteousness or justification (a right relationship with God). Thus he writes, "[We] know that a man is not justified by works of the law but through faith in Jesus Christ" (Gal. 2:16). Similarly, he dismisses pagan convictional systems by pointing out that they are centered upon convictions about "beings that by nature are no gods" (4:8), while, by contrast, the gospel is centered around convictions about the true God—the One God (4:9; cf. 1 Cor. 8:4–6). But the believers of any type of faith make the same claim. The Jews, as we shall see, claim that through the Law, through Torah (which stands at the center of their system of convictions), the Jewish believers are established in the right relationship with God. In the same way, each of the Hellenistic cults claims that it worships the true God (or Gods). For the Jews and the adherents to Hellenistic cults, this is self-evident. By definition the Jews and the Hellenistic worshipers are convinced of the validity of their respective systems of convictions and thus of the fallacy of any other system of convictions, just as Paul is. For each of them, their own system of convictions frees them from the "stupid" superstitions of the others. Thus far the Gospel is just a system of convictions as any other system of convictions. And we noted that Paul does acknowledge that it has power over him and other Christian believers.

Yet Paul seems to say more. Yes, the Gospel is freedom *from* other (false) systems of convictions, but he also speaks of the Gospel as providing freedom in a more absolute sense. He uses the term "freedom" by itself, as an absolute (without a qualification such as "from something"): "For freedom Christ has set us free" (Gal. 5:1). The Gospel means freedom from the Law (the Jewish convictional system), as well as from other systems of convictions (the Hellenistic convictional system of the Galatians). This is what he expresses by saying, "Christ has set us free." But it is "for freedom" that we have been freed from other systems of convictions, and not in order to find ourselves under a system of convictions like the others which enslave us by their power. The power of this new system of convictions (i.e., of the Gospel) is a freeing power, a power which frees us.[24] In the preceding passage (Gal. 4:21–31), Paul describes the Christian believers as free because they are "children . . . of the free woman" (Sarah) and not as free because they would have been freed from a slavery (the son of the slave Hagar is rejected and not freed). Thus, this complex interpretation of the story of Abraham, Hagar, and Sarah, and their sons, also implies a concept of absolute freedom which Paul closely relates to the Spirit (Isaac is described as "born according to the Spirit"; 4:29).

Thus Paul seems to claim that the Gospel is unique and true because it is a type of faith radically different from any other type of faith. Its uniqueness and validity do not reside merely in that it involves the worship of the true God (in contrast to the false gods of any other religion). In fact, Paul does not deny that the Jews are worshiping the true God, since he uses their quasi-dogmatic definition of God, "God is One" (Gal. 3:20). As far as he is concerned, they worship the true God—but badly. We could say that his faith as a system of convictions is unique and true for him because of the way it functions. The other systems of convictions involve bondage. The Gospel involves freedom.

Is this really what characterizes Paul's system of convictions as expressed in his letters? This is the question at hand. But how can we even imagine a system of convictions which would both have power and not involve bondage?

## A Gospel Open to New Revelations?

At this point we wish to anticipate some aspects of our discussion of Paul's letters by suggesting that it might be possible to make a distinction between *static* and *dynamic* systems of convictions. Usually a system of convictions is static in the sense that the cluster of fundamental convictions which establishes its convictional pattern is set once and for all. The believers express this by affirming in one way or another that they have the complete and final revelation. In such a case the believers' identity, the purpose and meaning of life, the view of society and of the world, and so on, established by such a system of convictions, is perceived as permanently true, as something which cannot change without losing its truth. In other words, these systems of convictions include as one of their fundamental convictions that truth is static, unchanging, eternal because they are viewed, for instance, as directly reflecting the divine, the eternal. In such a case a system of convictions encloses the believers in a specific vision of the world and life (as the couple during its honeymoon is enclosed in its "love world"). No new revelation is expected, and none can be perceived when one holds this faith. For Paul, the Hellenistic religions (i.e., the pagan religions) and also Judaism belong (rightly or wrongly) to this type of faith.

By contrast, other systems of convictions can be said to be dynamic in the sense that the clusters of fundamental convictions which establish their convictional pattern are not taken as set once and for all. In such cases, the believers do not claim that they have the complete and final revelation. Rather, they are expecting *new revelations* which will establish new clusters of fundamental convictions and will override or fulfill former revelations. Such systems of convictions do establish for the believers their true identity and a true view of the world and life, but their convictional pattern is such that the truth of these convictions is perceived as dynamic and open to changes. These convictions are not viewed as absolute and permanent. Thus, for instance, the believers merely conceive of them as indirect reflections of the divine, the absolute, the eternal. As Paul puts it, "For now we see in a mirror dimly" (1 Cor. 13:12) and not "face to face" (a statement we will need to understand in its context). In other words, convictions, despite their power to provide valid identity as well as valid views of the world and life, are not absolute. They are still perceived as inspired (as having a transcendent origin), but in a manner of speaking, the human (and thus relative) character of these perceptions is also acknowledged. Therefore it is expected that systems of convictions will change. In such a case a system of convictions does not bind the believers to a specific view of the world and of life. It is always, at least potentially, in the process of changing. Hence one can speak of such systems of convictions as involving freedom in an absolute sense rather than bondage. The question is then, Could it be that Paul's Gospel is a system of convictions of this type?

In order to raise this question properly, we need to understand more clearly what it entails. We can conceive of believers expecting new revelations. This is a prophetic attitude which refuses to confine God to his former revelations. God is free to reveal something new. At first it appears that this might be Paul's view. He saw in Jesus Christ a new revelation. Furthermore, in the texts we have discussed there are indications that he might have been constantly expecting new revelations. We have noted his claim that he went up to Jerusalem "by revelation" (Gal. 2:2). He also emphasizes the role of the Spirit in the believers' experience (e.g., 3:2–5; 5:16–25). Could this involve new revelations from the Spirit? Paul also speaks of the believers as "a new creation" (6:15). What does this mean?

At any rate, we can conceive of a dynamic system of convictions, but how does such a system of convictions function? How does it remain the same faith if it can constantly challenge itself and change itself when new revelations override former revelations? The answer to these questions emerges when we note that in order to be expecting *new* revelations, the believers need to have a peculiar attitude vis-à-vis the revelations they presently have. They live by these revelations, since they have nothing better. These revelations form the system of convictions which establishes the semantic universe in which their life has meaning and purpose, but at the same time they perceive these revelations as partial and thus not absolute, which is what allows them to expect other (partial) revelations. This means that they have a second system of convictions, that is, a *meta-system of convictions*, since it involves convictions about their system of convictions.

I used the phrase "meta-system of convictions" by analogy with "metalanguage,"[25] the language that the linguists use to speak about language. We can carry this analogy one step further. A metalanguage, so as to be able to express what characterizes a given language, must be able to speak about other languages as well. Similarly, a meta-system of convictions, in order to express convictions about the believers' own system of convictions, must also include convictions about other systems of convictions. Thus, a meta-system of convictions is made out of convictions about systems of convictions. These convictions allow the believers to identify real and good (true) new revelations and to reject illusions or "false" new revelations. Therefore, they make it possible to be receptive to new revelations. Furthermore, the meta-system of convictions establishes the value of the system of convictions by which the believers live. As such it also molds this system of convictions by establishing its pattern (a dynamic pattern). Therefore the cluster of fundamental convictions about systems of convictions (which the meta-system of convictions is) establishes the convictional pattern which characterizes such a faith. Certainly this meta-system of convictions has a binding power over the believers, but this power imposes as self-evident that the freedom from any system of convictions (including the Gospel) is real and good. According to such a faith, viewing any given system of convictions as absolute is taking as absolute what is not. In other words, it is idolatry. Is this why Paul can equate the Jewish faith and Hellenistic idolatry? But, if so, in what precise sense is Judaism idolatrous?

These remarks are highly theoretical and abstract because they anticipate our forthcoming discussion of Paul's letters, yet they are necessary here because they help us understand the first results of our readings of Galatians. We have found that one of the main features of Paul's system of convictions is that it involves convictions about various systems of convictions, including the Gospel. As we noted, this is true, to a certain extent, about any faith. But the static systems of convictions merely include convictions expressing the view that other religions are absurdities, illusions, superstitions. In the letter to the Galatians, we have already found that Paul's system of convictions involved much more nuanced convictions about the relative values of various religions, including various forms of the Gospel. These first results of our investigation, and Paul's emphasis on freedom, demand that in our readings of his letters we raise the following questions: Could Paul's system of convictions be a dynamic one? Could the cluster of fundamental convictions which establishes the characteristic convictional pattern of his faith be a set of convictions about systems of convictions? A reading of some passages of Galatians guided by these questions will allow us to assess in a preliminary way whether our suggestions about Paul's perception of freedom are valid. But only after reading all of Paul's letters will we be in a position to propose an answer to these questions.

## THE GOSPEL IN RELATION TO JUDAISM
## AND HELLENISTIC RELIGIONS

In order to begin addressing the above-noted questions, we need to study more precisely the nature, in the letter to the Galatians, of the relations between Judaism and the Gospel, between Hellenistic religions and the Gospel, and between the "other gospel" and the Gospel. These relations might be those which establish the convictional pattern that characterizes Paul's faith. We already know that they are opposed in pairs as various manifestations of the opposition between freedom and bondage, but they are interrelated in other ways.

### The Gospel and the "Other Gospel"

First, let us keep in mind that the relationship of the "other gospel" to the Gospel is different from the relationship between Judaism or Hellenistic religions and the Gospel. The "other gospel" is totally and violently rejected. There is no hope for those who are fully involved in it, that is, for those who preach it. They are *anathema* and should be completely rejected. The "other gospel" is an *anti-gospel*. The Gospel and the anti-gospel have totally negative relations. Nevertheless, they have much in common. As does the Gospel, the anti-gospel clearly involves convictions about the relations between the God who is One and humankind, and about the Christ Jesus. But these are "upside down" convictions. In Paul's view, ultimately the anti-gospel involves seeking to please humans instead of seeking to please God (Gal. 1:10), and instead of seeing the death of Christ as salvific it implies that "Christ died to no purpose" (2:21). Nothing can be salvaged from the "other gospel." It must be totally rejected.[26]

### The Gospel and Judaism

The relation between Judaism and the Gospel (with the Law for the Christians of Jewish origin) is quite different. Judaism is a wrong system of convictions, but it is not an anti-gospel in the strict sense of the term. For Paul it is, rather, a non-Gospel. Yes, it is wrong, but it should not be completely rejected; indeed, many things in it can be and need to be "salvaged." To begin with, the Jews believe in the One God, in the true

God. The Gospel also involves this conviction. The Jews believe that the Hebrew Bible is the word of God, revelation from God, Scripture. It is clear that the Old Testament is still Scripture for Paul. In Galatians he quotes it constantly as an authoritative warrant for his argument. The Jews also believed that this Scripture contained both promises (such as the prophecies) and expressions of the will of God (in commandments). Paul still accepts this, although he emphasizes the promise (cf. Gal. 3:15–29). Furthermore, Paul agrees that it expresses the will of God, which for him can be summarized (a view which is not foreign to Judaism[27]) in the love commandment ("you shall love your neighbor as yourself") that Christians need to fulfill (5:13–15). Furthermore, as we suggested earlier in discussing Gal. 2:1–14, Paul does not see anything wrong with the Christians of Jewish origin carrying out the Law, the commandments, as long as in so doing one does not contradict the Gospel, as Peter did at Antioch (2:11–14). The commandments are "holy and just and good" (Rom. 7:12). Paul does not reject Judaism in its totality. Indeed, in many ways he still considers himself a Jew. The Jewish system of convictions is different from and contradictory to the Gospel as a system of convictions, but they overlap. They can be compared to two overlapping circles, although our two-dimensional figure (Figure 1) does not allow us to represent all the relations between these two systems of convictions.

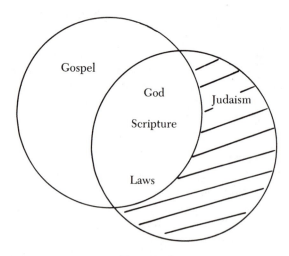

FIGURE 1

## The Gospel and Hellenistic Religions

The relation between Hellenistic religions and the Gospel is similar to that between Judaism and the Gospel. The validity of this statement is granted when one considers the implications of the fact that Paul preaches a Gospel without the Law to Hellenistic people (Gentiles). It means that they do not have to follow the Jewish Law. They do not have to be circumcised, they do not have to observe the dietary laws and the numerous biblical and traditional laws which govern all aspects of a Jew's life. In brief, they do not have a Jewish way of life. But what way of life will they follow in their daily routine? The answer can only be the Hellenistic way of life. In fact, Paul encourages them to keep their way of life as long as Hellenistic customs and views are not in contradiction to the Gospel. For Paul this is a general principle, which we shall find applied again and again. Whatever the convert's situation, the exhortation is always the same, although phrased in different ways: "remain as you are." It is most directly expressed in 1 Cor. 7:19–20: "For neither circumcision counts for anything nor uncircumcision, but keeping the commandments of God. Every one should remain in the state in which he was called." Then he applies this principle to various categories of people: to slaves, to married people, and to unmarried people. About the unmarried he repeats this principle: "It is well for a person to remain as he is" (1 Cor. 7:26). It is important to note the context of this saying. In 1 Cor. 7:25 he emphasizes that this is *not* a command of the Lord, but Paul's opinion. As he says later, remaining single is not necessarily good for everybody (1 Cor. 7:36–38). In the same way, he agrees that the Christians of Jewish origin should remain as they are. They may follow the Law in their life, but this is not a command of the Lord. Following the Law is all right, but only as long as this does not conflict with the Gospel, with "the commandments of God" (which are not necessarily written in Scripture; that is, these are the commandments of God according to the Gospel). In other words, the laws of Scripture, the Jewish laws, are not absolute, but they have their place in the life of the Christians of Jewish origin.

The situation of the Christians of Hellenistic origin is similar. Of course, the Hellenistic way of life is not an absolute and thus there is no ambiguity in this case (by contrast with the Jewish way of life, which is closely linked with Scripture). But the Hellenistic way of life is all right.

Hellenistic people should also remain as they are—Hellenistic. When this is understood, Paul's exhortations to the Galatians in 5:19–23 do not come as a surprise.

What do we find in these verses? A list of "works of the flesh" and another of "fruit of the Spirit." We shall come back to these important concepts. For the time being it is enough to say that we have here a list of vices that the Christians should not have, and a list of virtues that they should display in their lives. In other words, Paul describes first negatively then positively what should characterize the Galatians' way of life. Let us consider the list of vices: "fornication, impurity, licentiousness, idolatry, sorcery, enmity, strife, jealousy, anger, selfishness, dissention, party spirit, envy, drunkenness, carousing" (Gal. 5:19–20). In fact, all of these vices (with the exception of idolatry) are also denounced in Hellenistic philosophies and in many Hellenistic religions. They are what is commonly viewed as evil attitudes in the Hellenistic culture of the time. The same is true of the list of virtues: "love, joy, peace, patience, kindness, goodness, faithfulness, gentleness, self-control" (5:22–23). All these virtues (with the exception of love) are praised by the Hellenistic philosophers and are often affirmed in Hellenistic religions. They are what is commonly viewed as good attitudes in the Hellenistic culture.[28] They are not "commandments" derived from Scripture, even though Hellenistic Judaism (i.e., the Judaism which interacted with Hellenism in cities such as Alexandria [cf. the work of Philo, a Jewish philosopher of that time] and Tarsus, where Paul was raised) also affirmed them, adding "idolatry" to the list of vices. Thus it is clear that once more Paul's teaching to the Galatians can be summarized by the exhortation "remain as you are," follow your Hellenistic way of life and its convictions about good and evil. In fact, Paul says that "the works of the flesh are *plain*" (5:19), a term which can be translated as "evident" or, better, "self-evident"—the very definition of "conviction." But they should do so only insofar as this way of life and convictions do not contradict the Gospel. Therefore, to this traditional Hellenistic wisdom two things need to be added: a rejection of "idolatry" and a new positive attitude, "love."

It is most striking that Paul does not hesitate to call the Hellenistic virtues (such as self-control) "fruit of the Spirit." They do belong to the Gospel as a system of convictions. It is clear that the Hellenistic system of convictions and the Gospel do overlap, despite fundamental differences which call for a conversion when a person passes from one to the other.

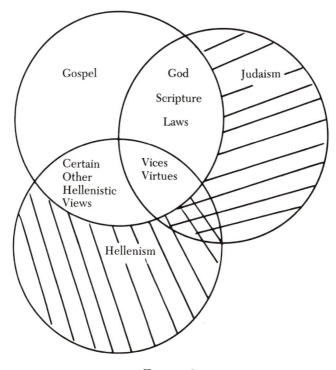

FIGURE 2

By representing the interrelations between the three systems of convictions as in Figure 2, we show that the Hellenistic and the Jewish systems of convictions overlap with the Gospel in different ways and also slightly overlap with each other. Paul suggests this about the list of virtues by noting that "against such there is no law." Although this representation is quite schematic, it nevertheless suggests a few characteristics of the interrelation of the Gospel, Hellenism, and Judaism. Note, for instance, what is found in the circle representing the Gospel as a system of convictions—which would be valid for all Christians. Certain convictions about God and Scripture, even though they have their "origin" in Judaism, become part of the system of convictions of any Christian and thus also of those of Hellenistic origin. It is clear that Paul taught them about the biblical God and Scripture. The reverse—"certain Hellenistic views" which would have to be adopted by Christians of Jewish origin—is merely a theoretical possibility at this stage of our study. We shall see whether or not it is valid. Again we emphasize that this two-dimensional schema cannot represent all the relations and actually misrepresents certain relations. In particular, the Jewish way of life (the laws) and the Hellenistic way of life (virtues) occupy proportionally a much larger place in their respective systems of convictions. Furthermore, it hides the difference between the Gospel of the Jewish Christians and that of the Gentile Christians.

The preceding observations suggest that the relations of opposition between Judaism and Gospel, and between Hellenistic religion and Gospel, are not as clear-cut as one might expect. Freedom from Judaism and from Hellenistic religions does not mean their pure and simple rejection, but it does mean freedom from their bondage, that is, freedom from the curse of the Law or freedom from the slavery to the elemental spirits of the universe. Thus we begin to perceive that the Gospel is a system of convictions which is open-ended in that it can incorporate parts of the system of convictions, whatever it might be, from which the believers converted, and conversely that conversion to the Gospel demands that only a part of one's old system of convictions be rejected—that part which makes out of it a power of bondage. But how can this be? And what does it mean? Let us go back to our love story to express it more concretely.

## The Gospel and Pharisaic Judaism

We have noted that the young couple is in love and that their love as a system of convictions has power over them in that it provides them with identity, meaning, and purpose for their lives. During their "honeymoon" (which we define as that period of whatever length before and after their marriage during which they are totally "in love") their love is an uncompromised system of convictions. The casual observers say of such lovers that they have lost touch with reality. Indeed, they do live in a world of their own, in their love world, a world totally shaped by their love; we could say that they live in a love ghetto which, despite their interaction with other people, separates them from the rest of society. In order to be together, they renounce many opportunities to interact with other people. For instance, they have withdrawn from their respective groups of friends with whom they were involved in a variety of cultural and sporting activities. Our couple in love can thus be compared with the Pharisees (as viewed by Paul), who because of their devoted involvement in their own system of convictions are in effect "separated" (a possible etymological meaning of the term "Pharisee") from any other group and live in their Jewish world.

But love stories do not end with the honeymoon. Sooner or later the couple goes through a crisis when its love system of convictions is challenged or even breaks down. What happens is that love as an absolute system of convictions is abandoned by the couple. This is always a crisis, which today too easily ends in divorce, that is, in total rejection of this system of convictions. This case does not correspond to what happens, according to Paul, when one converts from Judaism or a Hellenistic religion to the Gospel. In other cases, however, the couple goes through the crisis without separating, but the nature of the relation between the man and the woman has changed. They still love one another, even though love is no longer the absolute system of convictions it was for them before the crisis. We need to take the time to develop this parable in detail because it will help us understand how two systems of convictions can be interrelated;[29] what happens when one is freed from the bondage of a system of convictions; and what is, according to Paul, "justification through faith," that is, being in the right relationship with God through faith rather than through works of the Law.

Paul's conversion from Judaism to the Gospel is like the following story. This is a *parable*. It does not intend to say anything about married life, but to provide a concrete illustration of how *relations* (here between a man and a woman) are transformed when a system of convictions is replaced by another one.

A few months, a few years, have passed. Our lovers are still in love— or are they? The husband is. But he feels that their relationship is changing. His wife seems to be more distant. Are they drifting apart? On the surface, little has changed. They still have their love rituals and are doing many things together. Following his suggestion, she had abandoned her job as a social worker even though it meant living on his meager salary as a researcher in biochemistry. And she was glad to have done it, since their schedules would have been too much in conflict.

They do not need much money. The essential thing for them is to spend as much time as possible together. This remains the husband's view, but the wife begins to wonder if it is still true for her. A few months ago they were so attuned to each other that they could anticipate each other's thoughts and wishes. But now, when they are together, she seems to be absent-minded. No, that is too strong a word. Yet when they are together, she is no longer fully present with him. It is as if she were holding back. A part of her is out of reach.

In the following weeks his worst fears seem to be confirmed. She had dinner ready when he arrived home from work, so that they might have as much time together as possible. But now when he comes home, dinner is not ready. Moreover, when he had called home earlier during the day, she was not there. She explained that she goes out and visits her friends who work as social workers at the halfway house for teenage delinquents. Indeed, she does some volunteer work there. But what is going on? Is she not happy with him any longer?

One evening, when she mentions that there might be a position for her at the halfway house, he explodes. All his world, all their world, is crumbling. All their happiness is at stake (that is, also, as we are aware, his identity and the meaning and purpose of his life totally defined by their love). There is no need to describe the violent, emotional, irrational scene; the reader can imagine it. He accuses her of flirting (if not worse) with the director of the halfway house (from the perspective of his love system of convictions, only another love can be an actual threat; similarly, in the case of Paul, only "another gospel" is a real threat to the Gospel). No. She is no longer in love with him.

This last statement is correct. She has realized that social work is an important part of her life, a central part of her life that their love cannot replace. She attempts to explain this to her husband in her own words, but to no avail. No. There is no other man in her life. He is the only one she loves. But her husband looks so desperate that she promises to forget the whole idea and go back to their old routine.

Again, she stays home so that everything is ready when he arrives. And they can spend hours together listening to music and pursuing their love dialogue. But all this which was so rewarding and meaningful a few months ago—which was a "gain" for her, as Paul would say (Phil. 3:7)—she now finds absolutely frustrating, a "loss" (Phil. 3:7). She is stuck at home playing the devoted wife, instead of being able to devote her time and energy to what she feels is truly important. She now perceives their love system of convictions, which once made her so happy, as a burden, indeed, a bondage. She feels this bondage in the present situation, because she is kept away from the halfway house. But she also discovers that their love has always been a bondage blinding her to the importance of her vocation as a social worker. She was "bewitched" by their love. As she sees it now, it is and always was a "curse."

But she is again caught up in social work and freed from this love spell, this love curse. It is her turn to confront her husband. Her work must take priority over their love. She will not let herself be subdued by him again. Yes, she loves him, but the way they loved each other before was wrong. They cannot live as if no one else exists. After all, that was a purely egotistic attitude. Out there are kids in trouble, whom she abandoned to devote herself to her husband. These kids are in desperate need of help from somebody who would give of herself to them. It is irresponsible not to devote her energy and time to these teenagers. And what about him? Is not his work in the lab important? How can he view it as a mere nine-to-five job to make money for supporting their love life? Is not his team involved in experiments which could lead to significant progress in cancer research? How can he laugh at his colleagues, who are so devoted to this project that they often work sixty hours a week? Is he so blind that he does not see the urgency of this research? Out there are people dying from cancer and people grieving over the death of loved ones. It is irresponsible of him to abandon the lab and his colleagues in the middle of the experiments, as he has done several times so as to be with her. Does he not see this?

After several discussions of this type over a period of time, he begins to see her point. But he asks, "Since our love made us so egotistic by blinding us to the needs of others, should we separate?" "Divorce? Certainly not! By no means! Of course not," replies the wife. "Our love is beautiful. It is good." ("What then shall we say? That the law is sin? By no means! . . . The law is holy, and the commandment is holy and just and good" [Rom 7:7, 12].)

We can now tell the happy ending of our story. The man and the woman are now totally devoted to their new system of convictions, which is centered this time on concern for other people's needs. Thus the man is fully devoted to his research because, he hopes, it will help alleviate the suffering of many people. The woman, working full time at the halfway house is entirely devoted to "her kids" (as she calls them), who so often find themselves in impossible situations from which they cannot disentangle themselves without help. But the man and the woman still live together. They are not separated—what nonsense to suggest that! They deeply love each other. Their love life is going strong. And yet there is a big difference which an outsider might not perceive. Their love is no longer at the center of their life; it is a corner of their life (an important corner, and possibly several corners, but not the center). Their love is not what structures and gives meaning and purpose to their lives. Rather, their lives are structured by something else: their system of convictions centered on their common concern for other people's needs. Their love provides a home base for their respective work. It is the environment in which they can rebuild their energy, their strength; it is the place where they can again find the courage and the will to go ahead, despite a failure with a teenage delinquent or a setback in the research. Yet, despite its importance and its value, their love is secondary as compared with their concern for others. A part of their love-life is given up whenever necessary for their work for others.

## FOURTH READING: WORKS OF THE LAW, FAITH, AND RIGHTEOUSNESS

The preceding story about the man and woman is a *parable* of the *relations* between the Gospel and Pharisaic Judaism; it does not express the content of the Gospel and of Pharisaism as systems of convictions. This parable does *not* intend to say that the Gospel is a system of convictions centered on a concern for other people's needs. Certainly "love for the neighbor" has its place in the Gospel as a system of convictions, but as we shall see, this is not its center. Similarly, it does *not* intend to say that Judaism would involve an absence of concern for others.

This story helps us to understand in a preliminary way the relations, in Paul's system of convictions, between the Gospel and Pharisaic Judaism and also concepts such as "justification through works of the Law" (related to a *system* of convictions, Pharisaic Judaism, which corresponds to that of the lovers during their honeymoon), and "justification through faith" (related to a *meta-system* of convictions, the Gospel, which corresponds to the situation at the end of the parable).

The Pharisaic system of convictions from which Paul converted is in his view centered around the "Law." Thus he speaks of himself as having "died to the law" (Gal. 2:19). But what exactly does he mean by the term "law"? He uses this term both to designate the commandments and to designate Scripture in general (4:21). We can conclude that he follows the Jewish usage: he translates by the Greek term *nomos* (further translated in English by "law") the Hebrew term *Torah* which designates at once (a) the books of Moses (the Pentateuch), and thus in a more limited sense (b) the will of God expressed in the many laws contained in these books, as well as (c) the traditional interpretations of these laws, and also, in a more general sense, (d) the entire Hebrew Scripture, since these books are the most sacred part of Scripture for the Pharisees. So from now on we shall use the term "Torah" in order to preserve the ambiguity of Paul's use of the term "law." We need to add that he uses it in still another sense. When Paul refers indirectly to his conversion as dying "to the law," the term "law" (Torah) refers to the Jewish faith as a system of convictions. In the same way that the Christian system of convictions centered around the Gospel of Jesus Christ can be designated in a shorthand fashion by the term "Gospel" (or even by the term "Christ"), so the Pharisaic system of convictions centered around Torah (in Paul's view) can be designated in a shorthand fashion by the term "Torah" (or, in translation, "law").

### Justified through Faith (Gal. 2:15–16)

Keeping in mind our parable, and keeping in mind that we should read "Torah" each time we encounter the term "law" so as not to pre-judge in which of the above senses Paul uses the term, we can now begin to understand several aspects of the important argument of Gal. 2:15–16.

> We ourselves, who are Jews by birth and not Gentile sinners, yet who know that a man is not justified by works of the law but through faith in Jesus Christ, even we have believed in Christ Jesus, in order to be justified by faith in Christ, and not by works of the law, because by works of the law shall no one be justified. (Gal. 2:15–16)

From the Jewish perspective, Gentiles are by definition sinners since they do not follow the will of God. How could they? They do not consider Torah to be the word of God. But now as Christians "[we] know that a man is not justified by works of the law but through faith in Jesus

Christ." Here, by contrast with the discussion of justification in Romans (which we shall study in Chapter 6), "being justified" is *not* primarily opposed to "being condemned." As we have already noted, the words "being justified" refer to a relationship. Through justification, one is in the right relationship with God and Christ: Paul is "living to God" (Gal. 2:19); "it is no longer I who live, but Christ who lives in me" (2:20). Not being justified (because of putting one's confidence in the works of the Law) is being "severed from Christ" (5:4), that is, not being in this right relationship with Christ. The question is, How is one established in this right relationship with God (or Christ)? The answer is: through one's system of convictions. Our lovers were established in the right relationship with each other through their love during their honeymoon and, later on, through their concern for others. The Jews are established in the right relationship with God through Torah, the center of their system of convictions, while the Christians are established in the right relationship with God through "Christ," the center of their system of convictions. (But let us remember that what Paul means by the term "Christ" still remains to be defined.)

From Paul's perspective, the system of convictions centered on Torah involves focusing all of one's energy on this relation to God in order to maintain it and to sustain it: one has to act according to this system of convictions, to do "works of Torah," that is, to follow the laws. This could be understood if Paul also perceived the Jewish system of convictions as an absolute and thus as static. Such is also the situation of our lovers during their honeymoon; in order to maintain and to sustain their relationship, they devoted themselves to act in a loving way toward each other. Their love relationship depended upon their performing "works of love," because their love—system of convictions—was an absolute. Yet this suggestion concerning the "works of Torah" in Pharisaic Judaism is in large part made on the basis of the "parable of the two lovers." It needs to be verified in two ways: (1) through a study of the early Rabbinic system of convictions (the Jewish type of faith studied on its own terms—and not in terms of Paul's polemic against it—as it is expressed in the literature most directly related to the Pharisees), so as to show whether this view of the "works of Torah" and of "righteousness" has any relation to Judaism and whether Judaism can be viewed as involving a static system of convictions (see Chapter 3); (2) through further study of Paul's letters so as to verify whether it is such a view of the "works of Torah" and of "righteousness" that Paul rejects (see Chapters 4, 5, 6, 7).

By contrast with the Jewish attitude (as presented by Paul), for the Christians the right relationship with God is maintained and sustained "through faith in Jesus Christ." So far, according to our methodology, we do not know what this phrase means, but with Paul we can define it negatively: it means "not through works of Torah." Without repeating the preceding remarks in a negative form, we can note that, for Paul, the Christian system of convictions does not involve "works" for establishing oneself in the right relationship with God. We could say that this relationship with God happens, is maintained, and is sustained without any effort on the part of the Christians. Their system of convictions directs their attention, their concern, and thus their acts in a direction other than toward their relation to God. Our lovers, after their conversion to a system of convictions focused on concern for others, are in the same situation. Their right relationship with one another, their love, is maintained and sustained indirectly (and no longer directly by their "works of love"). They are in a true love relationship precisely when they do not consider their love—their system of convictions—as an absolute. Because all their attention, their concern, and their acts are focused on others (either in social work or in research), they are, without doing anything about it directly, in the right relationship with each other, in a love relationship. Note that this happens because the lives of both are focused on "concern for other people" (on the same thing), although this concern is manifested in different ways.

At this point we should note that, for Paul, "faith"—which among other things means not working toward establishing and maintaining the right relationship with God—does not mean passivity, absence of actions, absence of works. Indeed, in the concluding parts of the letter he exhorts the Galatians to act in certain ways and in so doing does not hesitate to say, "Bear one another's burdens, and so *fulfil the law of Christ*" (Gal. 6:2). By analogy with the lovers of our parable, we could say that it is because the Christians' acts, attention, and concern are focused upon "something" which is also the focus of God's (and Christ's) "acts, attention, and concern" that the Christians and God are in a right relationship with each other. They are in the right relationship with God, they are justified (2:16) and will be justified (5:5) without working at it, by "the grace of God" (2:21), while working at something else, fulfilling the law of Christ, that is, "walking by the Spirit," a phrase which could mean something similar to the phrase "co-worker with God" (RSV: "God's servant") that we find in 1 Thess. 3:2 (i.e., working together with the Spirit). If this were the case, the Gospel as a system of convictions would establish the believers in the right relationship with God precisely when they view the Gospel not as an absolute and static system but as a system pointing beyond itself toward "something else" (a situation) which is also God's concern and thus in which God intervenes. Then the phrase "through faith in Jesus Christ" should *not* be understood as merely referring to a belief about the revelation which occurred in the past—in the time of Jesus' ministry, death, and resurrection on the third day—but as also referring to *present* (and future) manifestations of God through the resurrected Christ. In other words, could the phrase "being justified through faith in Jesus Christ" mean being established in the right relationship with God by discovering (which is one dimension of faith) God/Christ at work in certain present situations and joining God in this work (another dimension of faith: the "work of faith" [1 Thess. 1:3])?

For the time being this is merely a question. It needs to be addressed through further studies of the organization of Paul's letters aimed at identifying his fundamental convictions, especially the convictions about God and his relationship with the believers, and the convictional pattern which they form. These convictions are expressed in Paul's descriptions of situations in which he sees the manifestation of God. After identifying these situations, we need to study the relative weight or importance he gives to each of them in his arguments. How does he perceive the relationship among past manifestations of God (in situations reported by Scripture and in Jesus), present manifestations (in his and other persons' experiences), and future manifestations (including at the time of the Parousia)? The above discussion of the freedom of the Gospel suggests that he would emphasize present and future manifestations of God as new revelations. Our discussion of righteousness suggests that he would view these manifestations of God as situations in which the believers can join God in his action. Thus the believers would be in the right relationship with God, not because they work at it but because God intervenes in certain situations and thus they can join him in his action. Whether this is the case will be shown by studying the organization of his arguments, and specifically the relative importance he attaches to their various parts. Our study of 1 Thessalonians, Philemon, and Philippians (Chapters 4 and 5) with these questions in mind will allow us to show the convictional pattern through which Paul interrelates various manifestations of God with the believers. We will then be in a position to examine the relationship of this pattern with the one we have begun to perceive in the way in which Paul interrelates various forms of the Gospel with Judaism and Hellenistic religions.

## The Works of the Law

We have noted that the Torah-centered system of convictions is homologable to the idol-centered Hellenistic system of convictions, that Torah is both evil (a curse bringing sin and death) and holy (belonging therefore to the Gospel). The only possible conclusion is that, for Paul, Torah is evil precisely when it becomes an absolute, when it is taken to be *necessary* for any valid relationship with God. Or should we say that Torah is evil when it structures the life of the believers to the point that all their attention, concern, and activity is focused upon their relationship with God? This is what our preliminary discussion of "righteousness through the works of Torah" would suggest. Paul admits that Torah is good and useful and has its place in the Gospel as a system of convictions, but it is not an absolute, and considering it as an absolute when it is not is nothing other than idolatry. Torah can be compared to the precious times our lovers spend together. During their honeymoon these times were absolute; they would have been desperate, lost, without these times, because it was through these times that their love relationship was maintained and sustained. After their conversion to the system of convictions centered on concern for others, these times are good, joyous, helpful, but no longer essential. Indeed, they often sacrifice them without hesitation.

We might be ready to agree with this interpretation of the parable. Making an absolute out of certain times in which the lovers' relation is directly manifested is considering as absolute what is not absolute. But is not the case of Torah quite different? Paul does affirm that Torah is Scripture, the word of God. Is this not recognizing that Torah has a divine and thus absolute authority? How can Torah, the Old Testament, be both word of God and not absolute?

Paul's argument against the Gentile Galatians who want to follow Torah makes it clear that for him Torah can be a curse which contradicts and nullifies (cf. Gal. 2:21) the Gospel (which is also God's promise), although by nature it does not or should not do so (3:21). In this argument, Paul seems primarily concerned with the heretic Galatians' wish to fulfill one of the commandments, that concerning circumcision. "If you receive circumcision, Christ will be of no advantage to you" (5:2).

In the report about his controversy with the "false brethren," he mentioned only one specific item: "Titus . . . was not compelled to be circumcised, though he was a Greek" (2:3). In the dispute at Antioch, he mentions that Peter wavered because of the "circumcision party." Yet this controversy over circumcision is not over the fulfillment of one biblical commandment but over an attitude toward the entire law (Torah), as he explains:

> I testify again to every man who receives circumcision that he is bound to keep the whole law. You are severed from Christ, you who would be justified by the law; you have fallen away from grace. (Gal. 5:3–4)

Indeed, through circumcision one becomes a member of the Chosen People. By being circumcised, the Gentiles adopt the Jewish faith centered on Torah. They signify their conviction that in order to be in the right relationship with God they need to fulfill the will of God as expressed in the laws of Torah, and thus they commit themselves "to keep the whole law." In the process they have abandoned the Gospel as their system of convictions, even if they still think that they believe in Christ. Christ has become a corner of their system of convictions instead of being its center, which is now occupied by Torah. Then they will no longer risk persecution (by the Jews) as Paul does (Gal. 5:11). They have joined them! The overlapping of the two systems has been reversed. Christ has been incorporated in the Torah-centered system of convictions instead of freeing the Galatians from it as from any other bondage.

We can understand how the Galatians could be deceived into adopting the Law. Are not the apostles themselves circumcised? Is not Peter, together with James, John, and all the Christians of Jewish origin, keeping the Law? Are they not good Christians? Then why should the Galatians not be like them?

Their situation is like that of a friend of the husband in our parable. He is himself fully involved and devoted to their joint research project because of its potential importance for the treatment of cancer. For him this involvement has also meant giving up a passion (a system of convictions), motorbike racing, which he now sees as a futile passion even though he still enjoys rides on his motorbike in the countryside. Now, he announces to his friend that he is falling in love. He expects congratulations from his friend, who he knows is happily married and has told him so many times how much his wife helps him when he is discouraged by a setback. To his surprise, his friend warns him, "Don't fall in love. It would be the end of your research career." "But are you not in love yourself, and does it not help you to be fully devoted to our research?" The friend then has to tell him the story we know. Despite appearances, they are no longer "in love," in the same way that he is no longer passionate about motorbike racing although he still enjoys riding his bike. (At this point our story is no longer adequate because the young husband might not want to tell his friend not to marry—which would correspond to Paul's exhortation that the Galatians should not be circumcised. This last part of the parable was nevertheless given because it helps illustrate the relations between the Galatians and the Jewish Christians, and also to show that Paul's Gospel as a system of convictions has additional characteristics which make it unlike most other systems of convictions.)

Despite appearances (and some temporary or permanent relapses), Peter has abandoned the Torah-centered system of convictions, as should any true believer of Jewish origin. No, the Galatians do not need to adopt the Jewish way of life which is helpful for the believers of Jewish origin (because it provides some meaningful order for their daily routine). Their Hellenistic way of life is just as good for this purpose. Yes, Scripture is the word of God. Yes, they need to hear Scripture and its promises, but they should not make out of it the center of their system of convictions. Something else should be the center. Indeed, Torah is Scripture precisely because it points beyond itself (and away from concerns about one's right relationship with God), that is, because it is "promise" pointing to "Christ" and to the Gentiles' experience of the Spirit.

These remarks again show that we need to study Paul's use of Scripture, yet it is already clear that, for Paul, the Gospel of Christ is not an enslaving power, not an idol (as the elemental spirits of the universe are), not a curse which keeps the believers in bondage (as Torah does), but still a system of convictions which has power over them.

## QUESTIONS FOR DISCERNING PAUL'S SYSTEM OF CONVICTIONS

Our successive readings have left aside important parts of the letter to the Galatians. We shall come back to them when studying Paul's use of Scripture (Chapter 6 will include a discussion of Galatians 3 and 4) and when dealing with his ethics (Chapter 8 will involve further discussion of

Galatians 5 and 6). Our concern in this chapter was to establish some of the central characteristics of Paul's faith, which involve a cluster of convictions expressing that for Paul the Gospel means freedom. Our study led us to conclude tentatively that the statement "for freedom Christ has set us free" seems to express the fundamental convictional pattern which is the distinctive feature of Paul's faith. Only at the end of our study will we be in a position to understand it fully. Through our reading of Galatians, however, we begin to perceive some of its characteristics. The complex interaction of this faith with other faiths (Jewish and Hellenistic faiths) shows the importance in it of convictions about systems of convictions. This is a first confirmation of our suggestion that the fundamental cluster of convictions of Paul's faith is a meta-system of convictions and thus that Paul's faith is dynamic in character, that is, characterized by its expectation of new revelations (see above, pp. 57–66). This is why the Gospel means freedom. As such it is to be contrasted with static types of faith, such as Judaism, which is in Paul's view a curse preventing the believers from being in the right relationship with God because it is a bondage that encloses them in the ghetto of an absolute system of convictions.

Our study of Galatians, and especially our reading of Gal. 2:15–16, helped us formulate more specific questions which will guide our study of the other letters.

First, we need to understand as clearly as possible the relationship between the Pharisaic system of convictions and the Gospel. We have seen how central this relationship is to Paul's system of convictions. We can even suspect that this relation manifests the fundamental convictions which establish the convictional pattern characteristic of his faith in the Gospel of freedom. We have also suggested that this relation in large part defines the central concept of "justification by faith." But in which sense is the Jewish system of convictions (centered around the Law), a curse? In which sense is it static? Does Paul's view of Judaism correspond to its reality? We need to study what characterizes the Jewish faith on its own terms, that is, as the Jews themselves expressed their faith in their own writings and practices. Chapter 3 will be devoted to this topic, in an effort to present a picture of the Pharisaic faith as a coherent system of convictions. This study will give us a picture of what the Gospel is not, without which we cannot hope to understand the distinctiveness of Paul's faith.

The following chapters will allow us to pursue our investigation of the characteristics of Paul's faith, and especially of the convictions about justification, by inquiring whether the dynamism of this faith can be found elsewhere. For this we need to elucidate the situations which are of utmost importance for Paul—those situations in which he sees God's interventions and revelations. We shall be able to discover these by studying how his arguments are organized. Our reading will be guided by these questions: What is the relative weight, importance, or role given to various parts of his arguments? We shall identify especially those textual elements which guarantee the validity of other parts of the discourse. In so doing, we shall identify the situations in which Paul found God's revelations and thus which established his fundamental convictions. Then, studying the interrelations of these convictions, we shall attempt to elucidate the convictional pattern they form. Such will be the goal of our reading of 1 Thessalonians (in Chapter 4) and Philemon and Philippians (in Chapter 5). Since Scripture, the Torah, is viewed by Paul as the word of God (even though it is also a curse), it is also a manifestation of God's revelations. The question will then be: What is the role of Scripture in Paul's system of convictions? How is it related to the patterns we will have found in 1 Thessalonians, Philemon, and Philippians? We will address these questions by reading a series of texts: Galatians 3 and 4, Romans 4, and 1 Corinthians 15, which have in common a heavy use of Scripture (see Chapter 6).

### SUGGESTIONS FOR FURTHER READINGS

Since our study of Galatians was designed to elucidate aspects of Paul's system of convictions (of Paul's faith), we did not raise a number of questions which would allow the readers to consider other dimensions of the meaning of this letter. Furthermore, even though we shall come back to Galatians in Chapters 6 and 8, our study does not deal with all the passages of the letter. The following studies of Galatians can be used both to complement the above reading and to compare and contrast the exegetical results of our approach with the results of other approaches.

For major English commentaries on Galatians, see H. D. Betz, *Galatians: A Commentary on Paul's Letter to the Churches in Galatia*; E. D. Burton, *A Critical and Exegetical Commentary on the Epistle to the Galatians*; D. Guthrie, *Galatians*; J. B. Lightfoot, *The Epistle of St. Paul to the Galatians*; M. Luther, "Lectures on Galatians," *Luther's Works*, vols. 26 and 27, ed. J. Pelikan; W. M.

Ramsey, *A Historical Commentary on St. Paul's Epistle to the Galatians*; J. P. Ropes, *The Singular Problem of the Epistle to the Galatians*.

Volumes 1 and 2 of the general work mentioned below deal directly with the issues of the Jewish and Gentile worlds and primitive Christianity. F. J. Jackson and K. Lake, *The Acts of the Apostles: The Beginnings of Christianity*, 5 vols.

For articles on Galatians in major reference works see H. D. Betz, "Galatians," in *IDBS*, pp. 252–53; J. Fitzmyer, "The Letter to the Galatians," in *JBC*, pp. 236–46; J. Knox, "Galatians," in *IDB*, vol. 2, pp. 338–43.

# 3

# The Pharisaic Faith and Paul

THE GOSPEL, freedom from the curse of Torah. The Gospel, fulfillment of the promises of Torah. These two formulas summarize the ambivalent relationship between the Gospel and Judaism as Paul saw it. Chapter 2 has shown how essential this complex relationship is in Paul's system of convictions. As a non-Gospel, Judaism provides the negative definitions of central convictions: the Gospel involves "righteousness through faith," the only possibility for establishing a true relationship with God, while Judaism misleadingly proposes "righteousness through works of Torah," which actually prevents any true relationship with God; the Gospel is freedom by contrast to Judaism, which is bondage under a curse. Furthermore, our reading of Galatians suggests that, for Paul, the Gospel is a dynamic system of convictions which is open to new revelations, while Judaism is a static system of convictions which holds certain revelations to be absolute and permanent. This would be why Judaism is a non-Gospel in spite of its worship of the true God, the God who is One, and its view of Scripture, Torah, as the revelation of the true God. Paul clearly bases this evaluation of Judaism upon his own experience as a zealous Pharisee. It is therefore certainly related to actual characteristics of Judaism. But this evaluation, as any evaluation, presents only a part of the phenomenon which is evaluated.

In Galatians as well as in other letters, Paul, as an apostle concerned to address the issues which confront his readers, expresses most emphatically what is wrong in Judaism from his perspective. More discreet statements and allusions show that he does not ignore—and does not object to—other aspects of Judaism. Indeed, Paul the former Pharisee presupposes in his own way of thinking a comprehensive knowledge of Judaism, but he discusses only those aspects which have direct bearing upon the issues at hand and which have their place in his Christian system of convictions either positively or negatively. Therefore, despite the many references to Judaism found in his letters, it is impossible to show clearly from them what characterizes the Jewish system of convictions.

In order to understand fully what characterizes the Gospel as a system of convictions we need to contrast it with what it is not. More precisely, we need to study the fundamental convictions which establish the convictional pattern of the Jewish faith, for Paul opposes the Gospel to Judaism at the level of their most fundamental convictions: those concerning the relations of humans with the divine (justification through faith versus justification through the works of Torah).

Such a study presents two difficulties. First, the study of early Judaism is a complex task because of the nature of the available documents and their diversity. Second, the preconceptions that modern readers hold about the Jewish faith are not easy to overcome, since they are based upon the partial picture of Judaism found in Paul's letters and other New Testament texts.

## THE CONVICTIONAL PATTERN OF
## PHARISAIC JUDAISM

Judaism can be defined, in a general way, as the religion which views the Hebrew Bible as its Scripture, and as such it cannot be identified with the religion of the ancient Israelites which is presented in the Hebrew Bible. The ancient Israelites did not have this multifold book as their sacred text. It is only during the exile (587–538 B.C.), and more clearly after the return from exile (which began in 538 B.C.), and in the time of Ezra and Nehemiah (fifth century B.C.) that one can date the beginning of Judaism as a religion which includes among its fundamental convictions that the Hebrew Bible is, in one sense or another, word of God. This religion of the book is closely related to the religion of the ancient Israelites expressed in its Scripture, but this new conviction about Scripture brought about a significant shift of the convictional system. Therefore we must speak of a new form, more precisely of several new forms, of the biblical religion. Indeed, several branches of Judaism progressively developed over the centuries. By the first century of our era, several parties can be identified.

The party of the Sadducees included the priests (of the Temple at Jerusalem) and their followers. Together with the Pharisees (a movement which emphasized the practice of the Jewish religion in the daily life rather than in Temple rituals), they formed what can be termed the mainstream of Judaism in Palestine at that time. Yet the situation is made more complex by the presence of various other movements: a mystical movement and the influential Apocalyptic movement. The latter was a movement made up of Jews who were convinced that the end of history was to be expected in the very near future. Parts of the Apocalyptic movement formed clearly identifiable splinter groups, and certain Apocalyptic believers withdrew from society to form religious communities in the wilderness; such is the case of the community of Qumran, whose library is known as the Dead Sea Scrolls and which might be one of the Essene communities described by the Jewish historian Josephus.[1] Other Apocalyptic believers were led by their beliefs to adopt radical political attitudes and to engage in revolutionary actions against the Romans; such are the Zealots who led the insurrection against the Romans which brought about the destruction of Jerusalem and of the Temple in A.D. 70.[2] Yet many apocalyptically minded people continued to participate in the worship and the life of the rest of the Jewish community.

Outside of Palestine, Pharisaism was the dominant trend of Judaism, but in the Hellenistic cities it entered into dialogue with the prevalent culture and gave rise to various forms of Hellenistic Judaism. The most developed form of Hellenistic Judaism is found in the writings of Philo of Alexandria (ca. 20 B.C.–A.D. 40),[3] who expressed the Jewish faith in terms of Neoplatonic philosophy. But elsewhere, and especially in Asia Minor, it is not clear that Hellenistic Judaism was so far removed from the mainstream of Pharisaic Judaism; in fact, it can be viewed as a form of Pharisaism.

Paul was a Pharisee (Phil. 3:5–6), and in his polemic against Judaism, Paul clearly attacks mainstream Judaism, Pharisaic Judaism. Our discussion of Judaism will be limited to the examination of the fundamental convictions which establish the convictional pattern of Pharisaic Judaism. In this book we shall present only the results of such a study, but first we need to explain briefly how we proceeded.

Any study of the Pharisees must grapple with two difficulties. First, the Rabbinic literature which contains most of the information we have about the Pharisees is quite extensive. It involves the Mishnah, the Talmud, and also Midrashim (plural of Midrash, "commentaries" on Scripture) and Targums ("translations" of Scripture in Aramaic). Second, these texts were written down much later (often centuries later) than the period which concerns us. They contain older traditions, but these are very difficult to date with precision. Yet our study remains manageable because of its specific focus on central characteristics of the Pharisaic *faith*.

Since our investigation is aimed at elucidating the system of *fundamental* convictions and its pattern, the examination of a cross section of representative texts is sufficient because, by definition, any text of a corpus (whatever be the size of the corpus) presupposes the fundamental convictional pattern of the system of convictions which undergirds the corpus as a whole.[4] If we limit ourselves to the study of the fundamental convictions regarding the relations of humans with the divine, and the convictions about the means by which this relation is established, we can be confident of reaching satisfactory results, even if we examine only a selection of texts which manifest these convictions in various settings.

The limitation of our study to the system of fundamental convictions resolves to a large extent the problem posed by the dates of the Rabbinic literature and of its traditions. If we wanted to trace the precise beliefs, ideas, and symbols of the Pharisees in the time of Paul, our task would be quite complex. We would need to demonstrate that each text we use records a tradition which can be traced back to that period. But by contrast to beliefs and ideas, a system of convictions, and especially its most fundamental parts which establish the convictional pattern, remains relatively stable. This has been demonstrated by anthropologist Claude Lévi-Strauss and his followers through their study of myths.[5] The story of the myth—its plots, its characters, its details concerning times and locations, its symbolism—can change quite radically, while the convictional pattern remains the same. All the variants of a given myth have the same "mythical structure" (Lévi-Strauss's term), that is, the same convictional pattern. This also applies to religions which are not mythological (i.e., religions which do not have mythological stories as their sacred "texts").

Pharisaism, when it became early Rabbinic Judaism, underwent many transformations. The ideas, the symbolism, the "stories" (used in sermons), the specific interpretations of the laws, and so on, changed in response to new cultural situations, and in the process, secondary convictions also changed. But the convictional pattern did not itself change. By contrast to the change of faith which occurred when convictions about Scripture were introduced among the fundamental convictions of the ancient Israelites, the passage from Pharisaism to Rabbinic Judaism does not seem to involve a change of the convictional pattern. If Judaism survived the destruction of the Temple and of Palestine by the Romans, it was because already for Pharisaic Judaism the primary place of worship was no longer the Temple but the Synagogue, and because the institution which authoritatively defined the norms governing the life of the Jewish community was the Rabbinic school (even though it was fully organized only after the fall of Jerusalem at Yavneh). This explains why the Pharisaic faith and its convictional pattern remained stable despite significant changes in the worship and life of the Jewish people. Actually the Rabbis in the third century viewed themselves as heirs of the Pharisees (heirs of the Sages, as the leaders of the Pharisees were often called). They perceived themselves as holding the same faith as the Pharisees.[6] This is not in itself a proof that there was no change in fundamental convictions and convictional pattern, but our study of such texts and traditions demonstrates that the convictional pattern they manifest did remain remarkably stable.[7]

Thus we need to discuss texts which were written much later than Paul's time and which manifest a variety of expressions of the early Rabbinic/Pharisaic faith in a variety of cultural situations. But since we shall limit our investigation to fundamental convictions and their pattern, we shall be able to speak of what characterized the Pharisaic faith that Paul shared before his conversion and that he confronted as an apostle.

Our goal is therefore to discuss the fundamental principles which governed the use of concepts, symbols, ideas, and interpretations of the Law in Pharisaic and early Rabbinic Judaism. These principles are the convictional pattern which motivated these Jews to lead certain types of life in specific cultural situations, to worship in certain ways, to interpret and appropriate Scripture according to certain rules. The result of our investigation will be the presentation of the Pharisaic faith as a coherent system of fundamental convictions which can be compared and con-

trasted with any other system of convictions, whether or not it is historically related to Pharisaic Judaism. Of course, we want to compare the
Pharisaic faith with Paul's Gospel as a system of convictions which happens to be historically related to it. Yet let me emphasize that despite
the historical interrelations of Paul and Pharisaic Judaism, our study of
the convictional pattern established by the fundamental convictions will
*not* allow us to say anything about the way in which Paul appropriated,
transformed, or rejected specific Pharisaic concepts, symbols, ideas, or
interpretations of the Law when developing his theological stances. It
will, however, allow us to show clearly the differences between, and
overlapping of, the most characteristic features of these two types of
faith: their systems of fundamental convictions and their respective convictional patterns.

## MODERN READERS AND PHARISAISM

Our study presupposes that Pharisaic Judaism is characterized, as is
any religion, by a coherent system of fundamental convictions. This
involves a positive attitude vis-à-vis Pharisaic Judaism which is in sharp
contrast with our preconceptions.

As modern readers of the New Testament, we have the tendency to
construct a negative picture of Judaism and especially of Pharisaic Judaism, based almost exclusively upon the polemical statements found in
these texts. While this attitude is understandable because of the emphasis put on negative features of Judaism in early Christian writings, it
is misleading in that it overlooks the more discreet positive statements
about Judaism. As a result we have a view of Judaism which leads us to
misunderstand the Gospel, since it is in part defined through its multifold relationship with Judaism.

The preconceptions which bring about this stereotyped view of Judaism are rooted in a conviction that since the Gospel proclaimed by Paul
is true, Judaism must be totally wrong. Indeed, early Christianity involves a rejection of the various forms of Judaism since it involves a
conversion from these forms of Judaism. But for the earliest church in
general and for Paul in particular, conversion to the Gospel is a conversion not to a new religion but rather to the true form of Judaism.
Believing and proclaiming that Jesus is the "Christ" (Greek term for the
Hebrew "Messiah") is a Jewish belief and proclamation. What was hoped

for in Judaism is now proclaimed as realized. Being "Christian" is nothing other than being a truly faithful Jew. Even the universalism involved in Paul's statement "there is neither Jew nor Greek" is not foreign to Judaism and its hope for the conversion of the nations which, at last, would worship the true God, the God who is One. And for Paul, this universalism is not the result of a rejection of Judaism, but the affirmation of what is "real" Judaism according to the prophet Jeremiah (Jer. 9:25). What is important is not the physical circumcision, but the circumcision of the heart. Thus both the circumcised (the traditional Jew) and the uncircumcised (the Greek) can be "real Jews."

> For he is not a real Jew who is one outwardly, nor is true circumcision something external and physical. He is a real Jew who is one inwardly, and real circumcision is a matter of the heart, spiritual and not literal. His praise is not from men but from God. (Rom. 2:28–29)

Thus it is clear that the Gospel does not involve a total rejection of Judaism. The Judaism from which Paul converted is not an anti-Gospel, but a non-Gospel, that is, a form of religion which has much in common with the Gospel even though it misses the mark (since in terms of the above text, it does not give the place it should give to the "circumcision of the heart").

Yet our preconceptions are tenacious. We feel justified in having a totally negative view of Judaism (and especially of Pharisaic Judaism), since it was rejected by the early church. When we concede that the Gospel and the Pharisaic faith overlap—a view which acknowledges that the Jews have access (e.g., in Scripture) to at least a part of the truth— we brand the Jews as hypocrites. We justify such a claim by means of superficial interpretations of such statements as those found in Gal. 5:13 and Rom. 2:17–29 as well as in the Gospels (cf., e.g., Matthew 23). Without speaking of the latent anti-Semitism (which so easily becomes virulent anti-Semitism with all its horrors) which this view of the Jews involves, such a negative view of Judaism prevents us from perceiving the challenging character of the Gospel preached by Paul. When we say that the Pharisees are hypocrites, we mean that they pretend to serve God while being, in fact, concerned only with attaining their own salvation by accumulating meritorious works of the Law in order to escape the wrath of God. But then we cannot understand how the Jewish faith could be a coherent system of convictions providing purpose and meaning for Jews' lives. If Judaism was characterized by such an incoherent and hypocritical attitude, the passage from Judaism to the Christian faith would not be a conversion (from one faith to another faith) but the passage from an absence of faith to a faith. Yet Paul makes it clear in his own case that he *converted* from a faith in which he was deeply involved—he was "extremely zealous" (Gal. 1:14)—and in the case of other Jews he writes, "I bear them witness that they have a zeal for God" (Rom. 10:2), even though this zeal "is not enlightened," that is, is misled. In other words, Paul makes it clear that for him the Jews are not hypocrites in the sense that they merely pretend to believe in something. On the contrary, they are totally devoted to their faith, a faith which is not totally wrong since "they are zealous *for God.*"

As long as we hold the above negative view of Judaism, we are led to conceive of the Gospel merely as the proclamation of the gracious love of God in contrast to a doctrine of the meritorious works performed to escape the wrath of God. In this view of the Gospel there is no place for the wrath of God, despite Romans 1 and 2 and many other passages. A superficial understanding of Judaism can only leave us with a superficial understanding of the Gospel.

The question then is, How can we overcome our preconceptions? Since our negative view of Judaism is based upon the erroneous conviction that since the Gospel is true, Judaism has to be totally wrong, we presuppose that everything Paul affirms positively about the Gospel must be said negatively about Judaism: since Paul proclaims the love of God, the Jews did not know it; since Paul emphasizes the grace of God, the Jews knew only the wrath of God; and so on. As we know, these statements are far removed from the Jewish faith as expressed in Jewish literature. But even when we recognize that Judaism and the Gospel as systems of convictions do overlap, we should not prejudge what they have in common. We must presuppose that, until it is shown not to be the case, any element of the Gospel as a system of convictions may also belong to the Jewish system of convictions. In fact, we can expect that the two systems of convictions have many elements in common (since Paul perceives his faith as a form of Judaism) and that the differences between Judaism and Christianity are to be found in the specific ways in which these elements are interrelated by different convictional patterns so as to form two distinct systems of convictions.

In order to discover what characterizes the Jewish faith, we need to listen to the faithful and zealous Jews as they express themselves in their own literature. In so doing we should not minimize or exclude these elements which are very much like those of the Gospel. As a result, the Jewish faith will be allowed to appear in its integrity and its coherence as a system of convictions which commands the zealous devotion of the believers, and we will be able to understand how the Jews could be so reluctant to convert to the Gospel, as well as why the challenging character of the Gospel demands that they turn away from even such a beautiful faith.

## THE MULTIPLICATION OF THE LAWS

As is well known, the bulk of the early Rabbinic literature, indeed, its most authoritative part, is made up of legal material. I refer in particular to the Mishnah, which appears as a code of laws covering all aspects of daily life. A brief description of the main topics dealt with in the six Orders (or "books") of the Mishnah makes this clear.

The first Order deals with laws concerning agriculture, that is, how a Jewish farmer must carry on his trade. This Order involves laws about the dues to the poor, tithes, the proper way to plant and cultivate, the sabbatical law, how to offer the "first fruit." The second Order deals with the various festivals, such as the Sabbath, Passover, the Day of Atonement, the Festival of Booths, the New Year's festival, and laws related to worship (the tax for the Temple, fasting). The third Order deals with matters concerning women and the laws about marriage and family relationship. The fourth Order deals with criminal laws (theft, robbery, and other damages), the civil laws (governing property rights, business transactions), and the judicial institution (the Sanhedrin) and procedures. The fifth Order deals with sacrifices and things devoted to God, "holy things," and thus also "profane things." The sixth Order deals with laws of purity and mainly with laws concerning what is impure in all aspects of the community life. In addition, each Order contains laws dealing with subject matter other than their main topics. Thus the first Order includes a tractate on benedictions and prayers (the first tractate of the Mishnah) and the fourth Order includes the famous "tractate of the Fathers," which is a collection of sayings by renowned teachers.[8]

This glance at the early Rabbinic literature seems to confirm one of our preconceptions: the Pharisees were legalistic. But at the same time it challenges another of our preconceptions, the one concerning their alleged hypocrisy, for indeed, all these Mishnaic laws demonstrate the early Jews' concern with having a life totally governed by their religion. In no way can we call the faithful Pharisees and their descendants part-time Jews. On the contrary, they strived to make their Judaism coextensive with their lives. Even the most trivial aspects of the zealous and devoted Jews' lives were informed by their religion. Their lives were totally devoted to the service of the God who is One. In itself this ideal is certainly not in contradiction with the Gospel, which also requires total devotion to the service of God.

Thus we can say that the early Rabbinic faith involves among its fundamental convictions the conviction that the Jews' lives should be submitted totally to the will of God. Because of this they see the necessity of complementing the biblical commandments of the Pentateuch with numerous other laws which have their origin either in traditions or in interpretations of biblical laws, for the biblical laws are not comprehensive enough to deal with all aspects of the believers' lives. The Mishnaic laws tell faithful Jews what to do in the situations not covered by the biblical laws.

At this point we need to note how demanding Pharisaic and early Rabbinic Judaism are. One cannot carry on a life so meticulously regimented by hundreds of laws if one is not strongly motivated. These laws would be an unbearable yoke from which the Jews would be only too glad to free themselves—forsaking their Judaism—if it were not for their system of convictions, which shows that through the fulfillment of these laws they are attuned to the true meaning and purpose of life. In brief, the conviction that their lives should be submitted totally to the will of God is itself based upon other convictions concerning their relation to God, Scripture, and the nature of these laws. We now need to elucidate these convictions.

## CHOSEN PEOPLE OF A GRACIOUS GOD

The Pharisees as well as the Rabbinic Jewish communities viewed themselves collectively as the Chosen People of God, as Israel of old was, and therefore they also called themselves Israel. This conviction about their true identity, their revealed identity (i.e., that they are the

Chosen People), is part of a network of convictions concerning their relationship with God: the covenant.

Through the concept of the covenant, the Jews expressed their relationship with God in a symbolic form which was used by the various branches of Judaism and early Christianity (cf. the "new covenant"). This is to say that this complex symbol could be used, as any symbol can, to express various sets of convictions. We therefore need to understand the specific view of the covenant of Pharisaic and early Rabbinic Judaism.

The term "covenant" refers to a contract between two parties, in this case between God and his people. Among other ways, this contract can be conceived as a business-like agreement or as a love partnership (comparable to that of marriage).

According to the Christian preconceptions, Pharisaic and Rabbinic Judaism are characterized by a business-like understanding of the covenant. In such a view the laws (or commandments) are the primary components of the covenant. God is perceived as a dictator who unilaterally imposes his rule upon his subjects. He dictates his will, expressed in the form of commandments: the Law, Torah. Then his subjects are bound to this Law by the covenant. If they fulfill the commandments, they are blessed, rewarded, but if they do not, they are punished. In this perspective the covenant can be represented as including two elements in the following relationship:

Laws

Blessings

God is perceived as a business-like figure, a strict God of justice in contrast to a loving and merciful God. The relationship between God and the believers is also business-like. If the believers accumulate good works (or merits) they earn God's blessing, their place in the covenant, their right relationship with God (their salvation). If they do not, they are punished and rejected by God, they are cursed and no longer in the right relationship with God.

As soon as attention is focused on the convictional pattern which governs the way Judaism functions as a religion (as E. P. Sanders does in *Paul and Palestinian Judaism*[9] and as I did in *Early Jewish Hermeneutic in Palestine*),[10] it becomes clear that this cannot in any way be the view of the covenant and of the relationship with God which characterizes Pharisaic and Rabbinic Judaism. It might be closer to the Sadducees' view, if we can trust the indirect information we have about them in the literature of their opponents and the interpretation of this material by Jacob Z. Lauterbach and other Jewish scholars.[11] Actually, with such a view of the covenant the Mishnah would not exist. Instead of multiplying the laws to make them coextensive with life, according to this view, one would be merely concerned with fulfilling the biblical laws to the letter, for all that is required in order to receive God's blessing (and to avoid punishment) is to fulfill the commandments God laid upon the believers. Such seems to have been the Sadducees' attitude. They were content to observe the laws as received, and they rejected the value and authority of the "new" laws developed by the rabbis on the basis of traditions or interpretations of the biblical commandments. As a consequence, the Sadducees, despite their strict observance of the biblical commandments (a strict religious life), were also those who were most open to interaction with the Hellenistic and Roman rulers in Palestine. Besides their religious life aimed at securing the right relationship with God, they had a "secular" life, that is, a part of their life was not governed by God's commandments.

This view of the covenant and of the relationship to God is very legalistic (in the negative sense of the term) and very formal and thus could be perceived as hypocritical. It involves doing works of the law in order to earn salvation. Yet this is not the view of the covenant found in the Judaism from which Paul converted and which he rejected, Pharisaic Judaism.

The commandments and their fulfillment do occupy an important place in the Pharisees' and the Rabbis' faith, but they are not, in their view, the primary component of the covenant. The election by God is. One's election, one's chosenness, one's status in a special relationship with God, now and in the other world (one's "salvation" in Christian terminology), is *not* earned. It is always presupposed in any discussion of the laws, of obedience, of rewards and punishments, that the Jews *are* the Chosen People of God and that they can rely on God's fidelity to the covenant.[12] This election which was for them the ultimate blessing was the gift of a gracious and loving God. Such is one of the fundamental convictions held by the Pharisees and the Rabbis.

The contrast between the two views of the covenant can be expressed as follows. According to the first view (the Sadducees') one fulfills the Law and performs good deeds in order to obtain the blessing of being a member of God's people. But according to the Pharisees' view one *cannot* do so, because one has received the ultimate blessing (chosenness) before doing any good deeds. This second view involves the opposite relation between blessing and laws:

Blessing

Laws

Observing the laws therefore appears as a response to the gracious gift of God.

The last observation directly reflects statements found in the early Rabbinic literature which emphasize that God had first chosen Israel before giving her the commandments.[13] The following parable is found in an early commentary (or midrash) on Exodus, the *Mekilta*:

> *I Am the Lord Thy God* [Exod. 20:2]. Why were the Ten Commandments not said at the beginning of the Torah? They give a parable. To what may this be compared? To the following: A king who entered a province said to the people: May I be your King? But the people said to him: Have you done anything good for us that you should rule over us? What did he do then? He built the city wall for them, he brought in the water supply for them, and he fought their battles. Then when he said to them: May I be your king? They said to him: Yes, yes. Likewise, God. He brought the Israelites out of Egypt, divided the sea for them, sent down the manna for them, brought up the well for them, brought the quails for them. He fought for them the battle with Amalek. Then He said to them: I am to be your king. And they said to Him: Yes, yes.[14]

As this parable, together with many other texts of the early Rabbinic literature, expresses it, the God of the covenant is first of all a gracious and loving God and not a despot. He does not impose himself and his will (the Law) upon his people. He offers himself by offering the covenant.

The covenant as a convictional network can be viewed as involving three components, which we will discuss first in terms of their presentation in Exodus 19 and 20: the election, the vocation, and the laws.

## The Election

The covenant first of all entails the revelation of the election of Israel. Through his acts in history, that is, through his intervention in favor of Israel, God manifests that he has chosen Israel as his people, with whom he will be in a special relationship. This election of Israel in the time of Moses is also the election of the Jewish people through the centuries.

Why were the Israelites chosen by God? This is a mystery over which the Rabbis ponder. Quite clearly God took the initiative to choose them, so it is the act of a gracious and loving God. But at the same time he is not a capricious and arbitrary God, so he must have had a reason. The Rabbis gave several explanations,[15] which are in conflict with one another. Certain texts emphasize that God's election was totally gracious, that the election was offered even though Israel had no merit. This view is summarized in the following statement from the *Mekilta*: "Thou hast shown us mercy, for we had no [meritorious] deeds."[16] Other passages explain that the covenant was offered to all the nations, but only Israel accepted it. Another type of answer argues that Israel was chosen because of her merits, because of the faith of the Exodus generation. Here the election is seen as a reward. But even in this case, the covenant is a given for the Jewish community of the Pharisees' and Rabbis' time. It has been established once and for all by a God who remains faithful to his promises. The Jews cannot earn their election, since it is established since the time of the Exodus. Similarly it is explained that Israel was chosen because of the patriarchs' merits, but this view merely displaces this question: why were the patriarchs (e.g., Abraham) chosen in the first place?

Two other explanations of Israel's election are found in Rabbinic literature. The Israelites were elected "on the condition of future obedience" or "for the sake of God's name." Such statements point out that the conviction about the election is necessarily related to convictions about the two other components of the covenant: the *vocation*, and the *law* as spelling out how to fulfill this vocation.

## The Vocation and the Law

By definition, an election involves a purpose. For instance, in our democratic system one is elected by the people for a specific office: president, senator, mayor. The same is true here. Israel is chosen for a specific "office," for a specific vocation. In Exodus 19, following the retelling of God's acts through which Israel is elected, the purpose of this election is stated: "You shall be to me a kingdom of priests and a holy nation" (Exod. 19:6). Just as a priest at the Temple in Jerusalem (but also at most worshiping places of the various religions of that time) was the necessary intermediary between the divinity and the worshiping community, so Israel, as an entire people, is to be the necessary intermediary between God and all the other nations. As a people of priests they are in a close relationship with God and therefore need be a "holy nation," since only a special holiness will allow them to be in this relationship with God and will make manifest for the nations their specific status. The Law, according to Exodus 20ff., spells out how to be holy, how to be a people of priests for the nations, how to be the intermediary between God and the nations.

In early Rabbinic literature the vocation of the Chosen People is expressed in even bolder terms by the phrase "sanctification of the Name."[17] The boldness of this phrase can be perceived when one remembers that the Jews, in order to avoid designating God by his name (i.e., in order to avoid taking the name of God in vain) simply said "the Name" instead of "God" (or "Yahweh"). Thus "sanctifying the Name" should, in fact, be translated "sanctifying God," that is, "making God holy." In other words, God's holiness in the world depends upon the Chosen People. Israel, the Jewish people, was chosen in order to make God holy in the world.

What a vocation! Claiming to have such a vocation would be sheer arrogance if it were not that it results from an election initiated by God. And we begin to perceive why the covenant can be viewed by the Jews as the ultimate blessing. God puts his fate in the world into the hands of Israel and the Jewish people. If they are a holy nation, if they observe the commandments which spell out how to fulfill their vocation, then the Name (God) is sanctified. In such a case, God is celebrated, his presence and his actions are celebrated by the Chosen People, and thus other peoples (the nations) are also led to bless God. Fulfilling the commandments, sanctifying oneself (even if this entails being persecuted or even martyred) is sanctifying the Name. Conversely, any transgression of the commandments is a profanation of the Name. God's sanctity in the world is actually diminished among people who, because of these transgressions, would not be placed in the presence of God and consequently would not bless his Name. Through the covenant God bound his fate to Israel. God and Israel are in such a close relationship that whatever Israel does affects God's sanctity in the world. In this context the multiplication of the laws (such as those found in the Mishnah) must be understood. With such a vocation, one cannot be a part-time member of the Chosen People. It is through each act, attitude, and thought that one needs to sanctify the Name. Otherwise these acts, attitudes, and thoughts could be profanation of the Name.

The Pharisees and the Rabbis expressed the same conviction in terms of Torah.[18] "Torah" designates Scripture as a whole, but also more specifically the Pentateuch, the books of Moses, which contains the revelation of the covenant. As such, Torah is also viewed as the supreme gift of God. Torah is blessing from God. One cannot expect more than Torah, because in Torah God gave everything to his people, that is, to the Jewish community. Indeed, Torah was identified with Wisdom, God's Wisdom (which was with him at the time of the creation). And thus the Rabbis could say that when giving Torah and the covenant to Israel and to the Jewish people, God gave himself to them.

When one becomes aware of what is involved in the covenant and, more specifically, in the election and vocation of God's people expressed in Torah, one can understand that for the Pharisees and Rabbis no blessing can surpass it. God chose the Israelites to be his people; he bound his fate in the world to them. A fantastic risk! But for the Jews this is a fantastic responsibility and blessing. To be a Jew means to be in this very special, very close relationship with God. As the prophets said, this is like the love in a marriage, when one takes the risk of being totally bound to someone else. Nothing can surpass this blessing. Yes, the Pharisees believed in the resurrection, but the Rabbis did not expect anything more in the "world to come" (i.e., paradise, in our terminology). There they will be God's Chosen People. The only difference is that then they will be perfectly faithful to their part of the covenant, as God is already faithful to his part. The ultimate blessing of God (or in another terminology, salvation) was already given to them. To be blessed, to be saved, is to be a member of the Chosen People.

While this covenant is graciously offered to the Jewish community, membership in the Chosen People is not automatic. This election has to be accepted by the individual Jew. The Rabbis speak of this acceptance as taking upon oneself the "yoke of heaven" or the "yoke of Torah."[19] The

kingship and authority of God as well as the authority of the commandments have to be "confessed."[20] As we understand now, this means both
to submit to the authority of God (who dictates what is to be holy) and to
accept one's responsibility vis-à-vis God, who binds himself to his people (the sanctification of the Name). In other words, this God who enters
into this loving relationship of the covenant is nevertheless "God," the
King, the One who has authority to give orders, to reward, and to
punish, and who indeed exercises this authority in the present as he will
in the future (at the final judgment).

Obedience is or will be rewarded by blessings. Disobedience is or will
be punished. The gracious God who gave the covenant once and for all
is also a God of justice in the sense that he is not arbitrary or capricious
in his dealings with humans. But this justice is exercised *in the context*
of the covenant. As E. P. Sanders shows, in early Rabbinic literature (by
contrast to the Prophetic literature) it is never threatened that God
might revoke his covenant. The covenant is given unconditionally and
cannot be earned. Believers, through their obedience, can obtain rewards and blessings, but these are not "the right relationship with God"
which has already been established once and for all. The covenant, the
election, the vocation, is always a given, a gracious gift. In other words,
"salvation" cannot be earned. It is always given. These rewards and
blessings are specific (material and spiritual) rewards appropriate to what
has been done.[21]

Humans can reject the covenant, refuse to be part of the Chosen
People, refuse the election, and thus deny God the right of giving them
commandments. They have that freedom. The covenant is not imposed
upon them, it is offered to them. As long as they want to remain in the
covenant, they can do so despite eventual disobediences. Transgressions
of the commandments (i.e., sins) are punished, but means of atonement
(e.g., the rites of the Day of Atonement, Yom Kippur) are provided for
repentant believers. Thus forgiveness from God through which he "*restores* the original relationship established by grace"[22] is part of the Pharisees' and the Rabbis' system of convictions based on the fundamental
convictions about the covenant. Sanders says, "Since atonement for individual sins *restores* the penitent sinner to the right relationship with
God, he originally *had* a right relationship with God, a relationship
established by God's mercy and maintained by the individual's obedience and repentance and by God's forgiveness."[23]

Such a statement, well substantiated by a careful study of early Rabbinic literature, directly contradicts our preconceptions about Pharisaism, according to which, as Sanders puts it, "Rabbinic religion was a religion of legalistic works-righteousness in which a man was saved by fulfilling more commandments than he commited transgressions."[24] And indeed, we might wonder, "Then, what did Paul mean when he said . . . ?" or, "What is the difference between Paul's gospel and Pharisaism?" In order to be in a position to compare fruitfully these two systems of convictions, we need to examine in greater detail how the covenantal convictional pattern functions in Pharisaic and Rabbinic Judaism. Here, again, Sanders is helpful:

> The pattern is this: God has chosen Israel and Israel has accepted the election. In this role as King, God gave Israel commandments which they are to obey as best they can. Obedience is rewarded and disobedience punished. In case of failure to obey, however, man has recourse to divinely ordained means of atonement, in all of which repentance is required. As long as he maintains his desire to stay in the covenant, he has a share in God's covenantal promises, including life in the world to come. The intention and effort to be obedient constitute the *condition for remaining in the covenant*, but they do not *earn* it.[25]

The last sentence of this quotation deserves special attention. Saying that the "condition for remaining in the covenant" is constituted by the "intention and effort to be obedient" is quite ambiguous. This could be interpreted as a psychological attitude or as a rational attitude, while Sanders wants to refer to a religious attitude. As he puts it elsewhere, it is a matter of "confession," of "confessing" the commandments, and of "confessing" the covenant.[26] In our terminology it means assuming a certain system of fundamental convictions which, as such, has the power to motivate the believers to carry out the commandments. Only by examining how this system of convictions structures the believer's life and way of thinking will we understand how it is organized.

## A CLOSED VIEW OF SACRED HISTORY

In early Rabbinic literature we find two types of documents: those which reflect the worship of the Jewish community at the Synagogue and those which represent the deliberations of the Rabbinic schools. We begin with an examination of the documents emanating from the worship experience of the community, since it is in such a context that fundamental convictions in any religion are established for the believers. We can assume that it is in and through their worship that the Jews discovered and appropriated their true, revealed identity as members of the Chosen People.

Even before the destruction of the Temple (A.D. 70) and although they participated in the Temple worship services (with the Sadducees), the Pharisees and Rabbis worshiped at the Synagogue, which was their own place of worship and later on the only one. For believers a worship service is the time and place in which the presence of God is apprehended. Therefore, worship services and their forms manifest the believers' convictions about God and their relationship to him.

For the Sadducees with their Temple worship, the presence of God is directly associated with a place (the Temple, and especially the Holy of Holies, is the place where one can find God) and with sacrifices (as ways to relate to God). Despite the conviction about the universal power of God, he manifests himself in a privileged way in that place. One cannot have Temple services and sacrifices anywhere else than in that place. Thus the destruction of the Temple marked, for all practical purposes, the end of the Sadducees' movement.

By contrast, the Synagogue service is not linked with any specific place. It can be anywhere. Its center—what manifests the presence of God, what allows a relationship with God—is Torah (i.e., Scripture). Wherever a group of believers may be, God is among them if they read or study Torah. Rabbi Hananiah ben Teradion (a second-century rabbi) said, "If two sit together and no words of the Law [Torah] [are spoken] between them, there is the seat of the scornful. . . . But if two sit together and words of the Law [Torah] [are spoken] between them, the Divine Presence rests between them."[27] Similarly, Rabbi Halafta ben Dosa of Kefar Hanania (a secondary rabbi) said about the Synagogue worship which must include at least ten men: "If ten men sit together and occupy themselves in the Law [Torah] the Divine Presence rests among them."[28] Thus in the same way that the Temple worship was organized around a place (the Holy of Holies where God is present), so the Synagogue worship was organized around Torah, or better, Torah provided the entire framework for it.

Synagogue worship included the following elements, all of which related to Scripture: prayers and benedictions (either taken directly from

Scripture, such as the Psalms, or composed of interwoven scriptural phrases); readings from Scripture in the original Hebrew (from the Pentateuch and the Prophets); "translations" of Scripture in Aramaic (the language of the community); and homilies (built on Scripture). Through these interactions with Torah—with Scripture—the worshiping community was set in the Presence of God, that is, established in the right relationship with God.

A detailed study of the ways in which Scripture was used, that is, of the ways in which Scripture was related to the worshipers and to various aspects of their experience, reveals much about the organization of the Pharisaic and Rabbinic system of convictions.[29] Here it is sufficient to present the results of my own investigation in general terms.

The fact that Synagogue worship is entirely structured by Scripture suggests in itself one essential way in which Scripture and the worshiping community are related. By entering the Synagogue and participating in worship, the believers "enter into Scripture." It is by being "into Scripture" that they are established in the right relationship with God. In the Rabbis' terminology, they take upon themselves "the yoke of heaven" and thus (in our terminology) assume their revealed identity as Chosen People. This relation between Torah (Scripture) and the worshipers implies that Torah is perceived as the *locus* of revelation. Furthermore, we can say that Torah is perceived as the complete and final revelation of the election and vocation of the Chosen People. Several observations substantiate this statement.

First, Torah—which in the strict sense refers only to the Pentateuch—is so much the essential part of Scripture that the other parts of the Hebrew Bible, the Prophets and the Writings (Psalms, Proverbs, etc.), are also viewed as Torah. These texts deserve the name Torah because, in the Rabbis' view, they are nothing else than interpretations of Torah (in the narrow sense of the term). Indeed, as the Rabbis often repeated in statements possibly originally directed against the Apocalyptists, "everything has been revealed on Mount Sinai." Thus, since there is no new revelation, the Prophets and the Writings have authority as revelation only insofar as they are authoritative interpretations of the complete and final revelation on Mount Sinai, the covenantal revelation.

These remarks are confirmed by a study of the way in which Scripture is used in the homilies (which have been collected and redacted in a series of books known as the Midrash) and in the "translations" into Aramaic known as the Targum (which were not literal translations but rather "free" translations involving commentarylike interpretation). To begin with, and this is very puzzling for modern readers, the interpretations in both the homilies found in the Midrash and the elaborations of the Targum do *not* follow a specific theme, theological or otherwise, which would be dictated by the interpreters' or the community's interest. Rather, the interpretation is fully structured by Scripture. Scripture is constantly interpreted by means of Scripture. A text from the Pentateuch is interpreted by a text from the Prophets, which is itself interpreted by means of other texts, and so on. The homilies appear, therefore, as a chainlike series of scriptural passages linked together in a circular fashion like the beads of a necklace. This use of Scripture presupposes that the explanation of a passage of Scripture can be found only in Scripture because Scripture is the complete and final revelation.

That the revelation is fully contained in Scripture and does not depend upon the believers' interpretation is further shown by the way in which the Scripture passages are chosen. When a text is used to interpret another text—for instance, when a Prophetic text is used to interpret a text in the Pentateuch—it is *not* chosen because it deals with the same topic or the same theme as the other text. Such a choice would involve an evaluation of the texts by the interpreters in terms of their own interests or experiences. Rather, these texts are brought together on purely formal grounds, that is, because they sound alike or, more precisely, because in their opening sentences they use phrases which in Hebrew have the same sounds (or at least, very similar sounds), whatever may be the words used and whatever may be their meaning. For us, this procedure seems to be artificial, but for the Rabbis it was the normal way of interrelating texts. It manifests the conviction that Scripture has in itself the authority to interpret Scripture without the intervention of the interpreter whose role is simply "to listen to the text of Scripture."[30] This "tallying" of biblical texts through the sound-resemblance of their opening statements has been shown by J. Mann[31] to be the principle governing the choice of passages from the Prophets to be read at the synagogue in conjunction with passages from the Pentateuch. This is also the principle governing the choice of a text for interpreting another text in the true homilies (in contrast to the "theological treatises" written in the form of homilies by later redactors of the Midrash). Our own study suggests that in the Targum the same principle is used in the interpretive sections of the translations. Therefore, interpreting Scripture means submitting totally to Scripture, letting Scripture interpret itself, and entering into it through listening.

The interpretation of Scripture by Scripture according to this principle involves the conviction not only that Scripture is in itself the complete and final revelation but also that the revelation is one as God is One. This implies that there is no contradiction in Scripture and, more positively, that the entire revelation is revelation of one thing: the covenant, and thus the election and the vocation of the Chosen People. This is manifested in the way in which the sacred history (i.e., the history of the interventions of God in human affairs) is interpreted. Since the various texts are interpreted by means of each other, an event taking place in the time of Abraham can be interpreted in terms of events taking place in the time of the Exodus, and/or in the eschatological future (in the Messianic times described, for instance, in Prophetic texts), and/or at the time of the creation.[32] As a consequence, a basic identity is found in these various acts of God, since all of them manifest God's election of his people. A study of the Targum also shows that everything in the Bible is interpreted as referring to a limited number of sacred events (acts or words of God) which involve revelation from God. All of these belong to the past sacred history (in biblical times), except for the eschatological event (the event taking place at the end of history, which for the Pharisees and Rabbis was viewed as belonging to a distant future). In other words, there is *no* reference in the Targum and Midrash[33] to *present* events ("present" to the interpreters, that is) which could be considered as having this basic identity with the events of past sacred history. To put it bluntly, it is as if, for the interpreters, God acted (in the strong sense of performing *revelatory* acts) in the past and will act in the ever-future eschatological time but is not acting in between.

Thus the principle of interpreting Scripture by Scripture manifests the conviction that sacred history is "closed." The whole of revelation was understood to be in Scripture. Consequently, it is only by "entering Scripture" that the believers could receive their revealed identity as Chosen People with a specific vocation.

The above observations begin to elucidate a fundamental difference between Pharisaism/Rabbinism and the Gospel as systems of convictions. For Paul, sacred history is not closed. Beyond the biblical acts of God, in the present of the believers, there are new acts of God which involve new revelations, that is (a) new election(s) and new vocation(s) and thus (a) new covenant(s). As we shall see, Paul held convictions that in Jesus—but also in happenings in the church—God is acting and thus revealing something new. For Paul, the sacred history of God's acts/revelations is not closed, and thus Scripture is not the complete and final revelation of the election and vocation of the Chosen People.

It should be emphasized that we have discussed only the convictions regarding the election and vocation—the revealed identity of the Chosen People in its relationship with God—as it is manifested in Synagogue worship and Scripture usage. We now need to consider the convictions regarding how to carry out this vocation, that is, regarding God's will for his people, the Law. At this level the relation between the believers' experience and Scripture is quite different. Scripture is no longer the complete and final revelation. Besides the written Torah (Scripture) there is the oral Torah, an ever-growing and authoritative formulation of *how to be* the Chosen People in various cultural situations. This second level of scriptural interpretation is found primarily in the (Rabbinic) schools, where the Rabbis and their disciples gathered to study Torah, but it is also present in the "moral" teaching of the Synagogue (in both the translations and the homilies). In order to have a better understanding of the relations between the convictions regarding, on the one hand, the election and the vocation and, on the other hand, how to carry out the vocation, we need to consider other uses of Scripture at the Synagogue and then in the teaching of the schools.

## DISCOVERING THE WILL OF GOD IN NEW CULTURAL SITUATIONS

Despite the fact that Scripture was interpreted by Scripture (and thus priority was given to Scripture), the interpreters' and the Jewish communities' experience nevertheless found their way into the interpretations. Both in the Midrash and in the Targum we find actualizations of

Scripture, that is, interpretations of the texts in terms of contemporary situations. Yet these actualizations are of a very specific kind. The biblical personages are often presented as struggling with issues, and adopting attitudes, which reflect the situation of the worshiping communities. Thus, for instance, the Patriarchs (before Moses and the giving of the laws) are often shown to be carrying out the laws as interpreted in Pharisaic and Rabbinic Judaism. For example, the dispute between Abel and Cain is described in detail as if it were that of a Pharisee and a Sadducee confronting each other on the question of whether or not there is an afterworld and a final judgment.[34]

What takes place in these actualizations can be summarized as follows. By "entering Scripture," which forms the framework of the Synagogue service, the worshiping community perceives itself as the Chosen People. As such it identifies itself with the biblical Chosen People. In the same way that, in the Passover ritual, the family members around the table retell the story of the Exodus by identifying themselves with the people who went out of Egypt (saying, for instance, "*we* went out of Egypt") so the Jewish believers at the Synagogue identify themselves with the various biblical personages. Through this process the worshiping community embodies Scripture. They are the Chosen People. It is not a matter of merely pretending to be the Chosen People, nor a matter of viewing oneself as being like the Chosen People of old. They truly are the Chosen People. This is their true identity, who they are. And thus the worshiping community embodies the revelation as it is "embodied" in Scripture. They are the very proof of the reality of the covenant. Indeed, God chose for himself a people, God put himself in the hands of this people which has as its vocation the sanctification of the Name. The proof of all this can be found here, in the Synagogue. It is the Chosen People who are worshiping. Thus the worshiping community manifests the revelation of the gracious covenant as much as Scripture does, and in the same way.[35] Its prayers, without necessarily repeating passages from Scripture, are expressed in scriptural terminology (they are made of scriptural words and phrases).

In this context another relation to Scripture takes place, that is, the interpretations involving actualizations. The biblical personages' behaviors are, for the believers, either models to be imitated if they are virtuous, or types of vices to be avoided if they are evil. Thus the interpretations express *how to be* Chosen People, that is, how to be "Abraham" or "Moses" and so on, in the contemporary cultural situation. At that point the closed circle of Scripture is broken open. Scripture is no longer the complete and final revelation.

The main convictions which characterize the Pharisaic and Rabbinic faith can now be perceived. On the one hand, Scripture is the complete and final revelation of the election of the Chosen People—the worshiping community which enters Scripture is the Chosen People as Israel of old was—and of its vocation, the sanctification of the Name. This election and vocation are gracious gifts from God. This Scripture, Torah, is a precious gift, since through it God puts himself in the hands of his people. By participating in the Synagogue worship, one confesses and takes upon oneself this election and vocation. But on the other hand, "how to carry out this vocation," "how to sanctify the Name," is *not* fully revealed in Scripture. The laws or commandments found in Scripture provide important guidelines, but they are *not* the complete and final revelation of the will of God. The ways in which the biblical personages are viewed as moral models and the manner in which the laws are interpreted in terms of various cultural situations show that the Pharisees and the Rabbis held the conviction that God's will (i.e., the way to carry out one's vocation as Chosen People or, in Jewish terminology, "the way to walk" [in Hebrew, *halakah*]) was to be discovered anew in new cultural situations.

Thus we find two levels of interpretation and two types of relation between Scripture and the Jewish community:

1. The scriptural "story" of the election and vocation is the complete and final revelation. Since its interpretation, called *haggadah* ("story") by the Rabbis and found in the Midrash and the Targum, is necessarily an interpretation of Scripture by Scripture, no single interpretation can be normative. In each case the interpreter has to submit to Scripture, to enter the closed circle of Scripture.

2. By contrast, the scriptural commandments are *not* complete and final. They must be interpreted in terms of the specific cultural situations in the context of which the Chosen People must sanctify the Name. These interpretations, the *halakah* ("the way to walk"), are at once normative—they dictate the conduct of the Jewish community in its daily life—and constantly in the process of changing in order to account

for new cultural situations. Even though the *halakah* has a place in the Synagogue (in the actualizations of Scripture and in other moral teachings) it belongs primarily to the Rabbinic schools.

## "THE WAY TO WALK" AS THE CHOSEN PEOPLE

The work of the schools has been collected first in the Mishnah (whose redaction is attributed to Rabbi Judah the Prince at the end of the second century of the Christian era), then in the Talmud (a collection of later Rabbinic teachings up to the fifth century). Although it includes "haggadic" material (comparable to the teaching of the homilies at the synagogue, i.e., the *haggadah*), the Mishnah is primarily composed of halakic material—spelling out "the way to walk," the *halakah*.

The Mishnah deals with the various dimensions of the "religious" life (rituals, prayers, etc.) as well as with the ways to conduct business transactions, carry on one's job, relate to other members of one's family and of the Jewish community and to Gentiles, and so on. This should remind us of the Pharisees' and Rabbis' view that Torah (i.e., one's vocation and its fulfillment) cannot but be *coextensive with life*. This is one of the general principles (convictional pattern) which govern the unfolding of what is called the "oral Torah" (even though it was finally written down).

As the phrase "oral Torah" suggests, this teaching supplemented and/or interpreted the written Torah, or more precisely, the part of the written Torah which spells out the way to fulfill the vocation—the commandments. This teaching had an authority comparable to that of the written Torah. It is Torah. This is the case even though the oral Torah includes customs and traditions which emerged in the experience of the Jewish community independently from Scripture as well as interpretations of the scriptural commandments. This observation confirms that revelation of the will of God is found both in Scripture and in the Jewish community's experience.

Another characteristic of the Mishnah (and of halakic interpretations of Scripture such as those found in early Midrashim like the *Mekilta* on Exodus and especially the *Sifra* on Leviticus and the *Sifre* on Deuteronomy) is that its teachings are presented in the form of "debates" between various Rabbis who often give conflicting points of view on an issue. This makes it clear that the Law is not an absolute imposed by a dictatorial God. As the noted Jewish scholar Jacob Z. Lauterbach said, "the Pharisees did not become the slaves of the Law; they were its masters."[36] Again, Torah was perceived by the Pharisees as a gift from a gracious God. The commandments express how to carry out the fantastic vocation for which they have been chosen. Their attempt to make Torah coextensive with life is a response to the gracious love of God manifested in the covenant. Thus it can be understood best in terms of their vocation, the sanctification of the Name.

In order to sanctify the Name, to make clearly visible the holiness of the true God who alone deserves praises, the Jewish community needs to be clearly identifiable as the Chosen People, a people different from other peoples because of its special relationship with God. This special relationship with God can best be manifested by the people's special holiness. They have to be holy as God is holy, separated as God is separated (as the Rabbis interpreted Lev. 20:26).[37] This leads to a first type of extension of the biblical commandments, "making a fence around Torah," as the Rabbis designated it. They adopted traditional customs and deduced new laws from the biblical commandments (according to precise rules of interpretation)[38] so as to make absolutely certain that they would not inadvertently transgress the biblical laws of holiness. For instance, among the dietary laws is the one which reads, "You shall not boil a kid in its mother's milk" (Exod. 23:19; also Exod. 34:26, Deut. 14:21). To be sure that this commandment would not be inadvertently broken, the oral Torah commanded: "No flesh may be cooked in milk excepting the flesh of fish and locusts." Thus the meat of fowl (such as poultry) is now included in the prohibition in order to avoid any possible confusion about different types of meat. The tradition went further by prohibiting the eating (and not merely the cooking) of meat together with milk (in any form including cheese). The school of Hillel went still further by saying that fowl and cheese should neither be served together on the same table nor eaten together. The school of Shammai had a more lenient position: "A fowl may be served up on the table together with cheese, but it may not be eaten with it."[39]

This example from among a vast number of similar rules about all aspects of life is enough to illustrate how meticulous the Pharisees were in their attempt to be a holy people. Such observances set them apart from the Gentiles and thus put them in a position to be witnesses of the

God whose will they followed. Carrying out all these rules without being deeply "motivated" by the convictions about their election and vocation would have been an unbearable burden, but with such convictions it is a joy—it is sanctifying the Name. In contrast, transgressing these laws would be profaning the Name.

Other interpretations of the commandments are more lenient. When these laws become too strict and burdensome, when one is therefore no longer able to carry them out joyfully, they do not contribute to the sanctification of the Name; the Jewish community cannot praise God. It may then be appropriate to interpret these rules so that they might be observed more easily. Furthermore, in order to carry out their vocation and to bring about the sanctification of the Name among Gentiles, the Chosen People must be in contact with them. The Jewish community must be separated, distinct, but not to the extent that they are unable to be with the Gentiles. It is good "to make a fence around Torah," but this fence should not be too high. So other rules were promulgated which made the observance of God's will easier, even when this actually involved not following a biblical law. In such a case the new rules were based upon a careful interpretation of the law which was being canceled. Only the law can cancel itself, so to speak. An example of such lenient interpretations will help us understand this process.

In Deut. 15:1–3 there is a law which prescribes the release of all debts on every seventh year. In this way "there will be no poor among you" (Deut. 15:4). It was a good law for a time when one had to sell oneself and one's family as slaves if one could not pay one's debts. The danger was that, as the seventh year grew near, rich people might refuse to give a loan (which would be canceled on the seventh year). Thus Deut. 15:9–11 stipulates that one should not refrain from giving a loan even if the seventh year, the year of release, is near. Yet in the time of Hillel (first century B.C.), people transgressed this second law. As a result of the seventh-year law, the poor had either to go hungry or to borrow from and eventually to sell themselves as slaves to Gentiles. In other words, this law had the opposite effect from the one it was intended to have. So Hillel promulgated a law, called the *prosbul*, according to which a loan was not canceled on the seventh-year if this loan was made "in court" ("prosbul" comes from the Greek, meaning "in court"), where it was stipulated that it could be collected whenever the lender so desired. This law, which directly contradicts the biblical law, was introduced because of the needs created by the economic life of the Jews in Hillel's time. How could a hungry family (or a Jewish family having to sell itself as slaves to Gentiles) praise God and thus sanctify the Name? Another example: Simon ben Shetah (first century A.D.) emended the law about the *mohar* (the sum of money the groom had to pay the father of the bride, a law based on Exod. 22:16). Instead of paying the *mohar*, the groom had to write a *ketuba*, in which he pledged all his property up to the amount of the dowry as a security for his wife in case of his death or of divorce. By such an interpretation of the law, the woman possessed rights of her own and was protected economically, instead of being considered the property of her father. Thus women were in a better position to sanctify the Name.

A series of new laws were promulgated in this way by abrogating or emending biblical laws or, more often, traditional laws (ritual as well as economic and civil laws), in order to adapt Torah to new cultural situations. The Rabbis proceeded with great caution. Yet the conviction presupposed by these expansions of the law is clear. The will of God is to be discovered not only in Scripture but also in the culture in which the Jewish community lives. Thus, discovering the will of God involves scrutinizing the culture in its many manifestations so as to discover the new values (e.g., "women's rights") which can be recognized as being "in the spirit of Torah" (my phrase) and therefore as deserving inclusion in Torah (i.e., in the oral Torah), and also to discover the ways in which to carry out the vocation in new cultural, social, or economic situations.

An excellent modern example of this process can be found in the play *Fiddler on the Roof*,[40] in which the new value "love" is recognized by a Jewish community as being valid, as being "in the spirit of Torah." The traditional authority of the matchmaker, and then that of the father, is abrogated to make room for love in the successive marriages of the daughters. Note that it is the grandmother, the matchmaker par excellence, who in the scene of the dream abrogates the authority of the matchmaker. Similarly, it is the father who uses his authority to abrogate his traditional role. All these traditions, all these laws governing marriage, all these ways to be the Chosen People, can be changed in view of the new cultural situation and of the new value, "love." But the last marriage (with a Gentile) cannot be accepted, because it would involve giving up their revealed identity, giving up their election and vocation. That *cannot* be changed.

Far from being rigid, the Law is constantly being expanded, emended, and supplemented by traditions and by reinterpretations in terms of ever-changing cultural situations. From outside the Pharisaic/Rabbinic faith, this attitude toward the Law might appear excessively "liberal" or even hypocritical, especially when the usually lenient interpretations of the school of Hillel are in view. While claiming to serve God they find ways not to obey what is literally demanded by scriptural commandments. But we can now understand that this whole attitude is actually aimed at fulfilling their vocation, that is, at fulfilling their part of the covenant in response to the gracious gift of the election.

Pharisaism can certainly be termed "legalist" because of the central place of the Law in its convictional view about how to fulfill the vocation of Chosen People. Despite the legal apparatus involved, however, it is not "legalistic" ("strict, even excessive, conformity to the law or to a particular code"). Indeed, such institutions as the Sanhedrin, which decided what interpretations of the law were binding, were necessary precisely because Pharisaism did not involve a literal and blind conformity to a law, yet as Lauterbach notes, "the Pharisees are masters of the Law." The Law must constantly be reinterpreted in terms of new cultural situations, but if each member or school would do so on its own, the Chosen People could not be identifiable as the one people of the God who is One. Thus the Sanhedrin ruled on which of the new ways of fulfilling the vocation in specific cultural situations were binding for the whole people (local communities could have, in addition, their own customs and practices).

The metaphors used to designate Torah further underscore that Pharisaic Judaism is not "legalistic." For instance, Torah is compared with "water" because it is at once gratis, priceless, bringing life and purifying, and with "wine" because it is kept in humble vessels (humble people), and rejoices the heart. Torah is also compared with a wife with whom one lives joyfully. And thus, since Torah rejoices the heart (as wine and wife) it can be read during the joyful day of Sabbath.[41] Torah rejoices the heart as the gift of the election and vocation, but its laws also rejoice the heart because they spell out how to carry out this vocation. In Torah, Jewish people have received all that they need to be the Chosen People. The election is theirs. Their vocation is astounding. The laws show them the way to walk. It is now their responsibility to respond to God's love. Certainly there are evil inclinations which push them to betray the covenant, but in Torah they have all they need to overcome it. God has put himself in their hands. Their responsibility is now to sanctify the Name.

## PHARISAIC JUDAISM AND THE GOSPEL AS SYSTEMS OF CONVICTIONS

This brief survey of some aspects of the early Rabbinic literature[42] has allowed us to elucidate the convictional pattern which characterizes the Pharisees' and Rabbis' faith. Yet it should be emphasized that the other Jewish groups—and especially the Apocalyptists—had quite a different kind of faith, which did not involve the conviction that Torah is the complete and final revelation of the election and vocation of God's people (see Chapter 6). For the reader of Paul's letters one thing is striking: the Pharisaic faith involved an amazing number of convictions which we also find in Paul's teaching. We might have wondered, how can one convert from such a beautiful faith? And we can begin to appreciate why the majority of the Jewish people did not convert to the Gospel, a painful fact for Paul (cf. Romans 9–11). Their faith did involve a total devotion to the true God and made out of them his zealous servants, but Paul converted and considered all this zealous service to God as a loss.

What is the difference between the Pharisaic faith and Paul's faith? At times what we found seems to contradict Paul's statements about Judaism. For instance, how could Paul write as he did about the "works of the Law" if the Pharisees believed in a gracious God and thought that their good deeds were actually in response to God's love? Does not Paul demand such a response to God's love from his followers? Did Paul misrepresent Judaism and actually attack a "straw man" made up for the occasion? But this cannot be the case since he himself converted from Pharisaic Judaism. Then did Paul attack a bastardized form of Judaism? No, for this is what the Rabbis were constantly doing themselves, and Paul would not have been calling his followers to a new faith. He would have urged them to become good Pharisees. But he certainly did not do so when proclaiming a Gospel free from the Law for the Gentiles!

What then is the difference? An obvious answer is that Paul acknowledged Jesus as the Christ, the Messiah, while the Jews did not. Yet we have to press this question further. What is the difference that this conviction about Christ makes? Paul writes, "Christ died for our sins" (1

Cor. 15:3). But the Jews already had access to the forgiveness of God. There is something new brought about by Christ's death only if "sin" and "forgiveness of sins" are themselves viewed in a new way. Paul writes, "God shows his love for us in that while we were yet sinners Christ died for us" (Rom. 5:8). But the Jews could say, "God shows his love for us in that while we were yet sinners he gave us the covenant." There is something new in Paul's statement only if, somehow, God's love is understood differently. There is something new in Christ only if somehow his coming involves a shift of the entire way of perceiving human experience in its relation to God, that is, a change in system of convictions. All these convictions which were so familiar to the Pharisees have been transformed by being interrelated in a different way. The convictional pattern has changed.

The question becomes: For Paul, how does acknowledging Jesus as the Christ change the Pharisaic convictional pattern? For the Pharisees, Torah is the complete and final revelation. Paul proclaims a *new* revelation in Christ. Sacred history (the history of God's revelatory acts), which was closed for the Pharisees, is now reopened for Paul. Thus we have proposed to distinguish Paul's dynamic type of faith—which involves the possibility of new revelations—from the Pharisees' static type of faith. I believe these categories to be valid. Now we are in a position to understand more concretely what they mean.

To begin with, let us keep in mind that we found two dimensions in Pharisaic Judaism. First, the convictions about the election and the vocation, which are absolute, established once and for all on Mount Sinai. Here revelation is closed. Second, the convictions about how to walk as the Chosen People, which are constantly changing to take into account new cultural situations. Here revelation is open. Thus, in this second dimension, there is dynamism.

By saying that the Pharisaic faith is static in character, I do not want to deny the dynamism involved in the ever-unfolding oral Torah. I simply want to say that the *convictional pattern* which characterizes that faith is static. Any system of convictions is "dynamic" in the sense that it always expands its semantic universe to include all the new situations and dimensions of human experience. This is done by repeatedly applying the same convictional pattern to the new data. Thus the Pharisees applied the convictional pattern of their covenantal relationship with God to all the new situations in which they had to live as God's Chosen

People. But for them, this convictional pattern, which was established once and for all in the scriptural revelation of the covenant, was always the same. In this sense their faith is static.

In contrast, by acknowledging that in Christ there is a new revelation, Paul also recognizes that a new convictional pattern is established. We could say, using a phrase that Paul himself rarely used, that in Christ a "new covenant" is revealed. In other words, a new way of being in relationship with God is established which involves a new way of perceiving all the relations in human experience. Sacred history, which was closed, has been reopened. New revelatory acts of God are to be found in Jesus, his death and resurrection. At this point there are two possibilities. One can view this new revelation, this new covenant in Christ, as the final and complete revelation establishing a new Chosen People, which has to determine how to carry out its vocation in various cultural situations. In such a case, sacred history has been closed again; one is not expecting any new revelation. Our reading of Galatians leads me to doubt that this is the type of faith Paul had. The Gospel would then mean freedom merely in the sense that it frees the believers *from* other systems of convictions (as any faith does) and not in a more absolute sense, as suggested in several passages. This static type of faith might be the one which characterized the "false brethren," who are appropriately called Judaizers, for their faith is not fundamentally different from the Jewish faith.

The other possibility is to view this new revelation in Christ as reopening sacred history and as announcing still other new revelations which constantly supersede the preceding ones. So the covenant is never established once and for all. The believers are constantly elected anew, and these elections involve a new vocation each time. For them, it is not merely a matter of scrutinizing the new situations to discover the will of God, that is, how to carry out in new ways an established vocation. Rather, it is a matter of scrutinizing these new situations to discover in them new elections (new acts of God which manifest an election) and new vocations. Yet Paul seems to avoid this covenant terminology, possibly because it was used in parts of the early church which had opted for the first possibility. Speaking of *a* new covenant in Jesus Christ would imply that this covenantal relationship has been established once and for all. We shall see that Paul uses a more dynamic symbolism (such as that of a footrace). We have noted that this dynamic type of faith involves a meta-system of convictions, a set of convictions about various systems of convictions, because from such a perspective any faith, including the faith that one holds, is relative (and not either absolutely right or absolutely wrong); it is the convictional pattern itself which is dynamic and changes. Yet these changes are not erratic. They themselves follow a pattern, the pattern established by the meta-system of convictions.

Saying that Paul's faith is dynamic, that it involves discovery of new elections and new vocations, does not mean that this process, this race, is going on at such a pace that one cannot catch one's breath. The believers, while expecting new revelations, have a given system of convictions for a certain length of time. In other words, they have the opportunity to carry out a given vocation and to discover "how to walk" in various concrete situations. And they have to follow an appropriate law, the "law of Christ" (Gal. 6:2). But their system of convictions bears the imprint of the meta-system of convictions—that is to say, the convictional pattern of their system of convictions is itself dynamic.

If these suggestions based upon our reading of Galatians and our discussion of Pharisaic Judaism are true, we should find a dynamic pattern in any part of Paul's system of convictions. This is what we now need to verify by studying Paul's other letters. Our readings can now become more ordered and systematic because they will be guided by more specific questions formulated in terms of our discussion of the Pharisaic convictional pattern.

## SUGGESTIONS FOR FURTHER READINGS

Our study in this chapter has been aimed at showing the characteristics of Pharisaic Judaism as a coherent system of convictions. It needs to be complemented by a study of Pharisaic Judaism, focused upon its interaction with the historical settings in which it progressively developed.

For a history or development of Judaism, particularly Pharisaic Judaism and its eventual relationship to Paul, see the following: E. Bickermann, *From Ezra to the Last of the Maccabees*; W. D. Davies, *Paul and Rabbinic Judaism*; R. T. Herford, *Pharisaism: Its Aims and Its Methods*; J. Klausner, *From Jesus to Paul*; G. F. Moore, *Judaism in the First Centuries of the Christian Era*, 3 vols.; J. Neusner, *Between Time and Eternity: The Essentials of Judaism*; J. Neusner, *From Politics to Piety: The Emergence of Pharisaic Judaism*; J. Neusner, *Method and Meaning in Ancient Judaism*; E. P. Sanders, *Paul and Palestinian Judaism*; S. Sandmel, *The Genius of Paul: A Study in History.*

For reference articles outlining Rabbinic Judaism and/or Hellenistic Judaism, see M. J. Cook, "Early Rabbinic Judaism," in *IDBS*, pp. 499–505; "Hellenistic Judaism," in *IDBS*, pp. 505–9; L. H. Silberman, "Judaism," in *Encyclopedia Britannica*, 15th ed., Macropaedia, vol. 10, pp. 284–302.

# 4

# First Thessalonians: Beloved and Chosen by God

As we open 1 Thessalonians, we find Paul in a strikingly different mood as compared with his mood in Galatians. This is a joyful letter in which Paul repeatedly praises the Thessalonians for their faith. It can be called a pastoral letter in the sense that Paul addresses himself to new converts and seeks to complement his oral teaching. Thus it is the pursuit of an ongoing dialogue. Throughout the letter we find phrases like "as you know" or "you remember," which allude to their common experience or to a former teaching as a basis for a new teaching. And so this letter gives us a glimpse of Paul's missionary preaching. It is a down-to-earth but powerful message aimed at strengthening his readers' faith and exhorting them to a sanctified life by referring to concrete situations and experiences.

Here we do not find heavy theological arguments such as those in Galatians about "righteousness by faith," but this letter in its concreteness will help us understand the convictional pattern that this concept expresses more abstractly. This pattern is in part evoked by the phrase "in Christ," which Paul so often uses. Therefore we need to consider the phrase "in Christ" as an "unknown" which can only be properly understood in the context of the network of relations which characterizes Paul's faith. In fact, when we have elucidated Paul's overall convictional pattern, the relations expressed by the phrase "in Christ" will have themselves been shown.[1]

Reflecting on Paul's conviction about righteousness through faith and not through works of Torah, we have suggested that the Gospel establishes the believers in the right relationship with God by focusing their attention upon something other than this relationship. The believers' attention, concern, and acts are directed by their system of convictions toward what is also God's concern, that is, toward the situations in which God manifests his concern by intervening in them. The question we must raise, therefore, is: in this letter, what are the events or situations to which Paul attaches great importance by virtue of their manifesting God's intervention? In other words, what are the events or situations which, in Paul's view, establish him and the believers in a right relationship with God, that is, as "co-worker with God" or "collaborator of God" (the phrase that Paul uses to designate Timothy and that he could also use for himself and other Christians [1 Thess. 3:2])?

For the Pharisees these questions would have only one answer. The scriptural events (God's acts in the biblical past) are the only ones which established them in the right relationship with God as the Chosen People. Thus in their present the only manifestations of their chosenness can be found when they "take upon themselves the yoke of Torah" both by participating in the Synagogue worship and by fulfilling their vocation in daily life. For them, no new revelation concerning their election is expected or found in the present. In light of our reading of Galatians and the discussion of the relation between Pharisaic Judaism and the Gospel, we can anticipate that, for Paul, there are new revelations and that the convictional pattern which characterizes his faith is dynamic. It is a matter not of "confessing a relationship to God" which has been established once and for all, but of discovering again and again this relation as it happens and takes ever-new forms. Consequently, we could formulate the above questions in Jewish terminology by asking, In what events or situations does Paul see revelatory acts of God which establish a new election of, and a new vocation for, the believers?

In order to progress in our study of Paul's faith, we prefer to read 1 Thessalonians in a way which will allow us to address these questions. This reading is a simple one. The letter is an argument whose main objective is to exhort the Thessalonians to lead a sanctified Christian life (as a first reading, a historical reading, of the letter will show). In any such argument there are two types of statements: those which express the main argument, in this case the exhortations, and those which warrant the validity of the statements of the main argument. The warranting statements, since they express the truth, the reality, and the validity of exhortations (and at times the falsity, the illusory character, the invalidity of wrong attitudes) manifest fundamental convictions among which are convictions about God and his relationship with humans. The exhortations are themselves undergirded by convictions, but these are secondary convictions regarding the reality and the value of various aspects of daily life. Thus it appears that, by reading this letter in such a way as to identify the warranting statements, we will also have identified the events and situations which Paul sees as establishing the believers in a right relationship with God. As we progress through this reading we shall consider the interrelations between these events and situations in order to show the distinctive and dynamic pattern which characterizes them.

## MODERN READERS AND 1 THESSALONIANS

For modern readers the main potential source of misinterpretation comes from underestimating the "historical distance" which separates us from this text. To begin with, 1 Thessalonians is the first letter written by Paul. As such it expresses theological positions which are much less developed than those found in the other letters. The tendency is to project upon this letter what Paul wrote later, especially concerning Christ and salvation. We know that of course Paul's theological thinking unfolded throughout his ministry, although the convictional pattern which characterizes his faith remained stable.

Second, one of Paul's convictions which plays a central role in this letter (and also in others, although in slightly different ways) is that the Parousia, the Second Coming of Christ, is expected to occur in the very near future. He presupposes that only a few people will die before this event (1 Thess. 4:13–18). Such a view is problematic for us, since it is clearly wrong—the Parousia has not yet come. Because of this we tend to leave this aspect of Paul's teaching aside. But then the coherence of his system of convictions cannot be perceived. Similarly, it is difficult for us to accept Paul's teaching about the wrath of God and other such concepts which are foreign to our modern way of thinking. A careful reading is in order.

## FIRST READING: HISTORICAL CONTEXT

This letter is addressed by Paul, Silvanus, and Timothy (Paul's companions) to the church at Thessalonica. From the detailed references to the circumstances of the Thessalonians' conversion, we conclude with most commentators that the letter was written shortly after (let us say four to six months after) Paul's missionary activities in that city. At the time of the writing, Paul was probably in Corinth, since the reference to Athens in 1 Thess. 3:1 seems to indicate that he is no longer there. On the basis of the account of Acts about Paul's missionary journeys, this letter is usually dated in 50/51 (see "Appendix: Chronologies of Paul"). But because of the theological and christological views expressed in it, I think this letter should be dated even earlier, more specifically, before the Jerusalem assembly and the conflicts between Paul and the Jewish Christians which was the occasion of this meeting.[2]

In 1 Thess. 2:2 we learn that Paul came to Thessalonica from Philippi, where he was persecuted. After establishing the church in that city (1:5–6), he left. He does not speak directly about the circumstances of his departure, unless 2:15–16 can be taken as an oblique reference to the Jews' driving him out and preventing him from speaking to the Gentiles "in Thessalonica," even though this city is not mentioned. Yet Paul might be referring to another situation (his persecution in Philippi, for instance) rather than to the situation in Thessalonica. At any rate, it is clear that he was not able to stay as long as he would have liked in order to establish the church on stronger foundations. Thus he attempted several times to return, but without success: "Satan hindered us" (2:18). Finally he sent Timothy to them from Athens "to establish you in your faith and to exhort you" (3:2). The Thessalonians were themselves persecuted by their "countrymen" (2:14), and he was afraid they would forsake their recently and incompletely established faith. When Paul writes, Timothy has returned to him with good news (3:6).

If we now compare this information with the account in Acts 17:1–10, we learn that Paul had to make a secret escape from Thessalonica because of a plot of the Jews against him. The Jews were "jealous" (Acts 17:5) of his missionary success among the Gentiles who attended the Synagogue (also called the God-fearers, people who were not yet Jewish proselytes but on their way to becoming proselytes). This fits well what we have found in the letter, with one important exception. While Paul is clearly saying that the church in Thessalonica is made up of pagans converted from idol worship (1 Thess. 1:9) and thus of Gentiles, in contrast Acts assumes that the church included both Jewish and Gentile converts as a consequence of Paul's preaching in the Synagogue ("as was his custom" [Acts 17:2–4]). But there is nothing in Paul's letters to suggest that this was Paul's practice. This does not exclude the possibility that Gentile God-fearers had also been converted and that this brought about the hostility of the Jews against Paul's missionary activity. In 1 Thess. 1:6 and 2:2 we find reference to a tense situation ("much affliction," "great opposition"), which was the occasion for Paul to warn the Thessalonians "that we were to suffer affliction; just as it has come to pass, and as you know" (3:4). But this later persecution suffered by the Thessalonians was apparently not directly from the hands of the Jews, but rather from those of their "countrymen."

Thus Paul wrote this letter to a young church that he had to abandon after a brief period of missionary activity. Yet he seems to have remained with them for several months, because the Philippians had the time to send gifts to him on at least two occasions (Phil. 4:15–16). This does not necessarily contradict the account in Acts, which does not say how long Paul was in Thessalonica, but only how long he preached in the Synagogue.

Paul was concerned about this church's ability to withstand persecutions which broke out after his departure. Unable to go there himself, he sent Timothy to strengthen them and to encourage them in their faith (1 Thess. 3:2). Upon receipt of good news about them (3:6) he writes to them. In effect, the goal of this letter is the same as that of Timothy's visit: strengthening them further in their faith. There is no specific problem (no false doctrine to fight against, no opponents teaching a wrong gospel) that he needs to correct. Paul simply addresses a young church which is still taking its first steps in the Christian life and needs to be guided and strengthened.[3] This is a pastoral letter of a missionary separated from recent converts.

Commentators unanimously agree that this letter was written by Paul, although some scholars argue that 1 Thess. 2:13–16 is a non-Pauline addition. This view stems from the fact that this passage is violently anti-Semitic and thus in contradiction with other teachings of Paul about the Jews. It also seems to break the literary organization of the letter. The latter objection will be answered as we study Paul's argument. Against the former, it can be said that even though we might deplore such anti-Jewish statements (and their illegitimate use as a justification for anti-Semitic attitudes), they are understandable from somebody who was suffering persecution from the Jews. At any rate, our study will show that it is not an anti-Semitic but an "anti-persecutor" statement. Therefore I view the entire letter as from Paul.[4]

## SECOND READING: THE ORGANIZATION OF THE ARGUMENT

The main purpose of this reading is to identify the passages which in this text are undergirded by fundamental convictions, that is, those which express the relation of the believers to the divine or, to use Paul's terminology, which most directly strengthen and confirm the Thessalonians in their faith. These are the statements which warrant the validity of the main argument.[5] A few remarks about the general characteristics of the letter will help us understand how to identify them.

This letter is part of an ongoing dialogue: Paul, Silvanus, and Timothy are the "we," and the Thessalonians are the "you." As a stage of this dialogue, the letter establishes its own time-frame. The present of the letter—the dialogic present—is a reference point in time in terms of which a past and a future are posited as times which are *not* those of the dialogue. It also establishes its own "space"—the dialogic space—which includes what is directly related to "we" and "you" and thus an "outside space" which includes everything else. In a first approximation we can recognize two dimensions or textual levels in this letter:

1. The level of the dialogue proper, which we shall call the *dialogic level*. It is made up of statements referring to the "present" interaction between "we" and "you." This level commands the unfolding of the overall argument of the letter.

2. Another textual level, which we shall call the *warranting level*, is formed of the statements that belong to other time and "space" frames such as past interactions between "we" and "you" and events which involve neither "we" nor "you." These statements do not make the main argument of the dialogic level progress. They are extraneous to it, but they play an important role in it. In fact, they establish the validity of the dialogic level; they are warrants for it. To put it another way, the dialogic level is based upon the statements of the warranting level. For instance, at that level we will find former teachings of Paul serving as the basis upon which new teachings can be unfolded. On this warranting level the fundamental convictions are found, while on the dialogic level there are only secondary convictions.

This last assertion can be understood when we consider another general characteristic of 1 Thessalonians. Its dialogic level aims at *causing* the Thessalonians *to do* certain things such as leading a sanctified life. But how does one cause somebody to do something? There are two conditions:[6]

1. One needs to explain to (or to teach) that person *how to do it*, that is, the various steps that one must take in order to do this action. This is what the dialogic level of the letter does. It explains how to have a sanctified life.

2. One needs to *convince* that person to do it, by showing why it is desirable, necessary, good, and so on, and why the instructions can be viewed as valid. This is the warranting level. In 1 Thessalonians it establishes the necessity of a sanctified life and the validity of the instructions by referring both to the fundamentals of the Christian faith accepted by the Thessalonians and to Paul as an example who implements this faith in his life.

The warranting level therefore has two functions: it establishes the fundamental convictional pattern which sets the believers in the right relationship with God (see esp. 1 Thess. 1:3—2:16); and it proposes example(s) of the way in which this pattern can be applied. In the present case, Paul expresses how he applied this pattern in his own behavior (esp. in 2:17—3:6). Thus the warranting level should not be construed as made up of a series of assertions verifying the validity of individual exhortations. Rather, it is providing the overall basis for the entire dialogic level, even though given parts of the warranting level are more directly related to specific parts of the dialogic level.

These brief remarks are enough to guide our reading of 1 Thessalonians. By reviewing the overall argument of this letter, we will first identify how the dialogic and warranting levels are interrelated. We will note especially the textual elements which belong to the warranting level to be studied later in greater detail.

## Paul, the Thessalonians, God, and the Lord
## Jesus Christ (1 Thess. 1:1–2 and 5:23–28)

This letter, in order to be a convincing discourse, needs to (re)establish a relationship between the addresser, Paul, and the addressees, the Thessalonians. The dialogic level, which includes the exhortations, posits and then takes for granted this relationship. The warranting level establishes the reality and the validity of this relationship. Yet, as we soon discover by reading the introduction and the conclusion, this relationship is not merely an "I-you" relationship but rather a complex relational network which forms the dialogic space and also defines who are the "I" and the "you."

The salutation, "Paul, Silvanus, and Timothy, to the church of the Thessalonians in God the Father and the Lord Jesus Christ" (1 Thess. 1:1), indicates that this letter is addressed by Paul, Silvanus, and Timothy, "we," to the Thessalonians, "you," who are in a relationship with "God the Father" and the "Lord Jesus Christ." The dialogue is opened by a greeting: "Grace to you and peace." It continues with a thanksgiving: "We give thanks to God always for you all, constantly mentioning you in our prayers" (1:2). This shows that "we" is also in a relationship with "God" (through prayers). Furthermore, through this relationship with God, Paul and his companions are also in a relationship with the Thessalonians.

The conclusion of the letter, 1 Thess. 5:23–28, reasserts the same dialogic space and specifies it. In 5:28 the greeting "grace to you" is repeated and made more explicit: "the grace of our Lord Jesus Christ be with you." It is a blessing (see above, p. 96–99) establishing the Thessalonians in a good (right) relationship with the Lord Jesus Christ. The other part of the greeting, "peace," is also specified in 5:23: "May the God of peace himself sanctify you wholly." "Peace" expresses the establishment of the relationship of the Thessalonians with God, a relationship which implies sanctification. How can one who is in relationship with God not be holy? Furthermore, it is clear that the Lord Jesus Christ and God take the initiative for their relationship with the Thessalonians. Similarly, in 5:26–27 "you" is further defined: it involves "all the brethren" and not merely a few leaders. "Brethren, pray for us" (5:25), which echoes the prayer by Paul for the Thessalonians (1:2), shows that "you" and "we" are in a symmetrical relationship. They have the same status before God and the Lord Jesus Christ. Both Paul (and his companions) and the Thessalonians are established in their true identity ("we" and "you" as Christian brethren in dialogue) through their relationship with God. But Paul did take the initiative in establishing this "we-you" relationship.

These two passages of the dialogic level posit a relational network which can be represented as a triangle. Both "we" and "you" involve a group. Even though this is in many ways a personal letter (as is clear from a few verses [2:18; 3:5; 5:27] where Paul writes in the first-person singular), Paul presents himself as associated with Silvanus and Timothy ("our brother and God's servant in the gospel of Christ" [3:2]). Similarly, he expects the Thessalonians to conceive themselves as associated with "all the brethren." The identity of the individual Christian cannot be conceived outside of a relationship with brothers and sisters (i.e., with people who have the same status). Furthermore, such a relationship in each of the groups, as well as the "we-you" relationship, exists only if each is in relationship with God and the Lord Jesus Christ. We can represent the relational network which forms the space of the dialogue as in Figure 3.

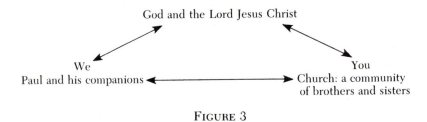

God and the Lord Jesus Christ

We
Paul and his companions

You
Church: a community
of brothers and sisters

FIGURE 3

Thus the introductory salutations and the conclusion posit a relational network among Paul, the Thessalonians, God, and the Lord Jesus Christ as the "space" (the partial semantic universe) in which the dialogue takes place. (For convenience, from now on we will say "Paul" to designate "Paul, Sylvanus, and Timothy.") This network involves the convictional pattern which characterizes Paul's faith and, in his view, also the Thessalonians' faith.[7]

In the context of this relational network the exhortations to a sanctified life (the bulk of the material in 1 Thess. 3:7—5:22) can take place. These exhortations all belong to the dialogic level. For instance, consider 4:1: "We beseech and exhort you in the Lord Jesus . . . to please God." This exhortation is set in the present dialogic relation of "we" and "you" and involves relations to the Lord Jesus and God. Consequently only if this relational network is accepted as true, real, and good by the Thessalonians will they perceive these exhortations as valid and trustworthy and thus as expressing what they will want to do. In other words, the Thessalonians will be true partners of Paul in this dialogue only if they perceive themselves in this relational network. Similarly, Paul can be this person he presents—a joyful and thankful Paul—only if this relational network actually exists and is perceived as good, that is, if the Thessalonians are truly in the right relationship, on the one hand, with God and Jesus and, on the other hand, with Paul as defined by this network.

Paul's thankfulness suggests that, as far as he is concerned, these relations do exist and that they are valid and good. He is convinced that the Thessalonians stand fast in their faith, but his pastoral concern for this young church under persecution pushes him to strengthen them in their faith, to reassert this faith rather than merely to presuppose that they have it. Thus the first part of the letter (which belongs to the warranting level) is devoted to reasserting the validity of the network of relations among Paul (and his companions), the Thessalonians, and the Lord Jesus and God and to expressing what justifies his thankfulness which he proclaims at the beginning of the letter (1:2), at the end of the warranting section (3:7ff.), and in the middle of it (by inserting the phrase "we also thank God" [2:13]).

## The Typological Pattern of Paul's System of Convictions (1 Thess. 1:3—3:6)

The entire first part (1 Thess. 1:3—3:6) belongs, generally speaking, to the warranting level. In a first approximation we can distinguish two parts in this passage.

In 1 Thess. 1:3—2:16 (and other verses interspersed throughout the letter) the warranting level establishes the validity of the relational network expressed in 1:1–2 (and 5:23–28). Its constitutive elements belong to a time frame other than the dialogic present, and even though they involve the same central personages (the Thessalonians and Paul), these are not set in the present we-you relationship. There is nevertheless in this part of the letter a series of phrases which belong to the dialogic level and are there as constant reminders that this material is presented to reassert the convictional basis for the rest of the argument. I refer to phrases like "remembering" (1:3), "we know" (1:4), "as you know" (1:5, 2:2, 5, 11), "you remember" (2:9), and "you are witnesses" (2:10).

Another part of the warranting level, 1 Thess. 2:17—3:6, has a slightly different function. It explains why Paul can be thankful. Consequently, it affirms the validity of the Thessalonians' faith and that this relational network is implemented both in the Thessalonians' life and in Paul's life.

We conclude that the purpose of the first part of the letter is to express what establishes and demonstrates that both Paul and the Thessalonians are in the right relationship with God and in the right relationship with each other. On this basis the exhortations found in the rest of the letter will be compelling for the Thessalonians.

### IN THE RIGHT RELATIONSHIP WITH GOD: THE ELECTION (1 THESS. 1:3–10)

In 1 Thess. 1:3–10 we find a series of elements which, for Paul, are demonstrations of the reality and validity of this relationship. The warranting material is clearly broken up into discrete units by the use of phrases which belong to the dialogic level.

1. *The Thessalonians' behavior: 1:3.* "Your work of faith and labor of love and steadfastness of hope in our Lord Jesus Christ." We find here the triad which for Paul is characteristic of Christian life (5:8; cf. also 1 Cor. 13:13, Gal. 5:5–6, etc.). Note that faith, love, and hope are manifested in concrete behavior ("work," "labor," "steadfastness," or "endurance"). This first element of the warranting level is introduced by the phrase of the dialogic level "remembering before our God and Father."

2. *God's action vis-à-vis the Thessalonians: 1:4–5a.* "We know," a phrase of the dialogic level, introduces a second element of the warranting level. The Thessalonians are "beloved by God," "he has chosen" them by intervening in Paul's proclamation of the Gospel which was "not only in word, but also in power and in the Holy Spirit and with full conviction" (1:5a). Thus Paul's proclamation involved the intervention of God (manifestations of his power, possibly in miracles, and of his Holy Spirit).

3. *The Thessalonians' response to Paul's ministry: 1:5b–6.* The next element of the warranting level is once again introduced by the phrase "you know." They "received the word in much affliction, with joy inspired by the Holy Spirit." As such they are "imitators" of Paul and of the Lord.

*The response of believers in Macedonia and Achaia to the Thessalonians' faith: 1:7–8.* In this element which is not actually separated from the preceding, the Thessalonians are said to be an "example" or, better, a "type" for these believers.

4. *The message about Jesus (the kerygma): 1:9–10.* This last element

is introduced by a phrase of the dialogic level: "they report," which implies, "we know." Jesus the Son of God will come from heaven; the "living and true God" raised him from the dead; he is the deliverer "from the wrath to come." We should note that all these elements are presented as related to the Thessalonians; they have turned to, and serve, the "living and true God," and they wait for his "Son from heaven."

The phrases which interrupt the development of the dialogic level allow us to identify these elements. But their identification is only approximate, and it does not show how they are interrelated. In most cases these elements seem to be merely juxtaposed and to be written down as Paul happens to remember them. Yet we can note that in this passage everything is related to the Thessalonians' experience, to which Paul directs the attention of the readers. Furthermore, Paul makes it clear that God intervened in their experience. Consequently, they are "chosen" by God. This already indicates that, for Paul, election is something *which happens in the believers' experience* rather than something established in the past. This important aspect of Paul's system of convictions sets his faith over against the Pharisees' faith. But then, in Paul's system of convictions, what is the place of this conviction about the election of the believers? And what is the distinctive convictional pattern which characterizes it? We begin elucidating it by considering how Paul relates the Thessalonians' experience to his own ministry, to the believers in Macedonia and Achaia, and to the Lord Jesus. Paul expresses this interrelation by means of two terms: "imitators" and "example" (as they are usually translated). We need to consider what kind of relations these terms refer to.

The Thessalonians are said to be "imitators of us and of the Lord" (1 Thess. 1:6). What does this mean? Note that they are said to be imitators of Paul and the Lord because they "received the word in much affliction, with joy inspired by the Holy Spirit" (1:6). We again find the term "imitators" in 2:14: "For you, brethren, became imitators of the churches of God in Christ Jesus which are in Judea; for you suffered the same things from your own countrymen as they did from the Jews." From this we can conclude that Paul uses the term "imitator" in a sense quite different from the modern sense of this term. What makes the Thessalonians "imitators" of others is not that they follow their example (although they also do this) but that the same things *happened* to them.[8] When they received the word, two things happened to them: they were in affliction, that is, other people inflicted suffering upon them; and they were joyful, but this joy was a gift from the Holy Spirit and not their own doing. Similarly, in 2:14 they are imitators because they were persecuted by their countrymen. Thus, if they are imitators of Paul and of the Lord, it is first of all because what happened in their experience is similar to what happened in Paul's experience and in the Lord's experience, and only secondarily because of what they did (receiving the word and acting accordingly).

The Thessalonians are also said to be an "example," or in a literal translation a "type," for the believers of Macedonia and Achaia. "Type" is a technical term for Paul, which we can understand when we note that the Thessalonians are a "type" for the same reasons they were imitators. The text reads, ". . . for you received the word in much affliction, with joy inspired by the Holy Spirit; *so that* you became an example [literally, "type"]. . ." (1 Thess. 1:6–7). Thus they are not so much a model to follow but rather a "type," that is, what happened to them is typical of what happens to those who receive the word, and thus their "experience" prefigures what will happen to other believers.

We now have an idea of how Paul perceives the relations among the various elements of this passage. There is an essential similarity among the experiences of Christ, of Paul, of the Thessalonians, and of the believers of Macedonia and Achaia, so much so that any one of these persons or groups can be said to be an imitator of those who precede him or them and a type of those who follow him or them in the unfolding of events.

In order to understand better this imitator/type relation among the Thessalonians' experience, Christ's experience, Paul's experience, and the Macedonian believers' experience, we will examine how Paul describes each of them. In a first approximation (which we shall refine as we progress) we can note that each of them involves three elements.

In the case of the Thessalonians' experience these three elements are (not necessarily in this order): receiving the word about the living and true God and acting accordingly (1 Thess. 1:3, 9b; cf. also 1:6); suffering (1:6); and the intervention of God (at work in Paul's proclamation), which is thus an election by God (1:4), and through his Spirit (1:6). In the case of Christ we can presuppose that he received the word (since he is God's Son, he is in the right relationship with God), he suffered (he died [1:10; 4:14], he was killed by the Jews [2:15]), and God intervened and raised him (1:10). In the case of Paul, we simply know that God intervened in his experience (in his ministry [1:5]). The following verses say that he suffered (2:2) and that he received the Gospel and acted accordingly (2:4–5). In the case of the believers of Macedonia and Achaia, we know only that they are believers and thus that they received the word. But in view of the preceding types which prefigure what their experience will be, they should expect both suffering and God's intervention.

Another experience is mentioned: the experience of the believers at the end of time. Again we find the three elements: the believers are those who have received the word; they will be suffering the wrath (1 Thess. 1:10) of God (cf. 5:9); God will intervene through the intermediary of his Son coming from heaven to deliver the believers (1:10).

These elements could form a chronological succession, a history: Jesus died and was raised; he appeared to Paul, who thus was elected to be Apostle to the Gentiles; Paul preached the Gospel to the Thessalonians, who thus were elected; the news of their faith is proclaimed throughout Macedonia and Achaia, and thus the believers of these regions are strengthened in their faith; and, at the end of time, Christ comes back from heaven to deliver the believers from the wrath to come. The text indicates clearly that Paul had in mind this historical development according to which one stage can take place only because the preceding stages have taken place and open the possibility for the next stages. But Paul does not present these elements in their chronological order. Such a presentation would have shown that for him the chronological and causal relations of this succession would establish the validity and the truth of the Thessalonians' faith. This would have implied either that the divine is discovered in a predetermined unfolding of history from its starting point (in the case of our text, Jesus) to its end (the Parousia) or that a complete and final revelation is found in its starting point (Jesus) and thus that the rest of the chronological succession is an implementation of this revelation in new situations.

Again, Paul does not ignore the historical development which links the experience of the believers on the one hand to Jesus and on the other hand to the Parousia. We will see that he perceived these stages as forming a sacred history which prolongs the sacred history of the Old Testament. At the same time, he sees (and emphasizes) among the elements of this history another kind of relationship, namely, a certain identity among them. What happens to the Thessalonians is the "same thing" that happened to Jesus, Paul, and the churches of Judea. This twofold understanding of the relations among Jesus, Paul, the Thessalonians, the Macedonian believers, and the believers at the Parousia is also reflected in his concepts of "imitator" and "type." On the one hand, the Thessalonians are imitators of Paul and the Lord because they *do* the same things they did: receiving the word, loving, hoping. The fact that the Thessalonians follow them as models is an expression of the historical link between them and those who preceded them. The same could be said about the statement that the Thessalonians themselves are models to be followed by the believers of Macedonia and Achaia. On the other hand, the Thessalonians are imitators of Paul and the Lord (and types for the Macedonians) because what happens to them is like what happened to Paul and the Lord (and what will happen to the Macedonian believers). In this case the historical, chronological, and causal link is discarded. The respective natures of the events/situations are compared and found to be equivalent. Since Paul does not stress in any way the chronological order of these various experiences, he makes it clear that this second kind of relation is primary for him, at least in this letter. In other words, he emphasizes the fundamental equivalence of these experiences.

It is also clear that he emphasizes the Thessalonians' experience. This suggests that the validity and truth of the Thessalonians' faith is found first in their own experience, where there is everything needed for establishing the truth of their faith. It is the experience of being chosen by God who intervened with power and with his Holy Spirit, and of having a joy inspired by the Holy Spirit in the midst of afflictions. Because of what happened in their lives, they are in the right relationship with God. Thus we can anticipate that Paul's experience and Jesus' experience simply verify the validity of the Thessalonians' experience. It is valid because it is of the same type as Paul's experience and Jesus' experience.

This provisional conclusion has far-reaching implications, since it means that the Thessalonians' faith is not centered on Jesus but on their own experience and what happened in it. More generally, it means that, according to Paul's faith, it is in the believers' experience that the convictional pattern is established for them. We have reached this provisional conclusion by noting that Paul focuses the attention of his readers on their own experience.

A first objection could be raised: this emphasis on the Thessalonians' experience was demanded by the thanksgiving literary form. But this emphasis is not accidental. Paul could have expressed his thankfulness about the Thessalonians' faith while focusing the readers' attention, for instance, upon Jesus' death and resurrection. This would have meant that he conceived of their faith—their right relationship with God—as primarily established by the events concerning Jesus. Such is, for instance, the pattern in Ephesians (an observation which raises doubts about its Pauline authorship). In such a case, faith would be primarily an appropriation of the message about Jesus' death and resurrection, as the Pharisees appropriated the Sinai covenant, but a study of the organization of the argument in 1 Thessalonians shows that this is not how he sees their faith. It is *not* because of what happened to Jesus, nor because of what Jesus did, that the Thessalonians are in the right relationship with God. Rather, it is because of what happened in their own experience. To put it in terms of our discussion of Pharisaic Judaism, Jesus is not the complete and final revelation of their election (their chosenness). There is a new revelation to the Thessalonians.

But do not these last statements contradict what Paul writes about Christ in other letters? We will also address this issue in the following chapters, when dealing with Philippians and central texts of Romans and 1 Corinthians. But in reading 1 Thessalonians we cannot reach any other conclusion. In fact, this letter says very little about what happened to Jesus and what he did in the past. It mentions that he was killed by the Jews (1 Thess. 2:15), but no particular significance is attached to his death. Paul simply says that Jesus was killed as the prophets were and as Paul and the Thessalonians are persecuted. There is no mention that he "died for our sins" and thus that his death establishes the believers in the right relationship with God. Actually his death is mentioned in only three other passages of the letter. In 1:10 and 4:14 his death is mentioned merely to point out that God raised him from the dead. What is significant is his resurrection.

What then is Christ's role? It is a *present* and *future* role, as is clear in 1 Thess. 1:10, "Jesus who delivers us from *the wrath to come*," and in 4:14, "through Jesus, God *will bring* with him those who have fallen asleep." The third reference to his death (5:10) also indicates that it is a future role. Christ "died for us so that whether we wake or sleep we might live with him" (5:10). As the context shows, this means that whether the believers are alive or dead they will be saved from God's wrath at the end of time. Again, Christ will bring about this salvation as the resurrected one (the believers will live with him), but in order to be the resurrected one who will save us, he needed to die. Thus he "died for us." This is all that our text says when one does not project on it what Paul writes in other letters.[9] The other passages about Christ in this letter also emphasize his future salvific role. At the end of time he will come (cf. 2:19; 5:23) from heaven to "deliver us from the wrath to come" (1:10; cf. also 5:9) by taking the believers (both those who are alive and those who died) with him to heaven (4:17). Thus one of the characteristics of the believers' attitude is "hope in our Lord Jesus Christ" (1:3).

Christ also has a role in the *present* experience of the believers. To begin with, as the resurrected Christ, he is the Son of the Father (1 Thess. 1:10) and is with God in heaven ("sitting at the right hand of God" [Ps. 110:1], a verse which was used by the early church to explain and make sense of the resurrection[10]). Therefore he is Lord, the Lord of the believers, and as such he has authority over them, and Paul links his exhortations to the authority of the Lord Jesus (4:1). Furthermore, the resurrected Christ, the Lord, also intervenes (or is expected to intervene) in the present experience of the believers as God does. So we read in 3:11–12 this prayer of Paul: "Now may our God and Father himself, and our Lord Jesus, direct our way to you; and may the Lord make you increase and abound in love. . . ." The intervention of God in the present life of the believers is associated, or even identified, with that of Christ. This helps us understand the strange statement found in 1:10: "Jesus who *delivers* us from the wrath to come." He delivers us *in the present.* The tense could easily be overlooked, since it is clear from the phrase "wrath to come" as well as from other passages that this deliverance will take place at the Parousia, that is, in the future. But the present tense indicates that this is the permanent function of Christ and that in a certain way it already takes place, although it will be fully carried out only in the future. Indeed, the wrath has already begun to come (on the Jews [2:16]). Furthermore, Paul uses technical terminology to speak about the present suffering and tribulations of the believers, which indicates that these are part of the sufferings expected at the end of time. And therefore the ability to persevere joyfully despite these tribulations might also be viewed by Paul as a present (and preliminary) deliverance of the wrath to come. Indeed, this ability is given to the believers by an intervention of God through his Holy Spirit (1:6). The end is close at hand. Paul so much expects to be alive at the time of the Parousia ("we who are alive, who are left until the coming of the Lord" [4:15]) that during his missionary activity among the Thessalonians he did not teach them anything about what happens to those who die before that time (cf. 4:13).

All this suggests that in 1 Thessalonians the believers are not established in the right relationship with God through something which happened in the past (e.g., Jesus' death or the event of his resurrection in the past), but rather through what happens in their present experience which involves interventions of God, of the Holy Spirit, and of the resurrected Christ as Lord. Jesus' past experience (his death and resurrection) and Paul's experience guarantee the validity of their experience insofar as it follows the same type or pattern as theirs. In effect, Jesus' and Paul's experiences prefigure the Thessalonians' experience in the same way as their experience prefigures what will be that of the believers of Macedonia and Achaia, as well as the believers' experience at the time of the Parousia (we shall come back to this). The decisive events which establish them in their faith and thus in the right relationship with God and the Lord Jesus Christ take place in their own experience. In Jewish terminology, the Thessalonians have been chosen, elected by God (1 Thess. 1:4), to be his servants (1:9) or, better, his "co-workers" (as Paul says of Timothy [3:2]; RSV: "God's servants") not because they appropriated a past election from the time of the Exodus or from the time of Jesus. They themselves are directly elected by God, who intervenes in their lives.

We should also note that Jesus Christ is a special kind of type. He might be viewed as the central type, since any new act of God can be viewed as Christ-like and even as manifestation of the resurrected Christ. Only when we have a more complete picture of Paul's system of convictions will we be able to understand Christ's uniqueness (see Chapter 7). But it remains that Jesus Christ is a type, a promise (and not a complete and final revelation).

The preceding verses have warranted one part of the dialogic space, the relationship of the Thessalonians with God and the Lord Jesus Christ (the resurrected Christ). The place of Paul in this relational network remains largely undefined. The following passage specifies it.

PAUL'S RELATIONSHIP TO THE
THESSALONIANS (2:1–12)

The Thessalonians' experience is closely interrelated with Paul's, indeed, their experience includes Paul's ministry among them. Through his proclamation of the Gospel "in power and in the Holy Spirit and with full conviction" (1 Thess. 1:5) God's call was manifested to them. This new section of the warranting level emphasizes this dimension of their experience and also the relation between their experience and Paul's, that is, the relation "we-you" of the dialogic space. On the basis of our reading of 1:3–10 we can now proceed more quickly.

As was the case in 1 Thess. 1:3–10, this passage of the warranting level includes phrases of the dialogic level which emphasize certain elements of Paul's and the Thessalonians' experience. The phrase "you know" is related to the Thessalonians' response to Paul's ministry in 2:1 (cf. 1:9) and to Paul's persecution in Philippi (2:2). The phrase "God who tests our hearts" (2:4; comparable to "as God is witness"), which expresses a present relationship with God and thus belongs to the dialogic level, is related to the affirmation that Paul's message was entrusted to him by God and was proclaimed to please God and not humans. This is reinforced by "as you know," in 2:5a, which points out that these are not words of flattery. "As God is witness" (2:5b) emphasizes that this is neither a disguised expression of greed nor an attempt to seek glory. On the contrary, Paul is both like a baby among them and like a nurse (2:6–8). The phrase "you remember" in 2:9 underscores that he worked night and day in order to avoid burdening them. The phrase "you are witnesses, and God also" in 2:10 calls his readers' attention to the holiness of his behavior among them. Finally, the phrase "for you know" in 2:11 is related to Paul's fatherly attitude toward the Thessalonians.

In order to understand how these components are interrelated, we consider successively those which concern Paul's experience prior to his interaction with the Thessalonians (Paul's own experience) and those which concern his ministry among the Thessalonians (Paul as part of the Thessalonians' experience). What does Paul say about his experience prior to his ministry in Thessalonica? Very little. He writes, "We have been approved by God to be entrusted with the gospel" (1 Thess. 2:4a). He also states that he proclaimed and still proclaims the Gospel to other people, as well as to the Thessalonians (2:6; cf. also 2:4b, which is a general statement about his proclamation of the Gospel). Despite their conciseness, these statements include the three elements we have found to be the characteristic pattern of the Thessalonians' experience: suffering; God's intervention in his experience (in order to test and approve Paul and thus to establish his true identity, i.e., his identity as "apostle of Christ" [2:6]); and receiving the word and acting accordingly.

The description of his ministry in Thessalonica demonstrates that it is a manifestation of God in the Thessalonians' experience. Thus he declares that his message is "the gospel of God" (1 Thess. 2:2) and not human, false, or greedy words (2:3, 5). He links his courage (in preaching the gospel despite great opposition) to God (having "courage in our God" [2:2]). He also emphasizes that his conduct among them was "holy and righteous and blameless" (2:10). This suggests the meaning "holy and righteous as God is." And he moves on to speak about "how, like a father with his children, we exhorted each one of you" (2:11). "Like a father," that is, like God the Father. Through his ministry Paul is indeed a manifestation of God for the Thessalonians. Using his terminology, we can say that Paul in his ministry is "imitator" of (or fulfillment of) the type "God in relation to somebody" (that is, with his Son, Jesus [1:10]). And thus, in the dialogic space, Paul (and his companions), "we," have authority over the Thessalonians, "you." Paul has the authority to exhort, to encourage, and to charge them.

In his ministry, Paul is also the fulfillment of the rest of the type "God in relation to somebody," that is, he is also the child under the authority of the Father, and as such he is concerned "to please God" (and "not to please men" and not to seek a benefit for himself [1 Thess. 2:4–6]). He writes, "We could have made demands on you, but we were babies among you" (2:7). (This is, in my view, the best translation of this verse, including the word "babies" found in very good Greek manuscripts, rather than "gentle" found in other manuscripts.[11]) This describes Paul in his relationship with the Father. Yes, Paul and his companions are apostles of Christ; they have authority. Yet at the same time they are children in their relationship with God, and thus they are like babies among the Thessalonians.

This brings about another metaphor: "As a nurse [nursing mother] taking care of her children [and giving them her own milk], so, having a strong affection for you, we were ready to share with you not only the gospel of God but also our own selves [or, our own life]" (1 Thess. 2:7b–8, my translation; I have added the parenthetical phrases to clarify the meaning). Concretely this means that Paul shared his life with them by working night and day rather than being a burden to them (2:9).

Thus Paul is in the following relationship with the Thessalonians: he is an apostle, called and tested by God, in whose ministry among them God manifests his power and his Holy Spirit (1 Thess. 1:5); but he is so as a child, submitted to and willing to please God the Father, and therefore he is a child with them, he is their brother (2:9); he is also a nursing mother who gives of herself (and who, in the family structure of that time, was submitted along with the children to the authority of the father); yet, in all this, he is a manifestation of God among them, and thus a father with his children. Paul is all this at the same time!

This is certainly a confusing use of metaphors, which we can better understand with the help of the imitator/type pattern we found in 1 Thess. 1:3–10. Conversely, these metaphors will help us to perceive more clearly the relations which characterize this pattern and to complement the description we have proposed above on the basis of 1:3–10. So we need to clarify the elements of Paul's, Jesus', and the Thessalonians' experience which correspond to the four metaphors.

Paul's experience involves: (1) Suffering, declaring to the Thessalonians the Gospel in the face of great opposition (persecution) because he has "confidence and assurance in God" (1 Thess. 2:2) and sharing with them his own life (or his own being). This is the nurse metaphor. (2) Being approved by God to be entrusted with the Gospel; having a ministry in which God manifests his power. This is being an apostle. (3) Being in a child/father relationship with God, pleasing God and not humans. (4) Having a father-like authority to exhort, to encourage, and to charge.

As such Paul's experience is the fulfillment of the type "Jesus," or in other words, he is an imitator of Jesus. Jesus' experience involves suffering and "dying for us" (1 Thess. 5:10); God's intervention, the resurrection; the Father/Son relationship between God and Jesus; and Jesus as Lord (with the authority of God).

The Thessalonians' experience is, in turn, the fulfillment of both Paul and the Lord Jesus as types, that is, they are imitators of Paul and of the Lord. It involves: suffering and spreading their faith (the Gospel [1 Thess. 1:7–8]) by their "work of faith, labor of love, and steadfastness of hope" despite persecutions; being called by God, having joy inspired by the Holy Spirit; being beloved by God their Father and being Paul's brothers; and being a "type" for the believers in Macedonia and Achaia.

As suggested earlier, Paul sees these three situations—Paul's, Jesus', and the Thessalonians'—as equivalent. In each of them there is the full manifestation and establishment of the right relationship with God. This is why Paul can direct his readers' attention to their own experience. But this also means that for Paul the various components of Jesus' experience, his own experience, and the Thessalonians' experience can be, and should be, understood together. As we saw, this is what he does in Galatians when speaking of his experience in terms of the Galatians' experience, and vice versa. Taking into account the equivalence of each of these components allows us to formulate some hypotheses and questions concerning Paul's system of convictions.

### Sharing One's Life with Confidence

We shall make two observations concerning the correspondence of the first element of Paul's, Jesus', and the Thessalonians' experience.

When interpreting the meaning of his own experience, Paul knows the kerygma (proclamation) about Jesus. For him, as we suggested, the kerygma is a type of what will happen or happens to him as believer. Thus he can perceive his own suffering (persecution) as equivalent to Jesus' suffering. But if this is so, he can then expect that God will intervene, as he did in the case of Jesus (when God raised Jesus from the dead). Thus Paul describes his suffering as follows: "But though we had already suffered and been shamefully treated at Philippi, as you know, we had courage [confidence and assurance] in our God to declare to you the gospel of God in the face of great opposition" (1 Thess. 2:2). So Paul "had confidence and assurance in God" (our effort to render the term usually translated "having courage" [2:2]). Could this mean that his confidence and assurance are based on the conviction that Jesus' experience as a whole is a type, a promise (Gal. 3:22: "What was promised to faith in Jesus Christ") of what will happen and happens in Paul's experience? Jesus faced "great opposition," but God intervened. This is a promise that the same will be true in Paul's case. Similarly, in the Thessalonians' case, what does "work of faith" mean? Could it mean work in the confidence and assurance based on the promises manifested in Jesus' experience *and* Paul's experience?

Paul's attitude toward the Thessalonians in the context of persecutions can be described as sharing his own life with others (like a nursing mother). And Paul does this by working night and day (1 Thess. 2:9). This could readily correspond to the Thessalonians "labor of love" (1:3).

The exhortations of the dialogic level suggest it further. In 4:9–12, after stating that they do not need to be taught anything about love, he nevertheless exhorts them to work with their hands to "command the respect of outsiders, and be dependent on nobody." This is what the labor of love should entail, as they already know and manifest by their own behavior. Furthermore, in 5:14–15 Paul writes, "Encourage the fainthearted, help the weak, be patient with them all. See that none of you repays evil for evil, but always seek to do good to one another and to all." This could be summarized "Share yourself with others."

In Jesus' experience all this corresponds to Jesus "dying for us" (1 Thess. 5:10). This should not be understood here as a sacrificial death for our sins (dying vicariously instead of the sinners). Rather, Jesus is sharing his life with us even up to death, a work of love comparable to Paul's proclamation of the Gospel despite persecutions and to the Thessalonians' labor of love.

### Approved and Elected by God

Because of the correspondences among the various experiences, we can conclude that on the one hand, the joy inspired by the Holy Spirit during the Thessalonians' afflictions (1 Thess. 1:6) and their election by God (1:4), and, on the other hand, God's approval of Paul (2:4) and the manifestation of God's power in his ministry (1:5), are equivalent to God's resurrection of Jesus. Thus Jesus' resurrection would be both a manifestation of God's power and an election. This would confirm our suggestion that, in Paul's view, through the resurrection Jesus became the Lord. Jesus is the Christ, the Lord, because God raised him not only *from* the dead but also *to* heaven, so that he might sit at his right hand. As we noted above, Paul's view of Jesus' death and resurrection seems to be based on the interpretation of those events as fulfillment of Ps. 110:1: "The Lord says to my lord: 'Sit at my right hand, till I make your enemies your footstool.'" According to this interpretation of the early Palestinian church, the resurrection is the vindication of Jesus and also his election (and establishment) as the Lord. Similarly, the interventions of God in the Thessalonians' and Paul's experiences are resurrection-like events, events through which they are delivered from death-like situations and through which they are elected, chosen for a specific vocation.

## *Having Authority*

Similarly, the equivalence of the authority of Jesus as Lord, of Paul as apostle with a father-like authority, and of the Thessalonians as "type" for other believers is clear. The Thessalonians are Lord-like or apostle-like figures for other people.

So this passage further establishes and defines the convictional pattern we found earlier. It does not add anything to our understanding of the believers' experience at the Parousia, except for the brief comment that this will involve participating in God's kingdom and glory (1 Thess. 2:12). In other words, the believers will then be fully Lord-like.

### THE SCOPE OF THE TYPE/IMITATOR PATTERN (1 THESS. 2:13–16)

In this passage, already discussed in part, we find the same pattern again. The attention is focused on the Thessalonians' experience (1 Thess. 2:13). Paul emphasizes that they are imitators of the churches in Judea (2:14) as well as implicitly of the Lord Jesus, of the prophets, and of Paul (2:15), since all of them have "suffered the same things" from their respective fellow citizens. We need only add two remarks.

First, the type/imitator pattern is expanded to include two additional stages: the churches in Judea and the prophets (of the Old Testament). Second, despite the diatribe against the Jews (2:16), the convictional pattern demands that this same harsh judgment be applied to the persecutors at each stage of the pattern, that is, to the Gentile fellow citizens of the Thessalonians as well as to the Jews (in the same way that in the letter to the Galatians both the Gentile idolaters and the Jews are under a curse). Thus this passage is not, in Paul's mind, anti-Semitic but rather "anti-persecutor."

### APPLICATION OF THE TYPE/IMITATOR PATTERN TO NEW SITUATIONS (1 THESS. 2:17—3:6)

This passage, which recounts both Paul's efforts to go back to Thessalonica and Timothy's visit, shows what Paul did as a result of his evaluation of the Thessalonians' situation as described in 1 Thess. 1:3—2:16. It presupposes the fundamental convictional pattern we have elucidated and therefore expresses less fundamental convictions. Actually, it shows how Paul applies this pattern to new situations. Yet, once again we find the phrase "as you know," which signals the presence of another element of the fundamental warranting level. I am referring to 3:3b–4, where Paul mentions that he had told them beforehand that they would suffer affliction. This had already been said once, but his explanation of this in 3:5 brings a new dimension. The afflictions are associated with the Tempter (also called Satan [2:18]). The afflictions are the manifestation of a satanic power which can eventually cancel the manifestation of God's power (and thus Paul's "labor would be in vain"). This begins to confirm our suggestion that the manifestation of God in the believers' (Thessalonians' and Paul's) experience is resurrection-like. Anticipating what we shall find in other letters, we can say that, in the same way that the resurrection is the overcoming of death by the power of God, so the election of the believers as well as the joy inspired by the Holy Spirit in the midst of persecution is the overcoming of an evil power. In light of our reading of Galatians, we can also say that this evil power which is overcome by the manifestation of God's power in the conversion of the believers is a power of bondage.

Similarly, 1 Thess. 2:19–20 involves elements of the fundamental warranting level (the rhetorical question form has the same role as the phrase "as you know"). The Thessalonians are described as Paul's "hope," "joy," "crown," and "glory." Thus he says that he will be able to boast of them "before our Lord Jesus at his coming." In other words, in Paul's experience the Thessalonians' conversion and faithfulness, which manifest that he is indeed an apostle with a father-like authority over them, is equivalent to the glory and the Lord-like position (cf. the crown) that he will have at the Parousia. They are his hope in the sense that they already prefigure what he will receive then. This suggests that while, for Paul, hope is the expectation of that which is not seen (Rom. 8:24), it is *not* a blind expectation. Rather, it is based upon manifestations in the believers' experience, of things which are like—or, better, which are of the same nature, which are preliminary manifestations of—what is hoped for. Thus this passage expresses the interrelationship of Paul's experience and the Parousia experience of the believers as conceived according to his convictional pattern.

About the rest of this passage we need only say that it is clearly the application to a new situation of the convictional pattern which had been previously established. In his concern for the Thessalonians, Paul is like a nursing mother to them (worrying about them and willing to sacrifice himself by being left alone in Athens [1 Thess. 3:1]), but also like a father, since he wants to strengthen them in their faith and to exhort them. He does so through Timothy (3:2), because he himself was "hindered by Satan" (cf. 2:18). Similarly, Timothy's report about the faithfulness of the Thessalonians shows that they are themselves applying the convictional pattern to the situation of persecution in which they find themselves.

### Implementing the Faith (1 Thess. 3:7—5:22)

The rest of the letter belongs almost entirely to the dialogic level, which expresses how to carry out this faith in various concrete situations, that is, how to apply the convictional pattern in their daily life. First, Paul states in 1 Thess. 3:7–13 how he applies this pattern in the present of the letter. He repeats in many ways what he has already expressed about the time he was without news from them (2:17—3:5), but adds now the dimension of thankfulness. This involves a veiled exhortation to lead a loving, perfect, blameless Christian life following Paul's example.

Then we find exhortations to a life free from immorality. This passage involves references to elements of his former teaching which belong to the warranting level (4:2, 6b–8) and which we have already found in other forms. This is followed by an exhortation to love (4:9–12), which also includes elements of the warranting level (4:9b–10a) that we have discussed above. Then Paul gives the Thessalonians a new teaching about the fate of those who died in 4:13–18 (with a brief reference to Jesus' death and resurrection).

The following exhortations to watchfulness (in the expectation of the Day of the Lord, which may come at any time [5:1–11]) also involve a reference to a former teaching on this matter (5:2–5). This shows that Paul included in his proclamation of the Gospel extensive teaching about the Parousia experience. But he primarily emphasized the relation between the believers' present experience and the Parousia. They are "children of light" who can hope (1:3; 1:10; 2:12; 2:19–20) because in their present there are prefigurations of what will be given to them at the end of time. But they have to be watchful. In the present there are people under the wrath of God (the Jews [2:16] and also possibly people under the power of the Tempter [3:5]), "children of darkness" who prefigure those who will be under the wrath of God at the end of time.

Finally, we find a series of exhortations about various issues (5:12–22). We need to emphasize only those found in 5:19–21a: "Do not quench the Spirit, do not despise prophesying, but test everything." These words presuppose that, for Paul, in the present of the believers and through the action of the Spirit, new revelations are received. They should not be neglected or set aside even though they always need to be tested.

## PAUL'S FAITH AS MANIFESTED IN
## 1 THESSALONIANS (4:13–18)

The teaching of Paul concerning those who died (1 Thess. 4:13–18) once more displays the pattern we found in 1:3—2:16. It applies the convictional pattern to a situation which heretofore had not been integrated into the Thessalonians' system of convictions (or semantic universe). As such, this passage gives us the opportunity to review the results of our reading of this letter.

The Thessalonians are ignorant concerning the fate of the Christians who died. This means that Paul failed to give them any instruction on the topic. But of what precisely were they ignorant? This is not clear. Were they ignorant of everything about the resurrection of the dead? The statement of 1 Thess. 4:13 seems to imply that they are without hope for those who died. Yet the following verses do not emphasize the resurrection in itself but rather that "God will bring with him those who have fallen asleep" (4:14b), that is, that the dead, after being resurrected will participate in the Parousia. They will be taken to heaven by Christ, together with the believers who are alive (4:17). At the Parousia, those who are alive will not precede those who are dead (4:15). Did the Thessalonians already know about the resurrection of the dead and merely not know how the resurrected believers will participate in the events of the Parousia? This seems to be the case. To be "without hope" is not to be ignorant of a doctrine (here, about the resurrection of the dead) but to be unable to perceive the correspondences of one's experience (which includes death) with, on the one hand, the promise (type) which Jesus' experience is and, on the other hand, the ultimate fulfillment at the Parousia. Paul then shows them what it is to hope.

Paul establishes his teaching about the resurrection by referring to Jesus' death and resurrection in 1 Thess. 4:14. As Jesus died, these believers died. As Jesus rose from the dead and to heaven at the right hand of God (see again our discussion of 1:10), God will bring these believers to him in heaven. This presupposes that he will also raise them from the dead (4:16). Therefore, the experience of the dead believers at the Parousia corresponds to and fulfills the promises contained in Jesus' experience. Yet, this correspondence, and therefore these promises, are not valid for everybody. They apply only to the believers, to those who died in Christ (4:16) or through Christ (a possible reading of 4:14). Whatever else the phrase "dead in Christ" means, it expresses that the believers' death corresponds to Jesus' death. Once the correspondence between this element of the believers' and Jesus' experiences is established, the correspondence between the other elements of their respective experiences is also established. So there is hope for the believers.

This is how the convictional pattern of Paul's faith is applied to new situations and how he incorporates them into his system of convictions. These remarks about 1 Thess. 4:13–18 also underscore that the most characteristic feature of this convictional pattern is the establishment of correspondences among various experiences (or situations). Furthermore, these experiences are not merely duplications of each other. In each there is something new. Each involves a specific election and vocation (those of Jesus, Paul, and the Thessalonians are not identical). Therefore none of these experiences can be viewed as a complete and final revelation. Rather, each is the promise or type of new revelations in new situations. Only one of these experiences can be viewed as absolute: the Parousia experience (that is, the experience at the end of time). But even though it is expected soon, this experience is still in the future. In the present there are only relative revelations, revelations which apply to specific believers in specific situations.

Consequently, what establishes specific believers in the right relationship with God is what happens in their own experience. Since Paul addresses the Thessalonians, he focuses most of his attention on their experience and on God's manifestation in it, and therefore also on his ministry among them. Jesus' experience as well as Paul's own experience (and the experience of the churches in Judea) are secondary for the

Thessalonians' faith, even though these experiences have an important role in ascertaining the validity of the Thessalonians' experience. Their experience cannot stand on its own. It is not an absolute. It is valid only insofar as it is related to other experiences either in the past or in the future.

For Paul the convictional pattern which characterizes the faith of the believers is centered on their experience (this is where they are established in the right relationship with God). But it has a threefold dimension, which Paul expresses by means of the three concepts "faith, love, and hope" (1 Thess. 1:3 and 5:8). In light of our reading of this letter, we can propose the following three hypotheses regarding the meaning of these concepts.

1. The concept of "hope" clearly expresses the relations of the believers' experience to future experiences and especially to the Parousia experience. Hope is identifying events or situations of one's experience which are preliminary manifestations (types) of what will be manifested in other people's experience (the Macedonians [1 Thess. 1:7]) in the near future, as well as, more fully, at the time of the Parousia. In Paul's experience, the faithful Thessalonians are his hope, his crown, his glory, that is, preliminary manifestations of what will be at the Parousia (2:19–20). Hope therefore involves identifying, in one's present experience, the preliminary manifestations of the Parousia and waiting with confidence for the ultimate manifestations.

2. Similarly, we can suggest that Paul's *concept* of "faith" (not to be confused with faith as a phenomenon which includes convictions about what Paul calls "faith", "hope," and "love") could express the relations of the believers' experience with *past* experiences (especially Jesus' but also Paul's, the Judean churches', and the prophets' experiences). "Faith" is identifying, in one's experience, events or situations which are fulfillments of what has been manifested in Jesus' or Paul's or the Judean churches' or the prophets' experiences (the types). Because of this correspondence, having faith means being at one with Jesus or with Paul or with the Judean churches or with the prophets. Could it be that the phrase "in Christ" is used in part to express that such a relationship is acknowledged by the believers? They are "in Christ" because, in their experience, there are Christ-like events.

The elements in one's experience discovered through faith as fulfilling the promises contained in the types Jesus and Paul, as well as in other types, are actually the same elements discovered through hope as being preliminary manifestations of what will be in the future and at the Parousia. Thus, in Paul's experience, the Thessalonians through their conversion are the fulfillment of the promises contained in Jesus' experience as well as preliminary manifestations of what will be Paul's crown and glory at the Parousia. By the discovery, through faith and hope, of the relations of these elements of one's experience with past and future experiences, one is established in the right relationship with God. In other words, it is by considering what God has done in Jesus' and Paul's experiences, as well as what he is beginning to do in the experience of others (the Macedonians) and what he will do at the Parousia, that one is established in the right relationship with God. Through faith (and hope) one is established in the right relationship with God, that is, that one discovers one is chosen by God, elected by God. In other words, it is only when one takes into account how God acted, is acting, and will act in the experience of *other* people that one can be in the right relationship with God. This does not occur when one's attention is focused exclusively on one's own relationship with God and on what God does in one's life.

3. Paul's concept of love could then express how this pattern (of the right relationship with God established through faith and hope) is applied in all the situations of one's own experience. It should not come as a surprise that the application of the faith and hope pattern to the believers' experience defines this experience as a specific kind of relationship with other people, love, for it is clear from our reading of 1 Thessalonians that a believer's experience is not a private experience. We are far from a view of religious experience (common in our culture) according to which a believer is in relationship with the divine by him or herself, through an individual, interior (mystical) encounter with the divine. For Paul, a believer's (religious) experience involves other people. Without even speaking of the Thessalonians' interrelation among themselves, we have noted that, at least, Paul was part of the Thessalonians' experience. And Paul is a necessary part of the Thessalonians' religious experience. Where did they discover manifestations of God? First of all, in Paul, in whom God manifested his power. Indeed, their conversion involved the discovery of God in Paul's ministry. Faith is not merely believing that God intervened in the past and will intervene in the future in other people; it is also the discovery that God manifests

himself in somebody else who is part of one's present experience. The Thessalonians first discovered God at work in Paul, and this was for them an election (1 Thess. 1:4–5). Only afterward did the Thessalonians experience God's intervention in their own private lives (e.g., the intervention of the Holy Spirit [1:6]). As a consequence of such a faith, the believers cannot but see themselves in a special relationship with those (or the one) in whom they discover God at work. Thus the Thessalonians "love" Paul (3:6), but now Paul is exhorting them to love one another as they already do (4:9–10) and also to "esteem . . . very highly in love" those who labor among them and are over them in the Lord (5:12–13). The inevitable question is: could it be that, according to Paul's system of convictions, the Thessalonians are in the same relation among themselves as they are with Paul? In other words, could it be that, through faith, they also discover God at work in their sisters and brothers? Could it be that love is this attitude that one has toward persons in whom one discovers God? Our study of the rest of Paul's letters will confirm that this is the case, despite the puzzling fact that Paul also appears to ask the Thessalonians to love nonbelievers (3:12; 5:15).

A last tentative remark about love, love as imitation of those who preceded the believers in the faith. Through hope and faith the believers are "imitators" of those who preceded them (the prophets, Jesus, the churches in Judea, Paul) and "types" of those who will follow them (the Macedonian believers, the believers at the end of time), because what *happens* to them is the same thing which *happened* or *will happen* to those who preceded them or will follow them. Yet through love the believers are "imitators" of those who preceded them and whose example they follow. As they did, the believers implement their faith in their daily life. They receive the word (1 Thess. 1:6), they turn to God from idols, they serve God (1:9), and they love one another and all people (3:12).

The convictional pattern of Paul's faith includes the same elements as the convictional pattern of the Pharisees' faith, although the patterns themselves are quite different. We have shown in Chapter 3 that in the Pharisees' faith there are two dimensions: (1) The election and the vocation is established once and for all in the biblical (past) sacred history. To be the Chosen People, the Pharisees only need to appropriate this past election by "entering into Scripture." (2) The way to walk (the *halakah*) involves carrying out this vocation in any new cultural situations by following the example of the biblical personages viewed as models and by fulfilling the commandments which need constantly to be reinterpreted so that they might be coextensive with life.

For Paul, the election and the vocation are discovered, through faith and hope, in the believers' experience. The revelatory acts of God, which are calls (elections), are to be found in the experience of the believers either in the recent past or in the present. Thus Paul writes, "He who *calls* you is faithful" (1 Thess. 5:24), not "He who *called* you in the time of the Exodus or of Jesus' death and resurrection." God acts (performs revelatory acts) in the present as he did in the past. These acts are calls, elections, and also vocations. Through faith and hope (which allow them to view events of their experience as God's acts, as elections), the believers discover that they are called to be God's Chosen People. This also involves a vocation, the vocation to serve God (as the Lord Jesus and as Paul the apostle did and do). In all this, Jesus, Paul, and others who preceded the believers are types whose experiences help them to discover their election and vocation.

Once this election and vocation are established, the believers must carry out their vocation. Because their vocation is not exactly the same as the vocations of those who preceded them, their way of carrying it out involves new dimensions. But those who preceded them—Jesus and Paul in this letter—are examples, models, that they can and should follow, as the Pharisees followed the examples of Abraham, Moses, and other biblical personages.

We now need to verify whether the overall convictional pattern we have discovered in 1 Thessalonians is found in the other letters of Paul. Especially puzzling is the fact that Jesus' experience, namely, his cross, appears to be not as central in Paul's Gospel as is usually thought. That Jesus actually has two "experiences"—a past experience including the cross and the resurrection, and a future one, his Parousia experience— certainly sets him apart from any other believer. But in 1 Thessalonians it is clear that his death is not a vicarious death for our sins and that Jesus, in his ministry, death, and resurrection, is not the complete and final revelation. Is this true also in Paul's other letters? Furthermore, if this convictional pattern characterized by the type/imitator relationships is shown to be valid, we need to understand more precisely the nature of these happenings in the believers' experience which Paul sees as revelatory acts of God through which they are chosen by God. In other words, we need to understand what is, according to Paul's system of convictions, the believers' experience, for it is quite different from our Western conception of "religious experience." It is not a private experience; it necessarily includes other people. Thus the phrase "in Christ" should not be understood as referring to a private mystical experience. Rather, it appears that because they can discover in their experience these new interventions of God which are fulfillments of the type "Christ," the Thessalonians can be said to be "in Christ."

### SUGGESTIONS FOR FURTHER READINGS

Our Study of 1 Thessalonians needs to be complemented both by other structural readings, similar to those presented in Chapter 2, and by studies aimed at elucidating dimensions of its meaning other than Paul's system of convictions. In the former case, the reader is invited to read this letter taking note of the oppositions found in the parts of the text which involve repetitions, strange reasonings, and metaphoric language. In the latter case, the reader is invited to consult the following studies and also to compare and contrast their interpretations of the letter with ours.

Few commentaries on 1 Thessalonians have appeared in English. However, these remain classic works for the study of the correspondence: E. Best, *A Commentary on the First and Second Epistles to the Thessalonians*; E. J. Bicknell, *First and Second Epistles to the Thessalonians*; J. E. Frame, *A Critical and Exegetical Commentary on the Epistles of St. Paul to the Thessalonians*; L. Morris, *The Epistles of St. Paul to the Thessalonians*; W. Neil, *The Epistles of Paul to the Thessalonians*.

For a more general overview of the Thessalonian correspondence, see F. W. Beare, "First Letter to the Thessalonians," in *IDB*, vol. 4, pp. 621–25; J. T. Forstell, "The Letters to the Thessalonians," in *JBC*, pp. 227–33; J. C. Hurd, "First Letter to the Thessalonians," in *IDBS*, p. 900.

# 5

---

# Philemon and Philippians:
# Consider Others as Better
# Than Yourselves

OUR READING OF 1 Thessalonians has shown that Paul views the believers as being chosen through the intervention of God in their experience, in which they discover the revelatory activity of God (in other people, such as Paul). In past situations—in Jesus' death and resurrection, in the Judean churches' experience, in Paul's past experience—there were also revelatory acts of God, but these do not establish the believers in the right relationship with God. God's intervention in the believers' experience does that. These past acts of God are "typical" of God's interventions in human affairs, and thus Jesus, but also the Judean churches and Paul, are "types" of manifestations of God that the believers can expect to discover in their experience. In order to discover these manifestations of God, the believers need to have "faith." Such a faith could be viewed as having three dimensions:

1. The believers need to have "faith in Jesus Christ," that is, they need to trust in the proclamation of the Gospel which affirms that God acted in Jesus.

2. They need to have "faith" that these past acts of God in Jesus are promises that God will act in their own experience. These first two dimensions of faith can be called "receiving the word."

3. They need to have that "faith" which discovers Christ-like events in their present experience.

All this suggests that, according to 1 Thessalonians, the past revelation in Jesus Christ is not the complete and final revelation but points beyond itself to new revelations which occur in the believers' experience. Through these latter revelations, discovered through faith, the believers are established in the right relationship with God. These revelations to the believers also point beyond themselves to further revelations in the future and ultimately to God's intervention at the end of history through the Second Coming, the Parousia, of Christ.

Such are the main features of the convictional pattern which, according to 1 Thessalonians, characterizes Paul's faith. If our reading of this letter is correct, and if Paul did not "convert" a second time during his ministry (and nothing suggests that he did), the same convictional pattern should be found in all of Paul's letters. This does not mean that in all his letters Paul expresses the same theological ideas or that he uses the same symbols or vocabulary. Rather, it means that no matter what ideas and symbols he uses, and no matter what the situation with which he deals, Paul interrelates the past, present, and future elements of human experience in the same way. Thus our task in this chapter on Philemon and Philippians, and in the following chapter on representative passages of Galatians, 1 Corinthians, and Romans, will be to verify that the convictional pattern we have discovered in a preliminary way in 1 Thessalonians undergirds the other letters as well.

Since we were surprised by the secondary place that this pattern assigns to Jesus Christ in Paul's faith, we chose to pursue this investigation by reading two letters which are as different as possible in their ways of dealing with Christ. In Philemon, Christ is merely mentioned. By contrast, in Philippians the famous hymn about Christ (Phil. 2:6–11) plays an important role in the argument. Through the reading of these two letters, we shall determine whether our understanding of Christ's place and role in Paul's convictional pattern is correct. If it is, the reading of these letters will help us better understand this pattern and how it functions.

Another aspect of the convictional pattern which needs to be further clarified concerns God's intervention in the believers' experience. In 1 Thessalonians, God's manifestations are closely associated with the believers' conversion. This gives the impression that, for Paul, God's interventions are primarily related to conversion. Yet we have to be cautious. This emphasis could result merely from the fact that Paul addresses recent converts. Indeed, we have already noted that other aspects of the believers' experience, such as their joy in much affliction, were described as Christ-like (as manifestations of God's intervention). We can hope that our reading of letters addressed to believers who are well established in the Christian faith will help us apprehend more clearly in what part of the believers' experience Paul perceives manifestations of God, that is, Christ-like events.

In this chapter, we shall perform the same kind of readings as those we performed in 1 Thessalonians. A historical reading will allow us to understand how these texts are related to specific situations insofar as they can be determined. Then an examination of the organization of the arguments will allow us to study the convictional pattern manifested in these letters.

## MODERN READERS AND PHILEMON AND PHILIPPIANS

The major difficulty we must overcome as modern readers of these letters is our deeply rooted pre-understanding that Jesus Christ is the complete and final revelation. This pre-understanding takes many forms. For instance, when Jesus Christ is viewed as the complete and final revelation, Paul's references to God's manifestations in the present of the believers are implicitly or explicitly taken as a reaffirmation for the individual believers of past revelations. Thus Paul's affirmation that the Thessalonians have been chosen by God is understood as meaning that they have become partakers in the (new) covenant established in Jesus Christ, as the Pharisees were partakers in the covenant established "in Moses." Other manifestations of God in the believers' experience are understood as God carrying out his part of the covenant by sustaining the (new) Chosen People. From the perspective of the Pharisees, God was also present in their experience, sustaining them, protecting them, intervening in their favor, vindicating them because of the eternal covenant which established them as his Chosen People. Consequently, according to this pre-understanding, Paul's descriptions of God's manifestations in the present of the believers are accounted for, but in such a way that they cannot be viewed as new revelations.

The pre-understanding of Jesus Christ as the complete and final revelation also brings about a specific interpretation of the believers' ethical life. It is thus understood that good Christians are people following in their life the teaching (commandments) of Jesus. The fact that Paul almost never mentions Jesus' ethical teaching should be a warning that this interpretation is problematic, but in order to avoid this objection, modern readers point out that another way to be good Christians (according to Paul's letters read with this pre-understanding) is to follow the example of Jesus, as the phrase "imitating the Lord" is then interpreted. The fact that Paul does not describe Jesus' ministry should be another warning of the weakness of this interpretation, but modern readers feel justified in continuing to interpret Paul according to this pre-under-standing, by pointing to such phrases as "in Christ." This is understood as "making one's life like that of Christ" or "making one's life conform to that of Christ" (as Phil. 3:10b is often interpreted, even though Paul's Greek text clearly says "*being* conformed" to Christ). Another form of this pre-understanding results in an interpretation of "in Christ" as "being in a mystical union with Christ" or "in communion with Christ" and in this way sharing the benefits of his death.[1] All these interpretations exclude from the outset the possibility that Paul might be speaking of acts of God which are Christ-like and thus that he might be speaking of new revelations for the believers.

Since our purpose is to determine whether or not the convictional pattern we found in 1 Thessalonians is truly characteristic of Paul's faith, we do not want to say at this point that these are misinterpretations. Our pre-understandings are not necessarily wrong. Nevertheless, we should recognize this pre-understanding for what it is. As long as we retain it as a pre-understanding, we are led to interpret everything Paul says as referring to Christ as the complete and final revelation, whether or not this was Paul's conviction. Through our reading, which requires patient study of how Paul interrelates various aspects of the believers' experience with past and future situations, we can hope to overcome this pre-understanding and to perceive what place and role Jesus Christ has in Paul's system of convictions.

## PHILEMON: FIRST READING—
## HISTORICAL CONTEXT

This brief letter is addressed by Paul (and Timothy) to Philemon (and to Apphia, to Archippus, and to the church in Philemon's house). It concerns Philemon's slave, Onesimus.[2] Paul is in prison (Philem. 1, 9–10, 13, 22–23). Where? Scholars have proposed either an imprisonment in Rome (cf. Acts 28) or in Caesarea (cf. Acts 23–24) or in Ephesus (on the basis of Paul's comments about fighting wild beasts at Ephesus in 1 Cor. 15:30–32 and about facing death in Asia in 2 Cor. 1:8–10). Since

Onesimus and Archippus are mentioned in the letter to the Colossians, it has been argued that Philemon lived in Colossae. Since Paul talks about his hopes of visiting Philemon in the near future (Philem. 22), we can surmise that Paul was being held prisoner in a nearby city. According to this reconstruction,[3] Paul would thus have written this letter from Ephesus in the early 50s rather than from Rome or Caesarea. The other viable alternative is to say that he was in Rome. In this case the letter would be written between 60 and 64.

In prison Paul meets a runaway slave, Onesimus, and converts him (Philem. 10–11). Paul sends him back to his master (v. 12) with this letter, following Roman law, which demanded that a fugitive slave be returned to his master. The latter could punish the slave as he saw fit; he could even kill him. Through this letter Paul urges Philemon to receive Onesimus as a "beloved brother" (v. 16), to receive his slave as he would receive Paul himself (v. 17). He also asks Philemon to charge to his own account whatever wrong Onesimus might have done to his master (v. 18). Beyond this, Paul does not specify what Philemon should do (he does not ask him to free his slave), although he suggests that Philemon send Onesimus back to Paul so that he might serve Paul (vv. 13–14). The concluding greetings mention Epaphras as Paul's fellow prisoner, and Mark, Aristarchus, Demas, and Luke as Paul's fellow workers (who are also mentioned in Col. 4:10–17).

This letter is comparable to one written by Pliny the Younger to Sabanianus about his runaway slave. A comparison of the two arguments shows interesting differences. Pliny first describes the slave's repentance and then urges his reader to exercise the Stoic virtues of clemency and self-control to overcome his legitimate anger. In contrast, Paul first expresses his thanksgiving for Philemon's love and faith, then urges him to welcome Onesimus "for love's sake" (v. 9).[4]

## PHILEMON: SECOND READING—
## THE ORGANIZATION OF THE ARGUMENT

As in the case of 1 Thessalonians, we can distinguish two levels in this brief letter: a dialogic level and a warranting level. A study of the dialogic level will allow us to elucidate the "dialogic space" and the goal of this letter which the warranting level needs to establish as real and valid so that the argument might be convincing for Philemon.

On the dialogic level, Paul intercedes for the slave Onesimus with the hope that Philemon will receive him as a beloved brother. This is a very personal plea addressed to a single person (the pronoun "you" in the singular, i.e., "Thou," is used through most of the letter). It is worth noting that the dialogic space of the letter is defined in other ways. In the introductory salutation the addresser is not Paul alone but Paul "the prisoner for Christ Jesus" and Timothy "the brother." Similarly, the concluding greetings (vv. 23–24) are sent by Epaphras, "my fellow prisoner in Christ Jesus," Mark, Aristarchus, Demas, and Luke, "my fellow workers." Thus the addresser is Paul in relationship, on the one hand, with Christ Jesus and, on the other hand, with people who are his co-workers and/or his fellow prisoners. So the addresser is Paul in relationship with people who have the same status as he does. They are in the same relationship with Christ Jesus as he is. Similarly, Philemon is not the only addressee. The letter is addressed to Philemon, "our beloved fellow worker"; Apphia, "the sister"; Archippus, "our fellow soldier"; and the church in Philemon's house. The blessings in verses 3 and 23 further establish the relationship of all these people with God the Father and the Lord Jesus Christ.

It is not by chance that Paul establishes such an elaborate relational network as the dialogical space of this personal letter. Even though in its main body Paul uses *singular* first- and second-person forms, the "I" (Paul) and the "Thou" (Philemon) remain defined by the entire relational network. The "I" and the "Thou" are in a brotherly relationship with each other and with other Christians. Thus, as soon as this relational framework is established and as soon as it has been shown that Onesimus has entered it, the problem of the runaway slave will be resolved. Philemon will not be able to treat him differently from the way he treats any other sisters or brethren. Indeed, he should treat Onesimus as he would treat Paul (v. 17), and Onesimus would then be free to join Paul (vv. 13–14).

One part of the warranting level expresses that Onesimus has converted. He is Paul's child: "my child, Onesimus, whose father I have become in my imprisonment" (v. 10). And thus, for Paul as well as for Philemon, he is now "a beloved brother . . . both in the flesh and in the Lord" (v. 16). If it can be established that the relational network is true, real, and good, the argument will be convincing for the reader. Paul uses the rest of the warranting level of the discourse to do this.

As usual Paul introduces such warrants for his argument in the form of a thanksgiving which mentions "Your love and . . . the faith which you have toward the Lord Jesus and all the saints" (v. 5); the "sharing of your faith" (v. 6); and that "I have derived much joy and comfort from your love, my brother, because the hearts of the saints have been refreshed through you" (v. 7). Another brief statement—"to say nothing of your owing me even your own self" (v. 19b)—is an allusion to Philemon's conversion by Paul and also belongs to the warranting level. In Paul's view, the validity and truth of this network of relationship is demonstrated for Philemon by his own experience characterized by love, by faith in Christ, and by the fact that he shares this faith with others.

As in 1 Thessalonians, the experience of the believers (here, Philemon) guarantees the validity of the exhortations. On the warranting level there is no direct mention of the kerygma (the message about Jesus' ministry, death, and resurrection), although it would have been easy to argue that Philemon should love Onesimus, as Christ loved us by giving his life on the cross for us. This would presuppose that for Paul (and Philemon) the fundamental convictions—one's true identity—are established in Jesus' experience. But Paul does not do so.

Similarly, Paul, using his authority as an apostle, could have commanded Philemon to act in a certain way toward Onesimus. Then the warranting level would have had to establish the validity of his authority. In such a case, what happened in Paul's experience would be the basis for Philemon's faith, and Paul would have given himself as an example. This is approximately how Luther interpreted the letter.

> This epistle gives us a masterful and tender illustration of Christian love. For here we see how St. Paul takes the part of poor Onesimus and, to the best of his ability, advocates his cause with his master. He acts exactly as if he were himself Onesimus, who had done wrong. Yet he does this not with force or compulsion, as lay within his rights; but he empties himself of his rights in order to compel Philemon also to waive his rights. What Christ has done for us with God the Father, that St. Paul does also for Onesimus with Philemon. For Christ emptied himself of his rights (Phil. 2:7) and overcame the Father with love and humility, so that the Father had to put away his wrath and rights, and receive us into favor for the sake of Christ, who so earnestly advocates our cause and so heartily takes our part. For we are all his Onesimus's if we believe.[5]

Actually this interpretation presupposes that for Paul the complete and final revelation is found in Jesus' incarnation and death and that Paul followed the example of Christ (doing the same good deeds) and thus proposed himself as an example for Philemon. But Paul does not put himself forward as an example, nor does he suggest that his experience (or Christ's) is the basis for Philemon's faith. He does write, "Even though I have full authority in Christ to command you to do what is required, I prefer to appeal to you for love's sake" (vv. 8–9, au. trans.). But this is just the point. He does not consider his authority as an apostle (and his experience) to be the basis for Philemon's Christian life. This is not simple modesty, but an expression of his conviction that Philemon's faith finds its foundation in his own experience.

What establishes Philemon's identity as a Christian—that is, the pattern of his faith which can be applied to ever-new situations, including that of a runaway slave—is therefore his own experience. Such is the conclusion we can reach in light of our reading of 1 Thessalonians.

An alternate interpretation could be that Paul merely emphasizes what Philemon is already doing—having faith, loving—and points out to him that it is in the logic of his behavior, of his good works, to adopt a loving attitude toward Onesimus. Yet this interpretation cannot be valid. If it were the case, Paul would begin this part of the argument by saying something like, "I *praise you* for your love and your faith." He does come close to saying this in verse 7, where he writes, "I have derived much joy and comfort from your love," but he introduces all this by a thanksgiving addressed to God: "I thank my God always . . . because I hear of your love and of the faith . . ." (vv. 4–5). This formula is so familiar that we often fail to notice it. Yet if we pay attention to it, we have to conclude that, if Paul can thank God, it is because, in his view, Philemon's love and faith are not merely his own doing but the results of God's intervention in Philemon's life. In 1 Thessalonians, Paul makes it explicit that the believers' "work of faith and labor of love" are indeed the results of God's intervention in their experience. We can further note that in Gal. 5:2 Paul speaks of love as a fruit of the Spirit (i.e., as the result of the intervention of the Spirit), and in 1 Cor. 12:9, he lists faith among the gifts of the Spirit. Thus, even though Paul is quite elliptic in this brief letter, we can conclude that he focuses Philemon's attention on his own experience because it is there that his fundamental convictions are established or, in other words, that God's revelation is manifested for him.

It is clear that this faith and this love are related to the Lord Jesus (vv.

5, 6, 16, 20) and also to Paul as an "apostle of Christ" (even though he does not use this term, the phrase "prisoner of Christ" [vv. 1, 9] has a similar connotation). While Paul does not make explicit the nature of these relations, nothing suggests that the type/imitator pattern we found in 1 Thessalonians would not be applicable here. Phrases such as faith "toward the Lord Jesus" and the allusions to the various acts of love performed "for Christ" can certainly be interpreted according to the relational network we found in 1 Thessalonians. Furthermore, Paul's relationship with the believers is described with the help of metaphors similar to those we found in 1 Thessalonians: it is a brother-to-brothers-and-sisters relationship (vv. 1, 2, 7, 16, 20), a father-to-child relationship (v. 10), an apostle (with authority)-to-converts relationship (vv. 8, 19), a nursing-mother-to-child relationship (although this metaphor is not used, this relationship is expressed in v. 12: "I am sending him back to you, *sending my very heart*"), as well as a co-worker (or partner) relationship (vv. 1, 2, 17, 23). Thus, if the type/imitator pattern is found in all the other letters (as we will show it to be), then we will be able to conclude that it is indeed presupposed here. In fact, Paul does not need to mention all the stages of this pattern. For a believer such as Philemon, it is enough to emphasize the stage upon which his faith is based. The brief references to the Lord Jesus Christ and to Paul's ministry and authority are enough to evoke for the reader/believer the rest of the pattern.

In order to resolve the problem of the runaway slave, it is therefore enough for Paul to remind Philemon of the relational network established in his own experience (by the intervention of God) and to show that Onesimus has entered this relational network since he has been converted. As soon as Onesimus is perceived in this light, he can no longer be viewed as a slave, as an inferior. He is Philemon's beloved brother. At the very least, Philemon has to consider him as having equal status with him, even as Paul considers Philemon his *fellow* worker, Archippus his *fellow* soldier (vv. 1–2), Epaphras his *fellow* prisoner in Christ Jesus, and Mark, Aristarchus, Demas, and Luke his *fellow* workers. This is not a call to consider and treat his slave Onesimus kindly, as though with a "paternalistic love." Rather, it causes Philemon to see Onesimus as an equal and no longer as a slave. In fact, Philemon should not count Onesimus merely as an equal but rather as someone "better than himself" (cf. Phil. 2:3), that is, as he views Paul (to whom he owes his own life [Philem. v. 19]). For Paul, it is in this context that the problem of slavery is resolved. The framework, the pattern of relations of the social and economic situation in which and through which slavery exists, is replaced by another pattern of relations. There is no point in saying anything against slavery itself. It is this overall pattern of relations which needs to be changed "through faith," that is, through the intervention of God which establishes a new pattern of relations that faith discovers and accepts. Our reading of Romans and 1 and 2 Corinthians will help us understand this more clearly (see Chapters 7 and 8).

Our reading of Philemon confirms the possibility that, according to Paul's faith, the fundamental convictions are those concerning the believers' experience, even though they are necessarily related to the kerygma and to Paul's experience. Yet the crucial test for the proposal we made on the basis of 1 Thessalonians will be our study of a letter which deals at length with the kerygma. The question we need to raise throughout our reading of Philippians is: What place and role does Jesus have in Paul's argument? At first glance the kerygma about Jesus is closely related to an ethical teaching (exhortations to the Philippians in chap. 2). But how is it related to this teaching? What kind of ethical teaching do we find in Paul's letters, and how is it linked to the convictional pattern which characterizes his faith? An examination of the organization of the letter's argument will allow us to address such questions. But we must first ascertain the nature of our text and its relation to concrete situations in Paul's ministry and in the church.

## PHILIPPIANS: FIRST READING—
## HISTORICAL CONTEXT

A first reading of Philippians aimed at understanding the development of its argument raises a number of problems. We can follow the development of the discourse without difficulty until Phil. 3:1. After the salutation and a thanksgiving for the Philippians (1:1–11), in which it is mentioned that Paul is a prisoner, Paul proceeds to discuss his present situation, that is, his imprisonment, and how it serves "to advance the gospel" (1:12–13). As a consequence, "the brethren . . . are much more bold to speak the word of God without fear," even though their motives are not always pure. Some proclaim the Gospel out of partisanship "to afflict me" and others "out of love" (1:14–18). He then reflects on his condition and on the possibility that he might die, but he hopes to survive for their sake (1:19–26). This leads him to exhort the Philippians to "stand firm in one spirit" and thus to overcome their divisions by having "this mind among yourselves, which you have in Christ Jesus" (2:5; cf. 1:27—2:18). Then Paul speaks about travel plans (sending Timothy to them and perhaps going to Philippi himself [2:19–24]) and discusses the health of Epaphroditus, his fellow worker from Philippi (2:25–30). Such comments about travel plans and news are usually found in the concluding parts of Paul's letters (see Philemon, 1 Corinthians, Romans). And in 3:1 we read, "Finally, my brethren, rejoice in the Lord." Then we find the sentence "To write the same things to you is not irksome to me, and is safe for you" (3:1b), which suggests that Paul wants to make an additional comment about a subject he has already discussed. But it is followed by exhortations which are anything but "rejoicing." "Look out for the dogs, look out for the evil-workers . . ." (3:2). One could understand Paul interrupting himself in the midst of his concluding comments and coming back to an issue he has already discussed (writing about "the same things"), but the content of chapter 3 is not related to the issues dealt with in the preceding chapters. He now deals with issues comparable to those we found in Galatians, that is, (probably) with the demands of the Judaizers (people "who mutilate the flesh" 3:2) that the Christians be circumcised or (possibly) with the teaching of Jewish missionaries. But such issues cannot be found in the rest of the letter.

This break has a character different from that of the breaks we found in Galatians, where despite interruption of the argumentative logic, a continuity in themes could be found. So, with many scholars, we have to conclude that this text is a composite. This is not the only case in which an epistle is made up of several Pauline texts. Both 2 Corinthians and Romans (Romans 16 does not seem to belong to that letter) are also composite letters. By this I mean that the text we have is made up of a letter from Paul into which passages of other letters from Paul have been introduced. We can conjecture that the composite came about when Paul's letters were circulated to churches other than the ones to which they were originally addressed. It was essential to preserve Paul's teaching rather than his letters in the exact form in which they had been first received.

When this is recognized, it appears that, as Francis Beare proposes,

Phil. 3:2—4:1 is certainly the central part of another letter of Paul.[6] To whom was this letter addressed? In this passage there is no indication of its destination, but because it is incorporated into a letter addressed to the Philippians, it is possible that it was addressed to this same church.

In Phil. 4:2 we find an exhortation to two women, Euodia and Syntyche, "to agree in the Lord." This can be understood as directly following 3:1, since it does repeat the exhortation to unity found in chapter 2 and applies it to a specific case. In 4:10–20 we find another interpolation. This passage is part of a letter of thanks to the Philippians for the gifts they sent to him through the intermediary Epaphroditus. This passage could not have been written at the same time as the rest of the letter, for in 2:25–30 it is said that Epaphroditus was seriously ill while he was with Paul and that the Philippians knew it and were concerned about it. This shows that the Philippians and Paul were in regular contact with each other during the period between Epaphroditus's arrival with the gifts and the writing of the main letter, so it is unlikely that Paul would have waited so long to express his thanks for the Philippians' gifts. But if 4:10–20 is viewed as part of a separate letter to the Philippians sent earlier, the difficulty disappears.[7]

Therefore we need to examine separately three parts of this epistle: Letter A = 3:2—4:1; Letter B = 4:10–20; and Letter C = 1:1—3:1; 4:2–9, 21–23.

Letter A (Phil. 3:2—4:1) was written against the same kind of opponents as was Galatians. It is clearly from Paul, as can be seen in the vocabulary and content, but it is not clear to whom it was addressed. If it was addressed to the Philippians, it reflects a significant change in the relationship between Paul and the Philippians, compared with the situation presupposed in the first part of the epistle. If one supposes that at first Paul only heard vague reports about opponents in Philippi, it can be argued that this segment was written after the main letter (Letter C). The mention of tensions in the Philippian church (1:28; 2:2–3) is then taken to allude to these opponents. Thus Paul sends the main letter with relatively general exhortations. After having received more detailed information about the situation in that church and about certain opponents there, he sends a harsh letter of warning concerning them. But it can also be argued that Letter A was written first and that as a consequence the Philippians rejected these opponents and their teaching. Letters B and C indicate a harmonious relationship between the Philippians and

Paul and make only slight allusions to the opponents (1:28), by whom the believers should not be frightened. Paul is satisfied with the Philippians' overall attitude. They have stood firm even though threatened with persecution by these opponents. Now he simply exhorts them to continue to stand firm and to make his joy complete (2:2) by overcoming the division among them. Thus, according to this hypothesis, Letters B and C were written after Letter A. Yet such reconstructions are always very tentative, and we do not even know for sure that Letter A was addressed to the Philippians. Therefore we shall deal separately with each letter.

Letter B (4:10–20) thanks the Philippians for their gifts. Through the intermediary Epaphroditus, they sent these to Paul when he was in prison, as they also did when he was in Thessalonica. So this letter was certainly written by Paul from prison to the Philippians.

Letter C (1:1—3:1; 4:2–9, 21–23), the main letter, was written by Paul to the Philippians a few months after Letter B. Paul was still in prison, although, as in the case of Philemon, we do not know where.

Once again Rome, Caesarea, and Ephesus are proposed by various scholars as possible locations. It seems that Caesarea can be excluded, but strong arguments can be made for Paul's imprisonment both in Rome and in Ephesus. Against the Roman hypothesis and in favor of the Ephesian hypothesis is the constant contact of the Philippians with Paul. The epistle presupposes at least four trips between Philippi and Paul's location: a message with the word that Paul is in prison, Epaphroditus's trip when bringing gifts to Paul, a message to the Philippians about Epaphroditus's illness, and a message from the Philippians expressing their concern about Epaphroditus's health. It has been calculated that a round trip between Philippi and Rome (by foot and boat) would take about five months (even longer between Philippi and Caesarea). This makes it difficult to explain the regular contact between Paul and the Philippians. By contrast, if Paul was at Ephesus, it would take only twenty days to make a round trip. Furthermore, Paul says that as soon as he is released from prison (if he is indeed released) he plans to visit the Philippians (Phil. 1:26). If he was in Rome, would he want to come back to Philippi? This would be surprising, in view of the travel plans mentioned in Rom. 15:24, 28, where Paul says that he wants to go from Rome to Spain.

In favor of the Roman hypothesis, the main arguments are that Paul mentions "the whole praetorium," "the whole praetorian guard" (Phil. 1:13), and "Caesar's household" (4:22), which seem to refer to a situation in Rome. Yet detachments of the praetorian guard were also found in major cities throughout the Roman Empire. Caesar's household can also refer to the imperial civil servants anywhere in the empire. And if "praetorium" is to be interpreted as a building, this term could have designated the residence of the proconsuls in Ephesus (as it designated Herod's residence). Another argument in favor of Paul's imprisonment in Rome is based on the descriptions of the conditions of Paul's imprisonment in this letter and in Acts 28:30–31 (about Paul's imprisonment in Rome), which fit together remarkably well. In both cases Paul is able to pursue his ministry and to receive visitors, and thus his imprisonment "served to advance the gospel" (1:12). But we do not know anything about Paul's imprisonment in Ephesus. Those who support the Ephesian hypothesis argue that the conditions of imprisonment could have been similar, but those who favor the Roman hypothesis argue that it is not certain that Paul was in prison at Ephesus for any length of time, while a long imprisonment at Rome is well documented.

We shall leave the question open, even though the hypothesis that Paul was a prisoner in Ephesus when he wrote Letters B and C appears to be more probable. In that case, these letters should be dated in the mid-50s (rather than in the early 60s, according to the Roman hypothesis).

### PHILIPPIANS: SECOND READING (A)—
### THE ORGANIZATION OF THE ARGUMENT OF
### A LETTER FRAGMENT (3:2—4:1)

As we noted, Phil. 3:2—4:1 is a fragment of a letter, and this makes its study more difficult. We have neither its introduction nor its complete conclusion, which would have disclosed its dialogic space, that is, the addressees and how they are related to the addresser (Paul, but certainly also his companions or a church).

This passage and Galatians 5 and 6 are comparable in terms of their contents and of their organization. The first part, Phil. 3:2–16, argues that the (Gentile) Christians should reject the teaching of people who urge them to be circumcised. This is also the content of Gal. 5:1–12. In Phil. 3:2–16 it is argued that the believers should have the same disposition Paul has (3:15); they should perceive "that to which they attribute a high value" as a loss, in the same way as Paul sees his former system of convictions, Judaism, as a loss. This is similar to the affirmation in Gal. 5:1–12 that the believers are free from the Law. But if the Jewish Law or other traditions (e.g., Hellenistic customs) are no longer absolute, then what will serve as guidelines for the believers' behavior? When one perceives oneself as free from Judaism and from other traditions, the danger is to fall prey to the extreme of immoral behavior. Since one is free, nothing is forbidden. Thus in Galatians, Paul exhorts his readers to walk according to the Spirit, to bear the fruit of the Spirit, and to fulfill the "law of Christ" (Gal. 5:13—6:10). Similarly, in this passage Paul exhorts his readers to a sanctified life by urging them to "imitate" him and those who live like him (Phil. 3:17—4:1). This broad comparison of the arguments in Galatians 5 and 6 and in Phil. 3:2—4:1 shows the unity of our text. For Paul, the proclamation of the freedom brought about by the Gospel (which includes freedom from the Law) needs to be balanced by a statement concerning the limits of this freedom (the freedom from the Law is not a license for immoral behavior).

We can thus proceed to identify the two levels of the argument: the dialogic level, which is made up of exhortations (as in 1 Thessalonians), and the warranting level, which manifests the most fundamental convictions. Through a first reading we need to identify these two levels before studying more closely the warranting level and its convictional pattern.

### The Type/Imitator Pattern of
### the Dialogic Level

The dialogic level includes only a few verses, the identification of which will help us understand the purpose of this fragmentary letter.

> Look out for the dogs, look out for the evil-workers, look out for those who mutilate the flesh. (Phil. 3:2)

This threefold exhortation is actually a series of puns. The term translated "those who mutilate the flesh" means literally "the incision" (*katatomē*). It is an ironic pun on "circumcision" (*peritomē*).[8] The Christians are the "true circumcision," as is expressed in the next verse. These people are merely the "incision" of the body. Similarly, "dogs" was a term used by the Jews to mock the impure Gentiles. But Paul uses this scornful term against the partisans of the circumcision, Christian Judaizers (or, less likely, Jewish missionaries). The third phrase, "evil-workers," is certainly also an ironic designation of those who advocate the importance of "good works" (the works of the Law). Understood in this way, the third warning makes it clear that Paul directs these exhortations against Judaizers who identify themselves with the Jews and advocate righteousness through works of Torah and circumcision. These Judaizers must be rejected by Paul's readers.

The warranting level of the argument establishes why these Judaizers are wrong and shows the reality of the danger they represent. Paul does this first by describing in Phil. 3:3 the believers' situation and status at any time (and not merely at the time of the dialogue), then by describing his own experience (3:4–14).

In the conclusion of this section, Paul can then express a new set of exhortations which belongs to the dialogic level.

> Let those of us who are mature [or perfect] be thus minded; and if in anything you are otherwise minded, God will reveal that also to you. Only let us hold true to what we have attained. (Phil. 3:15–16)

Despite the difficult wording of these exhortations, their general meaning is clear. Paul exhorts his readers to pursue a Christian life similar to his (3:15) and to continue what they have begun, a valid Christian life, rather than changing course and pursuing a different kind of life.

The dialogic level is prolonged by new exhortations: "Brethren, join in imitating me, and mark those who so live as you have an example in us" (Phil. 3:17). Then, still on the dialogic level, Paul reports to them, as he did earlier, that "many . . . live as enemies of the cross of Christ" (3:18). These people should not be imitated (or followed).

The warranting level establishes why these people should not be followed (their end is destruction [3:19]) and why Paul and other believers should be imitated (they will be saved [3:20–21]).

The concluding verse (4:1), which includes an exhortation to stand firm in the Lord, also belongs to the dialogic level. Thus the dialogic level of this passage is formed by six verses: Phil. 3:2, 15, 16, 17, 18, and 4:1. Positively, it is an exhortation to imitate Paul—more precisely, to imitate Paul and other believers, since once again Paul associates himself with others. So he writes, "mark those who so live" (3:17) or, better, "watch carefully [in order to see in them an "example" or a "type"] those who walk like this." Negatively, it means not imitating (or following the example of), on the one hand, the "dogs," the Judaizers, and on the other hand, "the enemies of the cross," the libertine believers who have an immoral life.

In order to express this relation between himself and his readers, Paul uses the vocabulary we have already found in 1 Thessalonians. In Phil. 3:17 Paul exhorts his readers to be "imitators" of him and of other believers who are the "types" (usually translated by the term "example"). A closer examination of the text shows that this "type/imitator" relation is the same as the one in 1 Thessalonians. Types and imitators are interrelated both because the same things happened (or happen) to them and because they do the same things (the imitators follow the model found in the types). This will be clearer when we study the warranting level, but the verses of the dialogic level already express it. In 3:15 Paul exhorts his readers to join him in adopting the attitude he has just described in the preceding verses (which belong to the warranting level). This verse could be translated "let all of us . . . have this disposition." This could be taken as a mere command *to do* as he does (to adopt the disposition that he has), but the rest of the verse makes it clear that it is not the believers' doing: "If in anything you have another disposition, this too God will reveal to you" (3:15b, au. trans.). Having the same disposition as Paul, being his imitator, is not so much doing something as having something happen to you. This is given to you by a revelation from God. The believers' (the imitators') role is to "hold true to what we have attained" (3:16), that is, to what they have received, to what happened in their lives, to what has been revealed to them. This is what "stand firm thus in the Lord" (4:1) also means.

Note also that Paul calls his readers "my crown" (4:1), suggesting the same kind of relationship we found in 1 Thess. 2:19. The believers are, in Paul's experience, a preliminary manifestation of the "crown" that he hopes to receive at the Parousia.

## Paul as Type for the Believers:
## The Warranting Level

The warranting level, Phil. 3:3–14 and 19–21, is not broken up into various segments by phrases of the dialogic level, as was the case in 1 Thessalonians. Its insertion in the dialogue of the letter is marked only (a) at the beginning, when Paul uses the first-person plural which includes his readers, "we are the true circumcision . . ." (3:3); (b) in verse

13 (toward the end of the first section of the warranting level), which mentions Paul's addressees: "Brethren"; and (c) at the end of the second section of the warranting level, when Paul again uses the first-person plural (3:20–21).

In fact, the warranting level deals only with Paul's personal experience (Phil. 3:4–14) and with Paul's and his readers' common experience. Because we do not have the introduction and conclusion (and possibly other parts) of this letter, we cannot evaluate why Paul emphasizes his own experience rather than that of his addressees. As we saw above, however, it is clear that he sees the relationship between his own experience and his addressees' as a type/imitator relationship. Since this warranting level is the basis for a twofold exhortation—that is, of positive exhortations to be imitators of Paul and other believers as types, and of negative exhortations not to follow the "dogs" and the "enemies of the cross"—we find in these warranting passages both a positive description of Paul's and the believers' experiences, and negative descriptions of wrong experiences (or attitudes). This feature of the text will allow us to understand more clearly what characterizes the experience of the believers (including Paul).

Paul proposes himself as a true "type" that his readers should "imitate," because unlike the "dogs" he puts "no confidence in the flesh" (Phil. 3:3). But what is "having confidence in the flesh" or "believing in the flesh" (as this phrase could also be translated)? Paul explains it by describing his own situation prior to his conversion. For him, it was being a Pharisee, a zealous Pharisee with the best qualifications. Thus it appears that "having confidence in the flesh" and more generally "being in the flesh" is for Paul having a false system of convictions (i.e., in light of our discussion of Galatians, an idolatrous system of convictions).

> Circumcised on the eighth day, of the people of Israel, of the tribe of Benjamin, a Hebrew born of Hebrews; as to the law a Pharisee, as to zeal a persecutor of the church, as to righteousness under the law blameless. (Phil. 3:5–6)

Paul's "good deeds" as a blameless Pharisee, who was in the right relationship with God through Torah, demonstrate that he was an "evilworker." Indeed, his "good deeds" included persecuting the church. Therefore he counts all this as a loss.

Here Paul uses the image of an accountant's balance sheet showing assets and liabilities. His Pharisaism, which he originally recorded in the asset column, he now records in the liability column. The "knowledge of Christ Jesus my Lord" takes its place in the asset column (3:7–8a). But what does the term "knowledge" (*gnosis*) mean? This word is usually interpreted by taking into account either its use in Hellenistic religions (in which case it should be understood as a *revealed* knowledge of the mystery of salvation) or its use in Judaism and in the Old Testament (in which case the "knowledge of Christ" should be understood as having a meaning similar to the "knowledge of God" in the Old Testament, that is, as a knowledge which is the response of faith to revelation).[9] According to our approach, however, we need to understand this term by considering how it is related to other elements of the text.

We again find the term "knowledge" (in a verbal form) in Phil. 3:10, which can be translated as follows: "that I may *know* him and the power of his resurrection and the fellowship of his sufferings, being conformed to his death." Thus knowing Christ is "knowing" the power of his resurrection and "knowing" the fellowship of his sufferings. It is clear that knowing the power of his resurrection actually means experiencing this power and recognizing that it is at work in one's experience. The same is true about knowing Christ's sufferings. It is experiencing the same sufferings, sharing in such sufferings. This is "being conformed to his death." The believer's experience has the "same form" as Jesus' death. Thus, knowing Christ is finding in one's experience both resurrection-like events (manifestations of the power of the resurrection) and Christ-like sufferings (i.e., situations which are like Christ's death). What kind of experience is in the "form of Christ's death"? What is "being conformed to his death"? The flow of the argument suggests that this phrase is related to the preceding statements about Paul's conversion. Perceiving his Pharisaic life as a loss is, for Paul, having a life conformed to Christ's death. This is confirmed by such passages as Gal. 2:19–20, where Paul expresses that dying to Torah is being crucified with Christ. This, in itself, is already "being conformed to his death," although in other texts Paul also says that his sufferings (due to persecution) and his weakness are "conformed" to Christ's sufferings. We shall see how this latter view is related to the former; for Paul they are two aspects of the same experience. But here we can conclude only that "being conformed to Christ's death" is "counting as a loss" his Pharisaic life. Paul's conversion from Pharisaic Judaism is not his doing; it is something which happened to him. "Counting as a loss" is merely recording on the balance sheet what happened to him, recording that *Christ Jesus has made me* his own" (3:12). Thus putting "no confidence in the flesh" (3:3b) is counting all that one believed in, one's former system of convictions (in Paul's case, his Pharisaic Judaism), as a loss, and sharing in Christ's sufferings or being conformed to his death.

Yet simultaneously the believers (and Paul) "experience the power of the resurrection." They are the (true) circumcision, the true Chosen People; they have the Spirit and thus can worship by the Spirit of God; they can be proud (and legitimately so) in Christ (Phil. 3:3a). But all this is not an end in itself. It is only a step toward the goal, toward the prize. Here Paul uses the metaphor of a race in the stadium (Phil. 3:12–14). The race is under way. The runner has progressed well but has not yet reached the goal and must therefore press on to reach it. Mixing the metaphors (as he often does), Paul also says he is not yet perfect. But these metaphors can easily be misinterpreted to mean that he, the runner, is responsible for the eventual success. Therefore he emphasizes that "Christ Jesus has made me his own" (3:12b).

These metaphors make it clear that, for Paul, his present gains—the Christ-like events in his present experience—are not an end in themselves, but promises, prefigurations, or preliminary manifestations of what he will receive at the Parousia, the prize. He summarizes the nature of this prize by the phrase "the resurrection from the dead" (Phil. 3:11). Through the resurrection, at the Parousia, the believers will not merely be people who experience the power of the resurrection and are conformed to his death (3:10) as they already are. Their bodies will also "be conformed" to Jesus' body of glory (3:21). At the Parousia the type, Jesus' death and resurrection, and the promises contained in the Christ-like events of their experience, will be totally fulfilled.

But they have not yet reached the goal. They are in the race. They should not look behind (to evaluate how much they gained). They should press on toward the goal, that is, look ahead, have hope, "await a Savior, the Lord Jesus Christ" who will come from heaven (Phil. 3:20). Here again we find the view that Jesus is the savior at the end of time, at the Parousia (and not in the past, i.e., not at the time of his death and resurrection).

This does not mean that the believers should neglect the present.

They must "hold true to what [they] have attained" (Phil. 3:16), which is not contradictory to looking forward to the Parousia. Holding on to what they have attained is also holding on to the promises contained in their experience. By holding to what they have attained, they look toward their heavenly homeland (3:20); they live in hope for the glory they will receive. The Judaizers (the "dogs") cannot share in this hope, because they put their confidence in the flesh instead of being conformed to Christ's sufferings. Similarly, those "who make out of the belly their god," those who boast of conduct that should be viewed as shameful,[10] those who have their "minds set on earthly things" (3:19) are "enemies of the cross." Despite their claim to have faith in Christ, their lives are not "conformed" to the cross. Thus their end will be not a glorious Christ-like body but destruction (3:19a).

It is therefore clear that the type/imitator convictional pattern we have found in 1 Thessalonians also provides the framework for this fragment of a letter. The vocabulary, the concepts, and the ideas are quite different. However, the convictional pattern is expressed, once again, through the type/imitator vocabulary (Phil. 3:17) and also by means of a new vocabulary: the phrase "conformed to," that is, "being given the same form as" (3:10 and 3:21). The use of such technical terms as "knowledge" and "perfection," as well as of metaphors such as the gain/loss balance sheet and the stadium race, suggests that Paul addresses readers who are quite different from those in Thessalonica. The specific situation (involving the heretical teaching of Judaizers and immoral believers) which he addresses has contributed to shaping the way he writes to his readers. Yet the convictional pattern remains the same.

## PHILIPPIANS: SECOND READING (B)—THE ORGANIZATION OF THE ARGUMENT OF THE MAIN LETTER

The main letter to the Philippians (1:1—3:1; 4:2–9, 21–23) is complete. Thus its introduction and conclusion express the dialogic space of the letter. The warranting level will establish the reality of this network of relations.

We can be very brief on this point, because the dialogic space of this letter is essentially the same as the one we found in 1 Thessalonians and Philemon. We need only note the differences. The relation between Paul (and Timothy) and Christ is specified. They are "servants" or, literally, "slaves" of Christ Jesus (Phil. 1:1a). As we shall see, this terminology is related to the description of Christ Jesus as taking the form of a "servant" or "slave" (2:7). The addressees are the "saints in Christ Jesus who are at Philippi, with the bishops and deacons" (1:1b). The terms "bishops" and "deacons" do not refer to institutionalized offices in the church (as suggested by the fact that the term "bishop" is in the plural form). Here these terms describe functions in the church and use a vocabulary common in Hellenistic society. They are "overseers" and "servants" of the community, but we do not know anything specific about their functions. Paul calls the Philippians "saints in Christ Jesus" (cf. also 4:21–22). Why does he do so? What kind of relationship with Christ does this phrase presuppose? The rest of the letter will provide answers to these questions, as well as explain Paul's relation to Christ and God and the interrelation between Paul and the Philippians.

## An Exhortation to Rejoice: The Dialogic Level

The dialogic level of this letter involves: the introduction (Phil. 1:1–2); the expression of his thankfulness (1:3–5a, 6a, 7a); his prayer for the Philippians (which is also a veiled exhortation, 1:9–11); a few phrases which directly address the readers and are interspersed in the presentation of his situation (1:12a, 18, 19a, 25a, 26a); a series of exhortations (1:27–28a; 2:2–5; 2:12–16a, 17b, 18); the description of the travel plans of Paul, Timothy, and Epaphroditus (2:19, 22a, 23–25, 28–29); a concluding set of exhortations (3:1; 4:2–5a; 4:6–9); and the conclusion (4:21–23).[11] The rest of the text belongs to the warranting level, which establishes the reality and validity of this thanksgiving, these exhortations, and these plans.

Upon looking more closely at the passages of the dialogic level, we can place all the textual elements into two categories. The thanksgiving (as expression of joy) and the many exhortations to rejoice, as well as the plans for travel (which are made either "so that I may be cheered by news of you" [Phil. 2:19] or "that you may rejoice" [2:28]) can be put in one category; the exhortations to unity and humility (1:27–28a; 2:2–5; 2:12–16a; 4:2–3) can be put in a second category. Yet these exhortations are themselves related to Paul's joy, and he summarizes them in 2:2 by the exhortation "complete my joy." This shows that the main goal of the dialogic level is to insure that both Paul and the Philippians will be joyful.[12] The Philippians are encouraged to make Paul's joy complete. On the other hand, Paul aims at convincing the Philippians that he is joyful and that they should also be joyful.

The letter has such a goal because of the situation which, at first glance, is quite grim. Paul is in prison and could be killed. In the church of the city (Ephesus or Rome) where he is is prison there is a faction which opposes Paul and attempts to afflict him (Phil. 1:15–17). The Philippians themselves suffer (persecution?) from opponents (1:28–30). Epaphroditus, one of the Philippians, was seriously ill (2:25–27). And finally there are tensions in the church at Philippi which tarnish the joy that Paul could have because of the Philippians' devotion to him. Their spontaneous response may have been that of anxiety and fear. Thus Paul exhorts them by saying, "Have no anxiety about anything" (4:6). He also writes, "so that . . . I may hear of you that you . . . [are] not frightened in anything" (1:27–28). And Paul says about himself that he hopes to "be cheered by news of you" (2:19) and be "less anxious" (2:28).

In this bleak situation, Paul's exhortation to rejoice can be received as valid by his readers only if he can convince them that one can actually be joyful in the midst of these events. This is what the warranting level of his discourse does. From the perspective of Paul's system of convictions the warranting level proposes a view of the situation which shows reasons for true joy. Yes, they should heed his exhortations to rejoice. Yet at the same time, in the perspective of this system of convictions, the community life of the Philippian church appears to be wanting. There are attitudes which contradict this system of convictions, and therefore Paul's joy cannot be complete (Phil. 2:2); indeed, the Philippians themselves cannot truly share in this joy, as long as they do not correct what is wrong in their community life (2:12–18).

We can expect from our reading of 1 Thessalonians, Philemon, and Philippians 3:2—4:1 that this bleak situation can be viewed joyfully for two reasons: First, because it is perceived as a fulfillment of promises contained in Jesus' experience, because there are Christ-like events in it, and because Paul and the Philippians are "imitators" of Christ.[13] Second, because it is viewed as involving promises, prefigurations, and preliminary manifestations of what will happen at the Parousia, and because as such Paul and the Philippians are types for future believers, including the believers at the Parousia.

But Paul does not use the type/imitator terminology here. So we need to see whether or not this convictional pattern undergirds this text, and if so, in what specific ways it is expressed. For this purpose we need to examine how Paul interrelates his own experience with that of the Philippians and that of Jesus. We shall focus on Phil. 1:1—2:18, which contains the main part of the warranting level.

## A New Vocabulary for the Type/Imitator Pattern: The Warranting Level

### PAUL'S EXPERIENCE

Let us first read, in the order of the text, the passages of the warranting level which describe Paul's experience as related to other people and God: Phil. 1:7b, 12b–17, 19b, 30.

"For you are all partakers with me of grace, both in my imprisonment and in the defense and confirmation [vindication] of the gospel" (Phil. 1:7b). Paul and the Philippians have the same status; they are "partakers" of the same grace.[14] But what is this "grace" that Paul in his imprisonment and ministry can share with the Philippians? The term "grace," which can also be translated "gift" (from God), is an important concept in Paul's letters. Therefore we need to consider it as an "unknown" term (as in an algebra problem). On the basis of this verse we can note that "grace" is closely related to Paul's imprisonment (his bonds) and to the "defense" and "vindication" of the Gospel. Here Paul uses the technical vocabulary for legal defense in a court of law. This terminology is appropriate for the defense and vindication of a prisoner, and by using these terms he links his imprisonment with the defense of the Gospel. In 1:16, speaking of his imprisonment, Paul says, "I am put here for the defense of the gospel." Thus grace is somehow manifested in his imprisonment for the Gospel, which is also a defense of the Gospel. We can therefore expect that Paul's description of his imprisonment will explain the nature of the grace mentioned here. Yet we also need to understand the sense in which the Philippians can be said to share this grace with Paul. Paul's description of the Philippians' experience will explain it, but if the convictional pattern we found elsewhere also undergirds this letter, then this grace, this "gift from God," should be, on the one hand, the manifestation of God in Paul's imprisonment and, on the other hand, the same "type" of manifestation in the Philippians' experience.

In Phil. 1:12–14 Paul points out that his imprisonment "served to advance the gospel" (1:12), since it is recognized by the whole praetorian guard and by other people as an imprisonment for Christ. Furthermore, most of the brethren are made bolder in their proclamation of the word. This is already a reason for rejoicing. But why are most of the brethren "gaining confidence" through Paul's imprisonment (1:14)? Should they not despair or be afraid? Could it be that they do not despair because they are "partakers of grace" with Paul in his imprisonment (whatever this phrase may mean)?

Yet some of these brethren "preach Christ from envy and rivalry" (Phil. 1:15), "thinking to afflict" Paul in his imprisonment (1:17); that is, these people preach the Gospel to show that they are better missionaries than Paul. But Paul can rejoice in this situation, because the outcome of this competition is that Christ is proclaimed. We will come back to this passage in order to explain more completely why Paul rejoices, but we can note here that Paul's attitude implies that for him the essential thing is not how he is treated, that is, whether he is in prison and whether these brethren agree with him and recognize his authority. The essential thing is that his vocation, the proclamation of the Gospel, be carried out. His imprisonment contributes to this proclamation. It does not matter if it is because his imprisonment is recognized as a defense of the Gospel or if it is viewed as an occasion to belittle his influence in the church. In both cases the Gospel is proclaimed. And thus his imprisonment allows Paul to carry out his vocation. He can rejoice.

In Phil. 1:19–25 Paul further evaluates his own situation. He is confident that "this will turn out for [his] salvation" (1:19, au. trans.; a phrase he borrows from Job 13:16). The term "salvation" must be understood as referring to his ultimate salvation and not to his deliverance from prison, as is clear from the following verses where he envisions the possibility of his death. He associates this hope for salvation at the Day of the Lord with his hope to "glorify Christ" in his body "whether by life or by death" (1:20, au. trans.). Not being saved is "being ashamed" or in other words, it is not glorifying Christ with "the courage which has its source in freedom" (as the term translated by "courage" in the RSV [1:20] can be rendered). According to the convictional pattern we found elsewhere, "glorifying Christ in his body" would mean manifesting ("making clearly manifest," as the verb could also be translated) Christ in one's life by having in it Christ-like manifestations. Paul's life is Christ-like (1:21, "to live is Christ"). Yet his death would also be Christ-like, and furthermore would be a "gain"; it would mean moving forward toward the Parousia and being with Christ (1:23). Both outcomes are good, and thus he does not know which one to choose (1:22b). He would prefer to die, but he sees that remaining alive is more necessary (1:24), that is, more "fruitful" (1:22a), "so that in me you may have ample cause to glory in Christ Jesus, because of my coming to you again" (1:26).

This latter verse could mean that the Philippians will be joyful because Paul has been delivered from prison. But Paul is saying more. In him the Philippians will have cause "for boasting" (for glorying) legitimately, in contrast to the false boasting of sinners. The only legitimate cause for boasting is an action of the Lord (God or Christ). Now, if they will have in Paul a legitimate "cause for boasting in Christ Jesus," it is because in Paul they will be able to see "Christ," that is, the fulfillment of the type "Christ." (The validity of this interpretation is confirmed by the term Paul uses to describe his coming, "parousia." This is the very term he uses in 1 Thessalonians to speak of the coming of the Lord.) Paul's coming among them is like the coming of Christ among them, because he is the fulfillment of the type "Christ." We may say that his deliverance (from prison) as a result of God's intervention would be prefiguration of the deliverance that Christ will effect at his Parousia.

Finally, in Phil. 1:29–30 Paul identifies the suffering of the Philippians with his own suffering. He points out that "it has been granted to you that . . . [you should] suffer for [Christ's] sake" (1:29). The words "it has been granted to you" translate a verb derived from the noun "grace." It could be translated "you have received the grace." So this grace the Philippians share with Paul (1:7) is "suffering" as well as faith (1:29). If suffering is indeed grace, a gift from God, it is not only because it is "for the sake of Christ" but also because it makes out of them "manifestations of Christ" (fulfillments of the type Christ), as Paul also is.

### THE PHILIPPIANS' EXPERIENCE

These last remarks have already led us into a discussion of the Philippians' experience as described by Paul in Phil. 1:6, 28b–30a, and 2:1. Their experience involves God's intervention. "He [God] who began a good work in you will bring it to completion at the day of Jesus Christ" (1:6). As we just saw, this work of God in the Philippians' experience involves the gift (grace) of faith and the gift of suffering for Christ's sake.

In addition, Paul says that in their experience there are "signs" of their salvation, "signs" given by God (1:28; the RSV translates the term "sign" by "omen"), which are also signs of perdition for their opponents. It is clear that the term "sign" should be understood as equivalent to the term "type" that we found in 1 Thessalonians and in Philippians 3. Indeed, these "signs" are interventions of God in certain parts of the believers' experience which point toward (and/or are preliminary manifestations of) what will take place at the Parousia: the believers' salvation and their opponents' destruction. As we shall see (Chapter 7), the fact that these are both signs of perdition and signs of salvation is a characteristic of any type. For instance, the type "Jesus crucified" is a sign of perdition, a stumbling block to Jews and folly to Gentiles, and at the same time a sign of salvation for the believers (1 Cor. 1:18–25). Exactly what are these signs of the believers' salvation and their opponents' destruction? The preceding sentence provides the answer. "[Standing] firm in one spirit, with one mind striving side by side for the faith of the gospel, and not [being] frightened in anything by your opponents" (1:27–28). Since their unity and striving for the faith, as well as their joy (not being frightened), are "signs" (types) of what will come about at the Parousia, these are also, according to the convictional pattern, fulfillments of the type "Christ." This is expressed in 2:1–2, which introduces the exhortations:

> So if there is any consolation in Christ, any encouragement of love, any participation in the Spirit, any affection and sympathy, complete my joy. . . . (Phil. 2:1–2, au. trans.)

Paul often uses "if" to express a real situation (rather than a supposition). So the beginning of the verse could be rendered, "Since it is true that there is consolation in Christ. . . ." But what is this actual experience to which Paul refers? Clearly it is related to what precedes (Paul introduces this passage by "so" or "therefore"). This verse is related to the Philippians' experience of the grace of God (their suffering and faith), which is also Paul's experience. We can even say that this verse specifies what this experience is: an experience "in Christ," that is, an experience in which there are Christ-like manifestations, in other words, an experience which is perceived in terms of the promises contained in the type "Christ" and in which one discovers fulfillments of these promises.[15] In their experience "in Christ," the Philippians find (or should

find) "signs" of salvation which are consolations,[16] since these fulfillments
of the promises contained in the type "Christ" are also signs (promises)
of what they can expect in the future and at the Parousia. Their experience also involves "encouragement of love," that is, manifestations of
love which encourage them. These are manifestations of the love which
exists between Paul and the Philippians,[17] as well as manifestations of
God's and Christ's love for them (God's intervention in the life of the
believers is also the manifestation of his love; cf. 1 Thess. 1:4). These
manifestations of love are also promises of what the believers can expect
in the future and thus are an "encouragement" for them. Their experience in Christ also involves "participation in the Spirit." They "enjoy a
share of the Spirit"[18] through which God is at work among them, fulfilling
his promise, and they also are in communion with each other in the
fellowship created by the Spirit. The last phrase, "any affection and
sympathy [or, better, mercies]" in Christ, should be interpreted in the
same way as manifestations of Christ's affection and mercies in their
experience. These manifestations involve Paul's relationship with them,
as is expressed in Phil. 1:8, "I yearn for you all with the affection of
Christ Jesus." But these manifestations of Christ's affection are also the
attitudes that they should have toward each other. In brief, the Philippians' experience is an experience in which they discover through faith
fulfillments of the promises in Christ. These fulfillments are themselves
signs (promises) concerning the future and thus encouragements. Therefore the Philippians' experience is one of the bases upon which Paul can
exhort them. The other basis is Christ's story, which Paul presents in
2:6–11.

### THE KERYGMA ABOUT JESUS CHRIST

Because of the poetic form of Phil. 2:6–11, we can say that it is a
hymn which Paul quotes. Whether this hymn was written by Paul or by
a member of a church founded by Paul is irrelevant for our purpose.
What interests us is how Paul understood it, as expressed by the way in
which he integrates it in his argument. Much has been written on this
famous passage, but we will simply emphasize a few features which play
a role in the overall convictional pattern of the letter.[19]

Christ Jesus was "in the form of God" (Phil. 2:6a). This is neither
being God nor being equal with God (2:6b). The phrase "in the form
of God" does not say anything about the nature of Christ. It merely

expresses a certain relation to God. Christ is in the same relation to God as the believers are in relation to Christ, as is expressed in 3:10 and 21, where it is said that the believers are or will be conformed to Christ's suffering and resurrection. Christ's condition is God-like (in the form of God), as the believers are Christ-like (conformed to Christ) because of what happens in their experience.

The relation between Christ and God is also expressed by the verb "look" or "consider" (Phil. 2:6). Christ looks at God. He considers God's condition, but not as a condition he should appropriate (or, literally, "plunder"). As we shall see, Paul uses the same verb "look" or "consider" to express the relation the Philippians should have among themselves (2:3). They should consider "others as better than themselves" as Christ considers God "better than himself."

Christ "emptied himself, taking the form of a slave, being made in the likeness of men and being found in the shape of a man" (Phil. 2:7–8a, au. trans.). Taking the form of a slave, the likeness of human beings (the shape of a man) expresses that he now has a human-like condition rather than a God-like condition. Here again these phrases do not say anything about the nature of Christ (whether he was fully human or not). They express a relation between Christ and humans. Yet this implies that the human condition is to be a "slave," that is, "obedient" (2:8). Slave to whom? Obedient to whom? This is not made explicit. Of course it means "slave" or "servant" of God, even as Paul and Timothy are "slaves of Christ Jesus" (1:1), and thus obedient to God, just as the Philippians are urged to be obedient to Paul and to God (2:12). But when humans are not "slaves of Christ," they are slaves of other powers (e.g., slaves of Torah or of the elemental spirits [Gal. 4:3, 9]). When Christ was "obedient unto death, even death on a cross," was he a slave of God or of evil powers (the "rulers of this age" who "have crucified the Lord of Glory," as Paul writes in 1 Cor. 2:8)? These verses by themselves do not allow us to answer this question. However, according to Paul's system of convictions, Christ by obedience to God made himself obedient and a slave to other powers (see Chapter 7).

In so doing, Christ "humbled himself." As a consequence "God has highly exalted him" (Phil. 2:9a). He made himself a "slave," and as a consequence God "bestowed on him the name which is above every name" (2:9b), the name "Lord." He made himself "obedient," and as a consequence God gave him authority over those "in heaven and on earth

and under the earth." This includes authority over the "heavenly powers" or "elemental spirits." The reversal of situation involved in these
verses suggests that he was a slave of and obedient to the heavenly
powers (elemental spirits), the earthly powers (humans), and the subter-
ranean powers (other evil powers) but that now he is given authority
over all of them.[20]

How does Paul use this hymn as a basis for his exhortations? This
"story" of Christ is directly related to, and indeed introduced by, an
exhortation: "Have this mind among yourselves, which you have in Christ
Jesus" (Phil. 2:5). Note that Paul does *not* say, "Have the same attitude
Christ had" (as this verse was sometimes interpreted). It is possible to
interpret this exhortation to mean "Have among yourselves the attitude
which you have as believers who are in Christ."[21] But the sentence is
constructed in such a way as to make clear that "among yourselves"
(literally "*in* yourselves") and "*in* Christ Jesus" are parallel phrases.
This suggests the meaning "Have the same attitude toward each other as
the attitude you have toward Christ" or "Have this disposition vis-à-vis
each other that you have vis-à-vis Christ." Understood in this way, this
verse summarizes well the exhortations found in the preceding verses.
"In humility consider others better than yourselves" (2:3b, au. trans.).
The believers consider Christ as better than themselves even as Christ
also considers God better than himself. Thus the believers should consider others as better than themselves (2:3).

Similarly, the next verse reads, in a literal translation, "Let each of
you look not only to his own things but also to the things of others"
(Phil. 2:4). What are the "things" to which Paul alludes? In the context
of these exhortations to overcome strife and divisions in the community
caused by partisanship and by vain ambition (rather than selfishness and
conceit, as suggested by the RSV [2:3]), "things" cannot mean "possessions" or "interests." Rather, Paul exhorts the Philippians to "look attentively" for the "qualities of the others." As the believers look attentively
for the "qualities" of Christ, that is, for the manifestations of God in
Christ's experience, they should look attentively for the qualities and
manifestations of God in others. This is humility and, indeed, the very
condition of true love and of harmonious community life (2:2). It is
not a humility which seeks to have the same moral disposition as Christ
had when he "emptied himself." Paul does *not* take into account this
aspect of the hymn in these exhortations. Rather, for him, humility is

looking attentively at the others as one looks at Christ, that is, looking at the others so as to discover in them Christ-like manifestations, their God-given gifts (graces), what God is doing in their lives. This is why the believers should look at others as better than themselves. In these others, God is at work. And thus it is not a matter of acting as if others are better than themselves (a moral attitude). Others are truly better than them, since they are manifestations of God or of Christ. Through the others, the believers have access to a manifestation of God, to a revelation. We could say, in light of 1 Thessalonians, that humility is looking at the others so as to see them as "types" (as Christ is a type) in the same way that the believers in Macedonia and Achaia saw the Thessalonians as types. Or again, as Paul expresses it in 3:17, the believers should "watch carefully those who so live, as you have a type in us" (Paul and other believers).

In having such attitudes they obey (Phil. 2:12), they are "slaves" (or "servants") as Paul also calls himself (1:1). They follow the example (the model) of Christ and "work out [their] own salvation" (2:12). They follow Paul's teaching and example: "What you have learned and received and heard and seen in me, do" (4:9). By obeying, they are "in the form of slaves," and thus they can also expect to be exalted (cf. also 1:6, 10–11; 2:16). But this obedience is "in fear and trembling" because they are in the presence of God. While it can be said that they "work out [their] own salvation," it should also be said that this is God's work in them or, better, among them: "For God is at work in you, both to will and to work for his good pleasure" (2:13).

In the same way that he urges the Philippians to discover God at work in others, so Paul sees God at work in them. In their experience Christ-like events are to be found. They are not perfect; they are not yet "blameless and innocent, children of God without blemish" (Phil. 2:15). Paul had to rebuke them. Yet God is at work among them; he has "[begun] a good work" in them (1:6). And thus they are already "set apart for God," that is, they are "saints," "holy people" (1:1; 4:21). This is why Paul can rejoice, why they themselves can rejoice. They can also rejoice because, as they can now see, God is at work in Paul's experience, even in his imprisonment, even if he should die, even if this letter is also his "farewell" speech (as may be suggested by Paul's allusion in these verses to Moses' farewell speech [Deut. 31:24—32:5]). Indeed, they can rejoice as long as they "[hold] fast the word of life" (2:16). This word of life is the

Gospel, which allows the believers to discover that God's promises in
Christ are fulfilled in their own experience. Once again we can perceive
what the broad term "experience" entails. Their experience involves
other people. In fact, it is primarily in other people that they discover
these fulfillments which are themselves additional promises (signs) of
their salvation at the day of Christ. These last remarks have many implications for our understanding of Paul's system of convictions (see
Chapter 7, on Romans).

## The Believers' Vocation

The main letter to the Philippians clearly manifests the convictional
pattern we have found in 1 Thessalonians and in Phil. 3:2—4:1. In the
believers' (Paul's and the Philippians') experience, the "grace" (of God) is
manifested in Christ-like events. These manifestations of God in their
experience are also a source of encouragement, since they are promises
of interventions of God in the future and especially "in the day of Christ"
(2:16). These are "signs" of their salvation, but for their opponents they
are "signs" of their destruction. Thus once more the vocabulary used by
Paul has changed, but the convictional pattern remains the same.

As we shall see when studying central passages from Galatians, Romans, and 1 Corinthians, the entire type/imitator pattern is not manifested in this letter to the Philippians. Only three stages are clearly
manifested: Jesus as type fulfilled in Paul, who consequently is himself a
type for the believers, who in turn fulfill both the type "Jesus" and the
type "Paul." The day of Christ, the Parousia, the (ultimate) salvation as
fulfillment of all the preceding types (or promises) is also expressed in
this letter, although more discreetly than in 1 Thessalonians. But the
Old Testament prophets (mentioned in 1 Thess. 2:15) and, more generally, all the scriptural types which are fulfilled in Jesus' as well as in the
believers' experience and which are underscored in other letters, are
not made explicit. Yet they are present. For instance, Paul, without
referring explicitly to these texts, actually quotes Job 13:16 in Phil. 1:19
and uses Deut. 31:24—32:5 (Moses' farewell speech) as a model for his
exhortations in Phil. 2:12–18 (and possibly elsewhere in the letter). As
Moses, at the time when he faced the prospect of death in Moab,
exhorted the people whom he had led out of bondage, so Paul, facing
the possibility of death, exhorts the Philippians, whom he "has led out of
bondage" (a vocabulary we found in Galatians). Paul sees himself as the

fulfillment of the type "Moses," despite quite different situations (therefore when in 2:15 he uses the vocabulary of Deut. 32:5, he has to do so with significant changes).[22] In view of Paul's use of Scripture elsewhere, these allusions are not accidental. But for well-established believers such as the Philippians, he does not need to rehearse the whole system of convictions; emphasizing a part of it is sufficient: the relations among Christ, himself, and the Philippians.

Because his readers are well established in the faith we have an opportunity to observe how Paul's convictional pattern is applied beyond the experience of conversion. Indeed, Christ-like manifestations are to be found in their individual and/or collective experience of conversion. In their personal lives and through faith, they have discovered and can still discover God at work. But through faith they should also look carefully at the other members of the community. Through faith, that is, with the confidence that in these sisters and brothers God is also at work, the believers can then discover in them Christ-like dimensions. They are Christ among them, because in them God is acting as he acted in Christ. Thus they are better than themselves.

Are these acts of God in other people's lives revelations of the believers' election? This is possible. But at least in the texts we found in this epistle, these appear to be more definitely revelations of "the way to walk" (the verb used in Phil. 3:17 [au. trans.]: "Watch carefully those who *walk* in this way," often translated "live"), revelations of the way to carry out one's vocation and at the same time revelations of one's vocation in specific situations. Instead of following a law (or commandments) and finding how it should be applied in ever-new cultural situations so as to fulfill a vocation established once and for all (as the Pharisees did), the Christians should constantly be on the lookout for what God is doing around them. Having identified people in whom God is at work, they should then consider them as better than themselves and follow them. This is their vocation and thus the way they should walk. In so doing they follow God in his work, they join God in his action. In turn, God joins in their action "both to will and to work for his good pleasure" (2:13).

Through faith which sees Christ-like events in others, the believers walk in humility and obedience. The results of such an attitude is love and harmonious community life. In such a context, love, even if it is "labor of love," is not a "good work." It is a byproduct of faith. Indeed, faith, by seeing in others Christ-like dimensions, establishes a new kind of relationship between the believers and others: love. This is true even in the case of "love for one's enemies," as Phil. 1:15–18 suggests.

Let us review the situation. There are brethren who "preach Christ from envy and rivalry" (Phil. 1:15), "out of partisanship, not sincerely but thinking to afflict me in my imprisonment" (1:17). But then, we can venture to say, that Paul, following his own exhortations to his readers, "watched them carefully" (3:17). He had toward them the same disposition he has toward Christ (2:5). He considered their things [gifts from God] (2:4). He looked at them as better than himself (2:3). And thus, through faith, he discovered that despite everything God was at work in them. Christ was proclaimed. So he can rejoice because of them. We can say that as a byproduct of this attitude of faith, he truly loves these enemies. Clearly this is not what happens each time. In other cases, through faith he sees in his opponents only signs of their destruction (1:28) even if he must talk about it "with tears" (3:18–19).

We now begin to perceive how love and faith are interrelated. We also understand more clearly how one is in the right relationship with God: not by focusing attention on one's personal relationship with God, but rather by focusing attention upon something else, namely, (a) upon what God has done in the past and especially in Jesus Christ (this is faith as trust); (b) upon what God is doing in one's present experience, that is, what God is doing in other people who are a part of one's experience (this is faith as discovering the fulfillment of God's promises, with love as its byproduct); as well as (c) upon what God will do in the future, in the day of Christ, the Parousia (this is hope grounded on the promises which God's manifestations in the present also are). Faith, love, hope, "but the greatest of these is love" says Paul in 1 Cor. 13:13. That is, the greatest is this love which is a byproduct of the faith through which one discovers in others Christ-like dimensions. Paul concludes his letter by urging his readers to "think about"—or, better, to "take into account," "to give weight in their decisions to" (i.e., "to consider," "to look at carefully")— what is "good" in others. This "good" which can be discovered in others he describes by using Hellenistic ethical categories, including "virtue," which was for the Stoics the highest good. As in Galatians, the Philippians can use their Hellenistic categories to designate and understand what is good, that is, to identify what God is doing among them in Christ-like manifestations.

Finally, brethren, whatever is true, whatever is honorable, whatever is right, whatever is pure, whatever is lovely, whatever is esteemed, if there is any thing which pertains to virtue, if there is anything which is praiseworthy—take these into account. (4:8, au. trans.)


## SUGGESTIONS FOR FURTHER READINGS

As in the case of 1 Thessalonians, our study of Philemon and Philippians needs to be complemented both by additional structural readings of these letters (as proposed in the "Suggestions for Further Readings" for Chapter 4) and by the reading of other studies of these texts to be compared and contrasted with our interpretation.

English commentaries on Philemon: J. Knox, *Philemon Among the Letters of Paul*; E. Lohse, *Colossians and Philemon*; M. R. Vincent, *A Critical and Exegetical Commentary on the Epistles to the Philippians and to Philemon*.

Reference articles on Philemon: J. Fitzmyer, "The Letter to Philemon," in *JBC*, pp. 332–33; M. E. Lyman, "Letter to Philemon," in *IDB*, vol. 3, pp. 782–84.

English commentaries on Philippians: F. W. Beare, *A Commentary on the Epistle to the Philippians*; J. F. Collange, *The Epistle of St. Paul to the Philippians*; J. B. Lightfoot, *St. Paul's Epistle to the Philippians*; R. Martin, *Philippians*; J. H. Michael, *Epistle of Paul to the Philippians*; J. J. Müller, *The Epistles of Paul to the Philippians and to Philemon*; M. R. Vincent, *A Critical and Exegetical Commentary on the Epistles to the Philippians and to Philemon*.

Reference articles on Philippians: G. S. Duncan, "Letter to the Philippians," in *IDB*, vol. 3, pp. 787–91; J. Fitzmyer, "The Letter to the Philippians," in *JBC*, pp. 247–53; H. Koester, "Letter to the Philippians," in *IDBS*, pp. 665–66.

For works dealing with a theological perspective of salvation history in Paul or with christological hymns, see J. Munck, *Paul and the Salvation of Mankind*; J. T. Sanders, *The New Testament Christological Hymns*.

# 6

# The Cross, the Resurrection, and Scripture

OUR READING OF 1 Thessalonians, Philemon, and Philippians has enabled us to elucidate several facets of Paul's system of convictions and important features of the convictional pattern which characterizes his faith. The specific kind of reading we used demanded that we follow the unfolding of the argument on several levels. As a result the various dimensions of Paul's system of convictions have been presented as a series of more or less discontinuous remarks. In order to present a clearer and more complete picture of the characteristics of Paul's faith, we need to interrupt this kind of reading. Instead of merely summarizing and recapitulating what we have found through our reading of Galatians, 1 Thessalonians, Philemon, and Philippians, however, we shall read various passages from Paul's letters, in the context of a discussion of the way in which central elements of Paul's system of convictions are expressed in theological formulations. This will allow us to understand more clearly certain fundamental characteristics of Paul's system of convictions, which should not be confused with his theological formulations of these convictions. Then we will be ready to consider the place and role of Scripture, as well as that of the cross and resurrection, in his faith. For this purpose we shall read three central texts—Galatians 3, Romans 4, and 1 Corinthians 15—in order to present more systematically the partial results and tentative conclusions we have reached so far.

As we compare the results of our reading of 1 Thessalonians, Philemon, and Philippians with the great epistles (Galatians, 1 and 2 Corinthians, and Romans), we must deal with a question raised several times in the preceding chapters, the question of the place of Christ (and especially of his death) in Paul's system of convictions.

## THE CROSS AS RECONCILIATION: CHRIST AS THE CENTER OF PAUL'S THEOLOGY

### The Cross: Salvation or Promise of Salvation?

The most puzzling result of our investigation of Paul's letters to the Thessalonians, Philemon, and the Philippians has been the secondary place apparently given to Jesus Christ in Paul's system of convictions. We find no mention in these letters that Christ "died for our sins," and he is consistently described as "savior" in the future (at the Parousia) and the present but *not* in the past ("he saves us or will save us" but not "he has saved us"). These observations seem to contradict certain passages in Galatians, 1 and 2 Corinthians, and Romans. For instance, in Gal. 1:3–4 we read, "Our Lord Jesus Christ, who gave himself for our sins to deliver us from the present evil age." There is no doubt that such a statement involves the view that Jesus' death (in the past) is salvific. Similarly, in 1 Cor. 15:3 Paul quotes and appropriates for himself a tradition which involves the statement "Christ died for our sins." Likewise in Romans, Paul emphasizes the salvific role of Jesus' death. For instance, in Rom. 5:6, 8 we read: "While we were still weak, at the right time Christ died for the ungodly. . . . While we were yet sinners Christ died for us."

The difference in attitude toward Jesus' death cannot be explained by a change of system of convictions and of convictional pattern or by a change in theological formulations (even though Paul's theological way of thinking underwent significant transformations during his ministry). In the major epistles both attitudes toward Jesus' death are found. This means that Paul simultaneously held both views of Jesus' death. On the one hand, he viewed the cross as a salvific event in the past (Jesus died for our sins) which is the necessary precondition for the believers' faith. On the other hand, he viewed the cross merely as a prefiguration (a type) of Christ-like events in the believers' experience which are the center of the believers' faith and speak of Christ's salvific role as future (at the Parousia). Clearly, for Paul, it was not a contradiction to hold both views. How is this possible? Some additional remarks about the way in which a system of convictions is organized and about how it functions will allow us to understand it.

## A System of Convictions and Its Expression
## in Theological Arguments

We discussed in Chapter 1 how a system of convictions can be viewed as a semantic universe. The elements of human experience are interrelated in the semantic universe so that they might be perceived as a *meaningful* world. Yet from another perspective this "meaningful world" is the context in which *purposeful* human life can take place. I stress "meaningful" and "purposeful" because these two terms describe two kinds of relations among the elements of human experience. Certain of these relations characterize the semantic universe itself. Others manifest the way in which a purposeful process can be elaborated on the basis of this semantic universe.[1]

1. *The systemic relations* are the most fundamental relations for the believers. These relations are those of the convictional pattern which organize the various elements of human experience so that they are perceived as a meaningful system. Thus, what is real is distinguished from what is illusory, what is good from what is evil. These are the relations through which the system of convictions has power over the believers. These fundamental relations include the oppositions in pairs (the opposition of a positive and a negative conviction in each pair) and the correlations (or homologations) of these pairs (see Chapter 2). The type/imitator relations that we discovered in 1 Thessalonians and elsewhere are a specific kind of correlation (or homologation). In our effort to elucidate these relations of correlations, we have so far focused upon the positive elements of Paul's system of convictions and their interrelations. But we can anticipate that to each type corresponds an "anti-type" (a negative type) to which this type is opposed. We shall see this when we study the negative dimensions of Paul's system of convictions (Chapter 7). Thus these type/imitator relations are fundamental relations which manifest in part what is most characteristic of Paul's faith: a part of his convictional pattern. These systemic relations of the convictional pattern define and delimit the elements of human experience in such a way that they can be perceived as meaningful in a given system of convictions.

2. Other relations which express *process and purposefulness* are also found among the elements of human experience. Because of these other

relations, the elements of human experience, as defined and delimited by the convictional pattern, are perceived as also having a specific place in life as an unfolding process. Once what is real and good is established, the goal of a purposeful life can be set. The elements of human experience are then viewed as being in spatial, temporal, and/or causal *continuity* with each other (even though they may have opposed meaning according to the convictional pattern). Thus, for instance, they may be viewed as being in a relation of cause and effect while simultaneously being either homologated with each other or opposed in a pair of oppositions according to the convictional pattern.

This second kind of relations manifests how a system of convictions and its convictional pattern find expression in a *purposeful* life which takes place in a *purposeful* and meaningful *unfolding* of *history*. These same relations are also those which are taken up in the argumentative logic. They express the purposefulness of the unfolding of a logical argument and thus also of theological arguments and theological ways of thinking. They are a reexpression of the convictional pattern (the convictional logic) they presuppose. As such the relations which express process and purposefulness should not be confused with the relations of the convictional pattern which characterizes a faith. Yet these two kinds of relations should not be viewed as independent of each other. A discourse or a way of thinking cannot express purposefulness outside of a semantic universe which establishes what is meaningful. Conversely, a semantic universe (a system of convictions) would remain a mere theoretical possibility if one does not make use of it, and thus activate it by conceiving in it purposeful processes. Therefore the same elements of human experience are simultaneously perceived in terms of the systemic relations of the convictional pattern and in terms of the process/purpose relations of the argumentative logic. This is true even though one or the other kind of relations comes to the forefront in a given discourse.

Insofar as Paul refers to the various elements of human experience, in order to establish for his readers the reality and validity of the system of convictions (i.e., in order to establish the "faith" of his readers), it is the convictional pattern which is manifested. Thus we saw that in Paul's system of convictions the interrelations of various "experiences" (for lack of a better word) play a central role. Jesus' experience and other experiences, including the believers' experience, are viewed in the type/imitator relationship of Paul's specific convictional pattern, while their chronological, historical relationship is left aside. Yet as we have already suggested, Paul does not deny that these experiences are also in a historical relationship with each other. We now need to consider how Paul sees these historical relations.

## Sacred History as the Framework of
## Paul's Theological Thinking:
## Reconciliation and Justification through Faith

We proceed by listing these various experiences in their chronological order (even if they were barely mentioned in the letters studied so far).

1. The experience(s) of Old Testament personages (the Prophets, 1 Thess. 2:15; Moses, Phil. 2:12–18; Job, Phil. 1:19). For instance, Paul emphasizes the experiences of scriptural personages in Galatians 3 and Romans 4, as well as in many other texts.
2. The experience of Jesus (his death and resurrection).
3. The experience of the churches in Judea (1 Thess. 2:14).
4. Paul's experience.
5. The experience of the believers (including the experience of people around them) to whom Paul writes.
6. The experience of believers of a "following generation" (such as the believers of Macedonia and Achaia who converted after the Thessalonians).
7. The experience of the believers at the end of time (i.e., at the Parousia).

In the texts we have studied, Paul does not emphasize the chronological continuity of these events, but clearly he presupposes that they succeed each other in a chronological sequence (even though some overlap with others; for instance, Paul's and the believers' experience overlap during his ministry). They form a history, the history of the revelatory interventions of God, in brief, a sacred history.

Since it was not emphasized by the letters studied so far, we have not considered the "historical" relationship among these experiences. Doing so will certainly help us address the question of the place of Christ in Paul's system of convictions and in his way of thinking, for our puzzlement concerns historical relationships. According to Paul, did Christ effect salvation in the past by dying on the cross "for our sins"? Or does he effect salvation only in the present and future? In other words, have the believers been saved once and for all by Christ's death on the cross, or are they saved in the present, or again, will they be saved only in the future, at the Parousia?

A historical relationship involves a chronological continuity (a succession) which often is expressed as a relation of cause and effect (*because* a first event took place *then* a second event can take place).[2] As we already mentioned, Paul perceived such a historical relationship between these experiences. For instance, *because* of Paul's previous experience, and because of Paul's proclamation of the gospel, the Thessalonians converted (as is expressed several times in 1 Thessalonians 1 and 2). Similarly, Paul's conversion was a result of God's revelation of his Son to him (Gal. 1:16). The context makes clear that God's Son is the resurrected Christ and that Jesus' death and resurrection were necessary so that Paul's conversion could take place. In the christological hymn of Phil. 2:6–11, another relation of cause and effect is mentioned, however surprising it may be. Because Jesus "became obedient unto death . . . God has highly exalted him" (note the "therefore" at the beginning of Phil. 2:9). And it is because of his exaltation that every tongue will confess that Jesus Christ is Lord at the Parousia (he was exalted "*in order that* at the name of Jesus every knee should bow . . . and every tongue confess . . ." [Phil. 2:10–11]). Thus, there is a relation of cause and effect between Jesus' death and resurrection and the Parousia. Even though this kind of causal relation at times bypasses several stages of the above chronological list, it is clear that Paul sees them as forming a kind of history, a sacred history.

### THE THREE MAIN PERIODS OF SACRED HISTORY

In Gal. 3:16–27 Paul suggests a general framework for this sacred history. He divides it into three periods. Two of these periods belong to the time of the Old Testament. First, there is *the period of promises* (to Abraham): "Now the promises were made to Abraham" (Gal. 3:16). Second, there is *the period of the Law* (or Torah) which brings to an end the period of the promises (at a precise date!): "This is what I mean: the law, which came four hundred and thirty years afterward . . ." (Gal. 3:17). Besides the "precise" chronological sequence expressed here, Paul also mentions that the periods are in a relation of cause and effect. Why was the period of the Law introduced, bringing about the end of the period of the promises? Paul expresses it in Gal. 3:19: "Why then the law? It was added because of transgressions" (against the covenant given to Abraham and its promises).

The period of the Law extends "until Christ came" (Gal. 3:24) and thus until the time of Christ which opens up *the period of faith*: "Now that faith has come" (Gal. 3:25). This is the period in which the believers live. This period is also linked with the preceding one through a relation of cause and effect. Because of the transgressions Christ came and "gave himself for our sins" (Gal. 1:4), and because of this "we are no longer under a custodian" (the Law; Gal. 3:25).

So this passage suggests that Paul viewed sacred history as a succession of three periods—the period of the promises (in the biblical time), the period of the Law, the period of faith—culminating with the Parousia, the Day of the Lord.

### SACRED HISTORY FOR THE APOCALYPTISTS AND PAUL

This view of sacred history as being divided into three periods is not without similarities to that of the Jewish Apocalyptists, whose movement was quite influential in Palestinian Judaism (see Chapter 3). The Apocalyptists believed that the end of history was imminent. One of their fundamental convictions was that the time in which they lived was the time of the "last generation," when new revelations were discovered and expected. Indeed, there were among them "prophets" who proclaimed the revelations of God for the end time (the last generation). This is why they are called "Apocalyptists," from the Greek word meaning "revelation." They were expecting a new covenant given by a new Moses and/or by the Messiah. Certain groups were even expecting two messiahs, a priestly messiah and a kingly messiah (both the priests and the kings were "anointed," the meaning of the term "messiah"). There were many Apocalyptic groups which held different views expressed by means of various symbolisms, but all of them held this conviction that the end of time was imminent and that they lived in the last period of history.[3]

Paul's views are closely related to those of the Apocalyptists. He was expecting the end of history in the very near future—before his death, according to 1 Thessalonians, somewhat later but nevertheless in the near future, according to other letters. Furthermore, he proclaimed that Jesus is the Christ, the Messiah. He even claimed that through his resurrection Jesus was "the first fruits" of the dead: "In fact Christ has been raised from the dead, the first fruits of those who have fallen asleep" (1 Cor. 15:20). In other words, Jesus' resurrection is the beginning of the general resurrection of the dead. We have also repeatedly noted that for Paul there are new revelations.

The Apocalyptists expressed the conviction that they were the last generation, in terms of a sacred history, which they also divided into several periods. This is one of the characteristics of the *Book of Jubilees*,[4] for instance. This Apocalyptic book is a "rewriting" (a kind of commentary) of Genesis and Exodus, emphasizing periods in sacred history that they called "jubilees" (one jubilee equals seven "weeks of years," i.e., 49 years) and "jubilees of jubilees" (i.e., 49 times 49 years). In this way the author maps out human history from beginning to end in terms of such periods. Major eras began on the "jubilees of jubilees" years. The Torah was given on such a year and thus marked the beginning of a new era (*Jubilees* 50:4).

These calculations varied from writing to writing. Paul's division of sacred history into three major periods does not correspond directly to this detailed breakdown of sacred history into jubilees, yet it is not without connections with the Apocalyptists' views. From their writings it appears that they also presupposed that sacred history involved three broad periods. To begin with, they perceived themselves as living in a special period, the period of the last generation. Before this, there was a period of wickedness, which had brought about the sorry state of affairs of the present situation. Still earlier there was another period, in which God revealed himself to his people.

Thus there was a first period in which God acted (i.e., performed revelatory acts) in history. When does this period end? It is often understood that such a period ended with the disappearance of the prophets, that is, at the time when Ezra proclaimed anew the Torah. In Galatians 3, Paul seems to say that this period ends with the giving of Torah, but in other texts he presupposes that God revealed himself in other periods of biblical history.

During the next period, from the end of prophecy until the present (or the recent past), God did not act in history. There were no (new) revelations. The Pharisees and the Rabbis themselves expressed this by saying that, at that time, God withdrew his Spirit (the spirit of prophecy) from Israel[5] because of the transgressions of Israel. The Apocalyptists had similar views. In other words, this second period was a time in which God did not and could not act in history because the Chosen People were disobedient (did not carry out their part of the covenant).

The third period of history was, for the Apocalyptists, the period beginning in their time. This period, during which God returns and acts again in human history, will involve, toward its end, a catastrophic cleansing of the world's sinfulness. Destruction, war, famine, a new "flood" (of fire) will destroy the wicked people or even the wicked world. And then there will be a "new creation," a new world, a new Jerusalem. Only the faithful remnant (the Apocalyptists themselves, of course) will be saved.

In light of this background and of our remarks about Paul's view of faith, we can begin to understand how Paul perceived sacred history in Galatians 3.

There is first a period when faith was possible, as in the time of Abraham. It is a time when God acted and when his acts could be recognized through faith. It was also a time when promises (the verbal promises to Abraham, but also God's previous acts as promises of future acts) could be received with confidence through faith.

The second period is the time of the Law, the time of "righteousness through the works of the law." It is a time when the believers are "under a custodian," a time when God does not act in human history because of transgressions. In other words, humankind is separated from God, alienated from God. Thus it is a time when faith is *not* possible. Certainly one can trust in the promises, but trust by itself is not faith for Paul. Faith also involves discovering new acts of God which fulfill the promises. How can one have faith as long as there is no (revelatory) act of God to discover and no new revelations to appropriate for oneself?

The third period, inaugurated by the coming of Christ (more precisely, his death), is a time when God acts again in human history and therefore a time when faith, as recognizing God's interventions in the present, is again possible. "Before faith came, we were confined under the law, kept under restraint until the coming faith was to be revealed" (Gal. 3:23, au. trans.). The coming of faith, the possibility of faith, is associated with the coming of Christ ("until Christ came" [Gal. 3:24]) and with revelations. For Paul the believers are in the last period of history. This is the eschatological time (the period of the end time), when God acts again in human history and thus when there are new revelations and when God's Spirit is again with his people.

Why does Paul propose a sacred history divided in three periods? What kind of presentation is this? How is this related to the convictional pattern we found in our reading of 1 Thessalonians, Philemon, and Philippians?

From the perspective of the believers' system of convictions, the essential thing is that God intervenes in their present. For Paul, it is through these interventions of God, discovered and appropriated through faith, that the believers are established in the right relationship with God and that they receive their true identity by discovering themselves as chosen by God for a specific vocation. The temporal succession of these periods is important only insofar as it indicates that Abraham and other biblical personages, Jesus, other churches and Paul belong to the past. For the establishment of the believers' faith and revealed identity, it is enough for them to hold the conviction that God intervened in the experience of those who preceded them *in the same way* as he intervenes in their experience. *As* their predecessors were elected and received a vocation through God's intervention in their experience, *so* the believers are elected and receive a vocation through God's intervention in their own experience. In order to appropriate these new revelations and to ascertain their validity, they need to discover what, in their experience, *is like* the experiences of their predecessors in the faith. It is a matter of *comparing* various experiences and situations. Finding in their experience the same type of situations and interventions of God as in the experience of their predecessors is what establishes for them the validity of their system of convictions and the reality of their relationship with God.

These comparisons establish the system of convictions that the believers experience as a mysterious power. Their system of convictions is a set of self-evident truths. For them it is true because they "know" (feel) it is true. But they also need to *understand* their system of convictions, that is, they need to make sense of their faith by formulating it in a "logical" or, better, theological discourse which will also make sense to others. How can they explain their conviction that God intervened in their experience and that he performs in it revelatory acts through which they are established in the right relationship with him? How can they explain their conviction that the Jews (the Pharisees) are not in this right relationship with God? How can they explain their convictions that Jesus is the main "type" for the interventions of God in their experience? And why should God intervene in such a radical way—performing revelatory acts—in their experience? Only a theological discourse (or a theological reflection with an argumentative logic) can express such explanations.[6]

A theology can take many different forms, depending on the system of convictions which it attempts to express and explain. But since Paul's (and his followers') system of convictions and its convictional pattern are characterized by the comparison of various experiences belonging to various periods of history, Paul could develop a theology based upon reflections about history. Thus his theology is a sacred history, that is, a history of the acts of God, understood in terms of their continuity and of their cause and effect relations.

### GOD'S RECONCILING ACT IN CHRIST

Why can the believers claim that God intervenes in their experience? And why is Jesus' experience such an essential type for what the believers discover in their own experience through faith? Paul's theological reflection on sacred history provides an answer: it is because the period in which the believers live is the last period of history. In this eschatological period God again intervenes in history.

But how is this possible? The world, humankind, is still characterized by evil and transgressions against God's will. One cannot even claim that there is a group without transgressions against God. As Paul puts it, "All have sinned and fall short of the glory of God" (Rom. 3:23). Thus God should still "withdraw his Spirit" from humankind and abstain from intervening in human affairs. But he does not. Somehow God is no longer separated or alienated from humankind. He intervenes in the believers' experience. Paul's theological explanation of this "fact" (i.e., of this self-evident truth, according to his system of convictions) is that Christ, or more precisely, his death on the cross (and his resurrection), has overcome this separation of God from humankind. He has *reconciled* humankind to God. Thus we can read the following statements. "While we were enemies we were reconciled to God by the death of his Son" (Rom. 5:10). He "was put to death for our trespasses" (Rom. 4:25); he "died for our sins" (Gal. 1:4; 1 Cor. 15:3), and thus God and humankind are no longer separated. In Christ "God was reconciling the world to himself, not counting their trespasses against them, and entrusting to us the message of reconciliation" (2 Cor. 5:19).

In this theological perspective expressed in the form of a sacred history, Jesus' death plays the central and essential role of reconciling God and humankind, removing the wall which separated them, namely, transgressions. God can again act in human history, not because wickedness and the wicked have been destroyed in a catastrophic cleansing (which is often viewed by the Apocalyptists as the role of the Messiah and which for Paul will also take place at the Parousia), but because Christ died for our sins. This is a theological/historical explanation (in terms of cause-and-effect relations) of the fact that, according to Paul's convictions, God is acting in the present while he was not acting in a period of the past. It is *not* this explanation which establishes the believers' faith, as can be seen when we realize that when Paul wrote 1 Thessalonians he apparently did not yet conceive of this theological/historical explanation (there is no mention in this letter of the view that Christ died *for our sins*; see our discussion of 1 Thess. 5:10, p. 144 above).

This sacred historical work which Christ performed once and for all should not be confused with "salvation" (even if Paul uses this word, or the corresponding verb, to designate it). The reconciliation of God with humankind is *not* salvation in and of itself. It merely opens the *possibility* of salvation. Similarly, this work of Christ—dying for our sins—is not to be confused with "justification through faith." It merely opens the possibility of new interventions of God which, when they are appropriated through faith by the believers, set them in the right relationship with God. This is what Christ means in this historical perspective, that is, when Paul's system of convictions is reexpressed in terms of a purposeful and meaningful unfolding of the believers' lives and of history.

What is confusing is that Paul expresses this *theological view* by means of a series of terms and phrases which, at times, he also uses to express his *convictional view*. When Paul speaks of this work of Christ which reopens the possibility of God's intervention in human history, he uses such terms and phrases as "reconciliation," "Christ dying for our sins," "not counting the sins or trespasses." In such cases, "sins" or "trespasses" are always understood as "transgressions" (of the Law or of God's will). Paul also uses the term "justification" in precisely the same sense as "reconciliation." In such a case this term designates "justification from sins" or "transgressions" (note that sins and transgressions are in the plural form, as above) and not the establishment of the believers in the right relationship with God, which is associated (as we saw in Galatians) with the deliverance from a curse or from an evil power or again from the power of sin (singular). Since Paul always expresses himself in a vocabulary that his readers will easily understand—he is Galatian with the Galatians, Roman with the Romans, as he is Greek with the Greeks and Jewish with the Jews (cf. 2 Cor. 9:19–22)—Paul's vocabulary has different meanings in different contexts.

So each time we study a text we need to ascertain in which sense Paul uses his terminology. Is it to express a theological explanation of the purpose of Christ's work and its place and role in the unfolding of sacred history? Or is it to express systemic relations of the convictional pattern which establish the believers' faith? Paul often uses the same vocabulary to express both. As long as this distinction is not clearly made, Paul's statements appear to be contradictory and confusing. The failure to make such a distinction led to the debate among scholars over the importance of sacred history in Paul's thought and over the meaning of his concept of justification. Thus scholars such as Johannes Munck,[7] Oscar Cullmann,[8] and Krister Stendahl[9] give priority to salvation history in their interpretation of Paul and in doing so reject the systemic interpretation of Paul proposed by other scholars such as Rudolf Bultmann.[10] In fact, as Ernst Käsemann has already noted,[11] it is not an either/or question but a matter of recognizing two dimensions of meaning[12] in Paul's letters:

1. The expression of Paul's system of convictions characterized by a convictional pattern involving the type/imitator relations and giving priority to the believers' experience as the place and time when they are established in the right relationship with God.
2. Paul's theological formulation of this system of convictions in terms of sacred history.

When this distinction is kept in mind, the statements Paul makes about the cross as reconciliation (or as "justification" in the sense of reconciliation) can be understood alongside the statements about "justification through faith," that is, about "the right relationship with God through faith." In other words, they are two sides of the same coin. The convictional views need to be reexpressed in theological statements so that the believers might understand how these convictions can have their place in the unfolding of their lives. But at the same time, these theological statements would be meaningless if they would not presuppose the system of convictions. Thus even in passages where the theological view comes to the fore, it remains framed by the convictional view which is its necessary foundation. The reading of two central texts in which Paul speaks about reconciliation (2 Cor. 5:17–21; Romans 5) will allow us to perceive how the statements about reconciliation (in the theological perspective) are related to those about "justification through faith" (in the convictional perspective).

The first text, 2 Cor. 5:17–21, reads:

> Therefore, if any one is in Christ, he is a new creation; the old has passed away, behold, the new has come. All this is from God, who through Christ reconciled us to himself and gave us the ministry of reconciliation; that is, in Christ God was reconciling the world to himself, not counting their trespasses against them, and entrusting to us the message of reconciliation. So we are ambassadors for Christ, God making his appeal through us. We beseech you on behalf of Christ, be reconciled to God. For our sake he made him to be sin who knew no sin, so that in him we might become the righteousness of God.

In verse 17 Paul refers to the believers as being "in Christ," a phrase which expresses that the believers' experience is Christ-like from the convictional perspective. The rest of the passage provides a theological explanation for this experience of the believers in terms of sacred history. To begin with, it means that the believer is "a new creation," or better, with C. K. Barrett,[13] that "there is a new act of creation" (emphasizing the process rather than the result). In other words, the time in which the believers live is the eschatological period, the end time, when God acts again and in which he establishes a new creation. Their experience "in Christ" is the manifestation of "a new creative act of God" (cf. also Gal. 6:15). Note that this phrase also implies that the present experience of the believers and God's intervention in it can be compared (according to the convictional pattern) to that of God at the time of the creation.

Now, "the old" (i.e., the old relation between God and humankind, as the following verses suggest) "has passed away." This "new" period in which one can be in this new relationship with God is the result of Christ's death through which God was reconciling to himself not only the believers (2 Cor. 5:18) but also the world (v. 19), that is, humankind as a whole. Reconciliation is not something which demands faith from people. Whether or not they know it and believe it, this reconciliation has taken place. It establishes the *possibility for faith*, and for the right relationship with God through faith, for all humankind.[14] It is part of the role (vocation) of the believers (in this case Paul and his companions) to proclaim that this reconciliation has taken place and to urge people (here the Corinthians) to "be reconciled to God" as God is reconciled to them. Accepting the reconciliation is the first step toward faith.

This reconciliation results from God's "not counting trespasses against them" (as we discussed) because "he made him [Christ] to be sin who knew no sin" (2 Cor. 5:21). This explanation of the meaning of Jesus' death on the cross is comparable to the one given in Gal. 3:13: "Christ redeemed us from the curse of the law, having become a curse for us—for it is written, 'Cursed be every one who hangs on a tree.'" Thus Christ took the position of sinners, of people estranged from God and under the wrath of God (see Chapter 7). Because of this reconciliation the believers can be in a new relationship with God; they can "become the righteousness of God," that is, manifestations of God's righteousness.[15] In other words, the believers (and their experience) can become the place where God acts and thus where God sets himself in the right relationship with the believers. These are the acts of God to which the believers can respond through faith and in this way be in the right relationship with God. It is this conviction that the theological concept of reconciliation reexpresses and explains.

The second central text in which Paul speaks about reconciliation is Rom. 5:1–11:

Therefore, since we are justified by faith, we have peace with God through our Lord Jesus Christ. Through him we have obtained access to this grace in which we stand, and we rejoice in our hope of sharing the glory of God. More than that, we rejoice in our sufferings, knowing that suffering produces endurance, and endurance produces character, and character produces hope, and hope does not disappoint us, because God's love has been poured into our hearts through the Holy Spirit which has been given to us. While we were still weak, at the right time Christ died for the ungodly. Why, one will hardly die for a righteous man—though perhaps for a good man one will dare even to die. But God shows his love for us in that while we were yet sinners Christ died for us. Since, therefore, we are now justified by his blood, much more shall we be saved by him from the wrath of

God. For if while we were enemies we were reconciled to God by the death
of his Son, much more, now that we are reconciled, shall we be saved by
his life. Not only so, but we also rejoice in God through our Lord Jesus
Christ, through whom we have now received our reconciliation.

In this passage we find a similar explanation of the conviction that God is
at work in the believers' experience, that is, how the believers "have
obtained access to the grace" in which they stand (5:2; see our discussion
of "grace" in Philippians). The linking of this passage with the concluding verse of Romans 4 makes it clear that if "we have obtained access to
this grace" it is because Jesus "was put to death for our trespasses and
raised for our justification" (Rom. 4:25).

Paul continues, "Therefore, since we are justified by faith, we have
peace with God through our Lord Jesus Christ" (Rom. 5:1). Here "justified by faith" means "to have peace with God," to "be reconciled to God,"
as Paul puts it in 5:10. This justification/reconciliation is brought about
by Jesus' death: "While we were still weak, at the right time Christ
died for the ungodly" (5:6); "while we were yet sinners Christ died for
us" (5:8b). This is a once-and-for-all "justification," the act through which
humankind is "made righteous" because God "had passed over former
sins" (3:25). Thus Paul can affirm, "We are now justified by his blood"
(5:9a). In the following verses, Paul repeats these statements but in
another terminology. Instead of speaking of "justification" he speaks of
"reconciliation." Yet it is clearly to express the same idea: "While we
were enemies we were reconciled to God by the death of his Son"
(5:10a); "now that we are reconciled" (5:10b). The parallelism of these
phrases makes it clear that, in this passage, "justification" and "reconciliation" have the same meaning. They designate the overcoming of the
separation between God and humankind, an event which has a specific
place in the past unfolding of sacred history. Reconciliation also precedes other events in the future unfolding of sacred history, namely,
salvation from the coming wrath of God. Thus Paul can affirm, "[we shall]
be saved by him [Christ] from the wrath of God" (5:9b), and "[we shall]
be saved by his life" (5:10c). This is a theological formulation in terms of
the believers' hope. But as we noted earlier, according to the system of
convictions, hope is based upon the believers' present experience.

The following verses (Rom. 5:12–21) make it clear that at this point
Paul is developing a theological explanation in terms of sacred history.
He proceeds to describe the "history" of sin, that is, that "sin came into

the world through one man" (5:12), Adam, and that as a consequence death spread to all humankind; that "sin was in the world before the law" (5:13); that "death reigned from Adam to Moses" (5:14); and that "the grace of God and the free gift in the grace" came also through "one man Jesus Christ" (5:15). But at the same time, according to the convictional pattern, Paul compares Adam and Christ. Adam is the negative type (the anti-type) of Christ, in other words, his negative prefiguration. Thus, for instance, he writes, "As one man's trespass led to condemnation for all men, so one man's act of righteousness leads to acquittal and life for all men" (5:18).

### RECONCILIATION AND JUSTIFICATION
### THROUGH FAITH

This reading of 2 Cor. 5:17–21 and Rom. 5:1–21 shows how Paul's system of convictions and its convictional pattern undergird his theological explanations in terms of sacred history. Speaking of reconciliation is valid only insofar as this event of the sacred history makes sense in terms of the type/imitator convictional pattern. This should be a reminder that the distinction we are making between system of convictions and theological explanation is a distinction between two dimensions of meaning which are simultaneously present in Paul's way of thinking. He cannot develop a theological argument outside of the semantic universe that his system of convictions is, and he cannot fully make sense for his readers if his discourse is not also, at least to some extent, a logical (theological) argument. It is a matter of discerning which dimension of meaning comes to the fore. Then, depending on the case, the words and phrases should be read in one way or another.

A case in point is Paul's uses of the word "justification," or "righteousness" (the same word in Greek), and the corresponding verb "being justified" or "being made righteous." For Paul, these terms can function equally well in the convictional and in the theological dimension of meaning because they always refer to a "right relationship with God" and its establishment. But they do so in quite different ways, depending on the dimension of meaning in which they are found.

According to the theological explanations, these terms refer to the "right relationship with God" which is established (or reestablished) once and for all through the overcoming of what prevents this relationship, namely, transgressions, sins. In this case, justification means approxi-

mately "forgiveness of sins," although the emphasis is on the reconciliation of humankind to God. This is what is achieved by Christ's death on
the cross as the central event of sacred history. As we noted when
discussing 2 Cor. 5:19, this justification/reconciliation is for the world,
that is, *humankind as a whole.* This is also expressed in Rom. 5:18: "One
man's act of righteousness leads to acquittal and life for *all men.*"

According to the system of convictions, these terms refer to the "right
relationship with God through faith," that is, to the right relationship
with God established through the interventions of God in the believers'
experience. These interventions are discovered and appropriated through
faith, thanks to a comparison with other people's experiences in which
God has previously intervened. In this case, the believers alone (and not
the whole of humankind) are in the right relationship with God and can
legitimately have the hope of being saved. Those who do not believe are
perishing and will be destroyed on the Day of the Lord—as is expressed
in such passages as 1 Cor. 1:18, where Paul opposes "those who are
perishing" to "us [the believers] who are being saved" (cf. also, e.g., 2
Cor. 2:15; 4:3; Phil. 1:28; 3:19).[16]

As long as this distinction between the two dimensions of meaning is
not made, one is led to conclude that Paul contradicted himself. Did
Paul want to say that humankind as a whole is justified, or only the
believers? Thus, for instance, E. P. Sanders concludes that Paul did not
mean precisely what he wrote in such verses as 2 Cor. 5:19 and Rom.
5:18 (and 1 Cor. 15:22): "He seems rather to have been carried away by
the force of his analogy."[17] But it is clear that justification as reconciliation
(in the perspective of sacred history) is the reconciliation of all human
beings to God. Because of this reconciliation, God can again intervene
in human history. This also means that Paul holds the convictions that
God does intervene in the experience of *all human beings* (as we shall
further see when studying Romans 1 and 2). But the believers alone
discover and take hold of these interventions of God through faith.
Therefore the believers alone are established in the right relationship
with God, and thus can hope to be saved.

For the believers, the cross is not simply the sign that their sins have
been forgiven and that they are reconciled to God. It is also the sign of
the manifestation of "the power of God" (1 Cor. 1:18) in their experience
where they can discover cross-like events. In this way, the "cross" is also
that through which they are delivered from (the power of) "the present

evil age" (Gal. 1:4) as well as from "the curse of Torah" (cf. Gal. 4:3–5). But in order to understand this point we once again need to focus our attention on Paul's system of convictions and how it is organized by a specific convictional pattern.

## SCRIPTURE, THE KERYGMA, AND THE BELIEVERS' EXPERIENCE

In order to progress in our elucidation of Paul's system of convictions beyond our reading of 1 Thessalonians, Philemon, and Philippians, we shall now examine three central texts: Galatians 3, Romans 4, and 1 Corinthians 15. Our study of these texts will allow us to see again how the type/imitator pattern functions in Paul's discourse. These texts will also give us the opportunity to discover new elements of Paul's system of convictions. In particular, they will allow us to understand the place and positive role of Scripture (Torah) in Paul's faith and thus to complement the results of our reading of Galatians.

### Scripture as Promise and Type (Galatians 3)

We shall not proceed to a complete reading of Galatians according to the approach we have used in Chapters 4 and 5, but we do need to identify the elements which belong to the warranting level, since it is on this level that the most fundamental convictions are expressed (yet, once again, convictions are also expressed on the dialogic level).

#### THE WARRANTING LEVEL

On the dialogic level of Galatians we find expressed the purpose of this letter. It is aimed at communicating to the Galatians a specific teaching—the Gospel that I preached to you and that you received is the true Gospel, any other "gospel" is not truly the Gospel (cf. Gal. 1:6–9)—and then at laying on them a series of exhortations. In order to warrant his statement that "the gospel which was preached by me is not man's gospel" (Gal. 1:11), Paul introduces, as a first element of the warranting level, the story of his conversion and of his interaction with the other apostles and the churches (1:12—2:14).

Beyond Gal. 2:14 the text's organization becomes more complex. The discourse frequently passes from one discourse level to the other. The dialogic level (and its argument aimed at showing that justification by faith and not justification by the works of the Law characterizes the "true" Gospel) takes a more important role in the organization of the text. Yet Paul constantly introduces warranting elements to establish the validity of his statements. Thus in 2:15–21 his statements are warranted by reference to the experience of the believers of Jewish origin, such as Paul: "We who are Jews by birth," who "believed," "died to the law," and "have been crucified with Christ" (2:16b–21). In this passage we also find brief warranting statements about Christ's experience: he "loved me and gave himself for me" (2:20); "Christ died" (2:21). Furthermore, it includes statements in the first-person singular ("I") and in the present tense (cf. 2:20–21) which function both on the warranting level (because they are true for Paul's past experience) and on the dialogic level. In this way the dialogic level is reintroduced in the discourse and plays an important role in Galatians 3.

A series of blunt statements directly addressed to the Galatians—"O foolish Galatians" (Gal. 3:1a and also 2a, 3a,c)—urges them to acknowledge that the Gospel preached by Paul is the true Gospel. These statements are warranted by the introduction of a series of references to the Galatians' experience (3:1b, 2b, 3b, 4a, 5) which are elements of the warranting level.

Then the argument of the dialogic level concerning justification through faith is further developed (Gal. 3:7, 9–10a, 11a, 12a, 14), but this time the warrants used to establish the validity of these statements are references to Scripture. Thus in 3:6 and 8 we find quotations referring to Abraham's story according to Gen. 15:6 and Gen. 18:18 (or 12:3); in 3:10b a quotation of Deut. 27:26; in 3:11b a quotation of Hab. 2:4; in 3:12b a quotation of Lev. 18:5; and in 3:13b a quotation of Deut. 21:23.

In Gal. 3:15 a "human example" is given as an additional warrant. From then on, until the end of the chapter, the argument unfolds on the dialogic level with the reintroduction of the warranting level in the form of references to the warranting elements already found earlier concerning Abraham, the Law, Christ, and the believers' experience.

By comparison with what we found in 1 Thessalonians, Philemon, and Philippians, what is new here is the place given to Scripture on the warranting level alongside Christ's experience and Paul's and other believers' experiences.

From our previous study of Galatians (following another kind of reading) we know that Paul considers his own experience (as a believer of Jewish origin) equivalent to the Galatians' experience (as believers of Hellenistic origin). We now understand why this is so. In the terminology of 1 Thessalonians, Paul is the "type" and the Galatians the "imitators" in whose experience the same things happen as in Paul's experience. Consequently, Paul can speak of their experience in terms of his own experience, and vice versa. We can therefore anticipate that he expresses the same kind of relations among all the elements of the warranting level. We have already discussed briefly how in Gal. 2:15–21 Paul presents his own experience as fulfillment of the type "Jesus": he "died to the law" (2:19), he has "been crucified with Christ" (2:20). And thus he can say in 3:1, "O foolish Galatians! . . . before whose eyes Jesus Christ was publicly portrayed as crucified." Paul's experience among them was the "public portrayal" of Jesus crucified; he was the fulfillment of the type "Christ crucified."

### ABRAHAM'S OFFSPRING AND HEIRS ACCORDING TO PROMISE

It remains to be seen how Paul uses Scripture in this context. To begin, note that he uses two kinds of texts: (1) biblical statements about curses and blessings, and (2) passages which refer to the experience of Abraham.

1. Deut. 27:26, Hab. 2:4, Lev. 18:5, and Deut. 21:23 are statements or, better, declarations of curses or blessings which can be understood as "promises" (negative promises in the case of the curses, positive promises in the case of the blessings). For Paul these promises are fulfilled. "Cursed be every one who does not abide by all things written in the book of the law, and do them" (Deut. 27:26; Gal. 3:10) is a curse (negative promise) fulfilled in the experience of those (the Jews and the Judaizers) "who rely on works of the law" (Gal. 3:10). Similarly, "he who through faith is righteous shall live" (Hab. 2:4; Gal. 3:11) is a promise fulfilled in the true believers' experience (i.e., Paul's and the Galatians' experience as described in the preceding verses). In the same fashion, in 3:12 the quotation of Lev. 18:5, "He who does them shall live by them," is presented as fulfilled in those (Jews and Judaizers) who perform works of the Law and do not live by faith. Finally, the quotation of Deut. 21:23, "Cursed be every one who hangs on a tree," is presented as fulfilled in Christ's death on the cross (3:13).

These quotations show that for Paul such statements from Scripture, including legal statements, have a function similar to that of "types." Even though they are verbal statements—rather than acts of God in the past which can be viewed as types or prefigurations of acts of God in later periods—they are perceived as promises of what happens in later situations, that is, in Christ's experience and in the believers' experience. Indeed, this is what Scripture, Torah (cf. Gal. 4:21), is when it is viewed as truly the word of God which is "holy and just and good" (Rom. 7:12). Far from being against the promises, it is itself promises: "Is the law then against the promises of God? Certainly not; for if a law had been given which could make alive, then righteousness would indeed be by the law" (Gal. 3:21). The Law, Torah, is not against the promises. The proof is that the Law cannot give life. It cannot establish the believers in the right relationship with God. But if it cannot do so, it can only point beyond itself and toward such a relationship with God. It can only be promises. Such is the positive role of the law, of Torah, of Scripture, which of course cannot be separated from its other roles, namely, of "[consigning] all things to sin" (3:22), of being a "custodian" (3:24), and of being a curse keeping people under its power.

2. As could be expected, the other quotations of Scripture—those concerning Abraham's experience—function as any other "typical" experiences. Abraham's experience is a type fulfilled both in the believers' and in Christ's experiences. In Gal. 3:6–9 the believers are presented as the "sons of Abraham." The image of the father/son relationship expresses the type/fulfillment relationship between Abraham and the believers (as it does between Paul and the believers in 1 Thessalonians and Philemon). The Gentiles who have faith and are justified by faith are fulfillments of the type "Abraham," who "believed God, and it was reckoned to him as righteousness" (3:6; Gen. 15:6). Abraham is also the type of the "Gentile believers" (a phrase expressed in Greek by one word, which can also be translated "nations") because he is the one to whom the promise was addressed, "In you shall all the nations be blessed" (3:8; Gen. 18:18 or 12:3). The Gentile believers, the "nations," are the fulfillment of this promise, but they are also the fulfillment of the type "Abraham to whom the promise is addressed" in that they are those to whom the Gospel is preached. The experiences of Abraham and of the believers are, for Paul, so much equivalent that he can speak of the one in terms of the others (as he speaks of his own experience in terms

of the Galatians', and vice versa). Thus Paul speaks of Abraham as if he were the Gentile believers to whom the Gospel is preached. He writes, "Scripture . . . *preached the gospel* beforehand to Abraham" (Gal. 3:8). So we find a twofold type/imitator (or fulfillment) relationship between Abraham and the Gentile believers. Abraham received a promise, the Gentile believers received the Gospel; Abraham was justified by faith, the Gentile believers are justified by faith.

This type/fulfillment relationship also involves a specific relation among the components of the experiences of Abraham and of the believers. Because of this relationship, the Gospel of Christ—the one Gospel (Gal. 1:6–7), the Gospel proclaimed by Paul (1:8), the Gospel that Paul received through a revelation of Jesus Christ (1:11–12)—is equivalent to the promise to Abraham. This in itself suggests that the Gospel is promise, a promise pointing beyond itself to (other) fulfillments. As we repeatedly noted, the Gospel, that is, the message or kerygma about Christ's death and resurrection, is not a complete and final revelation. It is a promise (see also 3:22: "that what was promised to faith in Jesus Christ might be given to those who believe").

And yet the Gospel as kerygma about Christ is itself fulfillment. In Gal. 3:13, Christ's death is presented as fulfillment of Deut. 21:23. This can be further seen in 3:16. In this verse Christ, and no longer the Gentile believers, is Abraham's offspring. The type is "Abraham and his offspring receiving the promise" (the various promises found in Gen. 12:7; 13:15; 17:7; 22:18; 24:7). Thus Christ is a fulfillment of this type. As was Abraham, Christ is the one to whom the promises have been made.

Thus in Galatians 3 we find a twofold fulfillment of the type Abraham: the type Abraham as fulfilled in the believers, the type Abraham as fulfilled in Christ. These distinct relations should be kept in mind. Yet in his text Paul brings them together as, for instance, in 3:29: "If you are Christ's, then you are Abraham's offspring, heirs according to promise." The promise to which they are heirs is both the promise made to Abraham and the promise made to Christ (or the Gospel as promise). Thus they are heirs (sons, offspring) of both Abraham and Christ. Paul does not explicitly express this relation between the believers and Christ in these terms (the closest statement to this effect would be Rom. 8:17, where the believers are described as "fellow heirs with Christ" or "heirs as Christ is"). Yet it is clear that what is involved here is a three-stage relationship: Abraham—Christ—believers. The believers are both Abraham's and Christ's offspring. Christ is an intermediary stage of the fulfillment of the type "Abraham" in the believers' experience. The same kind of relationship is found in Gal. 3:14: "that in Christ Jesus the blessing of Abraham might come upon the Gentiles."

When we bring these observations together we can see how in Paul's text the various components of each experience are interrelated. According to this passage the type "Abraham" involves three main elements:

1. Abraham received a promise.
2. Abraham has an offspring who received the promise with him.
3. Abraham was justified by faith.

Thus (1) Christ has also received a promise (3:16); (2) Christ is Abraham's offspring; (3) the title "Christ" implicitly expresses that he is in the right relationship with God. The (Gentile) believers are the fulfillment of the type "Abraham" in that (1) they received a Gospel/promise (3:8), (2) they are Abraham's offspring (3:29), and (3) they are justified by faith (3:7).

It also appears that the relation between the believers and Christ is similar to that between the believers and Abraham. More generally, we may say that the relation of the believers to Christ is the same kind of relation which exists between Scripture and its fulfillments in Christ and the believers. To put it another way, the kerygma about Christ functions for Paul as an "oral Scripture." This means that according to Paul's system of convictions, Christ, despite the fact that he is fulfillment of Scripture, has the same status as Scripture.[18] In the same way that Scripture should not be taken as an absolute—otherwise it becomes the curse-Torah—so Christ should not be taken as an absolute, otherwise he becomes an idol. Paul also had to confront this kind of issue in Corinth (see Chapter 8). In other words, the reconciliation which Christ has accomplished through his death on the cross should not be taken as an absolute. It has not resolved all the "problems" which are the daily lot of humankind, including that of the believers. The Gospel as proclamation of this message that Christ has reconciled the world to God is nothing but a promise. So that the believers might be in the right relationship with God through faith, God needs to intervene in their experience as radically as he did in Christ's. In this way the promises "in Jesus Christ" (3:22) are fulfilled by God. And this manifestation of God in the believers' experience is itself nothing but the promise of his ultimate intervention of the Day of the Lord.

Once more, this raises the question, Why does God need to intervene again and again in such a radical fashion in the believers' experience? What necessitates such interventions of God? The answer to these questions is: sin and/or evil. But we shall fully understand this answer only when we have elucidated the place and role of sin and/or evil in Paul's system of convictions. As a first step toward this goal, we shall consider successively Romans 4 and 1 Corinthians 15 in order to assess what kind of intervention of God is necessary to establish the believers in the right relationship with God and how this intervention of God is related to Jesus' resurrection.

## Justification as the Overcoming of a Hopeless Situation (Romans 4)

Turning to Romans 4, we can be confident that the convictional pattern found in other texts is also at work here. We came across it again in Galatians 3, and it allowed us to understand the "strange reasonings" we noted during our first reading of that letter (see Chapter 2). This first reading of Galatians allows us to understand other characteristics of Paul's convictional pattern, which will help us in our reading of Romans 4.

We have noted how Paul speaks of his own experience in terms of the Galatians' experience, and vice versa, because he views them as equivalent (see Chapter 2). We understand now that they are equivalent because, for him, they are in a type/fulfillment (or imitator) relationship. In other words, the same type of events—and especially the same type of interventions of God—is found in the various experiences. Because of this convictional pattern, Paul can speak of one situation in terms of all the others to which it is equivalent according to his system of convictions. Thus he speaks of the believers' experience in terms of the experiences of both Abraham and Christ; he also speaks of Abraham's experience in terms of that of the believers; and so on. Theoretically, all the stages of the type/fulfillment chain can eventually be collapsed into the description of one of its stages. According to his system of convictions, Paul conceives of the believers' experience as the fulfillment of the promises contained in Scripture, in Christ, and in earlier believers and as promise of later interventions of God and especially on the Day of the Lord. Consequently, he quite naturally speaks of the believers' experience in terms of all these types and these future fulfillments. We found several examples of this phenomenon in 1 Thessalonians and elsewhere, especially when Paul describes his own experience. But this is true about any stage of the type/fulfillment chain. For example, in Galatians 3 Paul describes the biblical type "Abraham" in terms of its fulfillment in the believers.

So a text which at first seems to speak about only one situation may nevertheless describe it in terms of other situations which are either its types or its fulfillments. This is precisely what happens in Romans 4.

## THE ORGANIZATION OF THE ARGUMENT

In Romans 4 the dialogic level involves an argument closely related to the one we found in Galatians 3. It aims at conveying that both the circumcised and the uncircumcised are "justified by faith apart from works of law" (Rom. 3:28). At the beginning of Romans 5, Paul is satisfied that, at least in large part, he has conveyed this point: "Therefore, since we are justified by faith . . ." (5:1). Romans 4 belongs almost entirely to the warranting level of this argument. Only a few elements (4:9a, 11b–12, 14–16, 23a) belong to the dialogic level. They concern the situation and status of the uncircumcised (Gentile) and circumcised (Jewish) believers. For all of them the only access to righteousness is through faith. These statements need to be established as valid by the warranting level.

Most of Romans 4 is devoted to Abraham, whose story is therefore the main unit of the warranting level. It includes a development (Rom. 4:4–8, with a quotation of Psalm 32) which speaks in general terms about "the man to whom God reckons righteousness." We can treat these verses together with Abraham's story, since he is clearly a "man to whom God reckons righteousness," even though this phrase also refers to other believers. Only the concluding verses, Rom. 4:22d–25, introduce, as part of the warranting level, statements about Christ.

In this text we find three experiences which are interrelated: Abraham's story (to which we can join the general development of Rom. 4:4–8), the kerygma about Christ, and the believers' experience (mentioned on the dialogic level).

## THE MAIN UNIT OF THE WARRANTING LEVEL: ABRAHAM'S EXPERIENCE

Since most of Romans 4 is devoted to Abraham, we need to consider the various features of his experience, which Paul underscores by repeating them at least twice. We list them in the order in which they first appear in the text.

- Abraham believed (Rom. 4:3 [Gen. 15:6]; 4:9b, 22), had trust in God (Rom. 4:5), "in hope he believed against hope" (4:18), "he did not weaken in faith" (4:19, 20, 21).
- His faith was reckoned to him as righteousness (4:3, 22; Gen. 15:6).
- He is indirectly qualified as "ungodly" (4:5) and as sinner (4:7, 8; Ps. 32:1–2); he is uncircumcised (4:10, 11).
- He has received the promise that he will be the father of many nations (4:17 [Gen. 17:5]; 4:20) this promise is from God, "who gives life to the dead and calls into existence the things that do not exist" (4:17).
- His body is "as good as dead," and Sarah's womb is in a "state of death" (4:19; literal trans.).

If we organize these elements according to an approximate narrative development, we obtain the following:

1. At first Abraham is uncircumcised, sinner, ungodly.
2. A promise is made to Abraham. It is, on the one hand, the verbal promise of descendants and, on the other hand, the "promises" contained in the creation story as type (promise of the creator God) and in the resurrection (promise by the God who gives life to the dead).
3. Abraham is in a hopeless situation: both his body and Sarah's body are qualified as dead.
4. Abraham has faith nevertheless, an unwavering faith.
5. Abraham's faith is "reckoned to him as righteousness."

### ABRAHAM, CHRIST, AND THE BELIEVERS

A quick glance at the above development makes it clear that in several instances the way in which these elements are presented is not inspired by the Genesis story about Abraham. Certain qualifications are strangely emphasized, others hardly fit the Genesis story about Abraham. In fact, as can be expected after the above discussion, the type Abraham and its fulfillments in Christ and in the believers are collapsed upon each other, so much so that the type "Abraham's story" is retold in terms of the fulfillments.

1. Abraham is qualified as ungodly and sinner as well as uncircum-

cised so as to make clear that he is the type (the father) fulfilled in the Gentiles and in the Jews (who are sinners, as is emphasized in the preceding chapters of Romans).

2. The promises involve, in addition to what could be expected (the verbal promise of descendants by the creator God), the reference to the God "who gives life to the dead." The terminology makes it clear that here Paul uses traditional Jewish formulations which refer to the general resurrection of the dead. But in this new context—which includes the subsequent mention of God who raised Jesus from the dead (4:24)—it becomes clear that the type "God who gives life to the dead" is a promise which also is manifested for the believers as "God who raised Jesus from the dead."

3. The hopeless situation of Abraham is described with much emphasis on the dead character of his and Sarah's bodies. This suggests that Abraham's situation is described in terms of its fulfillment "Jesus dead" or "Jesus crucified."

4. Abraham's faith is described as unwavering, despite the texts of Genesis (which Paul knows quite well) in which Abraham is shown as wavering in his faith and seeking to have a descendant through Hagar (Genesis 16; cf. Gal. 4:22ff.). The six children he had from Keturah (Genesis 25) are not mentioned. Of course, once more, he speaks of the type "Abraham" in terms of its fulfillment, the one who "became obedient unto death, even death on a cross" (Phil. 2:8), Jesus, who can thus be viewed as having an unwavering faith and full trust in the promise.

5. Abraham's faith is "reckoned to him as righteousness." This is manifested in the Genesis story as the fulfillment of the promises in his experience, that is, in the birth of Isaac. Yet here it is presented as the overcoming of a "death" situation. In other words, it is presented in terms of Jesus' resurrection.

When we consider the elements concerning the kerygma found either in explicit statements or implicitly in the retelling of Abraham's story, we find that Jesus is given over (to death) (Rom. 4:25) and is dead (corresponding to number 3 of the above list); that he is raised from the dead (4:24–25; corresponding to number 5 of the above list); that he has an unwavering faith (corresponding to number 4 of the above list).

About the believers we can note that they are qualified as ungodly (uncircumcised) sinners whether they are circumcised or not (4:9a, 11b–12; corresponding to number 1 of the above list); they have as promises the type "Abraham" (their father; 4:11b–12), the verbal promise made to Abraham, and also the promise contained in the type "God raising Jesus from the dead" (corresponding to number 2 of the above list); they also have faith (4:16, 25; corresponding to number 4 of the above list) and the "reckoning to them as righteousness" (whatever this phrase may mean; the network of relations should determine this).

Table 3 shows the various interrelations we have noted. Since the units "Abraham," "Christ," and "believers" have almost the same elements, they are represented as superimposed upon each other, to show the interrelation of their respective elements. These elements are represented in five columns titled in an abbreviated form: sinners; promises and types; hopeless situations; faith; fulfillments. In the case of Abraham, we merely note those elements which can eventually be found in Genesis. The words within parentheses anticipate the forthcoming discussion. A number of blanks in Table 3 can easily be filled (as suggested within parentheses) by reference to other passages in Paul's letters. Christ is also a "sinner." He was "in the likeness of sinful flesh" (Rom. 8:3). God "made him to be sin" (2 Cor. 5:21). He has "become a curse for us—for it is written, 'Cursed be every one who hangs on a tree'" (Gal. 3:13). In the column "promises and types" we can enter "Scripture," since in Christ's experience scriptural promises and types are fulfilled.

This table should clarify the correspondence among components of the experiences of Abraham, Christ, and other believers (Paul and the Romans). Abraham is sinner due to his noncircumcision. As such he is a type of Jesus as sinner and cursed. Both Abraham and Jesus are types for the believers, who are sinners either as ungodly, uncircumcised (Gentiles) or as "ungodly," circumcised under the Law (Jews).

The old body of Abraham and Sarah's barrenness is a type of the cross as hopeless situation, and both are types of the believers' situation, which is like the old body of Abraham and cross-like.

Similarly, Isaac as fulfillment of the promise to Abraham is the type of Jesus' resurrection: the "reckoning as righteous" of Jesus in his resurrection. Thus "the reckoning as righteous" of Abraham (manifested in the birth of Isaac) and of Jesus (his resurrection) are types for the believers' "reckoning as righteous." Their "Isaac" and their "resurrection" in their present experience is the reckoning as righteousness of their faith, that is, their experience of being in the right relationship with God through

## TABLE 3: TYPOLOGICAL RELATIONS IN ROMANS 4

| | 1. Sinners | 2. Promises & Types | 3. Hopeless Situations | 4. Faith | 5. Fulfillments |
|---|---|---|---|---|---|
| Abraham | Ungodly Sinner Uncircumcised | a. Type: creation story<br><br>b. Promise of a descendant and of being the father of many nations | Old body of Abraham and Sarah's barrenness | Faith, trust in the promises | Isaac (Faith reckoned to him as righteousness) |
| Christ | (Sinner) (Becoming curse for us) | (Scripture) | Confrontation with death on the cross, crucified | Unwavering faith, obedient unto death | Raised from the dead |
| Believers | Sinners Whether ungodly, uncircumcised, or circumcised | a. Type Abraham<br>b. Type Jesus<br>c. Scriptural promise of the reckoning of faith as righteousness | | Faith | Faith reckoned to them as righteousness |

faith. This is expressed in Rom. 4:25, "[Jesus our Lord], who was put to death for our trespasses and raised for our justification." Through this strange formulation, Paul expresses that justification is not merely a promise—that is, the reconciliation through Christ's death of humankind to God which opens the possibility of God's relationship with any believer in their present—but also the fulfillment of this promise, the resurrection-like events (or manifestations of the resurrected Christ) in their present.

Similarly, the faith of Abraham, the faith of Jesus, and the faith of the believers are homologable (equivalent). Note that here faith is primarily defined as "trust in the promises." For Abraham it is trust in the promises contained in God's act of creation and trust in verbal promises. For Christ it is trust in the promises contained in Scripture including Abraham's story. For the believers it is trust in the promises contained in Christ's story and in Scripture. But this faith is not merely past-oriented. It is also trust that God will intervene in their respective present situations. It is having hope despite hopeless situations. Faith as discovery of interventions of God in their present is not expressed here. This is so because Paul speaks of justification in the theological sense of reconciliation as in Romans 5. Faith as trust (when oriented toward the past promises) and as hope (when oriented toward their future fulfillment) expresses the conditions of possibility of being in the right relationship with God through faith (a present-oriented faith) in the same way as reconciliation of humankind to God, because of Jesus' "death for our trespasses" (Rom. 4:25), is the condition of possibility for God's intervention in the present (the "fulfillments" discussed above).

We could say the same thing about the promises and types as elements of each unit. Yet they occupy a special status which the figure hides to a certain extent. What are the types and promises for the believers? As we have seen, Abraham—that is, the entire story of Abraham—is a type (promise) for the believers. But as we found elsewhere, the entire kerygma about Christ is also type or promise for the believers. Furthermore, by the very fact that Abraham and Christ are types for the believers, what was for them types and promises also becomes types and promises for the believers. For instance, the type "creation story" and the promise to Abraham become type and promise for the believers (cf. Rom. 4:23–24). Thus all the types and promises of the preceding stages of the type/fulfillment chain are at least potentially types and promises for a later stage. Here this process culminates in the believers' present experience. As we have seen in other texts, however, the believers' future experience and ultimately their experience at the Parousia are still later stages of this process, which will be the fulfillment of the believers' present experience which becomes a type (or promise) that itself subsumes all the preceding types and promises.

### JUSTIFICATION AS "MIRACLE"

In light of this relational network we can now ask, What does it mean for the believers to be justified through faith? Justification, being in the right relationship with God, is like Isaac born despite Abraham's old body and Sarah's barrenness. Justification is like the resurrected Christ liberated from death. Justification is therefore something which is the result of the overcoming of a hopeless situation. Nothing less than a miracle can bring about the believers' justification. The birth of Isaac was a miracle, the result of God's intervention. It involved the overcoming of Sarah's barrenness and of Abraham's old age. It is like God's original creating act when he created the world out of nothing, that is, by overcoming nothingness (Rom. 4:17). Similarly, Jesus' resurrection was a miracle which demanded that God overcome death.

But then what is the cross-like situation in which the believers find themselves and which needs to be overcome so that they might be in the right relationship with God? Clearly, here it is not persecutions (as in 1 Thessalonians, in which case the resurrection-like situation was joy). It is a much more serious situation (of which persecutions are manifestations), a situation which is like the nothingness that existed before the creation, like the old age which overpowers our human bodies, like death, the supreme evil power from which no human being can escape. This hopeless situation in which the believers find themselves and which necessitates God's intervention is characterized by what can be called sin and/or evil, but in Paul's view sin and evil cannot be overcome by the believers. This is in contrast to the Pharisaic view, according to which the "evil impulse" could be overcome by the believers. Sin and evil hold human beings in their grasp so tightly that they cannot escape. Sin and evil keep human beings under their power. They are curses. Only a radical intervention of God can deliver those who are caught under their power.

This is why God needs to intervene so decisively in the believers' experience. Once again, we emphasize that throughout this text Paul speaks of the believers' justification (right relationship with God) not as something which has been established in the past but as something which is to occur in the believers' experience (present and future). In fact, Paul has a very pessimistic view of the present situation. Without the direct intervention of God in it—an intervention promised by the reconciling death of Christ—the situation is hopeless. This will become clear in our study of the negative dimensions of Paul's system of convictions (see Chapter 7). At this point we need to complement our discussion of the positive dimensions of Paul's faith by examining how his convictional pattern leads him to conceive of Christ's resurrection and of his own conversion experience.

## The Resurrection and the
## Believers' Experience (1 Cor. 15:1–19)

We will first determine the goal of the argument in 1 Cor. 15:1–19. For this we need to identify the parts of the text which belong to the dialogic level. Because of its importance, we shall also study the set of convictions which undergirds the dialogic level.

### THE BELIEVERS' EXPERIENCE AS THE BASIS
### FOR THEIR HOPE

Paul reminds the Corinthians of his preaching to them (1 Cor. 15:1a) through which they are saved if they hold it fast, unless they "believed in vain" (15:2). These few phrases of the dialogic level introduce a description of this preaching and its content (15:1b, 3–11, which includes the tradition that Paul received, vv. 3–7), which belongs to the warranting level. The other elements of the dialogic level show why Paul needed to remind his readers of his preaching. We reproduce in its entirety the argument of the dialogic level in 1 Cor. 15:12–19 as it stands after leaving out the elements of the warranting level which this passage contains. The warranting elements we are omitting are references to the content of Paul's message (15:3–11), whether they are positive references ("Christ has been raised") or negative references ("Christ has not been raised"), and to the fact that he proclaimed it. By leaving out these elements of the warranting level, we will be in a position to understand better Paul's argument in 1 Corinthians 15. (The last two verses, vv. 18–19, belong to the dialogic level because they describe the present situation of the dead and of the Corinthian believers.)

> Now . . . how can some of you say that there is no resurrection of the dead? But if there is not resurrection of the dead . . . then our preaching is in vain and your faith is in vain. We are even found to be misrepresenting God . . . if it is true that the dead are not raised. For if the dead are not raised, . . . your faith is futile and you are still in your sins. Then those also who have fallen asleep in Christ have perished. If for this life only we have hoped in Christ, we are of all men most to be pitied.

When we focus our attention solely on these elements of the dialogic level, Paul's argument becomes clear. He argues that if there is no resurrection (and no hope for those who died) then his preaching is "in vain" and it is misrepresenting God (or being a "false witness" of God), their faith is "in vain" or "futile," and they are still in their sins. In other words, in such a circumstance his preaching is "null and void," and does not have the effect it is supposed to have. It also appears that Paul presupposes that his preaching has a twofold effect. A first effect is a fruitful (and not vain) faith for the believers, a faith which establishes them in the right relationship with God. But their faith could not do so if Paul is a false witness of God. A second effect of Paul's preaching is that the believers are no longer in their sins.

Once more this argument does not follow an argumentative logic, but rather the convictional logic of Paul's system of convictions.[19] Note that the resurrection of the dead is directly related to what happens in the believers' experience. Having faith (and thus being in the right relationship with God) and "being no longer in one's sins" are, for Paul, preliminary manifestations or promises of what will be, the resurrection of the dead. These manifestations are the basis for the believers' hope (1 Cor. 15:19), as we also saw in our reading of 1 Thessalonians.

Since resurrection will deliver one from the power of death (the last enemy, or power to be destroyed, in 1 Cor. 15:24–26), there are resurrection-like deliverances in the believers' present experience which prefigure it. Faith, as a gift of God's Spirit (12:9), involves, according to Galatians, the deliverance from the curse of Torah and from the slavery to the elemental spirits of the cosmos. Yet this is not what is being said here. Rather, our text emphasizes that the believers' experience involves their deliverance from sins. Despite the plural form (sins), which is used because of the use of the traditional formula "Christ died for our sins" (15:3), it is clear that the phrase "you are still in your sins" should be understood as meaning "you have not been delivered from the power of sin."

In brief, Paul argues against some of the Corinthians: there will be a resurrection of the dead, and the proof of it can be found in your own experience, that is, in your faith and in the fact that you are delivered from the power of sin. Denying the resurrection of the dead would be denying your own experience. Thus once more we find that the believers' system of convictions is based upon what happens in their experience. Therefore, on the dialogic level we find expressed the relationship between the believers' experience (as promise) and its fulfillment in the future (at the Parousia).

### THE CROSS AND JESUS' RESURRECTION APPEARANCES AS INTERPRETED WITH SCRIPTURE

As another proof for the argument, the warranting level introduces the relationship of the believers' experience with the kerygma about Christ and with Paul's experience. According to Paul's convictional pattern, their experience is valid insofar as it is "conformed" to (fulfillment of the types) Paul's experience and Christ's resurrection, which also warrant (or should warrant) their hope for the resurrection of the dead.

The main part of the warranting level is the famous passage 1 Cor. 15:3–11 (15:12–19, consists of short statements referring positively or negatively to what is said earlier). First we should note that this proclamation of Christ's resurrection as witnessed by various disciples and Paul (which warrants the validity of the believers' experience and their hope) is itself warranted through references to Scripture. Thus in 15:3–4 we read:

> Christ died     for our sins          according to the Scriptures.
> He was buried, raised on the third day according to the Scriptures.

We positioned these two phrases to show their parallelism. In both cases we find three elements:

1. *An event*, that is, a historical happening that human beings can observe. In the first case the nature of this event is clear; it is Jesus' death on the cross (note that we did not write "Christ," since this in-

volves an interpretation of who Jesus is). In the second case "he was buried" is clearly an event. There is certainly more to this event than that, but there is no mention of anybody seeing Jesus in the process of being raised, and as we shall see, "on the third day" is not merely a date. Since the following verses emphasize that "he was seen" or "appeared" to various people, we can say that for Paul this event also includes the disciples' and apostles' experience of seeing Jesus after his death. Whatever the nature of this experience (we shall come back to it), it is historical fact that there were people who claimed to have seen Jesus after his death (human beings could observe that these people claimed to have had such visions). Therefore the beginning of the second phrase also refers to an event: Jesus' burial and his appearances after his death to certain people.

2. *Scripture.* In both cases we find the phrase "according to the scriptures."

3. *An interpretative element.* In the first case the death of Jesus, the event, is interpreted to mean that it was "Christ's death for our sins." In the second case, the event, burial and appearances, is interpreted to mean that "he was raised on the third day."

The process manifested by the interrelation of these three elements is worth noting, for it shows how Paul's system of convictions and its convictional pattern function. In this passage the believers who, according to Paul, hold such a system of convictions are Cephas (Peter), the "twelve," "five hundred brethren," James, "all the apostles," and Paul himself, who equates his own experience (at the time of his conversion) with that of the other apostles. Two things (events) happened in the apostles' experience: Jesus died on the cross and, after his burial, he appeared to them. Even when they are taken together, these two events can have many different meanings.

The death of Jesus on the cross could have been for the disciples a puzzle or a nonsensical occurrence. Why did he die? This could have been taken to show that his ministry was a failure, that his preaching about the kingdom was wrong. But if this event of the believers' experience is viewed "through" Scripture (as one looks through glasses), that is, if this event is viewed in terms of comparable scriptural events and in terms of scriptural texts speaking about similar situations, this event suddenly makes sense. Thus when one looks at the cross through the text of Isaiah 53, Jesus' death, far from being a failure, can be understood as a death "for our sins." This passage of Isaiah describes the suffering of "the servant of Yahweh":

> He was despised and rejected by men; a man of sorrows, and acquainted with grief; and as one from whom men hide their faces he was despised, and we esteemed him not. Surely he has borne our griefs and carried our sorrows; yet we esteemed him stricken, smitten by God, and afflicted. But he was wounded for our transgressions, he was bruised for our iniquities; upon him was the chastisement that made us whole, and with his stripes we are healed. (Isa. 53:3–5)

So the believers can conclude that Jesus' death on the cross is the fulfillment of this prophecy, and then Jesus' death is no longer meaningless or a failure. It makes sense. He is the righteous servant of God who suffers for the sins of the people. Jesus died for our sins. In this event the early believers can discover God at work in their present. Looking at the cross and at the appearances in terms of other texts of Scripture (from Acts 2 and 3 we know that the early church used such texts as Ps. 16:8–11, Psalm 18, and Ps. 110:1 for interpreting Jesus' death and resurrection),[20] the believer can see the crucified and raised Jesus as the Christ, the Messiah, the Lord.

In summary, without Scripture the cross is meaningless or a nonsensical occurrence. But through faith—which involves trust that Scripture is indeed promises of God, and confidence that God is at work in the present fulfilling his promises—the cross makes sense for the believers. Conversely, without the cross (and more generally, without events of the believers' experience which can be viewed as fulfillments of Scripture), Scripture itself is meaningless, it is an absolute and dead letter (Rom. 7:6) and indeed a "deadly letter" (cf. 2 Cor. 3:6), that is, Torah as curse.

The same is true for the second phrase of the statement. In and of themselves the appearances of Jesus to the disciples can receive many interpretations: they are illusions of people traumatized by the death of their leader, they are the apparitions of a ghost, and so on. But when this experience is viewed through Scripture, as fulfillment of Scripture, these appearances can be understood as meaning that Jesus is Christ who was "raised on the third day."

Once again our text does not specify the passages of Scripture which allowed the believers to reach this conclusion, but we can note that the "third day" was a symbolic date often found in Scripture. On the third day Abraham "sacrificed" Isaac, that is, on that day Abraham is delivered by an intervention of God from the agony of having to sacrifice his son (Gen. 22:4). Joseph delivers his brothers from prison "on the third day" by saying to them, "Do this and you will live" (Gen. 42:18). The spies sent to Jericho by Joshua are to remain hidden for three days, and then they will be able to escape without harm (Josh. 2:16). It is also on the third day that God appears on Mount Sinai and gives his Law to Moses (Exod. 19:15–16). We could also refer to Jon. 2:1 and to Ezra 8:32. Yet it is most probably the text of Hos. 6:1–2 which was used here:

> Come, let us return to the Lord; for he has torn, that he may heal us; he has stricken, and he will bind us up. After two days he will revive us; on the third day he will raise us up, that we may live before him.

The third day is therefore primarily the day of deliverance; indeed, for Judaism already it is the time of the eschatological deliverance and thus of the resurrection.[21] Whatever the exact date of the "resurrection," in light of Scripture these appearances of Jesus after his death and burial mean that he was raised from the dead and that this is the eschatological deliverance, the beginning of the general resurrection of the dead (of which Christ is the "first fruits"; 1 Cor. 15:20). His resurrection marks the beginning of the eschatological time of deliverance.

Here we need not discuss the various scriptural texts alluded to in these verses.[22] It is enough to note the way in which the convictional pattern functions. The believers (here the disciples), through faith, know that somewhere in their experience (i.e., in the events which surround them) God's promises are being fulfilled. Thus their task is to scrutinize their experience in order to identify, with the help of Scripture, these events in which God was at work. But conversely, they also need to scrutinize Scripture so as to be aware of the "type" of events in which they can expect to discover God at work in their present.

This twofold attitude was already that of the Apocalyptists, who were constantly on the lookout for the fulfillments of the scriptural promises and types in their time.[23] On this point the only difference between Paul's convictional pattern and that of the Apocalyptists concerns what is viewed by each of them as Scripture. Indeed, for Paul, Scripture is not merely the Old Testament Scripture, but also the kerygma about Christ, and the "story" of earlier believers' experiences.

## AN EVER-EXPANDING SCRIPTURE

If we can say that for Paul the message about Christ is also viewed as Scripture, it is not only because of its place in the convictional pattern we found in other letters, but also because of the way Paul introduces it here. "For I delivered to you as of first importance what I also received . . ." (1 Cor. 15:3). This phrase, which could be translated "I handed down to you . . . what I received," duplicates that of the Rabbis in the famous Jewish tradition about the transmission of Torah which reads: "Moses received Torah from Sinai and handed it down to Joshua, and Joshua to the Judges, [etc.]" (*Mishnah*, Tractate of the Fathers, 1:1). In other words, Paul presents the kerygma about Christ's death and resurrection and also the witness of the apostles and other disciples as "Scripture." The proclamation of the early church is indeed an "oral Scripture." Even though it is not written, it has the same function as the written Scripture.[24] The written Scripture, the Old Testament, is not for Paul a closed Scripture. It is open-ended. To it should be added not only the kerygma, but also the stories of the believers' experience which become Scripture for the following generation of believers.

This is no longer surprising for us. As we saw, Jesus' experience as well as the experience of earlier believers are "types" and promises that later believers can discover fulfilled in their own experience in the same way as they discover scriptural types and promises fulfilled in their experience. But this passage helps us better understand in which sense these experiences are "types" or "Scriptures," for it is not the raw material of Jesus' experience which is Scripture but rather "Jesus' experience as interpreted by means of the Old Testament Scripture." In other words the type "the Scripture about Jesus" is made out of those events of Jesus' experience which are viewed as fulfillments of the Old Testament Scripture and thus as manifestations of God in it. It is Christ (Jesus as anointed by God), crucified and raised from the dead (by God), who is the type for the believers, not Jesus of Nazareth. On the basis of the other texts we have studied we can similarly say that the experience of the apostles is type (Scripture) only insofar as it can be viewed as fulfillment of the types (and promises) found in Christ and in the Old Testament Scripture. Thus only those elements of the apostles' experience which can be viewed as fulfillments of previous promises are themselves "types." The same is true for Paul as a type, and then for the believers as types for later believers. Conversely, a type is defined by its fulfillment. In other words, only those elements of Paul's experience which are fulfilled in the believers' experience are types. Paul might recognize God at work in other parts of his experience, but these are not "types" as long as they are not fulfilled in the experience of other believers. Of course the same is true about Christ as type.

These observations allow us to understand several characteristics of Paul's letters. First, we can understand why Paul is not interested in giving his readers any detail about Jesus' life or even a detailed description of his crucifixion or his resurrection. It is enough to proclaim these events as interpreted through scriptural texts that they fulfill. A historical account, that is, a detailed factual account, would be useless for his purpose and might even hide the essential—God's typical work in Christ's experience. Furthermore, for him, the only (or almost only) parts of Christ's experience that are truly prefigurations of the believers' experiences are his death and his resurrection (and exaltation). And thus he does not say more about Christ.

Similarly, Paul speaks of his own experience. We understand now that he does so because in this way he proposes his experience as "Scripture," as type (or model), for the believers. With the help of this story of his experience the believers can discover where God is at work in their own experience. Consequently, Paul describes his own experience only insofar as it can be a "type" for the believers, so he does not speak of his "private" spiritual experience. When he does so to defend himself against opponents, as in 2 Cor. 12:1–10, he emphasizes that when he is speaking of his personal visions and revelations of the Lord, of his ecstatic experience (being "caught up to the third heaven"), there is nothing to be gained (2 Cor. 12:1). The only things he wants to speak about are "weaknesses, insults, hardships, persecutions, and calamities" (2 Cor. 12:10), for in his weaknesses the power of Christ is manifested (2 Cor. 12:9). It is through this public aspect of his experience that he is a "type" for the believers, because he can show that God is at work in it, that these events of his life are fulfillments of the promises contained in Christ (as type). Similarly, he emphasizes the details of his own experience only insofar as they can be seen as fulfillments of the promises contained in Scripture and in Christ. As a result, we are often frustrated in our hope of grasping the exact nature of Paul's experience. For instance, in 1 Cor. 15:8–10 Paul speaks of his conversion experience, which involved seeing the resurrected Christ. But what kind of experience is this? Was it an objective vision (seeing Christ as I see this friend who entered my office and that somebody else could also see)? Or was it a subjective vision, a dream-like spiritual vision (whom he alone could see)? What were the circumstances? This passage does not allow us to answer any of these questions, since the verb he uses in 15:8 is ambiguous. And the two other passages in which he speaks of this experience (1 Cor. 9:1 and Gal. 1:16) are just as ambiguous.

We are surprised. Should not Paul be very much concerned to give a detailed description of his experience in an argument which revolves around the question of whether or not Christ has been raised? Would not this be a decisive proof of Christ's resurrection? Throughout 1 Cor. 15:12–19 we expect a sentence such as "But Christ has been raised and the proof is that I have seen him and thus there is a resurrection of the dead." In such a case he would have given a detailed account of his encounter with Christ. Yet Paul does not do that. For him this is *not* the proof of Christ's resurrection, nor of the resurrection of the dead. The proof that Christ is risen is to be found in the Corinthians' experience. If their faith is not in vain and if they are indeed freed from (the power of) sin, then Christ is indeed risen. Their experience is the fulfillment of the type "Christ risen" and thus the type is true. Christ is really risen. Indeed, one can say that in their experience the resurrected Christ is at work. Similarly, Paul's experience (and the other apostles' experience) of "seeing" the risen Christ is true only if the promise (type) they contain is fulfilled in new believers' experience. In the same way, Scripture (i.e., the Old Testament) is promise (and not a complete and final revelation). Thus it is "holy and just and good," it is spiritual, it is word of God, it is true, only insofar as it is fulfilled.

But what exactly is this fulfillment in the believers' experience? Why does Paul limit the type "Christ" almost entirely to his death and resurrection? What does it mean for the believers to have a faith which is not in vain? What does it mean to be "no longer in their sins"? We have suggested that it means to be freed from the power of sin. But what is this power? How is it manifested? How is it related to the "rules, authority, and powers" that Christ will destroy (or is destroying? cf. 1 Cor. 15:24)? How is it related to the power of death (cf. 15:26 and 56)? Or, more positively, after all, what kind of interventions of God can the believers (and indeed anybody) expect in their experience, since God has reconciled the world to himself? Such are the questions we now need to address through our reading of Romans.


### SUGGESTIONS FOR FURTHER READINGS

In this chapter we have studied the interrelations of Paul's system of convictions with, on the one hand, sacred history, reconciliation, and justification and, on the other hand, Scripture. Many studies have been devoted to these themes. As a starting point, our interpretation can be complemented by, and compared and contrasted with, the following selected works.

For various interpretations of Paul's views of sacred history, reconciliation, and justification, see R. Bultmann, *Theology of the New Testament*; O. Cullmann, *Salvation in History*; E. Käsemann, *Perspectives on Paul*; J. Munck, *Paul and the Salvation of Mankind*; K. Stendahl, "The Apostle Paul and the Introspective Conscience of the West," in *Paul Among Jews and Gentiles*, pp. 78–96.

On Paul's use of Scripture, see W. D. Davies, *Paul and Rabbinic Judaism*; E. E. Ellis, *Paul's Use of the Old Testament*; B. Lindars, *New Testament Apologetic*; D. Moody-Smith, "The Use of the Old Testament in the New," in *The Use of the Old Testament in the New*, pp. 3–65.

# 7

## Romans: The Gospel as Power of God for Salvation

### An Overall Presentation
### of Paul's Faith

THROUGH A SERIES of readings of Galatians, 1 Thessalonians, Philemon, Philippians, and other texts, we have elucidated many elements of Paul's system of convictions and several characteristics of his convictional pattern. We can now gather together these partial results in order to obtain an overall picture of the convictional pattern which characterizes Paul's faith as system of convictions. This is another stage of the structural approach, which involves formulating, on the basis of partial results, a hypothesis concerning the overall organization of a system.[1] In our case, we shall formulate a hypothesis concerning the organization of Paul's system of convictions. Keeping in mind the rules which govern the organization of any system of convictions—the oppositions by pairs, the correlations and homologations of these pairs—we can now show how these various partial results are interrelated. This tentative overall picture of Paul's system of convictions will also point out that we still do not know anything about important aspects of it. In fact, we still do not understand the meaning of such central statements as "[the gospel] is the power of God for salvation to every one who has faith" (Rom. 1:16). After formulating this overall hypothesis, we will be in a position to proceed to a new kind of structural reading which begins with this tentative overall picture. In other words, our systematic presentation of the results reached so far will allow us to make proposals about elements of Paul's system of convictions which we have not yet encountered in our readings of his letters. Of course, we will need to verify these proposals, and we will do so by considering how Paul deals with these elements in the letter which is the most systematic presentation of his faith: the letter to the Romans.

232

## THE CHARACTERISTICS OF PAUL'S FAITH

When looking for ways to express what is most characteristic of Paul's faith, the three qualifications "charismatic," "eschatological," and "typological" seem most appropriate.

### A Radical Charismatic Faith

By the term "charismatic" I want to say that, according to this system of convictions, the revelation (the fundamental convictions) which establishes the believers' true identity as "chosen by God" and as "in the right relationship with God" is discovered primarily in the present experience of the believers and is not found in a tradition (it is not a past revelation that one appropriates). I also want to articulate that this revelation is discovered directly by the believers themselves and not through the intermediary of an institution (e.g., the institution of the Temple as the place where the believers can be in the presence of God through the intermediary of priests). In other words, the believers' faith is established through and because of God's interventions in their experience: God's gifts (*charismata*), grace (*charis*), and revelation. Yet, we need to remember that what we call "the believer's experience" is not limited to the private experience of an individual. It includes all that is related to this believer in the daily life, and thus also other people who are parts of his or her life experience.

This charismatic faith is of a very peculiar kind. Usually, charismatic believers view themselves and are viewed by their followers as having a religious authority over others.[2] Indeed, Paul has authority over the believers, and so he does not hesitate to designate himself as their "father" (cf., e.g., 1 Thess. 2:11; Philem. 10), a term which presupposes an authority comparable to God the Father, and claims for himself the title "apostle," a term which presupposes an authority comparable to the Lord (see Chapter 4). He mentions this authority to insure that the churches he founded will listen to his exhortations. At the same time, he constantly refuses to *use* this authority over his followers. Yes, he would have the authority to give them orders: he is an apostle (1 Thess. 2:6), he is an ambassador (of Christ) and a prisoner for Christ (Philem. 9), he is not inferior to "these superlative apostles" who, because of their spiritual gifts, are viewed by the Corinthians as having authority (2 Cor. 12:11). He can boast of such spiritual experiences, but as far as he is concerned, he is making a fool out of himself when he does so. No, he did not demand that the Thessalonians recognize his authority as apostle (and give him "glory"; 1 Thess. 2:6); he is rather a baby among them. Yes, he is their father, but not as one who demands something from his children but as the one who gives of himself (a nursing mother) to his children. Or, as he puts it in 2 Cor. 12:14, "children ought not to lay up [reserve their belongings] for their parents, but parents for their children." No, he does not use the title "ambassador of Christ" or "prisoner for Christ" to command Philemon. No, he does not want to boast of his personal spiritual experience to impose his authority upon the Corinthians. Rather, he boasts of his weaknesses because, in them, the power of Christ is manifested (2 Cor. 12:9–10).[3]

Thus while Paul does not see himself as a charismatic leader who, because of special gifts from God, can use his authority over his followers, he is not denying the charismatic character of his faith. In other words, he is not denying that the revelations he has discovered in his own experience are central for him. Indeed, they are the very basis of his faith, as he emphatically expresses in Gal. 1:11–17. His faith, which he aims at transmitting to others, is so fundamentally charismatic that he cannot conceive that the believers, in the churches he founded, could merely be followers who would be dependent upon his own charismatic faith (upon the revelations he received). In such a case the believers would have a different kind of faith as compared with the faith Paul has.

Paul's faith is a radical charismatic faith. Yes, Paul is a charismatic. He was directly chosen by God, from whom he received a revelation and the vocation of Apostle to the Gentiles without the intermediary of any human being and without recourse to a tradition (Gal. 1:11–17). But his preaching to the Gentiles is aimed not at transmitting to them a fixed system of convictions (the one which was revealed to him) but at helping them to have the same faith as he has, a faith through which they will themselves discover God at work in their present experiences and receive direct revelations from God. His aim is to allow them to discover the power of Christ, that is, Christ-like manifestations of God in their own experience. These direct revelations to the believers "supersede" those of Paul, not in quality (indeed, they are the same type) but in newness. These revelations to the believers concern what God is doing in new situations.

An analogy might be helpful here: mountain climbing. A charismatic leader who demands that the revelations which he or she has received be viewed as authoritative by his or her followers can be compared to the leader of an expedition who has reached the top of a mountain peak by using only his own strength and skills (which could be comparable to the charismatic leader's "superior insight, strength, goodness").[4] From the top, he guides the other members of the expedition in their climb by showing them where he has set pitons in the rock and helping them to climb with the rope that he has secured for them. In such a case, the followers do not have the same faith as the leader. They do not have a charismatic faith. By contrast, Paul can be compared to a member of a group of free climbers, that is, climbers who each climb as the leader of the expedition did in the preceding example. On this particular trip he climbs first, up to a ledge. Other members of the group, seeing that he was able to do it, feel challenged. They are confident that they can do as well as this first climber, who actually encourages them by suggesting how he overcame difficulties similar to those they are encountering, and he continues to do so even when they have passed him and climb higher than the ledge where he is. And all the while he applauds their accomplishments.

This analogy, despite its limitations, helps us understand how Paul can both claim that he has authority over the believers in the churches which he founded and at the same time see himself as having the same status as they. Because he preceded them in the faith, he is indeed a type for them, and thus he is in a position to exhort and to encourage the younger believers. Looking at him and at his experience in which through faith he discovered God at work, they can in turn make sense, through faith, of their own experience and discover in it God at work and thus revelations from God to them. Indeed, insofar as Paul is part of their experience, he might be (and often was) God's manifestation among them. Because his experience is a type for the new believers (and eventually a manifestation of God for them), he cannot tolerate his experience being distorted or belittled, because this would mean distorting and belittling the Gospel itself. But Paul is not the only type. Anyone who precedes the believers in the faith has a similar role and authority over them. Such is the case of Paul's companions, of the churches in Judea, of the other apostles and disciples mentioned in 1 Cor. 15:5–7, as well as of those Paul calls the "first fruits," the first converts in a region (cf. Rom. 16:5; 1 Cor. 16:15), who can also be God's manifestation in the experience of later converts. While this chronological priority gives a certain authority to some believers over others, it does not give them a different status. Everybody who shares this faith with Paul is a brother, a sister, a co-worker, or a co-soldier. Through faith, they are in the same relation to God. They discover God at work in their present, as does Paul. In this way, they receive revelations (elections, vocations) which supersede those received by Paul.

From the perspective of Paul's radical charismatic faith, the new believers themselves can be perceived only as having such a charismatic faith characterized by the same specific convictional pattern. Consequently, Paul cannot and should not impose a specific set of convictions upon other believers. Neither should the believers do this among themselves. They should look at others as better than themselves, because in others they can discover Christ-like manifestations (Phil. 2:3) as Paul can also see God's interventions in others (as he expresses in his thanksgivings to God about various believers). Since all have the same status, they should comfort one another, encourage one another, exhort one another (cf., e.g., 1 Thess. 4:18; 5:11, 14).

Paul expresses this part of his system of convictions again and again and in various ways. For the Corinthians, who are very much concerned about spiritual experiences (ecstatic experiences, prophecies, speaking in tongues), he expresses it in terms of the gifts of the Spirit. Against those who claim that they are superior to other believers because they have greater spiritual gifts (and thus should be viewed as charismatic leaders), he affirms that "all [the believers] were made to drink of one Spirit" (1 Cor. 12:13). He also writes, "Now there are varieties of gifts, but the same Spirit; and there are varieties of service, but the same Lord; and there are varieties of working, but it is the same God who inspires them all in every one" (1 Cor. 12:4–6). All the believers share in this charismatic faith through which they discover interventions of God in their present and receive revelations and gifts of his Spirit. There are different offices and functions in the community, but these offices and functions do not establish certain believers above others in the faith. All of them are fulfillments of the type Christ, and therefore all of them are Christ-like, and all together form the body of Christ (1 Cor. 12:27).

## An Eschatological Faith

Paul can hold this radical charismatic faith which demands that one see others as equal to oneself, because this faith is also *eschatological*.

Paul's faith can be called "eschatological" for reasons which differ according to the system of convictions and the theological explanations.

*According to Paul's system of convictions*—a meta-system of convictions—the only absolute and permanent convictions are the ones which will be established for the believers *at the end of time* (at the *eschaton*, at the Parousia). As Paul expresses it, "Now we see in a mirror dimly, but then face to face. Now I know in part; then I shall understand fully, even as I have been fully understood" (1 Cor. 13:12). Since the eschatological revelation alone is absolute, all other revelations are relative, partial, incomplete; they are "seeing dimly in a mirror." This is also true for the revelations that Paul or any other believer have received through their charismatic faith. But then, if true believers do not view their system of convictions as absolute, it also means that they can perceive other believers' systems of convictions as being, at least potentially, as valid as, and possibly better than, their own system of convictions (yet it does not mean that all the systems of convictions are valid). Thus, because the absolute, complete, and final revelation is expected only in the eschatological future, each believer (and not merely a leader) can have a charismatic faith, that is, each believer can be expected to discover new revelations in his or her experience.

Paul's charismatic faith also is properly designated "eschatological" because the manifestations of God discovered by the believers are prefigurations of the manifestations of God at the end of time (the Parousia). In other words, this charismatic faith is characterized by hope, eschatological hope. As Paul expresses it in 1 Cor. 15:12–19, "faith is null and void" (au.trans.) if it does not allow for such a hope. This is one of the criteria which permit Paul to distinguish between true and false charismatic faiths. The manifestations of God, which are discovered as revelatory by the believers, also have to be promises of the eschatological salvation, otherwise they cannot be true revelations. "If for this life only we have hoped in Christ, we are of all men most to be pitied" (1 Cor. 15:19).

In summary, Paul's faith, as system of convictions, can be designated as charismatic and eschatological because it involves the convictions that the believers discover in their present:

1. Interventions of God which are revelations of their revealed identity as chosen by God and as "in the right relationship with God," and which also establish for them a specific vocation defined, for

instance, by the "gifts" received by the believers (cf. 1 Corinthians 12).

2. Revelations which are promises or types for future manifestations of God and especially for those at the Parousia.

Such a system of convictions is thus intrinsically dynamic, and involves a meta-system of convictions as its basis or framework. It is not a complete and final revelation. It is promise, and as such it points beyond itself toward other revelations, the eschatological revelations at the Parousia.

*From the perspective of theological explanations*, this faith can also be designated as eschatological, but for different reasons. To begin with, the conviction that God intervenes in the present experience of the believers is explained by Paul in terms of the unfolding of sacred history. The believers live in the last period of history, in the beginning of the eschatological period. This period has been inaugurated by Christ's death and resurrection through which the world was reconciled to God, and God can (and does) intervene in the affairs of humankind in the present, as the believers discover through faith. In this theological perspective, Paul's faith is eschatological because the present already belongs to the eschatological period which will culminate in the Parousia. Similarly, the conviction that the present interventions of God are promises, prefigurations, or even preliminary manifestations of what will be fully manifested at the Parousia is explained theologically by emphasizing the imminence of the Parousia. But as with any theological explanation, this one can be changed to take into account concrete or cultural situations. Thus, while in 1 Thessalonians Paul expected the Parousia to occur in such a near future that most of his readers and himself would be alive at that time, later (e.g., when writing 1 and 2 Corinthians), he no longer has such an expectation, although he still conceives of the Parousia as occurring in a relatively near future.

## A Typological Faith

This eschatological charismatic faith also needs to be designated as typological. The present interventions of God and the revelations they involve are true and valid only insofar as they can be viewed as fulfillments of the types which are the experiences of former believers, of Christ and of biblical personages, and/or as fulfillments of former promises (the verbal promises and prophecies contained in Scripture, especially). The believers' faith is "null and void" if it does not bring them to see their experience as fulfillment of Christ's death and resurrection (cf. 1 Cor. 15:12–19).

In fact, for Paul, these types are the very conditions for the possibility of charismatic faith. In order to understand this statement, we must first note that Paul has the conviction that God is at work in the present experience of *every* human being. This conviction is repeatedly expressed in (or, more exactly, presupposed by) his theological statements about reconciliation and justification (in the sense of reconciliation). "In Christ God was reconciling *the world* to himself" (2 Cor. 5:19). "One man's act of righteousness leads to acquittal and life *for all men*" (Rom. 5:18). This is true even of the pagans who rejected God: "For what can be known about God is plain to them, because God has shown it to them. . . . Although they knew God they did not honor him as God or give thanks to him" (Rom. 1:19, 21). In the pagans' experience, there are revelations/manifestations of God. And, of course, this is also true of the Jews. The painful fact that they do not have faith (the charismatic faith) should not be interpreted to mean that God has rejected them. "By no means!" (Rom. 11:1). When reconciling the world to himself, God also reconciled the Jews to himself. But the Jews (or most of them) "were hardened." In sum, Paul has the conviction that God is at work and reveals himself in the experience of all human beings, including that of the Jews.

But the manifestations of God in the present of the believers are not in and of themselves sufficient to bring about faith. These manifestations of God are not such that they impose themselves upon all human beings so that the only possible response would be the amazed recognition that God is at work in their present. In other words, God's manifestations are "ambiguous" (we shall see below why this is so). The cross is indeed God's intervention (cf. 1 Cor. 15:3–4, pp. 224–26). It is an event which belongs to the experience of many people in Jerusalem at that time. But most of them did not see in this event God's intervention. The cross can be discovered as God's intervention in human affairs only with the help of Scripture, that is, with the help of the types and promises contained in Scripture and fulfilled by it. Similarly, without the help of Scripture, the appearances of Jesus after his death cannot be recognized as appearances of the resurrected Christ and thus as resulting from an intervention of God. We can add that the believers cannot recognize God's work in their experience without the help of these other types, which are expressed in the proclamation about Christ and the witness of Paul and other believers who precede them. The charismatic faith, which recognizes new revelatory manifestations of God, cannot exist as long as Scripture, the kerygma about Christ, and the testimony of earlier believers are not recognized as trustworthy types. Trust in the promises contained in former manifestations of God (the types) is a necessary part of Paul's charismatic faith.

Yet we can be more specific and say that it is *trust or belief in Christ as type which is a necessary part of Paul's charismatic faith*, for it is obvious that, among these types, Christ's death and resurrection have a preeminent place. In fact, it can be said that, for Paul, *Christ is the normative type*. Scripture, because of its association with the "dispensation of condemnation," is by itself unclear, tarnished, without splendor by comparison with "the splendor that surpasses it" (cf. 2 Cor. 3:7–11). Scripture and its types are veiled "to this day" for the Jews, but through Christ, and only through him, the veil which covers Scripture is taken away (cf. 2 Cor. 3:14–16). When this veil which hides the glory of God is removed, the believers can "behold the glory of the Lord," that is, perceive directly the manifestation of the Lord. Thus they "are being changed into his likeness," they become Christ-like (cf. 2 Cor. 3:18). We can therefore say that the types of Scripture become available for the believers as types only because they are first fulfilled in Christ. Similarly, Paul and earlier believers are types for later believers only insofar as they themselves are Christ-like, in his likeness. The validity of all the other types depends therefore upon their conformity with Christ, the normative type.

Thus, from this perspective, any manifestation of God is Christ-like. Consequently, the theological (sacred historical) expression of this conviction can say that before "taking the form of a servant" he was "in the form of God" (Phil. 2:6–7). Furthermore, what is said in Scripture about the Lord God can be viewed as applying to the Lord Christ. In other words, God's interventions in the biblical time are themselves Christ-like. Similarly, God's intervention or the manifestation of God's Spirit after Christ's resurrection can also be said to be intervention of the resurrected Christ by following the logic of the sacred historical development. Since Christ is resurrected and brought back to life as the Lord, he intervenes in the believers' experience and will intervene at the end of time. These observations help us understand why Paul so easily attributes the same role to God, to his Spirit, and to Christ the Lord. This is the same phenomenon we have discussed several times.

On the basis of Paul's system of convictions, it is possible to speak of any stage of the typological chain in terms of the others, to speak of a Christian of Jewish origin as if he were a Christian of pagan origin, of Abraham as if he were Christ, and so on. Thus, even though Christ plays a predominant and indeed a normative role in the typology, he remains a type, a promise pointing toward new interventions and revelations of God which are Christ-like. And thus the charismatic faith which discovers these new revelations needs to involve trust in the promises contained in Christ, in other words, belief or faith in Christ, in the sense of trust in the promises contained in Christ as type.

In his discussion of the situation of the Jews, Paul makes clear the conditions of the possibility of faith. We can now understand this statement in Romans:

> But how are men to call upon him in whom they have not believed? And how are they to believe in him of whom they have never heard? And how are they to hear without a preacher? . . . So faith comes from what is heard, and what is heard comes by the preaching of Christ. (Rom. 10:14, 17)

Faith, the charismatic faith which allows the believers to call upon the Lord, cannot exist as long as they do not believe in Christ, that is, trust that in him, and especially in his death and resurrection, God was at work and that these are promises that God fulfills in their experience. Without this trust in God's promises in Christ, the believers cannot discover what God (or Christ or the Spirit) is doing in the present. But in order to believe in Christ as type they must hear about Christ, and thus Christ must be preached.

Yet as we saw in several texts, Paul considers that the proclamation of his own experience and of that of other believers is just as necessary and effective for establishing the faith of his readers (cf. our discussion of 1 Thessalonians, Philippians, 1 Corinthians 15, and also that of Galatians). What then is the uniqueness of the type Jesus Christ? Before addressing this question we need to consider other aspects of Paul's system of convictions.

## Other Aspects of Paul's System of Convictions

Our description of Paul's faith is still incomplete. One essential dimension is missing. As we have emphasized in Chapters 1 and 2, a system of convictions also involves a series of "negative convictions." So far our discussion has focused upon positive convictions: upon revelations, upon interventions of God, upon salvation, upon freedom, and so on. But in a system of convictions all these have negative counterparts: the absence of revelations (the hardening of the heart, the spirit of stupor, the not-seeing, the not-hearing: cf. Rom. 11:7–8); the interventions of evil powers, the wrath of God and destruction; slavery; and so on. We cannot pretend to understand Paul's system of convictions as long as we have not elucidated this "dark side" of his faith. For instance, we do not understand why it is still necessary for God to intervene in the present of the believers, after the reconciliation operated once and for all by Christ's death and resurrection. Consequently, we do not truly understand the nature of these interventions of God, because we do not know what they are achieving. Yet after having elucidated, at least partially, the positive side of Paul's system of convictions, it will be easier to study its negative dimensions. Indeed, we know that the negative convictions are the counterparts of positive convictions.

Our study of Galatians has already shown that the negative counterpart of "being in the right relationship with God" is "being under a curse," or "being slave" to Torah, idols, and/or the elemental spirits of the universe, in other words, "being in the right relationship with beings which by nature are not gods." From this starting point, and on the basis of what we know about the positive dimensions of Paul's system of convictions, we can formulate hypotheses concerning other aspects of its negative dimensions.

Since the believers are established in the right relationship with God through God's interventions, we can expect that the nonbelievers are under a curse or slaves because of *interventions of a god-like negative power*. At first glance, this hypothesis is strange, because it almost says that Paul held the conviction that there is an evil god (or evil gods), while he affirms that he makes his own the Jewish belief that "God is One," for instance in Gal. 3:20. But, as this text also shows, he had to struggle with this issue. His view could easily be (mis)understood as a claim that there are gods other than the true God. Thus we can expect to find that Paul expressed this same negative conviction in different ways, namely, as the *negative interventions of God*, as the manifestations of the "wrath of God," a concept that we encountered several times.

We also know that God's interventions in the believers' experience are comparable to God's interventions in Jesus' experience. God intervened to raise Christ from the dead. His death is clearly both a positive type (as in Gal. 2:20 and other passages, where Paul can say that he was crucified with Christ) and a negative type (as in Romans 4, where it is a hopeless situation). In this latter case, it means that before God's interventions the believers are in a death-like situation. As in Romans 4, this death-like situation is a hopeless situation out of which there is apparently no escape, as there is apparently no escape from death. There we noted that Paul speaks of death as a power comparable to other powers. Thus Christ's work at the end of time will be to destroy "every rule and every authority and power. For he must reign until he has put all his enemies under his feet. The last enemy to be destroyed is death" (1 Cor. 15:24–26). The technical terms "rule," "authority," and "power" clearly designate "enemies," which keep human beings under their power, as death also does. But then, according to the typological pattern, if the ultimate intervention of Christ (or God) at the Parousia consists in fully destroying these powers, it means that Christ's resurrection from the dead as prefiguration, or preliminary manifestation, of the Parousia is also the overcoming of death viewed as a power. Thus, the Christ-like interventions of God in the believers' experience are also the overcoming of powers which, from a human perspective, cannot be overcome. But what are these "powers" which are death-like and deadly? To say that the terms Paul uses to refer to them are the Jewish designations of demons or spirits (good or evil)[5] does not truly answer this question. What are these demons or spirits? Or, to use the vocabulary we find in 1 Thessalonians, who is Satan or the Tempter? How do they manifest themselves in the experience of the believers?

One thing we can already say is that these powers constantly intervene in the believers' experience, that is, also after their conversion. Indeed, we have shown that God's interventions in the believers' experience are far from being limited to their conversion experience. To put it in another way, none of God's interventions in the believers' experience is the complete destruction of these evil powers. This will only take place at the Parousia. God's interventions are only punctual and partial overcomings of these powers in specific situations. From the perspective of the believers, this means that they are constantly in danger of being overcome by the evil powers, and thus need again and again to be delivered from them. There is always the possibility that they might have run in vain (cf. Phil. 3:11, where Paul speaks of his salvation as a mere possibility; he is still in the race toward that goal) and that Paul would have labored in vain (cf., e.g., 1 Thess. 3:5; Phil. 2:16). Persecutions as well as the killing of Jesus (cf. 1 Cor. 2:8) are manifestations of the evil powers. But so is being bewitched by a false gospel (Gal. 3:1). This is to say that these powers have both "concrete" and "spiritual" manifestations. Furthermore, these powers are clearly not manifested merely in the private spiritual experience of the individual person; they have a social dimension (persecutions, the separation of the Jews from the Gentiles, the separation of the slaves from their masters, the separation of the sexes, which are overcome through faith and thus through interventions of God; cf. Gal. 3:28) and even a cosmological dimension (the creation as a whole is in bondage; cf. Rom. 8:20–22). It is these evil powers which necessitate God's (or Christ's) continuing interventions.

The formulation of these hypotheses about the negative dimensions of Paul's system of convictions suggests that sin is somehow related to these evil powers. Therefore it is not surprising that sin is viewed by Paul as a power. The question is then, What kind of power is it? How is it related to these evil powers?

Such are the questions we will raise and the hypotheses we will test through our reading of Romans. Together with the positive dimensions of Paul's system of convictions that we have already tentatively elucidated, these questions and hypotheses will be the "model" (in the scientific sense of the term) which will guide our reading of Romans. Through this reading we shall verify this "model," complement it, and eventually modify it. Thus our reading of Romans will be devoted to the elucidation of the negative dimensions of Paul's charismatic, eschatological, and typological faith.

## THE ARGUMENT OF ROMANS AND ITS HISTORICAL CONTEXT

### The Nature of This Text

Paul's letter to the Romans is the most systematic presentation of his faith. But what kind of text is it?[26] Is it a systematic doctrinal presentation of the Christian faith? In such a case, this letter—which could then be called an "epistle"—would be comparable to a doctrinal encyclical. It could be termed "Paul's testament," the mature statement of his faith.[7] As such, this text would be quite different from the other letters, which were written in order to address the specific situations in which his readers were involved. If this text were a systematic doctrinal presentation, its historical reading would not need to take into consideration the specific situation in Rome. Indeed, it could be sent to any church. This epistle would then refer to, and thus should be understood in terms of, the general situation of the Pauline churches. It would be a statement made on the basis of Paul's overall experience as Apostle to the Gentiles and thus should be interpreted in this light. Therefore we must first consider the literary character of this text by asking, Why did Paul write it?

A first reason is given in Rom. 1:13 and 15:22–29. Paul plans to go to Rome and to visit the church in that city, as he has wanted to do for a long time (1:13). On the basis of Acts 20:3–6 and some indirect indications in Romans, scholars generally agree that Paul wrote this letter from Corinth around the year 57 (see Appendix: Chronologies of Paul). Indeed, he is ready to leave on a long journey which will first take him to Jerusalem and from there to Rome and Spain (15:24–29). As far as he is concerned, he has completed his missionary activity in Asia Minor and Greece. The churches he has established in these regions can continue the work by themselves, which means that the problems which developed in these churches (especially in Corinth; see Chapter 8) have been satisfactorily resolved. He is now free to go and proclaim the Gospel to countries in which it has not yet been proclaimed, and especially in Spain, which is the western end of the "inhabited world." On his way to this new missionary field he will stop in Rome. It is possible that he viewed the church in Rome as the base from which he would launch this new missionary activity.

Paul might have written this letter to the church in Rome in order to introduce himself and his teaching to that church which he had not founded, which did not know him, and which he did not know. This turning point in his ministry was the occasion for reflecting upon and presenting systematically the Gospel he preached in Asia Minor and Greece. If that were the case, Romans would be written without any reference to the situation in Rome. Then this text should be read as his "confession of faith" that he formulates on the basis of his preceding missionary activity and in light of the conflicts described in Galatians and 1 and 2 Corinthians. But this understanding of the letter to the Romans has to be rejected. This is not denying that Paul apparently thought his letter to the Romans could be useful for at least one other church, because of the comprehensive presentation of the Gospel which it involves. But it remains a letter written with specific addressees in mind.

Paul also might have written to the church of Rome because he thought that they had heard negative reports about him concerning his radical position in favor of Gentile Christianity and against Jewish Christianity, as well as about his tense relationship with Judaism. He alludes to such negative reports when he writes, "And why not do evil that good may come?—as some people slanderously charge us with saying" (Rom. 3:8). In that case, this text would be an apologetic letter demonstrating the well-balanced character of his proclamation, according to which the truth of the Gospel confronts both Judaism and paganism.[8] Then Romans should be read and interpreted primarily in terms of Galatians and the situation described therein. We cannot deny that one of the goals of this letter is to make an apology for Paul's view of the Gospel; a part of this letter does aim at establishing the validity of Paul's teaching. But this is not merely in order that he and his teaching might be welcomed when he arrives at Rome. In fact, chapters 12–15 contain specific exhortations to his readers. The "apologetic" part of the letter (chaps. 1–11) prepares the way for these exhortations, which are the actual goal of the letter.

Therefore Paul could also have written because he had some knowledge of the situation in the Roman church and wanted to address specific problems of that community. But since he did not found that church, he proceeds with great caution, taking the time to present at length his view of the Gospel before formulating exhortations addressing the concrete situation of the church in Rome. This view, advocated by Ernst Käsemann[9] and Willi Marxsen,[10] among others, is from our perspective the correct one.

## Addressing a Conflict Between Jewish and Gentile Christians

A full analysis of Romans aimed at elucidating the dialogic and warranting levels of this discourse could show in great detail how the argument unfolds so as to bring about the exhortations of Romans 12–15, but a few general observations will suffice to help us understand that this is indeed the purpose of the letter.

In the first verses of the letter, which belong to the dialogic level, we find a long description of Paul's apostolate and a brief description of the addressees: "to all God's beloved in Rome, who are called to be saints" (Rom. 1:7a). In other words, they are elected, chosen by God, and their vocation is to be "saints," thus "holy," because of their close relationship (right relationship) with God. As Israel was a "people of priests," a holy people which is the intermediary between God and the nations, so they are. Beginning with a thanksgiving, Paul expresses his wish to preach the Gospel to the Romans (1:8–15). Then through a long and involved development (1:16—11:36), he establishes the warrants for his wish and the exhortations addressed to these saints in chapters 12–15. These exhortations, which generally speaking belong to the dialogic level, are introduced with the following words:

> I appeal to you therefore, brethren, by the mercies of God, to present your bodies as a living sacrifice, holy and acceptable to God, which is your spiritual worship. Do not be conformed to this world. . . . (Rom. 12:1–2a)

This is what is demanded of "saints": to be "priests" offering sacrifices, and in light of the Gospel offering themselves as sacrifice; and to be separated from the world. This is followed, first, by general exhortations (chaps. 12 and 13) and then by more specific exhortations (chaps. 14 and 15). In these chapters the goal of the discourse is expressed. The material in the main body of the letter needs to be understood in terms of these exhortations that it warrants.

In Romans 14 and 15, Paul expresses his concern for the relations among two groups: those that he calls "the strong" and those that he calls "the weak." What are these two groups? Paul knows enough about the situation in the Roman church to say that they are divided over the question of food (some eat meat, the others only vegetables; Rom. 14:2), and drink (some drink wine, others do not; 14:21), and over the question of a special day that some observe while the others esteem all days alike (14:5). Thus there are, on the one hand, the strong who think that "nothing is unclean in itself" (14:14) and feel free to eat meat, to drink wine, and to esteem all days alike and, on the other hand, the weak, who are rigorists and follow certain practices. They judge and despise each other. In Romans 15 Paul comes back to the distinction between the strong and the weak and goes on to speak of the circumcised, that is, the Jews, and the Gentiles (15:1, 8–9). From this and the preceding chapters, one can conclude that this dispute is between Gentile Christians (the strong) and Jewish Christians (the weak). Paul does exhort the weak not to pass judgment on the strong (14:3, 10), yet it is clear that he addresses primarily the strong, exhorting them not to think of themselves as better than others (12:3), not to despise the weak (14:3, 10), but rather, out of love, to avoid "putting a stumbling block . . . in the way of a brother" (14:13). Here we simply note that these chapters seem to refer to a dispute between Gentile Christians and Jewish Christians in the church of Rome. Paul aims, through his letter, to exhort the Gentile Christians to "pursue what makes for peace and for mutual upbuilding" (14:19).

This is confirmed by the small but significant information we have about the historical situation of the church in Rome.[11] From the writings of Suetonius, a Roman historian, we know that the Emperor Claudius expelled the Jews from Rome because of disturbances caused by "Chrestos." This name certainly refers to Christ (the word "Chrestos," and "Christos" would have been pronounced almost exactly in the same way). And thus Claudius's edict was certainly the result of disturbances in the Jewish community caused by the development of the church. Acts 18:1–2 also mentions this edict in relation to Aquila and Priscilla, who were Jewish and had to depart from Rome. This means that, at first, the church in Rome included Jewish Christians. But these were expelled from Rome together with the rest of the Jews. Thus, only Gentile Christians remained in the church of Rome, which certainly went on growing.

At the time when Paul writes the letter, it seems that there is still a majority of Gentile Christians, but there are also Jewish Christians in the church at Rome. We know this because Claudius died in the year 54 and his successor Nero was favorably inclined toward the Jews. Thus the letter was written at the time when Jewish Christians were coming back to Rome. The church now had a majority of Gentile Christians and a sizable minority of returning Jewish Christians.

This would explain the conflict reflected in Romans 12–15. During the period following the expulsion of the Jews (and Jewish Christians), the remaining Gentile church developed along the lines of other Gentile churches. In other words, they followed a Gospel without the Law. As the Jewish Christians come back, they try to reinstitute the church as it was before their departure, a church following a Gospel with the Law. They "pass judgment" on the developments which took place in their absence. But the Gentile Christians consider them weak and despise them.

Paul, through his letter, intervenes in this delicate situation. For him this is not a new problem. He was confronted with a similar situation in Jerusalem (at the apostolic assembly). But here, addressing a church made up of Jewish and Gentile Christians, he has to be cautious. His readers will assume that he is on the side of the Gentile Christians, so his exhortations are primarily directed to the Gentile Christians. They should be the peacemakers. He does not demand that the Jewish Christians live like the Gentile Christians, therefore the latter should avoid being a stumbling block for them. Yet this is not a mere tactic, but rather what is demanded by his system of convictions, as we shall see. He also addresses exhortations to the Jewish Christians (the weak).

The main body of the letter (which warrants these exhortations) attempts, among other things, to establish that Jews and Gentiles are believers of equal status. Thus, sometimes he addresses the Jewish Christians (e.g., Rom. 7:1: "for I am speaking to those who know the law"), and at other times he addresses the Gentile Christians (e.g., 11:13: "Now I am speaking to you Gentiles"). There was no difference between them before the coming of Christ. Yes, the Jews had an advantage as compared with the Gentiles, but all had revelations from God and all are sinners (1:18—3:20). Similarly, after the coming of Christ, there is no difference between them with respect to righteousness (3:21—4:25). The righteousness of God through faith in Jesus Christ is for all who believe, both the Jews and the Gentiles (3:22). "Is God the God of the Jews only? Is he not the God of the Gentiles also? Yes, of Gentiles also, since God is one" (3:29–30). Then in chapters 5–8 he presents the results of justification by faith for all the believers. They are reconciled to God, freed from the condemnation (chap. 5). They have died to sin by being baptized into Christ's death (chap. 6). They are freed from the Law, in which sin found opportunity (chap. 7). They have a life in the Spirit (8:1–17) and they live in hope (8:13–39). Thus neither the Jews nor the Jewish Christians can make a special claim for themselves (3:9). All of them share this righteousness through faith. But at the same time Paul is careful to avoid giving the Gentile Christians an occasion for making a special claim for themselves, even though they are the strong. Romans 9–11 is in part devoted to making this point (see esp. 11:17–24, where Paul exhorts the Gentile Christians not to claim superiority over Israel by means of the parable of the olive tree).

In sum, Paul's text is indeed a letter addressing first of all the situation in the church of Rome. Because he has had very little contact with that church, he must develop at length the warranting level of his discourse, so that his exhortations might be accepted as valid. He therefore needs to provide a comprehensive explanation of his message which could be accepted by both Jewish and Gentile Christians, even if his exhortations will be aimed primarily at the latter. In fact, the discourse is organized in such a way as to have different effects upon the two groups he addresses.

Paul assumes that the Gentile Christians who form the majority of the community are in agreement with him concerning the understanding of the Gospel. The overall content of chapters 1–11 is therefore not new to them. It is basically a reminder of what they already believe, even if it includes new dimensions, so it can be used for establishing the legitimacy of the exhortations through which he rebukes them. Consequently, Paul can criticize quite strongly the attitude of the Gentile Christians who call themselves the strong by comparison with the Jewish Christians that they call the weak. For Paul, the Jewish Christians who have such a lack of freedom can indeed be viewed as "weak in faith," but they do have faith, and it is important not to make them stumble upon unimportant matters. The strong have to adopt the way of life of the weak. As Christ became a servant to the circumcised (the Jews) (15:8), they must become servants of the weak.

By contrast, Paul assumes that the Jewish Christians are suspicious of his teaching. They might well remain unconvinced by the arguments of Romans 1–11, and thus Paul cannot really use these developments as a basis for strongly exhorting and rebuking the Jewish Christians. He does not do so. Yet his rebuke of the Gentile Christians' attitude toward them is something they can view favorably. But if Paul's message is the basis upon which such "good" exhortations can be made, it means that this message and its view of the Gospel can itself be viewed as "good." Thus Paul's overall discourse would have the effect of convincing the Jewish Christians of the validity of this Gospel which gives equal status to the Gentile Christians (cf. 15:15–21).

## A Letter Sent Also to Ephesus?

Because this letter addresses equally Gentile Christians who can readily identify themselves to Paul, and Jewish Christians and others who might be suspicious of Paul's teaching, it can apply to different situations in other churches as well. Indeed, it is possible that Paul felt this letter could be useful elsewhere. It appears that he sent a copy of it together with a short letter of introduction and of greetings to Ephesus. Such is the conclusion reached by many scholars (following T. W. Manson). [12]

There are two problems regarding Romans 16. First, in the various manuscripts the doxology (Rom. 16:25–27) is found at different places: at the end of chapter 14, at the end of chapter 15, and at the end of chapter 16. It is known that the heretic Marcion had, for doctrinal reasons, cut off Paul's letter at the end of chapter 14, which explains the presence of the doxology at the end of that chapter. But why is it found at the end of chapter 15 in one manuscript? Could it be that the letter originally ended here? The use of a concluding formula at the end of chapter 15 suggests that this could be the case. This is confirmed by the content of chapter 16, which contains greetings to twenty-six people. Does Paul know that many people in Rome? He mentions Aquila and Priscilla (16:3), who we know were in Ephesus when Paul wrote 1 Corinthians (1 Cor. 16:19); of course, they were from Rome and might have returned there. He also mentions Epaenetus, "who was the first convert [the first fruits] in Asia" (i.e., from the region of Ephesus; 16:5). Furthermore, the sharp warning against false teachers (16:17–20) is in a polemical style which he carefully avoids in the rest of the letter.

Thus it is possible that Paul also sent a copy of this letter to Ephesus together with a short letter, Romans 16, involving a commendation for Phoebe (who might have carried the letter), greetings to the members of the church of Ephesus that he knew so well for having spent a long period with them, as well as a warning addressing a specific situation at Ephesus. [13]

## EVIL IN PAUL'S THEOLOGICAL ARGUMENT

Our second reading of Romans aims to elucidate the negative dimensions of Paul's system of convictions: his view of the wrath of God, God's judgment, death, evil powers, sin, and unbelief. For this purpose we will examine successively the role and place of evil in the sacred historical perpective of Paul's theological argument and in the perspective of Paul's typological system of convictions.

From what we know about the positive dimensions of Paul's system of convictions, we can expect to find that various manifestations of evil are comparable to each other. The manifestations of evil in the biblical time, in Jesus' experience, in the Judean churches' experience, in Paul's and other believers' experience, are typical of the present manifestations of evil in the believers' experience, which are themselves typical of the manifestations of evil at the end of time (the Parousia). According to the convictional pattern, what is essential is that these various manifestations are comparable and indeed homologable to each other. So Paul can speak of one specific manifestation of evil in terms of any one of the others, or even in terms of all the others. Such is the case, for instance, in Rom. 7:7–24, as Franz J. Leenhardt has pointed out.[14]

In the perspective of the typological system of convictions, the sequence of these manifestations of evil is important insofar as it determines what/who is "type" and what/who is "imitator"; sequence also plays a significant role in the theological argument. From our discussion of the concept of reconciliation, we can expect that various manifestations of evil are expressed in the theological explanations in terms of the unfolding of sacred history. This distinction between the theological and convictional dimensions of Paul's discourse will help us understand what appear, at first, to be contradictory statements about evil.

## Sinners without Excuse
## and under the Power of Sin

A first cursory reading of Romans aimed at identifying what Paul says about evil in its various manifestations reveals two apparently contradictory kinds of affirmations. On the one hand, Paul emphasizes that human beings are responsible for evil, or at least for some of its manifestations. The pagans are responsible for being idolatrous and sinners, so "they are without excuse" (Rom. 1:20b). Similarly, those who pass judgment upon the pagans, the Jews, have no excuse themselves (2:1). The Jews are responsible for breaking the Law (2:17–24), so God is not unjust when punishing both the Jews and the Gentiles (2:9; 3:5, 8). Yes, God does find fault in the Jews and is in the right when condemning them, even if this appears to be unjust (9:14, 19). In brief, humans are responsible for their idolatry and sin. Thus, they bring upon themselves this other evil which is the condemnation of God, his wrath, his destruction.

On the other hand, humans are under the power of evil. If the Jews do not believe, it is because they have hardened hearts, and this because God hardened their hearts (Rom. 11:7–8). That is why one could say that God is unjust when punishing them (9:14–24). God also gave the pagans up to sinful conduct (1:24, 26, 28). In other words, "all men, both Jews and Greeks, are under the power of sin" (3:9). They are "slaves of sin" (6:17). And this power of sin is such that there is no way to escape from it (7:7–24) without an intervention of God. Humans are under the power of evil, be it in the form of hardened hearts, of the power of sin, or of "tribulation, or distress, or persecution, or famine, or nakedness, or peril, or sword" (8:35) or of death (5:12–14). Even the creation is under this power of evil (8:20).

How can humans be at once under the power of evil and responsible for evil? We have to let ourselves be puzzled by this question which Paul himself raises (cf. Rom. 3:5; 9:14, 19). Furthermore, what is God's relationship to evil? We might be able to understand God's condemnation and punishment of sinners, although this seems to contradict statements describing God as the God of grace and of mercy. It is even more puzzling to find that God causes people to sin, as we can read in the passages mentioned above. We should not avoid this problem by saying that Paul could not have meant this and thus that these passages should be interpreted to mean that God tolerated sin. God "handed over" the pagans to sinful conduct even as the Jews "handed Jesus over" to Pilate (the same verb is used). And yet sin appears as a power independent from God (although God's Law is the occasion for sin).

These problems and apparent contradictions suggest that Paul's convictional logic is at work here. Elucidating how the various manifestations of evil are organized, according to both his theological/sacred historical way of thinking and his convictional pattern, will allow us to understand how Paul can make such statements without contradicting himself.

## Evil in Sacred History

This letter is, for Paul, the occasion for reflecting upon the message he proclaims and for explaining it at length to a twofold audience made up of Jewish and Gentile Christians. Since it is not a passionate plea (as Galatians is), but rather a calm and carefully balanced argument, the warranting part of the letter is often presented in the form of theological explanations using the classical form of argumentation in Paul's time: the diatribe. In contrast with Galatians, in which the convictional logic often commands the development of the argument (with many breaks in the argumentative logic), here Paul's argument unfolds more smoothly. In other words, the convictional pattern more consistently plays its usual role of undergirding a (theo)logical argument, although in certain passages this convictional logic has a significant part.

This predominant place of the theological explanations is manifested by the fact that the argument is based upon reflections concerning the unfolding of sacred history. Before considering how evil is viewed by Paul in this context, we shall emphasize some aspects of Paul's theological presentation of positive convictions.

In Rom. 5:1–11, Christ is presented in terms of his place in the unfolding of sacred history, that is, as accomplishing the reconciliation of humankind to God. Christ is presented as accomplishing a redemption and even "an expiation by his blood." Thus Jesus' death is described as an expiatory sacrifice (3:24–25). For Paul, this is an unusual way of speaking about the cross. Nonetheless, such statements can easily be understood as a theological/sacred historical explanation of his convictions which emphasize the correlation of the believers' experience with Christ's death. In the same theological/sacred historical perspective, justification is understood as the result of this reconciliation, that is, of forgiveness. Justification is thus often presented in a legal terminology. For instance, Paul says that God "had passed over former sins" (3:25) and that Abraham's faith "was reckoned to him as righteousness" (4:3–8, using biblical texts with such a legal terminology), as is also the believers' faith (4:24). But once again this theological argumentation should not be opposed to the convictional view of Christ (as type fulfilled in the believers' experience) and of justification (as being in the right relationship with God because of the manifestation of God's power in the believers' experience). This theological presentation is, so to speak, establishing the logical possibility for the convictions which are also expressed in these texts. Therefore, justification through faith is, in the perspective of the unfolding of sacred history, a "reckoning as righteousness," that is, the forgiveness of former sins, and faith is trusting in certain promises (faith thus has a content). But at the same time, as Ernst Käsemann has shown, faith is also used as an absolute, as referring to a relationship with God. Consequently, "justification through faith" is also "being in the right relationship with God through faith" and not merely being forgiven.[15]

Similarly, from the perspective of the unfolding of sacred history,

Paul's presentation of evil is not to be opposed to Paul's convictions about evil. It expresses in terms of chronological sequences and cause-and-effect relations what is perceived in the convictional system in terms of homologation and correlation of comparable manifestations of evil. Keeping these observations in mind, note what is, in Paul's view, the place and role of evil in the unfolding of sacred history. We can discern four steps in Paul's reasoning.

1. Paul places sin at the beginning of sacred history after the creation: "sin came into the world through one man" (Rom. 5:12), who is identified as Adam (5:14). Therefore, from the beginning all humans are sinners and under the condemnation. As a consequence of sin, death came into the world also at that time (5:12). Sin and death reigned before as well as after the giving of the Law to Moses (5:13–14), but before the Law sin was not counted (5:13), as in the case of Abraham (4:1–8). This is the time of faith.

2. What is the effect of the Law? On the positive side, the Israelites received "the sonship, the glory, the covenants, the giving of the law, the worship, and the promises" (Rom. 9:4). This election of Israel is irrevocable: "For the gifts and the call of God are irrevocable" (11:29). But the giving of the Law also has negative effects. The Law was for them a stumbling block (9:31–33), and thus "the law came in, to increase the trespass" (5:20). So that trespass might increase, the Law is necessary, because "where there is no law there is no transgression" (4:15) and thus "sin is not counted" (5:13). Without the Law there would be no need for a reconciliation of humankind to God. But because of the Jews' trespasses, salvation has come to the Gentiles (11:11). The Jews' trespasses constitute a necessary stage of sacred history demonstrating that "God has consigned all men to disobedience" (11:32). Not only the Gentiles but also the Jews need to be reconciled to God. Because of the Jews' disobedience, Jesus Christ could, through his death, accomplish the reconciliation of *all* human beings (be they Jews or Gentiles) to God (5:18).

3. So that this reconciliation might be extended to the Gentiles, God had to make the Jews stumble. They had to be made into "vessels of wrath" (Rom. 9:19–23). In other words, in order that the election might be extended by God to the Gentiles, the Jews had to be temporarily rejected by God. They had to be "predestined" to fail, that is, they had to be made to fail (9:6–18). For this, God hardened their hearts (9:18;

11:7–10), so that even though they hear (10:18) and have the promises (9:4), they cannot truly hear them and appropriate them (11:8). They have eyes, but do not see (11:8) the fulfillments of the promises. The promises are also theirs. They too have been reconciled to God. Indeed, God is at work in their experience. They could have faith. But they do not hear, they do not see. They have been given a "spirit of stupor" and have been hardened. Blindly they pursue "the righteousness which is based on the law" and do "not succeed in fulfilling that law" (9:31).

4. Yet the Jews are not rejected permanently (Rom. 11:1–2). Because of their trespasses, which have shown that all humans are sinners, God has reconciled the world to himself, and thus the Gentiles can be reconciled to God and have faith. But as the Gentiles convert, they will "make Israel jealous" (11:11). Then Israel will also convert at the end of time, "for if their rejection means the reconciliation of the world, what will their acceptance mean but life from the dead?" (11:15). This time of the general resurrection will also be the time of God's judgment and of the manifestation of God's wrath upon the wicked.

> There will be wrath and fury. There will be tribulation and distress for every human being who does evil, the Jew first and also the Greek, but glory and honor and peace for every one who does good, the Jew first and also the Greek. (2:8–10)

Such are the main elements of Paul's view of the place and role of evil in the unfolding of sacred history. Through this theological explanation, Paul aims at demonstrating that Jews and Gentiles are in the same position ("under the power of sin") and that righteousness through faith without the Law is indeed valid, and this without denying the irrevocable election of Israel. But this theological explanation also expresses and presupposes Paul's convictions about the reality of evil in human experience.

## EVIL IN PAUL'S SYSTEM OF CONVICTIONS

From what we know of the positive side of Paul's system of convictions, we can infer that the various manifestations of evil in the different stages of sacred history are in a typological relationship with each other as are also the various manifestations of God. A study of Paul's texts about evil will allow us to verify that this is indeed the case and to elucidate the features of evil which are typical, that is, what Paul views as the recurrent characteristics of the manifestations of evil which are the common lot of sinners of any period in sacred history.

## The Pagans as Typical Sinners (Rom. 1:18–32)

Several passages of the letter to the Romans speak of evil without reference to the sacred historical perspective discussed above. They are like snapshots showing manifestations of evil in various situations. This is the case in Rom. 1:18–32, which presents the manifestations of evil in the pagans' experience.

> For the wrath of God is revealed from heaven against all ungodliness and wickedness of men who by their wickedness suppress the truth. (1:18)

To whom is God's wrath revealed? Obviously not to people who are ungodly and wicked. They do not believe in God, and thus they cannot perceive what happens to them as manifestation of the wrath *of God*.[16] The manifestation of God's wrath against these people is revealed to those to whom is also revealed the righteousness of God (Rom. 1:17). In other words, there is a *twofold revelation* to the believers:

1. Through faith, the believers discover manifestations of the righteousness of God, manifestations of God's power for the salvation of the believers (Rom. 1:16). This revelation of God's righteousness is through faith (discovered and actualized through faith) and for faith (for those who have faith), as is expressed in 1:17a. This is the positive intervention of God in the believers' experience (involving other people) which is discovered and actualized in a life in the right relationship with God (1:17b).

2. Through faith, the believers also discover other manifestations of God in their experience, manifestations of the wrath of God. In their experience, they encounter people who are ungodly and wicked, that is, people who are in the wrong relationship with God. In these people they can perceive, through faith, the manifestation of the "wrath of God coming from heaven." This phrase is often used by Paul to describe the last judgment and destruction of evil people at the end of time (cf. Rom. 2:5, 7–9). Thus, according to his convictional pattern, Paul describes the negative interventions of God in the present of the believers, in terms of the negative interventions of God at the end of time. For Paul, these are

equivalent, the one being the preliminary manifestation (or prefiguration) of the other. We can note with Käsemann[17] that "wrath" is the power
of curse, that is, of condemnation which effectively brings destruction.
In the same way that the righteousness of God is actualized as power of
salvation (establishing the believers in a constructive relationship with
God) by means of faith, so the wrath of God is actualized as power of
curse (establishing the ungodly in a destructive relationship with God)
by means of the wickedness which "suppresses the truth."

In summary, beside the positive interventions of God, there are negative interventions of God. Both can be recognized through faith by the
believers. Both are actualized by human beings. The positive interventions of God offer salvation (the right relationship with God), which is
actualized if, through faith, these interventions are recognized for what
they are. But the negative interventions of God offer curse and destruction, which are actualized if truth is suppressed, that is, if the interventions of God are not recognized for what they are, the manifestations
of God, the God from heaven.

> For what can be known about God is plain to them, because God has shown
> it to them. Ever since the creation of the world his invisible nature, namely,
> his eternal power and deity, has been clearly perceived in the things that
> have been made. So they are without excuse. . . . (Rom. 1:19–20)

Human beings, whoever they may be, cannot use the excuse that God
does not manifest himself to them. Indeed, "ever since the creation of
the world," God has shown himself to them. Despite the vocabulary
borrowed from Hellenistic philosophy and from Hellenistic Judaism,[18]
this passage should not be understood as embodying a natural theology.
Paul speaks of the present experience of the believers and unbelievers
in terms of the type "humankind after the creation and before other
revelations," as he spoke of it in terms of the eschatological judgment in
the preceding verse. So these verses express what is, for Paul, the way
in which God reveals himself at any stage of the sacred history before
the Parousia, when he will be seen face to face.

To begin with, God is not hidden in such a way that humans would
have to seek him in a philosophical or religious quest which can either
be successful or not, according to the quality of this human quest. What
is knowable about God is manifest (or "plain"). Furthermore, God is not
passive. He makes himself known. He shows himself. He intervenes to

show himself to everybody (and not merely to the believers). In anybody's experience, God manifests himself.

What is the nature of this manifestation of God? It is not a face-to-face encounter with God, for his nature is "invisible." In other words, as we noted about the cross and the resurrection, a manifestation of God is not such that, when one is confronted with it, the only possible response is "This is God." For Paul, this kind of manifestation of God will take place only at the Parousia. A manifestation of God in the present needs to be apprehended by means of human intelligence. It must be "known," perceived, as is expressed in Rom. 1:20 (although the RSV does not express this clearly enough). In the present human experience, only certain aspects of God are knowable (1:19), namely, "his eternal power and deity" (1:20), God's divine power. This aspect of God's *invisible* nature is manifested in *visible* things. It is "clearly perceived" (Paul's play on the words visible/invisible is difficult to render in English). It is manifested in visible *works*. As is clear from the preceding mention that God actively shows himself, God manifests himself not merely in his creative act but "since the creation exists." He manifests himself in the creative act and in the creation which he sustains and in which he intervenes.[19] In sum, God manifests himself in the world in such a way that any human being can clearly perceive and know him.

> So they are without excuse; for although they knew God they did not honor him as God or give thanks to him, but they became futile in their thinking and their senseless minds were darkened. (Rom. 1:20b–21)

Human beings know God. They can see his manifestations and they can interpret them correctly. They have the intellectual capacity to do so (as is indicated in the preceding verse), but they do not honor him as God should be honored. They do not give thanks to God, even though it is the only appropriate response to the discovery of God's interventions.

Why did they fail to recognize and/or acknowledge God's manifestation in the creation? Paul does not explain it here, but he will do so in Rom. 7:7–13 when speaking of the role of sin in the Jews' experience. At any rate, because they failed to give honor and thanks to God, "they were made futile or vain in their thinking and their senseless minds were darkened." As the two passive verbs indicate, this does not mean that these people themselves made their thinking futile and their senseless minds (or hearts) darkened. This is something which happened to them. Who or what made their thinking vain and darkened their minds? From the perspective of Paul's system of convictions, this is already a manifestation of God's wrath, which these people experience as a curse. God's interventions and revelations are a blessing for those who recognize them for what they are and who therefore give honor and thanks to God. But for those who do not recognize these interventions and revelations of God for what they are, they are a curse which traps them in a futile way of thinking and in a darkened heart.

This is true of all God's interventions and revelations and not merely of those in the creation. This is true of the cross. "For the word of the cross is folly to those who are perishing, but to us who are being saved it is the power of God" (1 Cor. 1:18). For those who recognize the cross as God's intervention, and who give honor and thanks to God for it, it is a blessing. It is the manifestation of God's power, which is also manifested in the experience of the believers who, consequently, "are being saved." For those who do not recognize the cross as God's intervention, it is a curse, as Paul makes clear by quoting Isa. 29:14 and Ps. 33:10: "For it is written, 'I will destroy the wisdom of the wise, and the cleverness of the clever I will thwart'" (1 Cor. 1:19). God has made their wisdom foolish (1 Cor. 1:20). God's intervention in the cross, instead of being power of salvation, is a power which makes their thinking futile and darkens their minds. Thus their futile and darkened "wisdom" sees the cross as a folly, because according to their wisdom, "God" cannot manifest himself in such a way. Their wisdom has established for them an image of "God" (a perception of God which is, in fact, an idol) which is such that it is impossible for him to manifest himself in a cross. And thus they cannot see the cross as wisdom of God and power of God (cf. 1 Cor. 1:20–25). For them, the cross, instead of being a blessing, is a curse: "a stumbling block to Jews and folly to Gentiles" (1 Cor. 1:23).

Similarly, God's Law, Torah—which is "holy and just and good" (Rom. 7:12), revelation from God, promise of God, and thus power of salvation (by analogy with the cross)—is a stumbling block for those who do not have faith. Israel, "who pursued the righteousness which is based on law," failed to attain righteousness (the right relationship with God) "because they did not pursue it through faith" (9:31–32). The Jews failed to see in Torah the manifestation of the *power* of God. They failed to recognize it for what it is: the promises of new acts and revelations of God which would establish them in the right relationship with God.

Consequently, Torah became for them a stumbling block: "They have stumbled over the stumbling stone, as it is written, 'Behold, I am laying in Zion a stone that will make men stumble, a rock that will make them fall; and he who believes in him will not be put to shame'" (Rom. 9:32–33, quoting Isa. 28:16; see also Isa. 8:14).

Everybody can know or see (or hear about) manifestations of God's power and deity in the creation, in Torah, or in the cross. Everybody has the opportunity to give honor and thanks to God. Those who do not do so are then made vain in their way of thinking. They are made foolish, senseless. Their minds are darkened. God hardens them. "God gave them a spirit of stupor, eyes that should not see and ears that should not hear" (Rom. 11:8). And thus because of their senseless minds which they call wisdom (1 Cor. 1:20), they can no longer know God. In the case of the Jews, because they stumbled on Torah, not taking the opportunity to give honor and thanks to God for the promises contained in Torah, they are now unable "to see and hear" that God was at work in Jesus and is at work in their present.

The following verses describe in three parallel statements (Rom. 1:22–24; 1:25–27; 1:28–31) how this curse on the unbelievers takes effect in their lives.

> Claiming to be wise, they became fools, and exchanged the glory of the immortal God for images resembling mortal man or birds or animals or reptiles. Therefore God gave them up in the lusts of their hearts to impurity, to the dishonoring of their bodies among themselves. (Rom. 1:22–24)

In the case of the unbelievers who only benefited from God's manifestations and revelations in the creation, the outcome of this curse is idolatry. God had manifested himself to them in the creation, that is, in "mortal man," in "birds," in "reptiles." But instead of perceiving *manifestations* of God in these, they see absolutes. They worship the creatures instead of the Creator, as is expressed in Rom. 1:25. Instead of worshiping the glory of the immortal God, whose power and deity was manifested in the creation, they worship idealized and glorified images of the creatures. But their very idolatry is also the manifestation of God's wrath. God enslaved them to their idolatry. They are made slaves of their "selfish desires" (the term rendered by "lusts" in the above translation), which are not merely sexual desires but all kinds of selfish desires. And thus they dishonor their bodies. They corrupt the human body and the human relations which were supposed to be manifestations of God's power and deity.

In these verses, as well as in the following (Rom. 1:25–32), we find a list of vices. Paul's description of these vices reflects the traditional Jewish abhorrence of idolatry and is expressed with the help of Hellenistic categories. Here we simply note that in conclusion Paul emphasizes the responsibility of the pagans: "They know God's decree that those who do such things deserve to die" (1:32a). Indeed, they have all they need to know God and his will; they do not need Torah. As Paul puts it in 2:15: "They show that what the law requires is written on their hearts, while their conscience also bears witness and their conflicting thoughts accuse or perhaps excuse them." For instance, the Hellenistic tradition itself recognizes these things as vices, and the pagans also correctly identify virtues. But in their idolatry "they not only do them [these vices] but approve those who practice them" (1:32b). They are sinners. And so those who have sinned without the Law will also perish without the Law when the wrath of God will be fully manifested at the end of time, although this wrath of God is already manifested in their present corruption.

The Jews without faith are in the same situation. They have sinned under the Law, and thus they will be judged by the Law and will suffer the destruction and fury of God's wrath at the end of time (Rom. 2:12; cf. also 2:8–9). According to Paul's system of convictions, their situation is homologable to that of the pagans. And thus we can expect that they also perverted what was given to them as the manifestation of God's power and deity, namely, the Law, and that they were given up by God to their selfish desires so as to corrupt and destruct themselves. Their conduct is also a manifestation of God's wrath. This is what Paul expresses in 2:1–24, which he introduces by these words: "Therefore you have no excuse, O man, whoever you are, . . . because you . . . are doing the very same things."[20] The Jews will object to such a description of their life. They do not have such depraved behavior. And to Paul's accusations that they are stealing, committing adultery, robbing temples, and dishonoring God (cf. 2:17–24), the Jews could object: "You, Paul, the former Pharisee, should know better. Of course, there are always evil people in a community. But as you know, many of us are 'as to the righteousness under the law blameless' [Phil. 3:6] as you were. And we are striving to sanctify the Name and to keep the Name of God from being blasphemed among the Gentiles because of us [cf. Rom. 2:24]. This is a defamation of the Jews."

But Paul is not concerned with providing an accurate description of the Jewish way of life. He is merely pointing out that, according to his system of convictions, the Jews' situation is equivalent to that of the pagans, whom they so readily judge and condemn in the very terms used in the preceding passage. Whatever might be the concrete expression of their sinfulness, they are just as sinful as the pagans are. Indeed, their sin is the same. This is what we found expressed in Galatians, where Paul identifies his own experience as a Jew with the Galatians' experience as pagans (see Chapter 2). Thus, in the same way that the pagans are enslaved to the idols that they have made out of the creatures which manifested God to them, so the Jews are enslaved to the Law given to them by God and out of which they made an absolute means of salvation by viewing it as the complete and final revelation (see above, Chapter 3).

### The Jews as Typical Sinners and the Power of Sin (Rom. 7:7–25)

This enslavement to the Law has the same effect upon the Jews' life that the enslavement to idolatry has on the pagans. The pagans follow the demands of their bodies—this part of the creation out of which they made an absolute—because they believe that in so doing they do good (and thus they approve those who do such things; Rom. 1:32). Similarly, the Jews follow the demands of the Law—this revelation that they received from God and out of which they made an absolute—because they believe that in so doing they do good. By seeking to fulfill the Law, by doing works of the Law in order to attain righteousness, they fail to attain righteousness. Why? Because they do not succeed in fulfilling the Law (9:31). And how could they? By the very fact that they seek to establish their own righteousness instead of submitting to God's righteousness (10:3), they are transgressing the Law, or better, transgressing its very essence. They are corrupting the Law. Furthermore, the pagans "know God's decree that those who do such things deserve to die" (1:32), as their own lists of vices and virtues show. Nevertheless, they do these evil things. Similarly, the Jews know what sin is. The Law showed them what it is (7:7). They know also that sin brings death (5:12). And yet they do these very things that the Law condemns.

The Jews do have an advantage over the pagans: "The Jews are entrusted with the oracles of God" (Rom. 3:1–2). The pagans had only the revealed knowledge of God's decrees, concerning what is good and evil. By being given the Law, Torah, the Jews had not only a revealed knowledge of what is good and evil as expressed in the various laws, that is, a knowledge of the various sins as transgressions of these laws. They also had God's oracles, God's words, that is, his promises and verbal revelations. Among these is the revelation of the nature of sin. The pagans know God and know his decrees. They know that the way of life they follow because of their enslavement to idolatry is evil. Yet they do not know that the evil in which they are enslaved is a manifestation of God's wrath because they did not honor and give thanks to him. Furthermore, they do not know why they refused to give honor and thanks to God and why they became idolatrous. According to Paul, the Jews knew why. God's oracles reveal why people do not honor and give thanks to God. It is because of a power: the power of sin.

Yes, the pagans have no excuse. They know God and his decrees. Therefore they are under the wrath of God and will perish at the end of time. But the Jews will perish first (Rom. 2:9), because they have even less of an excuse since, in addition, they also knew the nature of sin (3:20). This additional revelation did not help them. They stumbled over it. They hear it. They know it. But they do not truly hear it. They have ears which do not hear.

In Rom. 7:7–25 Paul describes this situation of the Jews, which is also the situation of all sinners whatever their origin and the time in which they live. This passage first addresses the heart of the problem of evil, which is sin, and then moves on to describe the concrete experience of the sinners.

### SIN AND ITS POWER (ROM. 7:7–13)

What then shall we say? That the law is sin? By no means! Yet, if it had not been for the law, I should not have known sin. I should not have known what it is to covet if the law had not said, "You shall not covet." But sin, finding opportunity in the commandment, wrought in me all kinds of covetousness. Apart from the law sin lies dead. I was once alive apart from the law, but when the commandment came, sin revived and I died; the very commandment which promised life proved to be death to me. For sin, finding opportunity in the commandment, deceived me and by it killed me. So the law is holy, and the commandment is holy and just and good.

Did that which is good, then, bring death to me? By no means! It was sin, working death in me through what is good, in order that sin might be shown to be sin, and through the commandment might become sinful beyond measure. (Rom. 7:7–13)

In the context of a discussion about the Christians' freedom from the Law (Rom. 7:1–6), Paul had stated, "While we were living in the flesh, our sinful passions, aroused by the law, were at work in our members to bear fruit for death" (7:5). From this the reader could conclude that the Law is sin. Thus one of the purposes of this passage is to show that it is not sin, but revelation from God. We have already discussed how, for Paul, any revelation is both a potential blessing (for the believers) and a potential curse (for the unbelievers). Here he describes in greater detail why this is so.

To begin with, here the Law is described as the revelation of sin. Without the Law, one does not know sin, as Paul repeatedly affirms: "through the law comes knowledge of sin" (Rom. 3:20). Of course, the Law gives a knowledge of the transgressions of God's will, for "where there is no law there is no transgression" (4:15; cf. 5:13). Because of the Law (or, better, the laws), we can know our standing before God and be aware that we are sinners. But this is not what Paul means here. In fact, in these verses the Law conveys knowledge of sin in two ways:

First, "our sinful passions [are] aroused by the law" (Rom. 7:5). In other words, we "know" sin because we are sinners. It is the Law as curse which makes sinners out of us. We shall come back to this.

Second, the Law gives a knowledge of what sin is. The commandment "You shall not covet" is *not* given as an example (as would be the case if Paul had written, "for instance, I should not have known what it is to covet . . ."). This commandment is for Paul a summary of the whole Law. Paul follows a Jewish tradition which saw in this commandment the core of the Law.[21] In other words, the Law reveals that sin is primarily "coveting" or "desire," as the Greek word can also be translated. Furthermore, by quoting only the first words of this commandment, Paul makes it clear that this coveting is most general. It is the selfish desire to which the pagans were themselves enslaved (Rom. 1:24). Indeed, all the transgressions of the Law can be viewed as having their root in such a *selfish desire*. Any transgression is wanting and pursuing something *for oneself* rather than serving God. This selfish desire can take crude forms, such as stealing (taking for oneself what is not one's own), committing adultery (taking for oneself the spouse of someone else), or not honoring one's parents (by keeping things for oneself). But it can take more subtle forms. Seeking to establish one's own righteousness rather than submitting to God's righteousness (10:3) is a form of coveting. Serving God for oneself is also a form of coveting. It is sin. It is idolatry, as Paul suggested in Galatians. Any kind of idolatry has its roots in coveting.

Here and in the following verses Paul expresses the dramatic and tragic effect and power of sin upon any human being by speaking in the first person. Sin is not merely a problem for those infamous pagans about whom he spoke in Romans 1, or for those hardened Jews who reject the good news of Jesus Christ. It is also a problem for him, as well as for any human being. Sin as selfish desire is the source of all idolatries, including the idolatries which involve making idols out of the true God and out of Christ (see below, Chapter 8). In other words, it is because of sin that we view our systems of convictions as absolute and that they have power over us as self-evident truths, instead of viewing them as provisional views of life and of the world constantly pointing beyond themselves, as Paul's faith demands. Indeed, this view of sin—together with the complementary conviction about God's activity in the believers' experience—is the basis upon which Paul's entire meta-system of convictions stands.

### SIN AS SELF-ASSERTING DESIRE

We need to circumscribe Paul's use of the term sin/desire. First, it should not be limited to sexual desire. Paul refers to "desire" in the most general sense. It can take the forms of "all kinds of covetousness" (or desire) (Rom. 7:8). Thus sexual desire is only one form of sin/desire.

Second, for Paul, sin/desire is closely associated with death and life. "Sin revived and I died" (Rom. 7:9). The Law which reveals sin/desire is supposed to bring life: "The very commandment which promised life proved to be death to me" (7:10). Thus sin/desire tricks me into pursuing death instead of pursuing life (cf. 7:11). This implies that sin/desire deceived me into thinking that, by following it, I should have life although it was leading me to death.

Third, Paul notes that sin is "finding opportunity in the commandment" (Rom. 7:11). In other words, sin existed before the Law, as Paul says explicitly in 5:13, "Sin indeed was in the world before the law was given"—in the world since the beginning of humankind. Indeed, sin/desire is a characteristic of humankind. It pervades humankind: "All have sinned" (3:23). Sin/desire is a part of the human condition.

Thus, for Paul, sin/desire, which is related to idolatry, appears to be an integral part of the human condition. As such it is closely related to two other characteristics of the human condition: life and death. This suggests that Paul's convictions about sin/desire are, together with convictions about life and death, a part of the fundamental cluster of convictions which characterizes his faith. We know that Paul's cluster of fundamental convictions also includes convictions about the right relationship with God, that is, true faith which is opposed to idolatry (i.e., false faith). Before dealing with any specific manifestation of sin/desire, we must therefore raise a question: for Paul, how is sin/desire related to life, death, true faith, and idolatry?

There are a limited number of ways in which these five convictions can be interrelated. We already know that true faith and idolatry are opposed as life and death also are. It appears, therefore, that sin/desire brings about idolatry, which in turn brings about death (or destruction; Rom. 2:12). In contrast, it is freedom from idolatry which brings about true faith (the right relationship with God) and life (true life, honor, glory; 2:10). Yet it remains for us to understand what this means. How does sin/desire bring about idolatry?

It might be useful to describe this process with the help of concepts borrowed from a few contemporary thinkers who, like Paul, closely interrelate sin/desire, idolatry (false faith), and death. Of course, their vocabulary is different from Paul's; for instance, they do not speak about sin but merely about desire. In the following comments, I intend to borrow from these thinkers some concepts which will allow us to construct a kind of philosophical parable.

When reflecting on the characteristics of the human condition, social scientists often compare and contrast human beings and animals. The instincts of animals are sometimes seen as the major difference between humans and animals, because humans have little or no instinctive behavior.[22] In effect, instincts have the same function for the animals as a system of convictions has for human beings.

1. Instincts have power over the animals.

2. Instincts define for animals their "world," the relations that they must have with the world. Thus instincts dictate the habitat, the eco-

logical milieu, in which a given species must live and outside of which it would become extinct. For example, a certain species of wasps cannot reproduce itself without a certain species of caterpillars which they paralyze and in which they lay their eggs. Without such an instinct this wasp species would not survive, but it also could not survive in a world where there are no such caterpillars.

3. Instincts define for the animals their "identity" and the "purpose of their lives." There is no quest for identity and no real freedom for these animals. From birth a bird is a bird and has in its body complex instincts which allow it to migrate and to build a nest at the proper season. This is not to say that they do not learn anything, but what they learn is how to implement their instincts in specific situations. They can also lose their instincts, but in the process they lose their "identity"—for instance, when they are domesticated and become dependent upon people for their survival—for these instincts which determine the animals' identities, their destinies, their fates, are also what allow them to survive.

By contrast, human beings are born with almost no instincts and therefore without a predetermined identity. Therefore they have fantastic freedom. They can choose whom they shall be. Their society gives them a first identity, but they can choose to transform this society or to have a life different from the one imposed upon them by their society. Collectively they *construct* "semantic universes," and in this way *they* establish what is a good world and a good life. As individuals they can modify this semantic universe and "reconstruct" it to establish their own individual identities and thus the purposes of their lives.

Even though this view of the human condition does not include any thought about the divine, it is consistent with Paul's own view. As we saw, Paul presupposes that human beings are fundamentally free to choose their identity. Humans are able to view themselves in relationship with God or to view themselves in other ways, as the pagans chose to do. God does not impose upon them an identity, a destiny, a fate. But the identity they choose becomes their fate. For instance, they are enslaved to their idolatry. This is where desire intervenes.

Human beings are free to establish their own identity and their own semantic universe, but there are limitations to their freedom. People cannot fly like birds. They have to use aircraft. Sigmund Freud called this limitation the *reality principle*. People have to accept certain limitations, but within the framework of these limitations they can follow their own "drives," their own desire to be what they want to be. What is this drive or desire? Freud said it is the *pleasure principle*. People choose what will give them the most "pleasure," in the broadest sense of the term. As far as possible I will strive to be in a warm and dry place rather than in the cold and the rain. It is clear that this drive or desire, led by the pleasure principle, is not what Paul views as sin, as evil desire.

Herbert Marcuse and Norman O. Brown[23] appropriated Freud's insight and developed it further. Human beings follow the pleasure principle, but there is another important drive which explains people's behavior. Marcuse calls it the *performance principle,* a concept which could be related to Paul's concept of the "works of the law," the drive or desire to do good works. Brown describes it as a *drive to do death-defying works,* a concept we could relate to fulfilling the Law because the Law "promised life" (Rom. 7:10). Although in a different vocabulary, the philosopher Jean-Paul Sartre describes the same drive when, in the context of his discussion of "bad faith," he speaks of a *drive to become a being as things are.*[24]

For each of these authors this drive, this basic desire, has its origin in human freedom and insecurity. Humans cannot live in insecurity. They cannot be without an identity. They cannot stand the idea of not-being (nothingness), and therefore death is a constant source of anxiety. Humans want to live, to survive like the stones and the mountains which appear to be eternal. For this purpose humans struggle to overcome this insecurity, to find an identity, to make out of themselves "something" they feel will be worthwhile. For this reason, both collectively and individually, they "perform" all kinds of things which will give value to their lives. In this way they overcome the fear of death. They will survive in their works. On their tombstone will be written what they were, indeed, what they are: a hero who died for his country; a woman who dedicated herself to the betterment of society; a great philosopher; and so on.

This fundamental self-asserting desire, this performing principle, this drive to do death-defying works and to be "something" leads humans to create idols and absolute systems of convictions. Sartre illustrates this subtle process by taking the example of love. Our parable of the lovers and more precisely its very beginning—a man and a woman *in love*—has already described the result of this process. Their love is an absolute system of convictions, an idolatry. What we now need to understand is how they constructed this absolute system of convictions, how they became idolatrous. In other words, how did they fall in love? In brief, it is because of sin, that is, because of desire (coveting), or again because of the performance principle.

We are discussing the courting process. The man charms the woman and the woman charms the man. Let us take the case of the man, with the understanding that the same things could be said about the woman. Why does he charm the woman? Why does he do everything to cast a spell on her? Is it because of his sexual drive (or desire)? This might play a role, but it is not the actual reason. There are ways of satisfying sexual drive without falling in love. In fact, he is charming the woman in order to satisfy his performance principle. He wants somebody—in this instance, the woman—who will recognize some kind of value in him. He wants somebody he will be able to trust, somebody who will always recognize value in him, in the better as well as in the worst of circumstances. He wants her to see in him a hero when he succeeds and a martyr when he fails. He wants somebody who will always be on his side, whatever may happen, somebody who will constantly affirm and confirm his worthiness, somebody who will always understand him. For this purpose he charms the woman. He casts a spell on her in subtle ways. He manipulates her in such a way that she owes so much to him that she cannot but play her role. In other words, she will now satisfy his performance principle, his self-asserting desire, by constantly confirming his identity and the value of his life.

Of course, the woman charms the man in the same ways and for the same reasons. They allow themselves to be manipulated by each other and accept the role of asserting the value of each other's identity, because in this way they make themselves indispensable to the other, who therefore cannot but assert the value of their own identity. Thus they establish between them a network of relations which will govern their mutual assertion. In other words, they establish their love as a system of convictions which establishes their identities.

But consider the result of this process. The man loves the woman and asserts the value of her identity and of her life: she is a unique, exceptional person. The woman does the same things for the man. They are no longer affirming the value of their own life. There is no longer a need for self-assertion. The man is asserting the value of the life of the woman. Now she is what she desired to be. This value of her life is an objective reality, since it is no longer she who claims it but the man who recognizes it and affirms it. And the same is true for the man when the value of his life is affirmed by the woman. His life has value. He is a "good man" or a "great man," whatever the appearances and the circumstances. This is objective. He *is* a "good man" as the stones are stones. The performance principle, the self-asserting desire, fades into the background. He can and must deny this self-asserting desire and the performance principle which led to the establishment of their love as an absolute system of convictions. Acknowledging the origin of their love in this mutual manipulation would be acknowledging that his identity and its value are nothing but his self-assertion and therefore that he has no actual reality. Overt manipulation (i.e., charming) is no longer necessary. Expressing their love to each other (i.e., asserting that the other is a very special person) is enough of a manipulation to force the partner to remain in his or her role of asserting the value of the other's identity. Not remaining in this role would be running the risk of losing one's identity as an objective reality. Thus love as system of convictions is self-reinforcing.

Then we find this apparent paradox. The lovers can fully reveal themselves to each other. They do not need to hide anything from each other. They can be confident that even their weaknesses will be viewed positively by their partner. Loving is allowing oneself to be fully known. Love is not blushing when showing oneself to the other. Even one's self-asserting desire is unveiled and thus can be seen. For instance, the man will speak to the woman of his ambitions. But because of love this self-asserting desire is not seen for what it is. Thus love, which is by definition unselfish, has become the ally of selfish desire. The woman interprets the manifestation of self-asserting desire in the man's life as a noble, altruistic desire and asserts it in this way to the man who himself sees it as an altruistic desire, even though he "knows" that it is a self-asserting desire. This is what Sartre calls "bad faith." I know that I am not this person described by the other, but I nevertheless believe the other whom I have manipulated so that he/she will send me this image of myself. I need to be somebody, something. This is what Paul expresses by such statements as "they became futile in their thinking and their senseless minds were darkened" (Rom. 1:21); they "were hardened" (11:7); they have "a spirit of stupor, eyes that should not see and ears that should not hear" (11:8).

What should we say? That love is self-asserting desire and manipulation? By no means! Yet if it had not been for love I would not have known self-asserting desire. Indeed, I would not have known desire if love had not said, "Love does not insist on its own right" (cf. 1 Cor. 13:5). But self-asserting desire, finding opportunity in love, wrought in me all kinds of selfishness (cf. Rom. 7:7–8). Love multiplied the manifestations of self-asserting desire (cf. 5:20) by making believe that they are not selfish because "love bears all things, believes all things, hopes all things, endures all things" (1 Cor. 13:7).

This is the story of any idolatry, according to Paul. It involves three steps.

1. In our quest for identity, in our craving for identity, for meaning and purpose in our lives, for being something which has an objective reality, through our self-asserting desire we take hold of something which is good and/or has a real existence. This is to say that we take hold of something which is self-evidently real and good, that is, of a revelation: God's revelatory manifestations in the creation (Rom. 1:18–32); God's revelation in Torah (7:7–12); love as fruit of the Spirit; Christ as manifestation of God (cf. 1 and 2 Corinthians); the political authorities which "have been instituted by God" (Rom. 13:1); and so on. Each of them is "holy and just and good" (Rom. 7:12). Each of them reveals our true condition: that we are creatures whose meaning and purpose can be established only in relationship to our Creator; that we are people constantly desiring identity and whose identity can be established only by an election from God, who chooses us as his people; that we are people who cannot but be in relationship with other people because in them God manifests himself and thus they are better than ourselves (Phil. 2:3); that we are people who cannot have a true identity if it were not for Christ-like manifestations of God in our experience; that we are people who cannot live without order provided by political and cultural institutions, because without them we would not have any guideline for discerning useful from harmful conduct.

2. Our holding on to something which is good and/or which has a real existence demonstrates that "what can be known about God is plain to [us], because God has shown it to [us]" (Rom. 1:19). Furthermore, we know about our human condition because we know God's decree (1:32) and the nature of sin (7:7), and thus we "know that nothing good dwells in [us], that is, in [our] flesh" (7:18).

3. But our self-asserting desire (our performance principle) leads us to absolutize our relationship to one or the other of God's manifestations. In this way we will have an identity, an objective, permanent identity. It does not matter what this identity is. What we dread is *not having* an identity. If our identity, our fate, is to be a slave to the "weak and beggarly elemental spirits" of the cosmos (Gal. 4:9), this satisfies our self-asserting desire. We *are* something. This is what is essential for us. It does not matter if this something is a cog in a machine-like universe, a slob whose fate is to wiggle in the mud, a prostitute subjected to the most abject treatment (in sacred prostitution possibly alluded to in Rom. 1:24, or in secular prostitution as discussed by Sartre)[25] or a member of the holy Chosen People, which is "little less than God" and whom God "crowns with glory and honor" (Ps. 8:5).

In order to absolutize our relationship to one of God's manifestations, we need to transform it so that it might be a fixed mirror which always gives us the same image of ourselves. We need to manipulate this manifestation of God, to charm it, to fossilize it. The lovers of our parable make "idols" out of each other, that is, they reduce each other to fixed images with immutable qualities and roles. The pagans make out of this or that part of the creation an idealized and fixed image: a golden calf (to which Paul alludes in Rom. 1:23 by using the vocabulary of Ps. 106:20); stone or wood "images resembling mortal man or birds or animals or reptiles" (1:23). The Jews make out of the Law (i.e., out of Torah, as promises of God) the complete and final revelation. The Christians make out of Christ an absolute spiritual reality (which, as we shall see, some of the Corinthians did). Certain people make out of the state or of the Roman emperor, a god. And so on.

Once they are transformed into idols, these manifestations of God satisfy our self-asserting desire. They establish for us a permanent, objective identity. We no longer have to fear "nothingness." We no longer have to be anxious about death. In other words, our idols promise life to us. Such is the case for the Jews and their idol, Torah. They view Torah as promising life to them (see above, Chapter 3). Paul writes: "The very commandment which promised life" (Rom. 7:10). But despite our "bad faith," according to which we profess to believe this, we know and should be aware (although we are not aware of it because of our "bad faith") that this is not in fact true, since it is we who constructed this idol. This is nothing else than a death-defying attitude.

What is the result of this attitude? Yes, we have an objective, permanent identity. We have made it. We are lovers in love. We are forever the Chosen People. We are attuned to the universe (the cosmos) and participate in its eternity. We are spiritual beings saved from this world (I allude, once more, to the heretics in Corinth). We are a celebrity. We are rich. We are really something. But this also means that we are trapped in a role. We are condemned to play our role. When you are a celebrity, you cannot but behave accordingly. When you are a lover, you cannot but behave accordingly. We are "something" as the stones are. We are no longer truly alive. We are living dead. We are in hell where everything is fixed for all eternity. We are under the wrath of God. We have lost what makes us alive: our freedom. We are fossilized as much as our idols are.

We are nothing else than this something we desired to be. We are this something that our idols tell us we are. We are enslaved, bewitched, under the power of a curse. We are no longer truly persons. We have lost any authentic existence. We are "as good as dead."

Paul, speaking of the Jews and the Law (as well as of human beings under the power of any kind of idols), writes: "I was once alive apart from the law"—that is, as long as I did not "appropriate" the Law—"but when the commandment came, sin revived and I died" (Rom. 7:9). Taking advantage of this revelation of God, desire, self-asserting desire, which was dormant, became alive and active. And I died.

"The very commandment which promised life"—that is, which truly promised life as revelation of God and which deceitfully promised life as idol—"proved to be death to me" (Rom. 7:10). "For sin [desire], finding opportunity in the commandment, deceived me"—by causing me to see in it an absolute, the complete and final revelation—"and by it killed me" (7:11).

Despite my "bad faith" brought about by sin (self-asserting desire), I know that the Law is truly revelation from God. Paul can then affirm that this proves what is evil is not the Law itself but sin and what sin has made out of the Law: "So the law is holy, and the commandment is holy and just and good" (7:12). Therefore it is not the Law which brought death to me. "It was sin, working death in me through what is good" (7:13). In this way, since there is no doubt that the Law is good and from God, one can clearly see what the nature of sin is and what its role in human experience is. The Law magnifies sin and thus makes it clearly apparent (7:13).

LIFE UNDER SIN (ROM. 7:14–24)

Paul describes the life under sin as the life according to the flesh (7:14). This is a life governed by the idol which we have made for ourselves and which enslaves us. Paul is *not* describing the common experience of interior ethical conflict,[26] according to which, while our conscience tells us that we should not do something, we nevertheless go and do it. These are minor struggles which occur when we are caught between conflicting systems of convictions. But in Romans 7 Paul speaks about the situation of people who are totally committed to a system of convictions, in this case the Jewish system of convictions viewed as complete and final revelation.

"I do not understand my own actions" (Rom. 7:15a) or, more literally, "I do not know what I am doing." I "know that the law is spiritual" (7:14). "I agree that the law is good" (7:16). "I delight in the law of God, in my inmost self" (7:22). I know that it is the Law of God, revelation from God. And I want to serve God. Indeed, I strive to serve God. But by doing so I serve sin (my self-asserting desire), and thus my actions are against God. "I do not do what I want" (serving God), "but I do the very thing I hate" (acting against God and his will) (7:15). In fact, I practice the idolatry that I abhor (cf. 2:1).

So I am enslaved to sin. "It is no longer I that do it, but sin which dwells within me" (Rom. 7:17, 20, 23). "I can will what is right, but I cannot do it" (7:18; cf. 7:19). As soon as I undertake to do the good that I want, I end up doing evil.

This becomes clear when we put these comments in the context of what Paul says about the Jews. The more the Jews strive to do good works, that is, the more the Jews strive to "fulfill" the Law in order to sanctify God's Name, to be a faithful people, the less they "fulfill" the Law (9:31). I purposely used the phrase "fulfill the Law" twice but with different meanings, in the same way Paul does. In the context of Judaism as a system of convictions which sees Torah as the complete and final revelation, fulfilling the Law means carrying out the laws. It means striving to be the Chosen People, and to carry out one's vocation of sanctifying the Name. The Jews are aware that they do not totally fulfill the Law, that they transgress the laws and that as a result "the name of God is blasphemed among the Gentiles" instead of being sanctified (Rom. 2:24; cf. 2:17–29). But this is a "minor" problem. In Torah, as perceived in Judaism, there are means of atonement if they repent and thus if they commit themselves to striving even harder to fulfill the Law.

From Paul's perspective, however, the more they strive to fulfill the laws, the more they make Torah the complete and final revelation, the idol Torah. The more they do good, the more impossible it becomes to see in Torah the promises of new interventions and revelations of God. The more they strive to sanctify the Name of God, the less he is sanctified, that is, the less he can be recognized and thus honored and given thanks in his interventions in the present. The more they do works of the Law and the more they are striving to be in the right relationship with God, the less they are in the right relationship with God, for fulfilling Torah, from the Gospel perspective, is discovering in one's experience the fulfillment of the promises contained in Torah, and giving thanks and honoring God as revealed in these fulfillments. The true fulfillment of Torah is through faith and not through works.

When Paul attacks the Jews for seeking to establish their own righteousness, he does not want to say that they are consciously selfish, that they have selfish or greedy motives. No. They truly want to serve God. "I bear them witness that they have a zeal for God" (Rom. 10:2). But they are under the power of sin, which made them transform Torah into the complete and final revelation and thus darkened and hardened their hearts, eyes, and ears. And thus their zeal is "not enlightened" (10:2), not governed by a true understanding freed from the power of sin.

The more I want to do good, the deeper I find myself involved in evil. "So I find it to be a law that when I want to do right, evil lies close at hand" (Rom. 7:21). "So then, I of myself serve the law of God with my mind"—that is, "with my mind" I recognize that the Law is from God, as the pagans recognize "with their mind" the works of God in the creation (1:20), and thus I want to serve God, I am devoted to God —"but with my flesh I serve the law of sin" (7:25b) as the pagans "serve" the "creation," once submitted to their futile way of thinking and their senseless and darkened minds (1:21).[27] This is true for every human being. Sin is an integral part of living in the flesh, of being human. How could I not have self-asserting desire? How could I not seek to find an identity for myself? How could I not have a will to live and thus a will to overcome all kinds of death threats? How could I survive without such a death-defying attitude? As is well known, many patients survive terminal disease for unexpectedly long periods, when they have such a will to live, while people in good clinical health without such a will to live let themselves die. Is it not our nature to have such a self-asserting desire?

And thus how could we not make idols out of any revelation from God? How could we not get hold, grasp, and hang on to anything which would give us a clue about who we are and what is the purpose and meaning of our life? But then, how could we not destroy ourselves by becoming "something" as things are, living dead? And how could we not do evil, and bring death to ourselves, each time we strive to do good?

"Wretched man that I am! Who will deliver me from this body of death?" (Rom. 7:24). "No Exit," concludes Sartre in his well-known play.[28] Paul concludes, "Thanks be to God through Jesus Christ our Lord" (7:25a). "For the law of the Spirit of life in Christ Jesus has set me free from the law of sin and death" (8:2).

## THE GOSPEL AS POWER OF GOD
## FOR SALVATION

### Freed from the Law of Sin and Death

There is therefore now no condemnation for those who are in Christ Jesus. For the law of the Spirit of life in Christ Jesus has set me free from the law of sin and death. For God has done what the law, weakened by the flesh, could not do: sending his own Son in the likeness of sinful flesh and for [or in reference to] sin, he condemned sin in the flesh, in order that the just requirement of the law might be fulfilled in us, who walk not according to the flesh but according to the Spirit. (Rom. 8:1–4)

"Who will deliver me from this body of death? Thanks be to God through Jesus Christ our Lord." We begin to understand why God's intervention is needed in the believers' experience. Without it any human being is irremediably caught under the power of sin and condemned to death as his or her life—a living death—already manifests.

From a theological/sacred historical perspective, the need and role of the reconciliation performed by Jesus' death appears. On the one hand, all humans, including the Jews, are under the wrath of God. All are alienated from God. And thus, without reconciliation, there is no possible answer to the desperate cry of the sinner. On the other hand, this reconciling act of God needs to be extraordinary as compared with the previous interventions of God which were ineffective. The previous revelations were manifested in direct and positive interventions of God in his creation (in which God's eternal power and deity are clearly perceived [Rom. 1:20]) or in the giving of Torah to Israel (which was directly manifested as "holy and just and good" [7:12]). Another revelation of this kind, for instance, the revelation of a glorious and spiritual Christ, would not overcome the separation of human beings from God. On the contrary, as the Law did, it would increase trespasses, giving another opportunity for sin, idolatry. This is exactly what happens when some of the Corinthians want to proclaim a spiritual Christ rather than a crucified Christ. And thus God, in his wisdom, chose to manifest himself in sinful flesh by "sending his own Son in the likeness of sinful flesh" (8:3).

This verse is usually interpreted from the theological perspective to mean that Christ was sent "for sin," as a sacrifice for the expiation of sin (as in Rom. 3:25), so that sin might be forgiven and that the reconciliation of humankind to God might take place. "There is therefore now no condemnation for those who are in Christ Jesus" (8:1). But here this expiation of sin is not "passing over former sins" (pretending that sin does not exist). It is a judgment and a punishment of sin which so radically separates human beings from God and for which they have no excuse. This condemnation of sin in the flesh is accomplished by Christ, who is "in the likeness of sinful flesh." And this takes place so that what was the true purpose of the Law (its righteous effect) might be fulfilled in us, that is, so that we might walk according to the Spirit and not according to the flesh (8:4b). But from this theological perspective we cannot fully understand this "condemnation of sin in the flesh," a phrase with which commentators struggle.

This passage expresses important aspects of Paul's system of convictions and especially how God's interventions are related to the manifestations of evil. Paul does *not* say that Christ has set us free *from sin* or that sin in itself is condemned. He writes in 8:2: "Christ Jesus has set [us] free *from the law* of sin and death." Thus Paul says that Christ set us free from the law that "I see in my members" (7:23a), "the law of sin which dwells in my members" (7:23b), that is, in "this body of death" (7:24). Similarly, it is "sin in the flesh" which is condemned (8:3). And in 8:3b, Paul speaks of the flesh as "the flesh of sin" ("sinful flesh").

### The Power of Sin Is the Law

These statements can be understood when one notes that for Paul there are three basic manifestations of evil: sin, the Law as idol (or the creation as idol), and death. Furthermore, let us keep in mind that, by itself, sin is powerless. It is dormant (it needs to be "revived"; Rom. 7:9) as long as it is not joined with the Law (or God's revelation in the creation). The power of sin is the Law as idol. Yes, it is sin which brings death, and death would not exist if it were not for sin (5:12). But sin would be inoffensive without an idol, be it the Law or any other kind of idol. Thus Paul, in a passage where he does not mention the Law, exclaims in a formula he used many times, "The sting of death is sin, and the power of sin is the law" (1 Cor. 15:56).

It is clear, after our reading of Romans 1 and 7, that the Law and the creation are by themselves holy, just, and good. But sin, the self-asserting desire, establishes human beings in a perverted relation to them. They are manipulated and absolutized, instead of being taken for what they are, manifestations of God's power which are promises (or types) of new acts of God and thus occasions to honor and thank God. These perverted perceptions of God's interventions are the manifestations of sin. God's wrath is then manifested in that they are enslaved to these perverted perceptions of God's interventions, which then become fully idols which have power over sinners. This is the present situation of the sinners. They are enslaved to these idols and misled by them, so much so that the more they strive to do good the more they do evil. They have senseless and darkened minds, a spirit of stupor, hardened hearts, eyes that do not see, ears that do not hear. They are "in the flesh," "given up to the flesh," in other words, "given up in the desires of their hearts to impurity" (Rom. 1:24, au. trans.; cf. 1:26, 28).

Thus Paul distinguished two evil powers. First, *the power (or sting) of death which is sin*. This is the deeply rooted self-asserting desire. Even after Christ this power remains. It will be destroyed only at the very end of time: "The last enemy to be destroyed is death" (1 Cor. 15:26). In addition, Paul believes that the Christian believers are still under the power of death-bringing sin. They are not immune to death, and he constantly exhorts his readers to avoid selfish and self-asserting attitudes. Furthermore, Paul emphasizes, against the enthusiast Christians, that the believers are not purely spiritual beings but rather very human beings with all the limitations and weaknesses of this condition. Sin, the self-asserting desire which leads one to perform death-defying works and to make idols, is still present in the Christian believers. Although it is dormant (because its power is being destroyed), it can revive at any time if it is given the opportunity.

The second evil power that Paul distinguished is *the power of sin which is the Law or any other idol.* This is the power which enslaves the sinners. It is experienced by the sinners as the power of their idols. As a Christian, Paul can affirm that the idols have no real existence since there is only one God. But he acknowledges their power upon the pagans and even upon "weak brethren" (1 Cor. 8:4–13). In fact, Paul underscores the reality of this power by pointing out that it is a power given by God to the idols. It is the manifestation of the wrath of God. It is the power of a curse. From this power the Christian believers have been freed and are being freed. This is what Christ has done and what the resurrected Christ, in Christ-like interventions of God, is doing in the present (Rom. 8:2) and until the end of time. He is and will be "destroying every rule and every authority and power. For he must reign until he has put all his enemies under his feet" (1 Cor. 15:24b, 25).

The Law as idol is singled out by Paul as the most typical manifestation of the power of sin because it is the perversion of the most significant revelations of God before Christ. Torah is not merely the manifestation of the interventions of God, as the creation was, but also and primarily the words of God (Rom. 3:2), his verbal promises, as well as his covenants, his law, and his instructions about worship (9:4).

Under the power of the Law or of any other idol, human beings are helpless. They are dead (7:9). They are as good as dead, like Abraham's and Sarah's bodies (4:19). They are under a curse. We can understand this situation in terms of our reading of Galatians (above, Chapter 2) and of our discussion of the power of systems of convictions (Chapter 1). Such persons are fully under the power of a closed and static system of convictions which is centered upon that idol and which is therefore an idolatrous system of convictions, a curse. This system of convictions provides the idolaters with identity, meaning, and purpose. It provides them with what they view as the "only possible and true" life and with the only "true" perception of the reality of the world. As such, their idolatrous system of convictions gives them security, peace, and happiness, a feeling of wholeness in a secure identity, as lovers have during their honeymoon. They do not feel guilty about this idolatry. On the contrary, they have a guilty conscience when they step out of their idolatrous system of convictions. When they repent, it is in order to become once more faithful to their idolatry.

Anything which does not fit into their idolatrous system of convictions is therefore rejected by the idolaters as non-real, illusion, and/or evil. It does not belong to the "real world" formed by their semantic universe.

Thus they see it, but they do not see it as real. They hear it, but they do not perceive it as a meaningful thing. They know it, but they cannot even imagine that it could be good. And if there are any threats against their system of convictions, the idolaters will do everything in their power to protect it. They will vengefully attack those who constitute a threat, even at the risk of their own lives. If their idolatrous system of convictions was destroyed, they would lose their "true life" anyway. Such is the power of an idolatrous system of convictions which Paul describes in his own vocabulary in Romans 1 and 7 and elsewhere.

## Destroying the Power of an Idolatrous System of Convictions

From Paul's perspective, that is, from the perspective of his own faith which is a meta-system of convictions characterized by freedom from any given system of convictions (from any idolatry), there are only two ways in which the power of a given idolatrous system of convictions can be destroyed.

It can be radically destroyed *"from the outside,"* by destroying all the idolaters who sustain it and give it power and at the same time are under its power. For Paul, this radical destruction will be the transcendent and vengeful manifestation of the wrath of God at the last judgment. It will bring to its ultimate end the self-destruction that the idolaters are pursuing following their senseless minds. The other possibility is for God to destroy the power of the idolatrous system of convictions *from the inside*. This is a gracious alternative which spares the idolaters while delivering them from the power of their idolatrous system of convictions. How is this a theoretical possibility according to Paul's system of convictions?

The idolaters, who have eyes but do not see anything foreign to their system of convictions, can perceive and acknowledge as real an intervention of God only if it fits into their system of convictions. Thus God's manifestation has to be *conformed* to, in the *likeness of* (Rom. 8:3; Phil. 2:7), this idolatrous system of convictions. Because of the way any system of convictions is organized, however, this "conformity" of God's manifestation to the idolatrous system needs to be twofold. Thus the destruction of the power of the idolatrous system of convictions needs to be a two-stage process. The order of these stages does not really matter, at least theoretically. Yet in most instances Paul seems to prefer one order to the other.

In the first place, an idolatrous system of convictions, as any system of convictions, is twofold. On the one hand, parts of reality are viewed as good and/or as attuned to the "divine." These include "wisdom" and/or positive manifestations of the "divine" (as defined by this idolatrous system) in situations viewed as blessings and interventions of a positive power. On the other hand, parts of reality are viewed as evil, folly, and perceived as "weakness," "sinful," "blasphemous," and/or "curse."

Consequently, if the purpose of God's intervention is to destroy the power of an idolatrous system of convictions, this intervention should not merely be, and cannot merely be, conformed to the positive parts of reality as defined by this system of convictions. In such a case it would reinforce its power; it would confirm the validity of the idolatrous system of convictions. As such, God's intervention would have the opposite effect from the one at which it aimed.

So there is only one possibility. In order to destroy the power of an idolatrous system of convictions, God's intervention must *be conformed to the negative parts of reality* as defined by this system. God must manifest himself in what will appear, from the standpoint of this system of convictions, to be evil, weakness, sinful, blasphemous, and/or curse. In this case, the idolaters will perceive this "manifestation of God" as real. It is part of the reality that they can see, hear, and know, despite and because of their senseless and perverted minds. But they will not and cannot recognize the "manifestation of God" as a manifestation of the divine. For them it is part of this dimension of reality that they must strive to avoid, strive to reject so as to be "good" and to be attuned to the "divine" and to have "real" meaning and purpose in their lives (according to their idolatrous system of convictions). And thus they reject this scandalous manifestation of "evil."

Up to this point the idolatrous system of convictions and its power are intact. Indeed, the power of the idolatrous system of convictions is manifested most clearly in the violent rejection of this scandalous manifestation of "evil." In this way the idolatrous system of convictions condemns itself. It demonstrates unambiguously on which side it is, namely, against the true God.

In a second stage of this destruction of the power of the idolatrous system of convictions, God's intervention, this scandalous manifestation of "evil," is *also conformed to* (made in the likeness of) the *positive parts* of reality according to the idolatrous system of convictions. This happens when this scandalous intervention is such that it has also to be perceived as a positive manifestation of the "divine" according to the idolatrous system of convictions, that is, as manifestation of goodness, of wisdom, of positive power, or in other words, as a blessing. At this point the idolaters perceive this manifestation for what it is, a manifestation of God.

But from the perspective of the idolatrous system of convictions, this same manifestation of God is simultaneously viewed, on the one hand, as "evil" and thus as nondivine or even antidivine and, on the other hand, as divine, good, blessing. As a consequence, the inner logic, that is, the very systemic organization, of the idolatrous system of convictions is shattered. Nothing makes sense any longer. What the idolatrous system of convictions led me to perceive as "evil" and to *reject* in the name of the "good" is shown to be good, to be divine or attuned to the divine. Thus some of what I took to be good is evil and vice versa. But some of what I took to be good (according to the idolatrous system of convictions) is good and some of what I took to be evil is still evil. What confusion! But one thing is clear. This well-ordered view of the world, of reality, of life's meaning and purpose that the idolatrous system of convictions was providing for me cannot be absolutely true. The power of this idolatrous system of convictions, this particular manifestation of the power of sin, has been destroyed. I am freed from it.

Before discussing how Paul describes this destruction of the power of sin in concrete instances, note what this process entails for Paul's system of convictions.

It involves the conviction that the power of sin (the power of an idolatrous system of convictions) is real. It is so real for him that he can speak of it in a personified way, or as a series of "personages" that he calls "rulers of this age," "powers," "authorities" (which are kinds of demons manifesting themselves in what has power over human beings).

Paul's view of the destruction of the power of sin also entails the conviction that any idolatrous system of convictions is the perversion of true and valid revelations. In other words, the idolaters, although in a confused way, still consider as good, as real, as divine what is truly good, real, and divine. Theoretically speaking, if this were not the case, the intervention of God could not be conformed to (or made in the likeness of) the "divine," and "good" (according to the idolatrous system of convictions), and thus could not be recognized (as real) by the idolaters. This is why Paul emphasizes not only that the Law is a true revelation of God, but also that "what can be known about God is plain" to the pagans (Rom. 1:19) and that they know God's decree (1:32; 2:15).

As far as Paul is concerned, these two kinds of revelations—through the creation for the pagans, through Torah for the Jews—are holy, just, and good. They do not contradict each other (2:14), and they are not nullified by Christ or any other revelation from God. Because none of these revelations is absolute, none is complete. All of them are promises pointing to new interventions and revelations of God and ultimately to those at the time of the Parousia which alone will be absolute and complete.

The process through which an idolatrous system of convictions is established and destroyed by the power of the Gospel can be represented graphically by stages as follows:

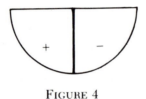

FIGURE 4

*First stage:* God reveals something (his power, deity, or "oracles") to people (Gentiles or Jews). This revelation is a partial system of convictions according to which parts of human experience are viewed as positive (+), that is, as real, good, and as attuned to the divine, while other parts of human experience are viewed as negative (−), that is, as illusory and/or evil, folly, sinful, blasphemous. We represent this revelation in Figure 4 as a partial circle to show that it is not a complete revelation (a complete system of convictions).

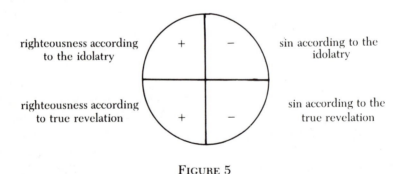

FIGURE 5

*Second stage*: This revelation is absolutized and transformed into an idolatrous system of convictions. We represent this process in Figure 5 by completing the circle. Idolatry amounts to deriving from the partial revelation (partial system of convictions) other positive and negative dimensions so as to have a complete system of convictions.

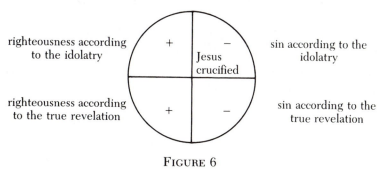

righteousness according to the idolatry    +    −    sin according to the idolatry

Jesus crucified

righteousness according to the true revelation    +    −    sin according to the true revelation

FIGURE 6

*Third stage*: Somebody (e.g., Jesus) performs certain actions which are sinful, blasphemous, evil, ungodly, *according to the definition of sin given by the idolatrous system of convictions*. This person is thus rejected and persecuted as a scandalous manifestation of evil (e.g., Jesus is crucified). But note that this person is *not* sinful according to the true revelation (against the true God).

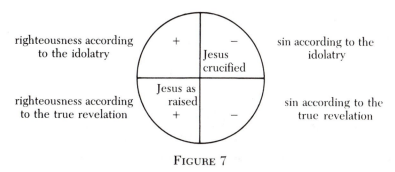

righteousness according to the idolatry    +    −    sin according to the idolatry

Jesus crucified

Jesus as raised

righteousness according to the true revelation    +    −    sin according to the true revelation

FIGURE 7

*Fourth stage*: God manifests himself in that person (Jesus, in our example) in such a way that the people who believe in this idolatry might recognize this manifestation as intervention of the divine (e.g., in the case of the Jews who believe in the resurrection, God raises Jesus from the dead).

At this point the logic of the idolatrous system of convictions is broken up and the power of the idolatry is destroyed, because what was rejected as being against "God" is also shown to be manifestation of "God." Thus, in our example, the event "Jesus crucified and raised" contradicts the logic of the idolatrous system. If the "reality" of this twofold event is acknowledged, the idolatry (the power of sin) is destroyed.

### The Uniqueness of Christ as the New Type of Divine Intervention

Such a view of the destruction of the power of sin involves the conviction that with Christ a new type of interventions of God begins. The previous revelations were primarily *constructive*. To the pagans is revealed God's "invisible nature, namely, his eternal power and deity" (Rom. 1:20). To the Jews are revealed God's covenant, Torah, the worship, the promises (9:4) and the nature of sin (7:7). But neither one of these revelations can set human beings free from the power of sin. Even the Law, Torah, could not do it (8:3). Rather, they have been "weakened by flesh," that is, by sin as manifested in the self-asserting desire of the flesh (8:3). Once weakened and perverted they became the ally of sin, which took advantage of them.

By contrast, with Christ a new type of divine revelations appears. These revelations are manifested in *destructive* interventions, which are aimed at destroying the power of sin or, better, all the powers of sin, "every rule and every authority and power" (1 Cor. 15:24). The destruction of these powers is a prelude to the destruction of the power of death at the very end. This is the uniqueness of God's manifestation in Jesus, according to Paul's system of convictions. Beyond its theological formulation in terms of reconciliation, God's manifestation in Jesus is eschatological in that it opens this last period of history, the end time, during which God will destroy all the powers of evil. And thus the only fitting titles for him are that of Christ, the Messiah king of the end time, the Son of God (who shares in God's power and destroys all powers; Ps. 2:7–9), the Lord who puts "all his enemies under his feet" (1 Cor. 15:25; Ps. 110:1). In Jesus Christ, the time of salvation from these powers is open.

Yet the revelation in Christ has many things in common with other revelations. First, the revelation in Christ can become an opportunity for sin as any other revelation. It is a scandal and a folly for those who are still lost in their sins (Rom. 9:32–33; 1 Cor. 1:18–25; 15:17), that is, for those who are still under the power of their idolatrous system of convictions and thus refuse to acknowledge his resurrection. It is also a new idol for those who ignore the cross and worship only the spiritual Christ as absolute revelation (see below, Chapter 8). Thus, for the unbelievers the Gospel of Christ is the manifestation of the wrath of God (Rom. 1:18). But the Gospel of Christ "is the power of God for salvation to every one who has faith, to the Jew first and also to the Greek" (1:16).

Second, despite the fact that the Gospel of Christ proclaims a new type of divine interventions, it is the fulfillment of the promises contained in previous interventions of God. For instance, as we saw when discussing Romans 4, the deliverance from the power of sin that it achieves for the believers is a fulfillment of the types "creation out of nothing" and "overcoming of the hopeless situation" such as Abraham's and Sarah's death-like bodies.

Third, the revelation in Christ is not a complete and final revelation. As with any revelation, it is the promise of new interventions of God (cf. Gal. 3:22). This means that according to Paul's system of convictions what is manifested in the believers' experience is homologable to what was manifested in Jesus Christ. In the same way that in Christ's experience a power of sin (the Law as power of sin) was shattered, so in the believers' experience other powers of sin are shattered.

## Christ as Manifestation of God's Power for the Salvation of the Jews (Rom. 8:1–4)

First and foremost, for Paul, Christ is a Jew among Jews: "of their race, according to the flesh, is the Christ" (Rom. 9:5). For the Jews, the power of sin is the Law transformed into an idol (Torah as complete and final revelation). According to this idolatrous system of convictions, "sin" and "blasphemy" are transgressions of the laws.

Now—and this is the first step toward the destruction of this idolatrous system of convictions—Christ, as the manifestation of God (as God's Son), was made "in the likeness of sinful flesh *in reference to sin*" (8:3, au. trans.). In other words, he was in the likeness of sinful flesh *according to the definition of sinfulness given by the Law as manifestation of sin.*[29] Christ commits transgressions of the laws. This is how Paul presents the cross in Gal. 3:13, where he interprets it in terms of Deut.

27:26: "Cursed be every one who hangs on a tree." The crucifixion is perceived as a punishment for transgressions, and Christ has "become a curse." The crucifixion is also the proof that Christ has been rejected by the Jews. According to their idolatrous system of convictions, such a transgressor, such a blasphemer, must be cursed and indeed is cursed by their "god," that is, by the idol god they have made out of God by viewing his revelation in Torah as the complete and final revelation. For Paul one can say that the Jews killed Jesus (1 Thess. 2:18), but according to his system of convictions it would be better to say that it was "the Jews under the power of sin," the Jews who do not understand what they do (Rom. 7:15). It would even be more exact to say that it was "the power of sin" which crucified Christ. This is precisely what Paul writes in 1 Cor. 2:8: "None of the rulers of this age understood this [the secret and hidden wisdom of God]; for if they had, they would not have crucified the Lord of glory." The power of sin (i.e., the perverted Law) is here personified and called the "rulers of this age."

In Rom. 8:1–4 Paul does not describe the process of deliverance from the power of sin but emphasizes its results. He does not speak of the resurrection or of the exaltation of Jesus in order to demonstrate that he is indeed the Son of God, the Lord. Yet he assumes that it is made manifest that this Jesus who is "in the sinful flesh in reference to sin" is the Son of God. According to Rom. 1:4, it is by means of the resurrection that Jesus is manifested as Son of God; he was "designated Son of God in power according to the Spirit of holiness by his resurrection from the dead." The resurrection, as demonstration that Jesus is God's manifestation, is something that the Jews can recognize as a divine manifestation. The Pharisees were expecting the resurrection from the dead as the supreme manifestation of God's power.

By being a sinner according to the idolatrous system of convictions of the Jews, Christ as manifestation of God, as his Son, condemns this idolatrous system, this sin as power. He demonstrates that its view of evil is wrong and not from God, as it blasphemously claims. This condemnation is in itself the shattering of the Law as an enslaving power of sin. So Paul writes, "Christ redeemed us from the curse of the law, having become a curse for us" (Gal. 3:13a); "Christ Jesus has set us free from the law of sin and death" (Rom. 8:2).

But what is the result? Sin is condemned and destroyed "in order that the just requirement of the law might be fulfilled in us" (Rom. 8:4a). The

Law is not in itself rejected. It is holy, just, and good. The aim of God's revelation in Torah as promises (and not as complete and final revelation) was to provide the possibility of being in the right relationship with God. Thus Christ reveals the end (the purpose) of the Law: "For Christ is the end of the law, that every one who has faith may be justified" (10:4).[30] The purpose of the Law was to establish in the right relationship with God not merely the Jews but also the Gentiles.

God has achieved in Jesus all that is necessary for the salvation of the Jews from the power of sin, the Law. All the conditions of possibility for faith are established. Faith is offered as a gift, but in order to benefit from this salvation and be established in the right relationship with God, one needs to accept and to appropriate this gift of faith. The Jews need to respond to God's intervention in their own experience. Faith involves trust in God's promises, a hope which is the confident expectation that God will intervene despite the apparently hopeless situation which "being under the power of sin" is. But faith is also seeing and appropriating God's intervention in the present. The Jews need to recognize this intervention of God. They know that Jesus has been crucified. But through faith the Jews also need to acknowledge that this Jesus crucified is indeed the Christ, the Lord, the Son of God. Or—and this amounts to the same thing—they need to acknowledge that the crucified Jesus has been raised from the dead. "If you confess with your lips that Jesus is Lord and believe in your heart that God raised him from the dead, you will be saved" (Rom. 10:9).

But most of the Jews do not do so, and so they are still under the power of sin, which is for them the Law. Yet some of the Jews—Jesus' disciples, Paul, and the Jewish Christians—had faith and have been freed from the power of sin and thus from the Law as curse.

Such was God's intervention in Jesus Christ. This took place in the past and was only the deliverance from the Law as power of sin. Yet it was the first intervention of God of this type: an intervention through which a power of sin was destroyed. As such it is the type, the promise, of comparable interventions of God aimed at destroying all the powers of sin. The power of sin is manifested in different ways for different persons and groups. It is manifested in the various "good things," various revelations or gifts from God whatever they might be, which sin (the self-asserting desire) has transformed into an absolute. As such these revelations or gifts from God have become an enslaving power. Torah was the gift of God and the manifestation of God's power through which the Israelites were elected and through which they receive a meaningful, although not absolute, order for their lives (the convenantal laws). Similarly, the creation was a manifestation of God's power for the Gentiles and provided a meaningful although not absolute context for their lives. And there are many other "good gifts" from God through which God's power is manifested and provides a meaningful, although not absolute, order for life.

## Political Authorities as Servants
## of God (Rom. 13:1–7)

In Rom. 13:1–7 Paul deals with the question of the attitude of the believers toward Roman political power. Of course, political power in the Roman Empire is far from being perfect; it is not characterized by love (discussed in 12:9–21). Yet it is a manifestation of the power of God, "for there is no authority except from God" (13:1). It has been given to human beings for their good: "he [the political ruler who embodies such an authority] is God's servant for your good" (13:4). Political authority provides a meaningful order for life in society and for its economic well-being (13:6–7), and so human beings should accept these gifts of God and the order they provide for life. They should submit to this order and to political authority, and even honor it. This is honoring God (1:21). This is seeing the political and economic order as a promise, a type, of the perfect life "in harmony with one another" (12:16). One must be thankful for this prefiguration even if it is not perfect. But as any intervention of God, it is a two-edged sword. It is a power unto salvation, and promise of ultimate salvation for those who acknowledge it. But it can also be a power of destruction for those who do not acknowledge it for what it is. As in the case of any manifestation of God, it can become a form of the wrath of God, if it is not acknowledged or if it is absolutized and thus transformed into an idol.

We can understand this by comparison with God's manifestation in Christ, which according to Paul's system of convictions is homologous to God's manifestations in the political authorities.

God's intervention in Christ became a "stumbling block to Jews and folly to Gentiles" (1 Cor. 1:23), who do not recognize it for what it is. Because of the Gospel, they are even more enclosed under the power of sin, under a manifestation of the wrath of God which makes them adopt self-destructive attitudes. Similarly, the political authorities, if they are not acknowledged for what they are—as legitimate authorities or, better, as a manifestation of God's power and thus as an occasion to honor and give thanks to God by submitting to them—become the manifestation of God's wrath. "He [the political ruler] is the servant of God to execute his wrath on the wrongdoer" (Rom. 13:4b). This is the warning we find in this text addressed to Christians who have no inclination to see an absolute (an idol) in political power.

The other possibility, which Paul does not mention, is that this political power might itself become a power of sin by being absolutized because of the self-asserting desire. Such was the case when the Romans viewed the emperor, who represented the Roman political order, as a god. Such is the case when a people perceives its political authority (or order) as an absolute (the only true and good political order). Elsewhere Paul uses the very terms by which he designates the political powers ("authorities," "rulers") to refer to powers of sin which "persecute" the Christians who challenge these idolatries, as the Law as power of sin crucified Christ. To repeat, in this text Paul, who addresses Christians, does not speak of political powers as idols, as power of sin. Yet according to the logic of Paul's system of convictions, sin can and does find opportunity in any good manifestation of God's power.

### Gentile Believers as Manifestations of God's Power for the Salvation of the Jews (Rom. 11:13–14)

There are as many forms of the power of sin as there are revelations of God and manifestations of his gracious power. Consequently, according to Paul's system of convictions, the destruction of each of these powers of sin demands a specific intervention from God. God's manifestation must be conformed to (made in the likeness of) the "sinful flesh," as viewed by this specific idolatrous system of convictions, so that the latter's power might be destroyed from the inside. Of course, these new interventions of God are of the same *type* as the one in Christ concerning the Law as power of sin. They are the fulfillment of the promises contained in Christ. These interventions of God against other powers of sin are Christ-like and can also be called manifestations of the resurrected Christ as well as of God's or Christ's Spirit. Because of their typological homologation, one can speak of one in terms of another.

Here we briefly comment on the cases of two interventions of God through which people are (or will be) saved from the power of sin beyond the time of God's intervention in Christ.

Paul still has hope for the Jews who did not convert. They did not recognize God's manifestation in Jesus Christ. But he is confident that they will recognize another intervention of God in their experience and thus be freed from the power of sin through faith. This is what Paul says in Rom. 11:13–14: "Inasmuch then as I am an apostle to the Gentiles, I magnify my ministry in order to make my fellow Jews jealous, and thus save some of them." This passage must be read in light of what Paul says about salvation in the passage we have discussed. For the Jews, the Gentile Christians are blasphemous, evil, sinful. They do not follow the laws; they do not have a Jewish way of life. Thus they are "in the likeness of sinful flesh" from the perspective of the Law as idolatrous system of convictions. But if it is made clear that God is at work in them, for instance, if it is shown that they have been freed from idolatry (which is also abhorred by the Jews), the Jews' idolatrous system of convictions, centered on the Law as an absolute, will be shattered. They will be made jealous. And thus some of them will be saved. This is why Paul "magnifies" his ministry, by "showing off" the Gentile Christians to Jews.

As a consequence, the Gentile Christians and their apostle are violently rejected by the Jews. They are persecuted because they do not carry out the Law (Gal. 5:11), while "blasphemously" pretending to serve "God." In two ways they are Christ-like, fulfillments of the cross, as type. On the one hand, as Christ, the Son of God, was in sinful flesh, they are sons of God, because of God's intervention which freed them from their pagan idols, and "sinful" because they are "uncircumcised," people following a Gentile way of life rather than carrying out all the laws. On the other hand, as Christ was crucified, they are rejected and persecuted. But they are also Christ-like, fulfillments of his resurrection, in that they are in the right relationship with God, freed from the power of sin. They "are in the Spirit" (Rom. 8:9a). This is so because "the Spirit of God really dwells in [them]" (8:9b), and this Spirit is indeed the fulfillment of the resurrection in their lives. "The Spirit of him who raised Jesus from the dead dwells in you" (8:11).

In summary, Paul's ministry and the Gentile Christians are indeed, in the present experience of the unconverted Jews, a salvific intervention of God, through which Paul hopes some of the Jews will be saved. Once freed from the power of sin, which for them is the Law, the Jews will then be in the right relationship with God and will confess that Jesus Christ is Lord, that in him God intervened to defeat the power of sin, and that Christ is a promise which has been fulfilled in their own experience in the form of Gentile Christians.

## Paul as Manifestation of God's Power for the Salvation of the Gentiles

Similarly, Paul was a manifestation of God for the salvation of the Gentiles from the power of sin, which for them is their idolatrous Hellenistic system of convictions which keeps them in bondage. To begin with, he appears to them as "crucified" (Gal. 2:20; 3:1). Consider the case of Paul's ministry among the Corinthians. For them, according to their idolatrous Hellenistic system of convictions, a good person, a person attuned to the divine, is a wise person and a great rhetorician who speaks eloquently (1 Cor. 1:20). A fool (1 Cor. 4:10) and a poor debater can only be despised and rejected. This is what people who are not attuned to the divine are, even more so if they are not of "noble birth," that is, if they do not belong to the educated, rich, and influential social group; for belonging to such a group demonstrates in another way that one is blessed and attuned to the divine. Similarly, people who are "weak," that is, without power and the confidence given by power (cf. 1 Cor. 1:26), cannot be "good."

Now Paul is among them as a "fool," speaking folly rather than wisdom, speaking about implausible things. His speech is far from being eloquent (cf. 1 Cor. 1:17), a rambling of unconvincing words. Furthermore, he is a weakling, lacking confidence and in fear and trembling. Thus he writes, "I was with you in weakness and in much fear and trembling; and my speech and my message were not in plausible words of wisdom" (1 Cor. 2:3–4). He does not appear to them as of "noble birth" but rather as a member of the lower social strata who has to work with his hands. "We hunger and thirst, we are ill-clad and buffeted and homeless, and we labor, working with our own hands" (1 Cor. 4:11–12, in contrast to the false apostles). Thus he is "reviled," "persecuted," "slandered." "We have become, and are now, as the refuse of the world, the scum of all things" (1 Cor. 4:13, au. trans.). As such, from the perspective of the idolatrous Hellenistic system of convictions, Paul is "in the likeness of sinful flesh" (although "sin" is not a Hellenistic concept) or, better, he is cursed and rejected: he is crucified.

At one and the same time, Paul is as an apostle of Christ, a son who can say to God, "Abba! Father!" (Rom. 8:15). This relation of Paul to God is also manifested in such a way that it might be recognized according to the idolatrous Hellenistic system of convictions. For the Gentiles, ecstatic and spiritual experiences (such as in the mystery cults) and miracles were manifestations of the divine. Such manifestations of the divine are found in Paul's life. God intervenes in his ministry "in demonstration of the Spirit and of power" (1 Cor. 2:4). In his ministry there are manifestations of God's power (and not of human power which could result from human wisdom; 1 Cor. 2:5) which Hellenistic people can recognize through their system of convictions. These manifestations of the Spirit are not the complete and final revelation (as heretic Corinthians view them), but rather *resurrection-like manifestations for Hellenistic people*. According to their idolatrous system of convictions, a resurrection in itself would have been meaningless; they were expecting not resurrection of the body but immortality of the soul. But they can recognize as divine these demonstrations of the Spirit and of power in the ministry of this "good for nothing" Paul.

In this way Paul's ministry is a salvific intervention of God for Hellenistic people. Once freed from the power of sin, they will recognize that this manifestation of God in their experience is the fulfillment of the type "Jesus crucified and raised," and they will confess that he is the Lord and that he is resurrected.

Christ, the Gentile believers, and Paul are typical salvific interventions of God aimed at destroying various powers of sin. Those who believe and agree to come out of their shattered idolatrous systems of convictions live in "the glorious liberty of the children of God" (Rom. 8:21), in the freedom of faith which is also the insecurity of hope (rather than holding to a complete and final revelation and identity). But what will their life be?

This life in faith does not involve the rejection of everything which constituted one's idolatrous system of convictions. Each idolatrous system of convictions is a perverted revelation of God, but when the idolaters are freed from it as power of sin, this revelation is also "freed." It appears for what it really is: a manifestation of God's power providing a provisional (and not absolute) order for life. The believers must give honor and thanks to God for it, otherwise they will be once again, although for a different reason, under the wrath of God, which will be manifested for them in this power and this order offered by God as a gift. Yet they must not make an absolute out of it again.

This difficult balancing act would be impossible to maintain if it were not for another characteristic of the believers' life or, better, if it were not for another demand placed upon the believers which insures that they do not consider anything as absolute. The believers themselves have to become the instruments that God uses for other salvific interventions. Their salvation from a power of sin is also an election; they are chosen and beloved by God (1 Thess. 1:4). Together with this election there is a vocation. They have to join God in his actions. This will often require abandoning one's way of life, for it involves becoming Jew with the Jews, Greek with the Greeks, and so on. This is what participating in God's salvific work entails (cf. 1 Cor. 9:19–23). "We are ambassadors for Christ, God making his appeal through us" (2 Cor. 5:20). We have been saved so that "we might become the righteousness of God" (2 Cor. 5:21). How are they to become ambassadors for Christ? How are they to join God in his actions? First, they need to allow God to use them as he used Christ, to allow God to send them "in the likeness of sinful flesh" into the world of various idolatrous systems of convictions. So Paul exhorted the Christians to "do evil that good may come" (Rom. 3:8). The charge against Paul on this issue is from people who slanderously interpreted this to mean "do evil against God," while Paul meant "do evil according to the definition of evil given by a sinful system of convictions." In fact, this exhortation to "do evil that good may come" means almost the same thing as the exhortation we find in Rom. 12:2a, "Do not be conformed to this world." In other words, do not adopt for yourself the definition of good given by the world. By agreeing to become "in the likeness of sinful flesh," they also agree to be persecuted, slandered, humiliated, sacrificed. If they can accept all this, it is because they can be confident that just as they are in the likeness of the crucified Christ, so God will manifest in them his resurrection-like power.

> I appeal to you therefore, brethren, by the mercies of God, to present your bodies as a living sacrifice, holy and acceptable to God, which is your spiritual worship. (Rom. 12:1)

## SUGGESTIONS FOR FURTHER READINGS

Our study of Romans needs to be complemented by and compared and contrasted with two kinds of works: studies entirely focused on the letter to the Romans and studies of Paul's theology (to be contrasted with our overall presentation of Paul's system of convictions).

English commentaries on Romans are numerous and varied in their approaches. Those listed below offer a number of different readings and understandings of Romans. C. K. Barrett, *A Commentary on the Epistle to the Romans*; K. Barth, *The Epistle to the Romans*; C. E. B. Cranfield, *A Critical and Exegetical Commentary on the Epistle to the Romans*; C. H. Dodd, *The Epistle of Paul to the Romans*; K. P. Donfried, ed., *The Romans Debate*; E. Käsemann, *Commentary on Romans*; F. J. Leenhardt, *The Epistle to the Romans*; P. Minear, *The Obedience of Faith: The Purpose of Paul in the Epistle to the Romans*; A. Nygren, *Commentary on Romans*; V. Taylor, *The Epistle to the Romans*.

Reference work and journal articles on Romans: F. W. Beare, "Letter to the Romans," in *IDB*, vol. 4, pp. 112–22; W. D. Davies, "Presidential Address: Paul and the People of Israel," *NTS* 24 (1977): 4–39; J. Fitzmyer, "The Letter to the Romans," in *JBC*, pp. 291–331; G. Klein, "Letter to the Romans," in *IDBS*, pp. 752–54.

For works that deal with Romans (or parts of it) in the context of a general study of Paul's theology, see G. Bornkamm, *Paul*; R. Bultmann, *Theology of the New Testament*; E. Käsemann, *New Testament Questions of Today*; E. Käsemann, *Perspectives on Paul*; L. Keck, *Paul and His Letters*; H. J. Schoeps, *Paul: The Theology of the Apostle in the Light of Jewish Religious History*; J. H. Schütz, *Paul and the Anatomy of Apostolic Authority*; R. Scroggs, *Paul for a New Day*; K. Stendahl, *Paul Among Jews and Gentiles*.

# 8

---

# First and Second Corinthians: Faith, Hope, and Love

## Implementing Paul's Faith in the Life of the Church

THROUGH A DIVERSITY of structural readings, we have elucidated the main characteristics of Paul's system of convictions. We can be reasonably confident that the results of our investigation are valid. Yet it should be clear that our proposals are tentative and incomplete.

These results are *tentative* because we have read each text using only one structural approach: studying in Galatians the anomalies in the argumentative logic so as to identify homologations and oppositions of the convictional logic; studying in 1 Thessalonians, Philemon, and Philippians the interrelations of levels of discourse so as to identify the dialogic space and what is used for warranting the main argument; constructing the first partial model (in the scientific sense of the term) of Paul's system of convictions on the basis of the provisional results of earlier readings and of study of Galatians 3, Romans 4, and 1 Corinthians 15; using this partial model in a reading of Romans aimed at testing and completing it. Now these results need to be verified by reading each text with the approaches we have not yet used when reading it. A structural study involves reading texts again and again, constructing models, then verifying them, refining them, complementing them. As we have said, this book is an invitation to read Paul. Much reading remains to be done. It is hoped that this book will be taken as an invitation to pursue this exploration of Paul's system of convictions through readings which will verify or modify our tentative results and complement them by examining the many other dimensions of Paul's faith.

The results we have reached are *incomplete* because we have deliberately focused our attention on Paul's fundamental convictions. For this reason we have discussed certain passages and left aside others which did not seem to manifest clearly these fundamental convictions. Of course, these other passages manifest convictions which themselves characterize Paul's faith, although not in the same fundamental way. Our reading needs to be complemented and broadened by investigations which take into account these passages. Furthermore, beyond the broad structural approach presented and used in this book, the systematic and detailed structural exegeses of these letters need to be taken up by scholars in order to establish these results on firmer ground. Only such detailed structural exegeses will allow us to refine our proposals and to complement and eventually to revise our interpretation of certain passages. Thus it is clear that our proposals concerning the main characteristics of Paul's faith should be viewed as questions—invitations to read further into Paul's letters.

In this concluding chapter we shall examine how, according to Paul, the believers should implement the fundamental convictions of this faith in their daily life. We chose to deal with these dimensions of Paul's system of convictions in a reading of Paul's letters to the Corinthians for two reasons. First, these letters deal with many ethical issues which will allow us to observe how Paul implements his faith in concrete situations. Second, they confront a misunderstanding of the faith that Paul proclaims. As such these letters were for Paul the occasion to clarify certain aspects of his message. We will also benefit from these clarifications.

## PAUL'S STORMY RELATIONSHIP WITH THE
## CORINTHIAN CHURCH

Paul's correspondence with the Corinthians reflects a stormy relationship. At first, Paul appears to be concerned by divisions in the church in Corinth. He seems to believe that it is only a misunderstanding concerning basic principles of the Christian faith (1 Corinthians). Yet later on, the correspondence shows that the tension between Paul and the Corinthians worsened. His ministry has been attacked and he must defend it and justify it (2 Cor. 2:14—6:13; 7:2–4). Indeed, the attitude of the Corinthians is such that it might lead to their irremediable separation from Paul and from the Gospel he preached to them (2 Cor. 10–13). Yet other passages of 2 Corinthians (1:3—2:13; 7:5–15; 8:1–24; 9:1–15) show that Paul and the Corinthians are reconciled.

Before considering the nature of this dispute and attempting to determine what problems Paul had to confront, we need to look closer at the exchange of letters and news between Paul and the Corinthians in order to elucidate the sequence of events. In the process, we will raise the question of the unity of these texts. Second Corinthians presents problems which are similar to those we encountered in Philippians and which led us to conclude that it was made up of fragments of several letters.

We will first note the various exchanges of letters and news mentioned in 1 and 2 Corinthians. In 1 Corinthians, Paul mentions that he had written earlier (cf. 1 Cor. 5:9). Then he received a letter from the Corinthians (1 Cor. 7:1: "Now concerning the matters about which you wrote . . .") in which they raised questions he explicitly addresses in 1 Cor. 7:1ff., 7:25ff., 8:1ff., and 12:1ff. (a series of passages beginning with the phrase "now concerning"). His first letter, which we do not have,[1] apparently did not resolve the problems encountered by the Corinthians. Thus he writes 1 Corinthians, his second letter to that church. Paul, who is in Ephesus (1 Cor. 16:8), writes after receiving news about the Corinthians from "Chloe's people" (1 Cor. 1:11) as well as from Stephanas, Fortunatus, and Achaicus (1 Cor. 16:17). Paul has sent to them Timothy (1 Cor. 4:17), who has not yet arrived at Corinth (having gone by land route while the letter is sent directly by sea). Paul seems to be concerned about the situation in the church, since he urges the Corinthians to send Timothy back to him as soon as possible (1 Cor. 16:10). He seems to be eager to receive news concerning the situation in the Corinthian church.

Various remarks in 2 Corinthians show that some time after 1 Corinthians the relationship between Paul and the Corinthians drastically deteriorated. Apparently Paul had received news about the church which was so disturbing that he decided to go there himself in order to straighten out the situation and to rebuke those who in his eyes had forsaken the Gospel. This is expressed in 2 Cor. 2:1, where Paul mentions that he made a "painful visit" to Corinth, that is, a visit during which he caused pain to the Corinthians (2 Cor. 2:2). This implies that Paul visited them during the period of the exchange of letters, for his first visit, during which he established the church, could not be described in this way. In fact, in 2 Cor. 12:14 and 13:1 he mentions that he is ready to go to Corinth for the third time and that during his second visit he warned them he would not spare those who sinned when he comes back (2 Cor. 13:2). During this second visit there was a violent confrontation between Paul and a member of the church (2 Cor. 2:5ff.).

How is this sorrowful interim visit related to the material we find in 2 Corinthians? In 2 Cor. 2:4 another letter from Paul to the Corinthians is mentioned, written "out of much affliction and anguish of heart and with many tears." It is doubtful that this is a reference to 1 Corinthians, which is relatively serene and involves a thanksgiving for the Corinthians. Thus Paul wrote to the Corinthians a "Sorrowful Letter" when the controversy was at its peak, that is, during the period between 1 Corinthians and 2 Corinthians 2. Where is this letter? Most scholars agree that this Sorrowful Letter (or at least a major part of it) is found in 2 Corinthians 10–13. These chapters—which are a violent polemic against Paul's opponents and against the church as a whole, since it took the part of these opponents rather than Paul's—cannot belong to the same letter as chapters 1 and 2, which show that the Corinthians are on Paul's side. These chapters presuppose that they have rejected Paul's opponents and even punished the person who had a violent quarrel with Paul, and now Paul begs them not to punish him too harshly. Thus, after his brief interim visit Paul would have written two letters: first a violent attack, the Sorrowful Letter (chaps. 10–13); then, after receiving good news from the church, he wrote a "joyful letter," to which belongs chapter 1 and at least a part of chapter 2.

Three other passages presuppose different situations: The first, 2 Cor. 2:14—7:4 (with the exception of a few verses which might not be from Paul [6:14—7:1]) is a defense of Paul's ministry which presupposes that the validity and authority of Paul's ministry are challenged (no longer the case in the Joyful Letter, to which belongs 1:3—2:13) but not rejected (as presupposed in the Sorrowful Letter, chap. 10–13). Thus this material belongs to a letter written after 1 Corinthians but before the interim visit and the Sorrowful Letter.

This material has been inserted in the Joyful Letter which presupposes a complete reconciliation and announces Paul's (third) visit to Corinth by way of Troas and Macedonia (1:3—2:13), where he was reunited with Titus (7:5ff.). At that time he presents the Macedonians as examples to the Corinthians for their contribution to the collection "for the saints" (in Jerusalem) (8:1–24). One can also argue that chapter 8 is an independent letter of recommendation for Titus.[2]

The third passage is chapter 9, which again deals with the collection in almost the same terms as in 2 Corinthians 8 and mentions Paul's continuing activity in Macedonia, is certainly another letter. He now presents the Corinthians (and their region, Achaia) as an example to the Macedonians, presumably because he received news that the Corinthians were already gathering gifts for the collection.

Without going into further details,[3] we can now present the succession of events after the writing of 1 Corinthians.

1. Having received news that his letter (1 Corinthians) had not resolved all the problems and that the validity of his ministry was challenged, Paul wrote *Letter A* (2 Cor. 2:14—6:13; 7:2–4).

2. But once more this was without result. So Paul goes to Corinth himself. This is the brief, sorrowful visit. He left them after a violent controversy without being able to correct the situation.

3. Paul writes the Sorrowful Letter, *Letter B* (2 Cor. 10:1—13:14).

4. The combination of the interim visit and of the Sorrowful Letter brings the Corinthians back on Paul's side. He can therefore resume his earlier plans (cf. 1 Corinthians 16) concerning the gathering in Corinth of the collection for the saints of Jerusalem. He writes the Joyful Letter, *Letter C* (2 Cor. 1:3—2:13; 7:5—8:24).

5. Later, as he progresses in his activity in Macedonia and shortly before his arrival in Corinth, he sends them another note about the collection, *Letter D* (2 Cor. 9:1–15).

All the events from the writing of 1 Corinthians to *Letter D* of 2 Corinthians took place in a relatively short period of time, at most eighteen months around the years 55–56 (see "Appendix: Chronologies of Paul"). This makes it doubtful that several different kinds of heresy developed in the Corinthian church during the exchange of letters. We can therefore assume that Paul had to confront a single group of opponents.

## PAUL'S DEFENSE OF THE GOSPEL AS POWER OF SALVATION

What were the problems, positions, and views found in the Corinthian church that Paul had to confront? We must keep in mind that in 1 Corinthians, Paul answers a list of queries he received from that church. This means not only that the Corinthians continue to recognize Paul's authority but also that they do not know what attitude to take with respect to outsiders who have come to the church and who oppose Paul. They are confused by teachings and behavior which they feel are not right but which they hesitate to reject. We shall not attempt to reconstruct the teachings of these opponents, but we shall deal with the views the Corinthian church held as a result of the presence of these outsiders. Although Paul addresses the church, and not his opponents directly,[4] we can perceive some of the views of these opponents from the Corinthians' attitude and Paul's direct references to his opponents.

## A Special Structure of Authority in the Church (1 Cor. 1–4)

At the beginning of 1 Corinthians, Paul abruptly scolds his readers because of their division into four parties: the party of Paul, the party of Apollos, the party of Cephas (Peter), and the party of Christ (1 Cor. 1:12). This situation certainly results from the presence of these opponents in the church. We can assume that the Corinthians adopted one or the other of these four positions, either because they submitted to the influence of Paul's opponents or because they attempted to take the part of Paul in one way or another.

As he develops his argument, Paul refuses to take sides in this dispute. Rather than supporting one or the other party, he endeavors to show in chapters 1–4 that they are all in the wrong because they are divided.[5] From Paul's argument in these opening chapters of his letter and in other parts of the correspondence, we deduce that certain of the Corinthians, the party of Christ, claimed to have received salvation and revelation (a knowledge or a wisdom) directly from the resurrected Christ or his Spirit. They emphasize the relationship of the believers to the resurrected Christ and thus minimize the crucified Christ.

In 1 Cor. 1:13—2:16 Paul attacks this view of Christ and of revelation by emphasizing that the Gospel is first of all the proclamation of the crucified Christ who is "the wisdom of God" (1:24) by contrast to any "human wisdom." Yet Paul undercuts any possibility for the believers to conceive of themselves as belonging to the party of any one of the apostles (1:13; 3:1—4:7). Paul and Apollos are merely "servants through whom you believed" (3:5), while it is through God's intervention that the Corinthians are saved, as Paul expresses by an analogy: "I planted, Apollos watered, but God gave the growth. So neither he who plants nor he who waters is anything, but only God who gives the growth" (1 Cor. 3:6–7). Thus they cannot say "I belong to Paul" or "I belong to Apollos." They are God's, "God's field" (3:9). Indeed, they are Christ's, that is, they belong to Christ (3:23). In this way Paul expresses views that the Corinthians of the party of Christ would have readily made their own.

Yet Paul does not want to deny the authority of the apostles over the believers. The apostles "are God's fellow workers" (3:9), they are the believers' fathers. "For though you have countless guides in Christ, you do not have many fathers. For I became your father in Christ Jesus through the gospel. I urge you, then, be imitators of me" (4:15–16). But the apostles have this authority because of cross-like experiences (they are "weak," the "refuse of the world"), unlike the Corinthians, who see themselves as having resurrection-like experiences (they "have become kings, [etc.]"; cf. 4:8–13).

Thus in his argument against the Corinthians of the party of Christ Paul has to adopt an ambivalent attitude. On the one hand, he has to assert the validity of their claim that the believers belong to Christ and to rebuke those who took his part by saying "we belong to Paul." On the other hand, he rebukes those of the party of Christ for their misrepresentation of the believers' relationship to Christ—as a relationship to the resurrected Christ rather than to the crucified Christ—and asserts the validity of his followers' claim that the apostles have authority over them, provided it is clear that they have authority as "crucified," as fulfillments of the type "Christ crucified."

It appears that in Paul's view the Corinthians are confused. The Corinthians that Paul perceives as forming the party of Christ might very well have been supporters of Paul, the very people who addressed to Paul a letter of inquiry. In attempting to defend him against these opponents, they inadvertently adopted part of the views of Paul's opponents. As is expressed in 1 Cor. 4:8–13, for the Corinthians, being in Christ is to be "filled," "rich," "kings," "wise," "in honor" or, better, "in glory." In other words, being in Christ is having a resurrection-like experience or even being in a mystical union with the resurrected Christ, sharing in his glory. For them, as is also expressed in 2 Corinthians 10–13, those who have authority have these spiritual gifts, and Paul's supporters might have claimed that they followed Paul because he had such gifts. Such an attitude might have been full of good intentions with respect to Paul, but it contradicted the Gospel he preached to them. In fact, this view of the believers' relationship to Christ contradicts Paul's convictional view of salvation. For Paul, the believers' faith and salvation can be true faith and salvation only if they acknowledge that other believers who preceded them in the faith are both manifestations of the crucified Christ by accepting to be folly, weakness, poor debaters, and powerless among them and manifestations of the resurrected Christ by God's intervention among them "in demonstration of the Spirit and of power" (1 Cor. 2:4). For the believers, faith and salvation are a call to offer themselves in living sacrifice, that is, to accept making themselves manifestations of the crucified Christ, with the confidence that God will intervene in resurrection-like demonstrations of power. But by making of these resurrection-like experiences ends in themselves or (and this amounts to the same thing) by denying that the believers' vocation is to be a manifestation of the crucified Christ for others, the Corinthians (and possibly Paul's opponents) reduce the Gospel of Jesus Christ to a powerless imitation of itself. Even though they still believe that "Christ died for our sins" (1 Cor. 15:3; note that Paul does not need to argue this point), "the cross of Christ [is] emptied of its power" (1:17).

Thus it appears that the Corinthians' confusion over the teaching of these opponents arises from a subtle deformation of Paul's teaching. Unlike the teaching of the Judaizers which was clearly in contradiction with central elements of Paul's teaching, the teaching of these opponents appears to be a mere application of his teaching. This is also clear when examining the more concrete information Paul gives about the identity of these opponents.

## Paul's Teaching Deformed by the Corinthians

Paul's opponents are a group of Christians who arrived in the Corinthian church from elsewhere with letters of recommendation (2 Cor. 3:1–3). They emphasize that, like Paul, they are Israelites by birth, that is, Hebrews, descendants of Abraham (2 Cor. 11:22), yet according to Paul they do not claim to be "Jews," the term Paul used in Galatians to describe the Jewish Christians and the Judaizers. In other words, they do not follow the Jewish way of life, and consequently they do not demand that the Corinthians carry out the requirements of the Law, as is made plain from the fact that the Corinthians under the influence of these opponents could have a clearly immoral conduct (cf., e.g., 1 Cor.

5:1; 2 Cor. 12:21). So we can view these opponents of Paul as Christians of Jewish origin who could accept a Gospel free from the Law, as Paul does. These opponents could also accept the Corinthians' emphasis on freedom. They apparently did not object to Paul's slogan "For freedom Christ has set us free" (Gal. 5:1). Indeed, the Corinthians who were under the influence of these opponents had for a motto "All things are lawful" (quoted by Paul in 1 Cor. 6:12 and 10:23), which could well have been part of Paul's own teaching. Similarly, they emphasize a life in the Spirit, which is also a part of Paul's teaching.

As such these outsiders can easily be welcomed by the Corinthians, but the rest of their views puzzle and confuse the Corinthians. Their views seem to be in the "logic" of Paul's basic teaching but are not what Paul taught them.

The first four chapters of 1 Corinthians seem to reflect the Corinthians' confusion regarding their relationship to people (such as Paul, Apollos, and Peter) whom, through faith, they view as having authority. The outsiders apparently emphasized that the resurrected Christ is the only one whose authority they should recognize. For the ones who received from Paul the gospel *of the Lord Jesus Christ,* this reasoning certainly appeared attractive, even if they defended the apostle. Indeed, for Paul also the Gospel is "Christ-centered" in the sense that there are fulfillments of the type "Christ" in the believers' experience.

We begin to see why the Corinthians were perplexed by the teaching of the outsiders. While under the influence of these outsiders the Corinthians could keep essential elements of Paul's teaching, but then they were led to reinterpret them implicitly by setting them in a different system of convictions. Thus, the Corinthians could still hold that the believers are "justified by faith in Christ" (Gal. 2:16). Together with Paul they understood this phrase to mean "being established in the right relationship with God because the believers are freed from the powers of sin and thus from their idols." And they could still repeat Paul's own teaching: "You are not in the flesh, you are in the Spirit" (Rom. 8:9); "For the law of the Spirit of life in Christ Jesus has set me free from the law of sin and death" (Rom. 8:2). Thus the Corinthians could still emphasize with Paul, that the Christians are new creations. But they distorted this teaching by absolutizing it. In many ways the outsiders' teaching led the Corinthians to a misunderstanding of Paul's proclamation. Looking at their views, on the basis of Paul's own statements, will give us the opportunity to point out what Paul's system of convictions is *not*.

## The Corinthians' View of the Cross as Vicarious Sacrifice

A surprising passage, in which Paul answers one of the Corinthians' written questions, needs attention first:

> Now concerning spiritual gifts, brethren, I do not want you to be uninformed. You know that when you were heathen, you were led astray to dumb idols, however you may have been moved. Therefore I want you to understand that no one speaking by the Spirit of God ever says "Jesus be cursed!" and no one can say "Jesus is Lord" except by the Holy Spirit. (1 Cor. 12:1–3)

The Corinthians' question can be approximately reconstituted as follows. "There are Christians who, under the influence of the Spirit, are saying 'cursed be Jesus.' What should we do about them?"[6] It is surprising that the Corinthians had to ask for Paul's advice on such a matter. Should it not be clear that a Christian cannot say "cursed be Jesus"? Since this issue is related to the matter of the gifts of the Spirit, we can conclude that these are Christians in a state of ecstasy or prophesying who proclaimed "cursed be Jesus." But in such a case the Corinthians should know that it is not the Spirit of God who inspires such sayings. The pagans in the Hellenistic mystery cults also had ecstatic spiritual experiences. Thus the Corinthians know that they should "test the spirits." Indeed, Paul mentions among the spiritual gifts that the Corinthians do know the gift of "[distinguishing] between spirits" (1 Cor. 12:10). Thus the context of this cursing of Jesus in ecstatic experience does not explain why they could not resolve this problem on their own.

The Corinthians are asking *Paul* to clarify an issue. Therefore we can assume that for them the proclamation "cursed be Jesus" is somehow related to a part of Paul's teaching that, under the influence of the outsiders, they are distorting, consciously or not. What could this be? What does Paul say about Jesus? Very little. Outside of 1 and 2 Corinthians, Paul almost never uses the name "Jesus" by itself. In most instances, he speaks of "Jesus Christ," "Christ Jesus," the "Lord Jesus," that is, of Jesus as the resurrected Christ who has been crucified or who is God's son. He uses the name "Jesus" by itself only in passages where he quotes a traditional formula (see, e.g., 1 Thess. 1:10; 4:14; Rom. 4:24; 10:9) and in two other passages: in Gal. 6:17 he compares his suffering with Jesus' suffering, and in Rom. 8:11, in a context where he makes a distinction between Jesus according to the flesh and the "Christ who is in you." All the other instances are in 1 and 2 Corinthians in the context of his polemic against the Corinthians' views (1 Cor. 12:3; 2 Cor. 4:5, 10–11, 14; 11:4). In his original teaching to the Corinthians, Paul certainly did not say much about the earthly Jesus, emphasizing the resurrected Christ and his manifestation in the experience of the believers (where Christ-like events can be found). As in his letters, he merely said that Jesus was crucified.

How does Paul speak about the crucifixion? In fact, as a curse (whatever might be the vocabulary used to express it). The crucified one has "become a curse for us—for it is written, 'Cursed be every one who hangs on a tree'" (Gal. 3:13).[7] As we now understand, for Paul, Jesus has become cursed, that is, has become sin, from the perspective of an idolatrous system of convictions, although from the perspective of the true faith he remained in the right relationship with God: "he knew no sin" (2 Cor. 5:21). For Paul, Jesus, by becoming human with humans, puts himself under "the wrath of God." Yet as we saw in our discussion of Romans 1, Paul uses this concept in a specific sense. The wrath of God is manifested in the idolaters' enslavement to their idols and their being under the power of their idolatrous system of convictions. Thus Jesus shares the idolaters' (the Jews') situation under the power of their idolatrous system of convictions which manifests the wrath of God. But because he remains in the right relationship with God (and thus without sin), he transgresses the demands of this idolatrous system and thus is rejected and viewed as cursed *by the idolaters*.

If one does not understand that Paul is speaking about Jesus' crucifixion from two perspectives when he says in the same breath that "he [God] made him [Jesus Christ] to be sin who knew no sin" (2 Cor. 5:21), how is such a statement to be understood? Apparently Paul's opponents, and the Corinthians following them, interpreted it to mean that Jesus truly became sin, truly became "sinful flesh" (Rom. 8:3), while as the spiritual Christ he did not know sin. Thus for them he was cursed by the true God (rather than by the false god of the idolatrous system of convictions and by the idolaters). Consequently, for them, when one claims in ecstasy, "Cursed be Jesus," it is under the influence of the Spirit of God (and not of an evil spirit).

Against this view, Paul replies, This cannot be the case! "When you were heathen, you were led astray to dumb idols" (1 Cor. 12:2). From this idolatrous perspective, you perceived Jesus as cursed rather than as the Lord, but now that you have been freed from these idolatries and now that you have the Spirit of God, rather than the spirit of an idol, you can recognize Jesus as Lord. He emphasizes that it is impossible to say "Jesus is Lord" as long as one is under the power of another spirit.

Against Walter Schmithals,[8] I do not think this means that Paul's opponents and the Corinthians saw Jesus as cursed because the flesh is evil, an execrable dwelling, as Gnostics in the second century believed. In order to explain the views and attitudes of the Corinthians, it is enough to presuppose that they held a view of the cross which was found in early Jewish Christianity: the cross as a vicarious sacrifice. For them, Christ died for our sins (Paul expects them to agree with this statement in 1 Cor. 15:3) because, in their view, he was cursed by God instead of us, he was punished by God instead of us. As we noted, originally (in 1 Thessalonians) Paul did not proclaim this salvific view of the cross. In fact, we can assume that such a view developed in Jewish Christianity by interpreting the cross in terms of Isaiah 53. Paul's opponents as Christians of Jewish origin and the Corinthians following them would have thus held that view of the cross.

After engaging in dialogue with Jewish Christianity, Paul himself adopted the phrase "Christ died for our sins" and other formulas expressing the cross as vicarious sacrifice (cf. Rom. 3:24–26), but limited their use to the expression of the *reconciliation* operated by Christ. Furthermore, he radically reinterpreted this view of the cross by redefining the concept "wrath of God." The wrath of God is not merely the "anger" which led God to "withdraw his Spirit from Israel" and by extension from humankind. For Paul the wrath of God is primarily manifested in evil powers (powers of sin, Satan, authorities, principalities) which keep human beings in bondage and which have an "existence" of their own, in a quasi-independence from God. Through a transcendent intervention, God can "destroy" these manifestations of his wrath (as he will do at the day of the Lord), but in doing so God would also destroy the people who are under the powers of sin instead of freeing them. Jesus offered himself "as a living sacrifice" by entering these sinful systems of convictions (sinful flesh) and therefore by submitting himself to these evil powers. Thus, for Paul, Christ is not punished by God to satisfy God's justice (or anger). His death is not a vicarious sacrifice but a pascal sacrifice (1 Cor. 5:7), a sacrifice liberating people (sinners) from bondage (the powers of sin). So Christ's death establishes the believers in a convenantal relationship with God, in the right relationship with God. In brief, Christ died because he became "sinful flesh according to sin" so as to destroy the power of sin as manifested in a specific idolatrous system of convictions.

By contrast, for Paul's opponents and the Corinthians, Jesus' death is viewed as a vicarious sacrifice, a sacrifice to appease God's anger. As soon as God's justice is satisfied and through faith the believers claim for themselves the benefits of this vicarious death, they are totally freed from any manifestation of the wrath of God. From this perspective Jesus is cursed by God. But then he is raised as the Christ, the Lord. For them, it is in the resurrected Christ that we must believe, and as believers we are and should be in the likeness of the resurrected Christ and not in the likeness of the crucified Christ. Since Christ died for us, instead of us, it is clear that we should not be punished as he was.

Against this view Paul emphasizes that as an apostle he decided "to know nothing among [them] except Jesus Christ and him crucified" (1 Cor. 2:2) and to be foolish and weak among them. While Paul is foolish, they are wise. While he is weak, they are strong. While he is held in disrepute, they are honored (1 Cor. 4:10). Unlike the Corinthians who are "rich" and "kings" (1 Cor. 4:8), "God has exhibited us apostles as last of all, like men sentenced to death" (1 Cor. 4:9). Similarly, in 2 Cor. 4:10–12, while contrasting his ministry to that of his opponents, Paul emphasizes that he is "always carrying in the body the death of Jesus" and that he is "always being given up to death for Jesus' sake, so that the life of Jesus may be manifested in our mortal flesh." And he concludes this passage by saying, sarcastically, against the Corinthians who follow his opponents: "so death is at work in us, but life in you." They believe that in their present experience God makes them like the resurrected Christ and so they already have a glorious life. Paul does not disagree with this. Indeed, the promises contained in Christ's resurrection are fulfilled in the believers. Thus he writes, "We all, with unveiled face, beholding the glory of the Lord, are being changed into his likeness from one degree of glory to another" (2 Cor. 3:18). But for Paul the believers as believers are also the fulfillment of Jesus crucified. Not so for his opponents and the Corinthians who follow them. Before their conversion, that is, before their salvation from the wrath of God (the anger of God), they were cursed as Jesus crucified was. But now, as believers, they should not be and are not like Jesus crucified. They are no longer cursed by God. They should not be like the Jesus who was cursed by God.

The Corinthians correctly believe that Jesus died for our sins by becoming cursed, but they misunderstood the nature of this curse and now believe that the crucified Jesus was cursed and rejected *by God*. Paul sees this as a complete misunderstanding of the crucifixion, a denying of the power of the cross and a misunderstanding of the entire Gospel. He describes the Corinthians' readiness to accept the teaching of these outsiders as follows: "For if some one comes and preaches another Jesus than the one we preached, or if you receive a different spirit from the one you received, or if you accept a different gospel from the one you accepted, you submit to it readily enough" (2 Cor. 11:4). This means that, from Paul's perspective, the Corinthians also have a wrong understanding of faith.

## Faith and Knowledge

Paul proclaimed salvation by faith in Jesus Christ crucified and raised. By contrast, the Corinthians under the influence of Paul's opponents proclaimed a wisdom (1 Cor. 1:18—2:13). They claimed to have "knowledge" (cf., e.g., 1 Cor. 8:1–3). We are faced here with another, frequent misunderstanding of Paul's teaching. Is not faith believing in a certain teaching, in a doctrine? Is not the Gospel a certain body of religious knowledge that one has to appropriate in order to be saved? Is not one justified by believing specific doctrines about Christ (e.g., that Jesus was punished by God instead of us) and from Christ and his Spirit? This seems to be what the Corinthians thought. Against them Paul writes:

> Love never ends; as for prophecies, they will pass away; as for tongues, they will cease; as for knowledge, it will pass away. For our knowledge is imperfect and our prophecy is imperfect; but when the perfect comes, the imperfect will pass away. When I was a child, I spoke like a child, I thought like a

child, I reasoned like a child; when I became a man, I gave up childish ways. For now we see in a mirror dimly, but then face to face. Now I know in part; then I shall understand fully, even as I have been fully understood. So faith, hope, love abide, these three; but the greatest of these is love. (1 Cor. 13:8–13)

First note that Paul emphasizes that faith, hope, and love are eternal, by contrast with "knowledge," which is partial, imperfect, and will pass away. Faith and knowledge do not belong to the same category. Faith is *not* knowledge. It is not knowing specific doctrines or even specific revelations received through the Spirit in prophecy or other ecstatic experiences. Paul does not deny the importance of knowledge, of revelations, of prophecies, but for Paul these are not absolute. For him any system of convictions is merely provisional. It is the promise of new revelations.

By contrast, the Corinthians see this revealed knowledge as an absolute (cf. 1 Cor. 8:1–2). We could say that, for them, one is justified through knowledge, through "believing in" (in the sense of holding to) certain specific revelations. What are these revelations? Revelations received through the Spirit, but also the Gospel of Jesus Christ. Paul accepts as valid most of this knowledge and these revelations that the Corinthians held. But for Paul they cannot be viewed as absolute, for three things show their limitations: faith which demands that they be seen as promises fulfilled in the present experience of the believers; hope which demands that these revelations and the believers' experience be seen as promises of the complete revelation and salvation at the end of time; and love which demands that other believers who have their own beliefs and knowledge be respected and honored.

Thus through the Gospel we know that idols have no real existence (1 Cor. 8:4), that they are only manifestations of the power of sin. We are freed from their power. So why not eat food sacrificed to idols? This is what some Corinthians do.

They also view the freedom of the Gospel as an absolute, a freedom without limitations. Since "all things are lawful" (1 Cor. 6:12; 10:2–3), they were apparently engaged in various kinds of immorality (cf., e.g., 1 Corinthians 5 and 6; 2 Cor. 12:21). Paul preached this kind of knowledge and this freedom. In a sense, for him also they are "absolute," since they are from God. But they are not transformed into a closed system of convictions. They are promises. They open up upon new vistas. This knowledge and this freedom are for him the freedom to love and to offer himself as a living sacrifice.

Paul therefore must address two interrelated issues. On the one hand, there are in Corinth misunderstandings concerning the nature of the Christian faith and the characteristics of the Christian ministry. Progressively these misunderstandings will become the main preoccupation of Paul in his correspondence with the Corinthians. The letters provide us with a rare opportunity to examine how Paul proceeds to correct these misunderstandings. On the other hand, there are in Corinth serious problems concerning community life. Paul addresses them primarily in the second part of 1 Corinthians, after chapters 1–4, which he hopes have resolved the main misunderstandings concerning the nature of the Christian faith (although these chapters have not succeeded in doing so, as we know from the rest of the correspondence). So 1 Corinthians 5–14 provides us with a series of concrete examples showing how Paul's faith is implemented in the daily life of a community.

We shall therefore examine how Paul brings back the Corinthians to his Gospel and how he deals with moral issues of community life.

## The Power of the Gospel Unleashed Against the Corinthians (2 Cor. 10–13)

We can summarize the view of the Corinthians under the influence of Paul's opponents: a certain understanding of the Gospel of Christ has become the complete and final revelation instead of being a promise of new interventions of God. Jesus' vicarious death has freed the believers once and for all from God's judgment and punishment. In this way the believers no longer have to suffer the consequences of sins, that is, weakness, poverty, shame. They can live in the glorious liberty of the children of God (cf. Rom. 8:21) in communion with the resurrected Christ and his Spirit. They do not need to hope for anything more. Thus Paul can imply that they have hoped in Christ only for this life (1 Cor. 15:19). Although it is difficult to reconstruct what they believed or did not believe about the resurrection,[9] it is clear that these Corinthians should be viewed as enthusiasts who hold that the true believers are already fully saved. It is enough to hold on to the revelation they have received, which is an absolute knowledge and not a partial or a provisional one, and to remain in communion (mystical union) with the resurrected Christ. For them, the Gospel of Christ has become a static system of convictions, an idolatrous system of convictions: human wisdom. As such it is no longer a power of God for salvation (1 Cor. 1:18; Rom. 1:16), but rather idolatry, and therefore the manifestation of God's wrath (Rom. 1:18ff.). Paraphrasing what Paul expresses about the Law, we can say that sin, finding opportunity in Christ, deceived them and by him killed them, even though Christ is holy, just, and good. Christ has become the ally of sin. Indeed, for them, the power of sin is Christ.

In 1 Corinthians, and until his interim visit, Paul apparently did not perceive the situation in this extreme way. Paul develops an argument aimed at correcting serious misunderstandings and problems, but at this point it is clear that he does not feel he has to win the Corinthians back to the (true) Gospel. Their writing a letter asking for advice on several issues shows that they still recognize his authority and his Gospel. Consequently, his argument aims at showing the implications of having such a faith in a variety of specific cases. In 2 Cor. 2:14—6:13 and 7:2–4 (*Letter A*, written before the interim visit) we find the same kind of argument, focused this time on the nature of the Christian ministry. This is an apology for his ministry and authority which presupposes that they have been challenged. But Paul is still convinced that the Corinthians are on his side.

After the interim visit, Paul's letter (the Sorrowful Letter, 2 Corinthians 10–13) has a different character. He now presupposes that the Corinthians have forsaken him to follow his opponents and that they now believe in another gospel. In his view they have accepted a "different gospel," "another Jesus," and a "different spirit" (2 Cor. 11:4). In other words, they have adopted a different system of convictions which is a false one. They have been deceived "as the serpent deceived Eve by his cunning" (11:3). They follow his opponents, whom he calls "false apostles, deceitful workmen, disguising themselves as apostles of Christ" (11:13). He even calls them servants of Satan (11:14–15). In our terminology, Paul views their gospel as an idolatrous (satanic) system of convictions.

The goal of the sorrowful letter becomes apparent. The letter aims at converting the Corinthians from their new idolatry and thus at freeing them from the power of their system of convictions. We can therefore view it as a "missionary" discourse, a proclamation of the Gospel through which the power of God for salvation is manifested. We will examine how this specific power of sin—the Christ-centered idolatrous system of convictions—is destroyed for the Corinthians. The Joyful Letter (2 Cor. 1:3—2:13; 7:5—8:24) shows that the Sorrowful Letter had this effect.

It is clear that this idolatrous system of convictions is a perversion of a true revelation, namely, the Gospel of Jesus Christ that they received through Paul and that Paul as Christ-like apostle had manifested among them. But as a result of the absolutization of the Gospel, the believers perceive themselves as freed from any punishment from God and as being in communion with Christ as the exalted Lord. From this perspective, the "true" believers are in a mystical union with the resurrected Christ. They are spiritual beings (filled by the Spirit and with many gifts of the Spirit), sharing the glory of Christ. As we saw, all this is true revelation for Paul. But they view themselves as "filled," "rich," "kings," "wise in Christ," "glorified" (1 Cor. 4:8–13), which are, according to this system of convictions, the only characteristics of the "true" believers attuned to the divine. And thus an apostle, somebody who has "true" spiritual authority, is someone who exemplifies in a superior way all these qualities and blessings. Conversely, the characteristics of a "sinner" who lives in the flesh rather than being in communion with the divine are poverty, foolishness, humiliations, and the absence of spiritual gifts. An apostle cannot have any of these characteristics.

In order to destroy the power of this idolatrous system of convictions, Paul needs to show both that he is "sinner" according to their view of "sin" (that he is in the likeness of sinful flesh according to their sinful perspective) and that in him God manifests himself, according to their view of the divine interventions. In this way, Paul would manifest himself as Christ-like among the Corinthians. They would perceive the contradiction of their system of convictions, whose power would then be broken.

This is precisely what Paul does in the Sorrowful Letter. First, he makes it a very personal letter. It is Paul alone (and not with Timothy and other co-workers) who addresses the Corinthians (2 Cor. 10:1). He is the one who was humiliated ("crucified") among them during the interim visit, and therefore he is the one who must show himself as manifestation of the power of God. He is the one who must continue to be the Christ-like manifestation of God for them. Yet, in his view, he does so not to defend himself or his authority, but to bring about the "conversion" of the Corinthians.

His Gospel is abandoned by the Corinthians because they (or some of them) view him as "having a way of life in the flesh" (2 Cor. 10:2, au. trans.), the life of an ungodly, lost person, according to their system of convictions. He does not deny it. He does live "in the flesh," but in his life and ministry God's power is also manifested (10:4).

He describes the purpose and means of his ministry with the help of military imagery (2 Cor. 10:3–6). His ministry with divine power aims at destroying strongholds, that is, powers, and especially the power of reasonings which are an obstacle to knowing God, which is the power of human wisdom (1 Cor. 2:5). The result of such a ministry is that every thought is made obedient to Christ (2 Cor. 10:5). Thus, for Paul, the major obstacle, the power of the idol, is defined as a certain way of thinking (cf. Rom. 1:21–22). And Paul affirms at the outset that he intends to carry out this mission with them (10:6).[10]

For this he needs to "magnify himself" (as he magnifies his ministry among the Gentiles so as to save the Jews; Rom. 11:13–14). In other words, he needs to make a show of himself, to boast (as he will say several times in this letter), so that they might see in him both the crucified Christ and the resurrected Christ. He does so right away. "Look at what is before your eyes" (2 Cor. 10:7). Look at me! You say that you are in Christ. So am I! Yes, he will boast, but unlike his opponents he will limit his boasting to boasting in the Lord.

Before doing so, he wants to make clear that in his view they are being deceived by these "superlative apostles" (2 Cor. 11:1–15) whom he ridicules, in 10:12, for comparing themselves to each other, and in 10:13–18, for boasting of other people's (Paul's) labor when assuming the leadership of a church founded by Paul. He makes it clear that they are Satan's. He also ridicules the Corinthians for accepting the authority of these superlative apostles (11:16–21). At last he does what he repeatedly announced he would do (10:7, 13–18; 11:1, 16–18): he begins to make a show of himself.

He boasts of his Jewish origins (2 Cor. 11:22). He boasts of being a servant of Christ, indeed, a better one than these "superlative apostles" (11:23). How does he go about showing this? By talking about all his humiliations, his imprisonments, his persecutions, his weakness, the shamefulness of his ministry (11:23–33). Among these weaknesses he even lists "the daily pressure upon me of my anxiety for all the churches" (11:28). What a lack of confidence in God! From the Corinthians' view, all this is a demonstration that God is not with him.

He continues to boast. But this time it is to show that this weakling is also the one who has the Spirit, special revelations in ecstasy (2 Cor. 12:1–4), indeed, extraordinary revelations (12:7). This is, for the Corinthians what a true believer and true apostle should have. Yet he again makes himself a sign of contradiction. Yes, he is such a man filled with the Spirit, but he is at the same time a weakling (12:5–10) with a thorn in the flesh—which is nothing less than "a messenger of Satan." Yes, he should be rejected, but then what about his spiritual gifts?

He can then point out to the Corinthians the conclusions they should draw from this boasting. He displayed when he was among them the signs of a "true" apostle, even though he is nothing. His ministry among them included "signs and wonders and mighty works" (12:12). He defends himself against accusations of wishing to exploit them financially (through the collection he is gathering for the Jerusalem church; 12:13–18). No, he did not aim at defending himself through this letter, but rather at bringing them back on the right path before his third visit, so that he will not have to scold them when he is with them (12:19—13:4). It remains for them to test themselves to see if they really hold to the faith and if Christ is really in them (13:5). And he hopes that this letter will have the desired effect (13:6–14).

His boasting had the desired effect, as is expressed in the Joyful Letter and especially in 2 Cor. 7:7–16. The Corinthians were deeply hurt. They were in mourning (7:7) and sorrowful (7:8). After sending it, Paul had some regret for having written such a letter, but now he does not regret it, because their sorrow was a "sorrow according to God" ("a godly grief," 7:9, 10) rather than a "sorrow of the world" (a "worldly grief," 7:10). The sorrow of the world produces death (7:10b). As we know, for Paul it is sin which produces death. The sorrow of the world is thus a sinful sorrow, a sorrow according to an idolatrous system of convictions. Such is the case of somebody who is sorry for having done something "wrong" according to an idolatrous system of convictions, for instance, a Jew who feels guilty for having transgressed a commandment of the Law or a Hellenistic idolater who feels guilty for having failed to offer a sacrifice to the idol. This feeling of guilt has the effect of bringing about a resolution to do "good" according to the idolatrous system of convictions. In so doing, such a person once more commits himself or herself to the service of the idol and therefore is even more enslaved to a specific power of sin. From Paul's perspective, such a guilt feeling produces a deeper enslavement to sin, which in turn produces death.

By contrast, "the sorrow according to God produces a repentance [or, better, conversion] that leads to salvation" (2 Cor. 7:10a, au. trans.). In this case, the person feels guilty not for having transgressed the idolatrous system of convictions but for having held such a system of convictions. This is the sorrow, the grief, the guilt-feeling of discovering with horror that the good which one was zealously pursuing was in fact evil, that the purpose one had for one's life was in fact totally misguided, that the gains one treasured were in fact losses. It is a painful experience. It is dying to one's idolatrous system of convictions. It is being crucified, as Paul puts it when speaking of his own personal experience (Gal. 2:19–20). Such a sorrow brings about "conversion," the turning away from this idolatrous system of convictions.[11] Such a "sorrow according to God," followed by conversion, brings about freedom from the power of sin to which one was enslaved, and thus salvation.

Paul has no regret at having caused sorrow for the Corinthians; on the contrary, he rejoices. Because of this sorrowful letter, the Corinthians have not suffered any loss (2 Cor. 7:9b), and they have gained conversion and salvation. Now they are taking seriously the problems raised by these opponents. They are eager to clear themselves. They show fear (a fearful respect for Paul), longing (for him), zeal (for him), and indignation (with Paul's opponent, possibly a member of the church) and desire for punishment (or justice against Paul's opponent) (7:11a). They reaffirm their allegiance to Paul. We can imagine that they were saying to Paul through the intermediary of Titus, "We did not mean to reject you in this affair." And Paul reassures them, "At every point you have proved yourselves guiltless in the matter" (7:11b). But Paul does not regret having sent this letter, for it was not "on account of the one who did the wrong," the opponent (7:12a), that he wrote. In fact, this opponent should not be punished too harshly and should even be forgiven (2 Cor. 2:6–8). Neither was it "on account of the one who suffered the wrong," Paul (7:12b), as he had already expressed in the Sorrowful Letter by asking rhetorically, "Have you been thinking all along that we have been defending ourselves before you?" (12:19). In fact, this opponent has caused pain not so much to Paul but to the Corinthians (2:5). And thus this letter was written for the Corinthians' sake, "in order that your zeal for us might be revealed to you in the sight of God" (7:12c). You had a zeal for us and our Gospel. But this commitment to the true faith had been obscured for you. It had been perverted. You could not see it any longer because you were deceived by these satanic superlative apostles. Thus the goal of this letter and of all its "foolishness" and boasting was to reveal it to you again before God. As in the case of any conversion, the Corinthians discovered the true nature of the revelation that they had previously received and that because of their senseless, idolatrous mind they had perverted.

## ETHICAL LIFE IN A CHRISTIAN COMMUNITY

### Community Life: Faith, Hope, and Love

For Paul, consistent ethical conduct can be expected only from persons who have been freed from the powers of sin, that is, from their idolatries. Prior to this deliverance, a part of their conduct is certainly good, since they know the "decrees of God," but this good conduct is mixed together with evil conduct resulting from their idolatries. We can therefore anticipate that, for Paul, ethical issues can be raised only in the community of believers, the community of those who have been freed from the powers of sin. There is no point in exhorting any other person to good conduct or in judging their evil conduct (cf. 1 Cor. 5:12). In the case of the outsiders the problem of evil is not an ethical problem but the problem of their bondage to powers of sin, which can be addressed only by their deliverance from this bondage.

As we have been able to observe again and again, the Gospel is the power of God for salvation. The believers are freed from the power of sin, which was their idolatry. Certainly they have to be watchful and to test themselves constantly in order to avoid being enslaved by another power of sin. They have to be freed again and again from such powers, yet they can live in the glorious liberty of the children of God. The question is: How should they live?

Now we need to examine the provisional results of our previous investigation, to formulate a hypothesis (a model) concerning the way in which Paul's system of convictions can be implemented in the daily life of a Christian community. We shall attempt to determine the main principles which should govern the organization of a Pauline community of believers. Then we shall test this general view by discussing how Paul dealt with specific concrete situations in central passages of the second part of 1 Corinthians.

It may seem that Paul's specific type of faith undermines any possibility of true community life, an impression one could have when it is noted that his faith can properly be called a "radical charismatic faith" and that his Gospel can be termed a gospel of freedom. For him, through faith the believers constantly discover in their experience new interventions of God which are elections and thus new revelations of their vocations. Consequently, we wonder, Will not the Christian community constantly be pulled apart as its various members follow their own vocations? Since no revelation can be viewed as an absolute, the community cannot be united by a joint commitment to a given core of beliefs. Pluralism is a necessary characteristic of a Pauline community. With such a dynamic system of convictions, the community cannot have a stable center. In fact, any attempt to have such a stable center is tantamount to forsaking the Gospel. Furthermore, God's interventions are the breaking apart of idolatrous systems of convictions; they are setting the believers free from any stable system of convictions. "For freedom Christ has set us free" (Gal. 5:1).

Pluralism, dynamism, and freedom are essential characteristics of Paul's faith and therefore have to be characteristics of a Pauline community. Consequently, as we attempt to understand how a community of believers is gathered together, we need to make sure that these characteristics are not left aside and thus relativized or contradicted. Paul must be taken seriously when he emphasizes that the various members of the community can be, and should be, as different among themselves as the various parts of a body are. He also must be taken seriously when he emphasizes that the unifying factor of this diversified body of Christ is the most unpredictable, most unmanageable, most dynamic feature of the believers' experience: the Spirit of God (1 Cor. 12:4–26). The Spirit of God is not a "spirit of slavery" but a "spirit of sonship" (Rom. 8:15). It is a Spirit which "bears witness with our spirit that we are children of God" (Rom. 8:16; cf. Gal. 4:1–11), and thus it is a Spirit bringing about freedom, "the glorious liberty of the children of God" (Rom. 8:21; cf. Gal. 4:21—5:1). But this pluralism, this dynamism, and this freedom should not be taken outside their context in Paul's system of convictions, where they are closely interrelated to other fundamental convictions.

### TYPOLOGICAL FAITH AS A BASIS FOR THE
### COMMUNITY OF BELIEVERS

At the outset, let us keep in mind that Paul's faith is a *typological* faith. This characteristic provides a first element which allows us to conceive of a Christian community and establishes a first link among believers of various periods. God's interventions are not haphazard. There is a continuity between the experiences of former believers (of any preceding period of the sacred history) and that of the present believers. The present believers are "imitators" or "fulfillments" of the types that the believers who preceded them are. And Jesus Christ is the most important of these types. He is the normative type. Thus the community composed of the believers who discover themselves through faith as fulfillments or "imitators" of the type Jesus Christ can conceive of itself as a community "in Christ," a Christian community. This community is in continuity with Jesus Christ as well as with the believers who preceded them in the faith. Similarly, through their hope that the promises contained in their own experience will be fulfilled, these believers also perceive themselves as linked with all subsequent believers until the Parousia. Thus the typological convictional pattern which characterizes Paul's faith demands that the community of believers conceive of itself as a part of a larger community which encompasses past and future believers. This is what is entailed, for Paul, by faith and hope.

The typological character of Paul's faith also establishes a preliminary structure for the organization of the community life. Those who were the first to receive faith have authority over those who followed them in the faith. They are types that the new converts have "imitated." Thus both the apostles and the first converts in a region are in a position of authority. Yet, as we have noted, their authority is not an authority to command others or to impose their own views. Their role is merely to encourage, to admonish, to guide, and to be types.

### THE INTERPERSONAL CHARACTER OF FAITH

A second feature of Paul's faith contributes even more to the establishment of the community of believers: faith *cannot* be a private experience. From our study of Paul's convictions about the deliverance from the powers of sin—the interventions of God necessary for the establishment of faith—we conclude that, for Paul, a believer cannot have faith by himself or herself. Faith is *not* an *individual* experience. God's intervention is not and cannot be a private matter, for God's intervention in a believer's experience is Christ-like. At first, would-be believers are enslaved under the power of sin, that is, under the power of a specific idolatrous system of convictions. So that this power might be destroyed, somebody who is not enslaved to this power of sin—and thus, *someone other* than these would-be believers—must be sent, to be a manifestation of God "in the likeness of sinful flesh" according to this idolatrous system. For the apostles, the first persons who were delivered from the power of sin manifested in the Law, Jesus Christ crucified and raised was the person who was God's manifestation in their experience. Similarly, for any other believers there is necessarily somebody who was Christ-like and in whom they could recognize the manifestation of God. God is recognized as manifesting himself in *somebody else*, a Christ-like figure, who is a part of the experience of would-be believers. *Faith is first of all recognizing that God manifests himself in somebody else.* It is only afterward that individual believers can truly recognize God's intervention in their own individual lives and in other aspects of their personal experiences. Therefore faith necessarily involves other persons in whom individual believers discover God's intervention, other persons whom the believers see as better than themselves (Phil. 2:3). When they were enslaved to an idolatrous system of convictions, these Christ-like persons appeared as better than themselves, as better than this identity the would-be believers had.

This interpersonal character of faith can be expected to play an important role in Paul's view of the relations among believers in a community as well as of the relations between believers and other people.

On the one hand, the believers constantly have to make sure that they "stand firm in [the] faith" (1 Cor. 16:13; cf. Gal. 5:1; Phil. 1:27; 4:1; 1 Thess. 3:8). They are a new creation (2 Cor. 5:17; Gal. 6:15) and thus no longer in the flesh (Rom. 8:9), that is, no longer under the power of sin which is manifested in the flesh; for them the powers of sin have been destroyed. But "sin" itself, or Satan (2 Cor. 2:11; 1 Thess. 3:5), or the flesh (i.e., the desires of the flesh, sin; Gal. 5:13), or again the power of death, has not yet been destroyed and thus can take opportunity in any revelation (including in the revelation of freedom; Gal. 5:13). Consequently, the believers are constantly tempted to, or in danger of, again being enslaved to sin and one of its powers. In order to ward off this danger, they must constantly discover new Christ-like figures in their experience. For instance, Paul exhorts the believers "to respect those who . . . are over you in the Lord and admonish you, and to esteem them very highly" (1 Thess. 5:12–13). They must see in them, as well as in others, Christ-like persons. By seeing in the other believers Christ-like persons (Phil. 2:3–5), they are constantly freed from the risk of making an absolute out of what they have themselves received (a special gift, a special revelation, their freedom).

On the other hand, their vocation is to offer their body as a living sacrifice and thus to agree to become Christ-like for others and especially for unbelievers (idolaters of one kind or another). This involves becoming Jewish with the Jews, Greek with the Greeks, pagan with the pagans, weak with the weak (1 Cor. 9:19–23), as Christ "emptied himself, taking the form of a slave, being born in the likeness of men" (Phil. 2:7). As Paul makes clear by his own ministry to the Gentiles, this is not merely a superficial conformity to these other people ("speaking their language so as to be better understood") or a matter of sharing with them the Gospel message; it is also and primarily to share one's own self with them (1 Thess. 2:8). It is really becoming a Gentile with the Gentiles.

But how can one do so in good conscience, that is, without falling prey to all kinds of vices and without betraying one's relation with God? The answer is given in Romans: even the worst of idolatries is nothing other than the perversion of a revelation from God to these people. Becoming a Greek with Greeks first involves recognizing through faith the revelation they have received, recognizing how God intervenes and manifests himself in their experience. Being Christ-like among the unbelievers means partaking of this revelation and living accordingly, but doing so without becoming idolatrous with the unbelievers. This involves transgressing certain demands of their idolatrous system of convictions and thus doing "evil," being "sinful," from the perspective of this idolatrous system of convictions. The result of this attitude might well be that the believer will be rejected and persecuted by the idolaters as Christ was crucified. But if God, according to his promises, also makes this believer like the risen Christ, demonstrating that he or she is indeed a manifestation of God among them, these people's idolatrous system of convictions will be broken up. They will be freed from the power of sin and be able to "see" the revelation of God that they had previously received for what it truly is.

So this interpersonal character of faith demands that the believers be involved in a specific kind of relationship: on the one hand, with other believers (seeing in them Christ-like persons) and, on the other hand, with unbelievers (becoming Christ-like for them). It is this twofold kind of relationship that Paul calls love.

### FAITH, FREEDOM, AND LOVE

It is often said that for Paul love is a limitation of the believers' absolute freedom. In a sense, this is true, but such a formulation of the relation between love and freedom is in many ways misleading, for it leads one to conceive of love and freedom as being opposed to each other. It is as if the freedom of the Gospel was a dangerous and potentially evil dimension of the Christian faith which must be checked, warded off. Is it not the source of all the excesses—immorality of all kinds—against which Paul had constantly to fight, as is expressed not only in the Corinthian correspondence but also, for instance, in 1 Thess. 4:1–7, in Gal. 5:13—6:10, and in Phil. 3:18–21? Yet when Paul finally confronts the Corinthians directly (in 2 Corinthians 10–13), he does not see fit to address the issue of freedom, even though he mentions their immorality (2 Cor. 12:20–21). For him the source of the problem is not with freedom.

Love, a specific kind of relationship with other people, is the very source of the believers' freedom. This freedom that they have in faith results from their deliverance from the powers of sin which takes place through this specific relationship with believers who preceded them in the faith. Since through this love relationship they have been established in the faith and chosen by God, their vocation is a call to enter into this same relationship with other people so that they, in turn, might be saved. Their freedom, this absolute freedom from any idolatrous system of convictions, gives them the possibility of entering into this love relationship with others. Without love (the love for those who preceded them in the faith, and their love for them) they would not have been set free. Conversely, without this freedom they could not love others, that is, become Jews with the Jews (or Greeks with the Greeks), by boldly entering their idolatrous system of convictions in order to be a sign of contradiction in it and thus to save some of them. Thus freedom and love are intimately interrelated. Far from being opposed to each other, or a limitation of each other, according to Paul's system of convictions, one cannot exist without the other.

## IDOLATRY AS LIMITATION OF FREEDOM
## AND LOVE

There is nevertheless a strict limit to freedom and to love. Freedom is true freedom and love is true love if, and only if, they are exercised without trespassing a well-marked borderline, that of idolatry. Idolatry is a constant danger which can take many forms.

In order to fulfill their vocation—thanks to their freedom and for love's sake—the believers have to offer themselves in living sacrifice, they have to enter the idolatrous system of the people who are around them. In so doing, they discern through faith what is the true, although partial, revelation which characterizes this idolatrous system of convictions despite its perversion. Thus they do not go to these idolaters in order to teach them the truth. On the contrary, they will receive from the idolaters a revelation that they, as believers, do not have. For the idolaters, however, this revelation is perverted and veiled. The believers have to unveil for these idolaters this revelation, so as to show them what it truly is by becoming sinful flesh in their view. In all this process there is always the danger that the believers might themselves become caught in the idolatrous system of convictions and thus themselves become idolaters.

According to what we know about Paul's system of convictions, there are two ways in which the believers offering themselves as living sacrifice can become idolaters. On the one hand, the believers might confuse a perversion of the true revelation as being that revelation. In such a case, by appropriating this element of the idolatrous system of convictions (e.g., a certain behavior that they took to be expressing the will of God), they themselves become idolatrous. On the other hand, the believers might take as a perversion of the true revelation something which is actually a true revelation. In such a case, in an effort to become "sinful flesh according to sin," they sin against the will of God (the true revelation).

## THE COMMUNITY OF BELIEVERS AS
## WARDING OFF IDOLATRY

How could one ward off such twofold danger? What are the criteria which would allow the believers to determine whether or not an element of a pagan system is true revelation, true expression of the will of God? Paul clearly affirms that such criteria are provided by the rest of the Christian community with which the believers have to remain in this love relationship. What other believers have abandoned when converting from their idolatrous system of convictions cannot be from God. Furthermore, the revelations they discover in a specific idolatrous system of convictions cannot be in contradiction with what other believers who have converted from different idolatrous systems of convictions have discovered as the true revelation (which was perverted in their former idolatry). These criteria are in fact the direct consequence that, in Paul's view, any believer should consider the other believers as types, as better than themselves.

Thus the community of believers (with its past, present, and future dimensions) is the necessary context from which any "missionary" activity can be launched. Without it the missionary believers will constantly fall prey to the very idolatry they aim at challenging with the help of God.

Idolatry is also a constant danger inside the community. There is always the danger of absolutizing, of transforming into an idol, the partial revelation one has received. The absolutization of a (love) relationship is itself idolatrous and thus is no longer true love. Love is necessarily a multidirectional relationship. Attributing an absolute authority to certain people (such as the superlative apostles) is idolatry. This is why, when Paul does "magnify his ministry," he emphasizes that he does not do so in order to establish his own authority, or at least not to establish himself in a position of strength or superiority over them. He does have authority over them, but when he is weak among them and when they are strong (cf. 2 Cor. 13:9: "For we are glad when we are weak and you are strong"). He has authority as the fulfillment of the crucified Christ, and as a type, a promise which they can discover fulfilled in their own experience. The same is true of any relationship within the community which is governed by the exhortation to "count others [any other] better than yourselves" (Phil. 2:3). And thus a given believer cannot but perceive the revelations or views that he or she has as partial, incomplete, or provisional, since the other believers have other revelations and views which are equally valid.

Thus Paul's system of convictions can be implemented only in a community. The relationships in this community are very fluid, defying any strict institutionalization. The community life has to be as dynamic as the faith upon which it is based. The community is necessarily open to the world, necessarily "missionary" by being with others. Yet the community remains a tightly interwoven network of relations and the necessary basis upon which the faith of each believer is sustained and can flourish. Without the types found in the community (the present and past community of believers), faith would be impossible, since the believer could not discover the new revelations and interventions of God.

## THE COMMUNITY OF BELIEVERS AS A BASIS
## FOR THE ETHICAL LIFE

The community of believers is also the basis upon which ethical judgments can be made. From our investigation, we can anticipate that for Paul there is no fixed norm on the basis of which one can conclude that a given behavior is good and another evil, and so we are not surprised to find in Paul's letter a great tolerance for a diversity of conduct. But it is also clear that Paul is most intolerant of certain kinds of behavior.

Paul makes it abundantly clear that many different ways of life, such as the Jewish and Hellenistic ways of life, are valid. Similarly, many different kinds of conduct, such as eating or not eating meat sacrificed to idols, and marrying or not marrying, are acceptable. No one way of life or kind of conduct is absolutely good or perfect; all of them are acceptable despite their imperfections. For Paul there is no way to classify in the abstract (i.e., outside of the community life) certain kinds of behavior and ways of life as either good or evil. There is no moral or ethical dualism. But Paul also vehemently rejects certain kinds of behavior such as immorality.

Paul's apparently contradictory attitude can be understood if one recognizes that his ethical teaching is governed by two principles: his view that any system of convictions is based on some true revelations, and his view of the power of sin.

Since any system of convictions, even if it has become idolatrous, is based upon a true, although partial, revelation, it can involve a valid system of moral values. Just as the political system, despite its imperfections, provides a valid and useful order for society life (see above, Chapter 7, on Romans 13), so any system of convictions, despite its imperfections, provides a valid and useful order for the lives of individuals and communities. Since the believers still belong to this (imperfect) world, they need to avail themselves of these (imperfect) orders. Therefore they need to follow, for instance, a Jewish or a Hellenistic way of life. On the basis of this principle alone there is no reason to prefer one way of life over another. All are equally valid and acceptable as long as their imperfection is acknowledged and as long as none is perceived as an absolute. The believers have the freedom to adopt one or another of these ways of life.

Yet Paul vehemently rejects persons who have adopted certain kinds of behavior. He does not hesitate to curse these people, such as the immoral man mentioned in 1 Cor. 5:5, or to proclaim that God's wrath will come upon them, as in 1 Thess. 4:6 or Phil. 3:19. We are now familiar with this vocabulary and its meaning in Paul's system of convictions. These people are in bondage to a power of sin and thus under the power of Satan or, again, under the wrath of God. By their way of life, they show that they are idolaters. Therefore Paul believes they must be rejected from the community of believers since they do not truly belong to it.

Without using such strong language, Paul vigorously scolds various believers for certain kinds of conduct: for instance, the immoral Galatians (Gal 5:13–24); the Romans who judge or despise each other (Romans 14); Peter, who refrains from eating with the Gentile believers (Gal. 2:11–18); and the Corinthians (as we shall see below). As far as Paul is concerned, these believers have sinned, they are once again under a power of sin. They have made an absolute, an idol, out of something. As such they exclude themselves from the community of faith, or worse, since they are inside the community, they risk destroying the community of believers. They sin against their sisters and brothers (cf. 1 Cor. 8:12). They also betray the community of faith by not carrying out their vocation, for a good kind of behavior is a behavior which is helpful in the process of fulfilling one's vocation as Christian, which involves offering oneself as living sacrifice so that some might be saved.

The community of believers and its characteristic network of relations, as well as its vocation, provide for Paul the basis upon which a "good" behavior can be defined. Such are the tentative conclusions we can draw from reflecting on the characteristics of Paul's system of convictions which we have elucidated so far. We will now verify, complement, and refine these general remarks through the study of a central section of 1 Corinthians in which Paul deals with concrete ethical issues: 1 Corinthians 5–10.

## Immorality and the Community of Believers (1 Cor. 5:11—6:20)

In this passage Paul deals with three concrete issues:

1. A member of the community is living with his father's wife (1 Cor. 5:1–13).
2. Certain members of the community have lawsuits before the court against other members of the community (6:1–8).
3. Certain members of the community use prostitutes (6:9–20).

The entire unit is about immorality. The passage about lawsuits is an aside brought about by Paul's comments on the community's right to judge and condemn those guilty of immorality.

Immorality was a recurring problem in Pauline communities (cf. again 1 Thess. 4:1–7; Gal. 5:13—6:10; Phil. 3:18–21), not only in Corinth. Our passage suggests that this is the case because the believers have a two-fold attitude with respect to immoral people. On the one hand, they have to associate with immoral people (1 Cor. 5:9–10). According to Paul's system of convictions the believers cannot form an ascetic community which would withdraw from the impure world. Their very vocation demands that they associate with immoral people of all kinds: with the greedy and robbers, the idolaters, revilers, or drunkards (5:10; cf. 5:11). Paul implies that the believers should not judge these outsiders, for God judges them (5:12–13a; cf. Rom. 2:1–2). The believers must coexist with the immoral idolaters in order to save some of them.

On the other hand, the believers should not themselves become immoral people, for this would amount to becoming idolaters with the idolaters (1 Cor. 5:11). Any immoral believer should be rejected from the community (5:2, 11, 13). The community should not even eat with such people (5:11; but they can eat with pagans [10:27]). It should judge immoral believers (5:12) and give them over to Satan for the destruction of the flesh (5:5). Because the Greek text (without punctuation) can be constructed in different ways, 1 Cor. 5:4–5 is difficult to interpret,[12] but it is clear that Paul alludes to a church meeting in which such immoral believers are to be cursed in the name of God. They are to be excluded from the community and sent back to where they belong: the idolatrous world under the power of Satan. As Paul writes in Phil. 3:19, "their end is destruction." The idolaters were given up by God to their immorality, with the result that they destroy their bodies (Rom. 1:24, 26, 28), so the community should give up these immoral believers to Satan for the destruction of their flesh. But this painful rejection of immoral believers is not without hope; it is done "that his spirit may be saved in the day of the Lord Jesus" (1 Cor. 5:5b)—a difficult phrase to interpret. It could mean that this is done with the hope that the immoral believer will repent and be reinstated in the community of faith (as Paul exhorts the Corinthians to reinstate the offender in 2 Cor. 2:5–11, a passage which also refers to the necessity of "keeping Satan from gaining the advantage over us").

What is most revealing is the attitude of the Corinthians prior to Paul's intervention. He mentions that they have an "arrogant" attitude (1 Cor. 5:2), that they are proud of having among them such an immoral believer. In 5:6 Paul says that they are boasting about it. This implies that the Corinthians do not perceive this situation as wrong,[13] that they do not see it as being in contradiction with their faith. This also seems to be the case in Gal. 5:13—6:10, where Paul presupposes that certain believers do not perceive it is contradictory to the Gospel to lead immoral lives.

The Corinthians apparently do not expect Paul to object to such behavior, despite his preceding letter (1 Cor. 5:9). The same is true of another kind of immorality, using prostitutes (cf. 6:12–20). They justify this behavior by the motto "All things are lawful for me." In other words, they conceive the freedom given by the Gospel as an absolute freedom which includes the possibility of immorality. This is the same problem anticipated (or encountered) by Paul when writing to the Galatians (Gal. 5:13).

We now understand how the Corinthians (and the Galatians) could misinterpret Paul's teaching. Yes, they have the freedom to associate with immoral people; indeed, doing so is part of the church's vocation. But this does not mean that they can become immoral themselves. A study of the arguments that Paul uses to refute the Corinthians' position will help us understand on which basis immorality should be rejected by the community of believers.

In 1 Cor. 5:6–8, by using leaven as a metaphor for impurity (as in the Jewish tradition),[14] Paul introduces a first argument against immorality in the church. The church is a community which constantly celebrates "Passover." Christ is the passover lamb who has been sacrificed. The church is thus the chosen people of the eschatological time—the period from Christ's death and resurrection until the Parousia. This is the time when the powers which keep human beings in bondage are destroyed (1 Cor. 15:24–28). Thus a part of the community's vocation is to celebrate Passover, the deliverance from bondage. The Christian community's worship should be festive. The community should "rejoice in the Lord always" (Phil. 4:4; 1 Thess. 5:16). We have noted that this is the pervading theme of the main letter to the Philippians. The organization of Paul's discourse in his letters also shows that the believers should constantly be celebrating. A thanksgiving acknowledging God's interventions in the present experience of the believers is the basis of any other aspect of the believers' life, in the same way that it is the basis for Paul's activity as apostle (and therefore a part of the opening statements in most of his letters). Indeed, any prayer and supplication should be made with thanksgiving (Phil. 4:6). The believers should "give thanks in all circumstances; for this is the will of God in Christ Jesus for you" (1 Thess. 5:18). A Christian community is a community which "together . . . with one voice glorify the God and Father of our Lord Jesus Christ" (Rom. 15:6; cf. also Rom. 15:7–13). It is also now clear that this is not a glorification of God's eternal majesty in the abstract, but rather of God as the One who manifests himself in the present of the community. By nature, the church is a community of believers who "contemplate" the concrete situations around them, discover through faith God at work in these situations, and give thanks with one voice to God. They are united because of this joint celebration.

Paul implies that since the community is constantly celebrating the "Passover" it must remain free from immorality and from evil, as the Jewish house is cleansed from any remnant of leavened bread for the celebration of the Passover. Immorality in the community is impossible because, by nature, this community is a celebrating, a thanksgiving community. This argument by itself would hardly be sufficient. Yet for

Paul this celebrating community must be perceived in terms of his typological convictional pattern. It is a community which is related, on the one hand, to the community of the Parousia and, on the other hand, to Christ.

Paul's second argument against immorality is again based upon the vocation of the Christian community, but this time more specifically upon its eschatological vocation. At the Parousia, "the saints will judge the world" (1 Cor. 6:2). Indeed, they "are to judge angels" (6:3) and "will inherit the kingdom of God" (cf. 6:9, 10). Because of its eschatological vocation as judge of the world, the church has the authority to judge and to condemn immoral people *inside the community*. This presupposes that for Paul the church should view itself as the community of the Parousia. In the perspective of Paul's typological convictional pattern this is not surprising. The church is already the prefiguration or a preliminary manifestation of the community of the Parousia. Internally it is *already* the eschatological community, even though it is *not yet* in a position to judge the outsiders. Thus the church is in a position to judge all the various kinds of evil which are found within itself, so it is nonsense for a believer to seek justice by going to court against another believer (6:1–8).

The members of the church must be saints also because the church is destined to inherit the kingdom of God (1 Cor. 6:9–11). Indeed, they are already this saintly, eschatological community: "You were washed, you were sanctified, you were justified in the name of the Lord Jesus Christ and in the Spirit of our God" (6:11).

The third argument against immorality of believers (1 Cor. 6:12–20) is based upon a third aspect of the nature of the church. The believers are members of the body of Christ and temples of the Holy Spirit. Being a member of the body of Christ means being "united to the Lord." It involves "becoming one spirit with him" (6:17). It is clear once more that this union with Christ is, for Paul, a typological relation. It involves being crucified with Christ, that is, having cross-like experiences (as Paul emphasized in 2:18—4:13). But here Paul does not mention this aspect of the experience of the believers as members of the body of Christ (although the phrase "the [believers'] body is . . . for the Lord" might allude to this). Instead he stresses that being a member of Christ's body means that one will be raised as Christ was raised (6:14). So the community of believers is united because all its members are "in Christ."

Immorality is impossible, because their bodies are for the Lord as the Lord is for their bodies.

Similarly, their bodies are temples of the Holy Spirit (1 Cor. 6:19–20; cf. also 3:16–17). Here this statement does not appear to define further the community of believers. As we have already noted, however, Paul shows in 1 Cor. 12:4–31 that the church can also be defined as the community of believers who each have gifts of the Spirit. Each believer is a temple of the Holy Spirit which is one as God is One.

The problems concerning immorality in the church are therefore arising out of a misunderstanding or, better, an incomplete understanding of the church's vocation and nature. The church is a community whose vocation is to associate itself with immoral people and thus to stay in the world. The freedom they have received allows them to do so. But the church is also a community constantly celebrating and giving thanks to God; a prefiguration of the community which will judge the world and inherit the kingdom; the body of Christ; and a community whose members are temples of the Holy Spirit. As members of such a community, the believers who must associate with immoral people cannot become immoral with them.

Abstention from immorality is demanded by the very nature and vocation of the church. We shall see that this is true of Paul's ethical teaching as a whole. For Paul, ethical and good behavior is based upon the discernment of what is good and evil made in the context and in terms of the community of believers. As we proceed in our investigation of Paul's moral teaching, we shall elucidate the nature of the church, that is, how a community of believers functions. Yet 1 Cor. 5:1—6:20 does not allow us to understand fully why Paul systematically rejects immorality. Is the nature of the church defining a new law which would include, as one of its basic tenets, abstaining from immorality? This would be in contradiction with Paul's convictional pattern, which establishes freedom for the believers. But what is the basis for this systematic rejection of immorality?

## Other Arguments Against Immorality
### (Phil. 3:17—4:1; 1 Thess. 4:1–8; Gal. 5:13–25)

In Phil. 3:17—4:1 a much shorter argument against immorality is made on the basis of the eschatological future of the believers and their relationship with Christ. In the present they share in Christ's sufferings by being conformed to his death (Phil. 3:10), but they will be conformed to his glorious body (3:21). Furthermore, their commonwealth is in heaven (3:20). Being immoral is forsaking all this; it is being enemies of the cross (rather than being cross-like; 3:18) and thus going toward destruction (3:19; instead of toward resurrection, 3:10), an argument against immorality similar to the one we found in 1 Cor. 6:9–18. In addition, it is based upon relations in the church. This warning against immorality is introduced by an exhortation to join in imitating Paul and other believers who are types for them (3:17). Thus, for Paul, the type/imitator relation *in the present church* is an additional reason for rejecting immorality. On the basis of this text, we cannot understand why this is so. Other texts will show it.

In 1 Thess. 4:1–8 the argument against immorality is quite short. It is based upon the vocation (call) of the believers. "This is the will of God, your sanctification" (4:3), "for God has not called us for uncleanness, but in holiness" (4:7). Furthermore, it is based upon a warning about eschatological punishment (4:6). In conclusion we find this cryptic statement: "Therefore whoever disregards this, disregards not man but God, who gives his Holy Spirit to you" (4:8). We need to be cautious in our interpretation. This letter was written much earlier than Galatians, 1 and 2 Corinthians, and Romans, yet we can say that Paul expected his readers would be accustomed to making distinctions between "human" and "divine" views of good and evil. It is clear that the believers had been taught to "disregard" what is human, because without explanation Paul exhorts them to "test everything; hold fast what is good, abstain from every form of evil" (1 Thess. 5:21–22). Thus the argument against immorality is based upon the assumption that the believers should discern through the Spirit (cf. 1 Thess. 5:19–20) what is good (from God) and evil (from humans). Since no other system of convictions is mentioned in this letter, we must assume that the Thessalonians had to discern what is good and evil by testing everything which belonged to their former idolatrous system of convictions. Unfortunately, Paul gives us few clues about how this testing of everything was to take place. The only thing we can say is that it was *not* done by an individual believer on his or her own. The exhortations against immorality underscore that the Thessalonians should have a pure life, as they have learned from Paul and Timothy (4:1). Similarly, the exhortation to test everything is preceded by exhortations concerning the community life (5:12–15). Since in this letter Paul emphasizes that other believers (Paul, Timothy, the Judean churches) are types for the Thessalonians, it is possible that this "testing of everything" is to be made by comparing one's behavior with that of the "types."

In Gal. 5:13–25 the problem of immorality and other evil behavior is directly related to excessive freedom, as in 1 Corinthians 6, but the argument is quite different, except for the warning that immoral people will not inherit the kingdom of God (Gal. 5:21). This is certainly one of the bases for Paul's overall argument against immorality. But Paul never uses it by itself, since it could give rise to a new kind of legalism, an eschatological legalism, which would cancel the freedom of the Gospel. At first it seems that the argument against immorality is based primarily upon the concluding statements: "Those who belong to Christ Jesus have crucified the flesh with its passions and desires. If we live by the Spirit, let us also walk by the Spirit" (Gal. 5:24–25). But this cannot be the case. "Being crucified with Christ" and "living by the Spirit" cannot be the basis of an argument aimed at limiting the believers' freedom and thus at excluding immorality. Paul has already spoken of the believers as crucified with Christ primarily to express that the believers are freed from bondage (cf. Gal. 2:19–20), so the statement of 5:24 is a summary of what precedes, not the basis for the argument. Similarly, the statement about the Spirit cannot be the basis for the argument, for Paul does not here suggest that the believers are temples of the Spirit; they are merely led by the Spirit. And when one examines how Paul defines the Spirit in this letter, one discovers that it is also primarily associated with the believers' liberation from bondage. It is the Spirit of God's Son (Gal. 4:6) through which the believers themselves become sons rather than slaves (4:6–7). Walking by the Spirit should not involve immorality, but this statement does not really provide any clear limitation of freedom and thus no basis for avoiding immorality.

This argument against immorality is based upon statements concerning the Law. "Do not use your freedom as an opportunity for the flesh, but through love be servants of one another. For the whole law is fulfilled in one word, 'You shall love your neighbor as yourself'" (Gal. 5:13–14). "Against such [the fruit of the Spirit] there is no law" (5:23). In this concluding part of a letter in which Paul has so violently attacked the Law, it is clear that he does not intend again to propose the Law as an absolute which would allow the believers to discern what is good and evil. The Law to which he refers is clearly the partial revelation from God which provides the promises and types which help any believer to discern the new interventions of God, a provisional way of life which the believers of Jewish origin can follow.

In this text the list of vices and virtues (fruit of the Spirit) is borrowed from the Hellenistic system of convictions (possibly through the intermediary of Hellenistic Judaism), that is, from the Galatians' former idolatrous system of convictions (see above, Chapter 2). The criterion for discerning what is good (fitting for a life in the Spirit and in Christ) is seeing that these virtues are not in contradiction with the "Law" or, more precisely, with what is the "true revelation" found in the Law when it is freed from the idolatrous system of convictions in which it was perverted. Hellenism (at least in some of its manifestations) identifies immorality as a vice. This is not enough to affirm that it is evil. The Hellenistic idolaters could have viewed as evil what is good before God, but now the believers of Jewish origin who were freed from the idolatrous system of convictions centered on the Law have discovered that one of the true revelations found in the Law is the law of love (Gal. 5:14). So the Jewish Christians hold to the law of love and abstain from anything which contradicts it. Since the Jewish Christians are types for the Gentile Christians, the latter should be conformed to the former. In other words, the Gentile Christians' behavior should not be contradictory to the Jewish Christians' behavior. Now all the vices listed in Gal. 5:19–21—the first of which is "immorality"—are contradictory to the law of love, as is evident when they are contrasted with the virtues/fruit of the Spirit. Consequently, one must conclude that immorality should be rejected, since it would contradict the true revelation discovered through faith in the Law by the Jewish Christians.

It is not a matter of the Galatians' adopting the Jewish way of life of the Jewish Christians and thus viewing them as examples they should follow step by step. This is clear from the overall argument of the letter. In light of our discussion of Philippians 3 and 1 Thessalonians 4, we conclude that Paul's exhortation to a life free from immorality is based upon the type/imitator relations inside the church. The Jewish Christians, and the churches in Judea, are types for the Galatians, in the sense that the promises contained in the experience of the Jewish Christians are fulfilled through God's interventions in the Galatians' experience. While this also implies that the Galatians' way of life should be "conformed" to that of the Jewish Christians, it does not mean that they should have identical ways of life. Indeed, the Galatians should keep their Hellenistic way of life as long as it is not idolatrous. This is demanded by their vocation, which is to save at least some of the people among whom they live. They must be Hellenistic with them so as to become, thanks to God's intervention, a sign of contradiction for them. In order to be a true sign of contradiction for their compatriots, however, their lives must also be "conformed" to that of the Jewish Christians, in the sense that their behavior should not be in contradiction with that of the Jewish Christians, that is, of other members of the church. Concerning the main characteristics of the Galatians' behavior, a Jewish Christian should be able to say, "Against such there is no law" (Gal. 5:23).

The Jewish Christians should have the same attitude. They should follow their Jewish way of life because of their own specific vocation to be Jews with the Jews. The Jewish way of life is good. It provides a useful order for their life. But it is not an absolute. Thus the Jewish Christians' way of life should also be "conformed" to that of the Gentile Christians. It should not be in contradiction with the Gentile Christians' way of life so as to avoid becoming Jewish idolaters again. This is, according to Paul, the attitude that Peter and the Jewish Christians should have had at Antioch (Gal. 2:11-18).

So that these very different ways of life might not be in contradiction with each other, they must have a common ground. But what will this common ground be? According to Gal. 5:13-25, it is love. Love is expressed in the form of the law of love in Torah and was revealed to the Jews. But for Paul love is not a law; it is a fruit of the Spirit (Gal. 5:22). Because of the way in which love is conceived by Paul, it does not provide any stable norm for deciding what is good or evil.

> Love is patient and kind; love is not jealous or boastful; it is not arrogant or rude. Love does not insist on its own way; it is not irritable or resentful; it does not rejoice at wrong, but rejoices in the right. Love bears all things, believes all things, hopes all things, endures all things. (1 Cor. 13:4-7)

These verses can be summarized in Paul's other formula: "Count others better than yourselves" (Phil. 2:3). A concrete instance of this attitude in a community is the one we just described: the Gentile Christians conforming themselves to the Jewish Christians, and vice versa. This is what is involved in "not being arrogant," "not insisting on one's own way" (not seeking one's own advantage), and "believing everything." It is not a law dictating what is good or what should be done.

Yet for Paul love serves as a negative principle. This is how Paul uses love to define evil behavior in Gal. 5:15: "But if you bite and devour one another take heed that you are not consumed by one another." The relationships which would destroy one person or the other are evil. Idolatry is evil because it is "boastful," "arrogant," "insisting on its own way," and believing only one thing, the absolute "truth" that it has. Thus love (seeing others as better than oneself) is impossible. Furthermore, idolatry is bringing about the destruction of all the normal interhuman relations, as Paul emphasized in Rom. 1:18–32, but so is immorality. Because it is a manifestation of selfish desire (self-asserting desire), which is the source of idolatry, it is also destroying all true interhuman relationships (love relationships), and therefore it is evil. Immorality, which is rejected both by the Jews (and the Law) and by the Gentiles because it makes it impossible to have a community life, is thus a true evil (an evil according to the partial but true revelations received by the Jews and the Gentiles) and not merely an evil according to their respective idolatries.

All that love allows us to define is a domain in which good behavior can take place. This domain of love is the community of people who are in such a relationship: the community of believers, of those who have been freed from various powers of sin (various idolatries). But this community of believers does not include the false believers, those who are once again under the power of an idolatry (e.g., the Judaizers or the enthusiast Corinthians).

Because of their faith the believers are free to consider others as better than themselves, as types to whom they should be conformed. This is love in the community according to which nobody can be subordinated to anyone because the relations of authority are constantly reversed, each seeing the other as better than oneself. "There is neither Jew nor Greek, there is neither slave nor free, there is neither male nor female" (Gal. 3:28). And this love relationship serves as a basis for ethics. Their behavior should be conformed to the conscience of the other believers. Their conscience is not an absolute, and so they must acknowledge the value of the conscience of other believers.

Because of their faith and hope, the believers trust that God's interventions in their own experience are promises and types of new interventions of God in the experience of others. Because of their love these believers have a vocation which demands that they associate with immoral people and idolaters. This is love for the outsiders, through whom they will recognize the revelation that these outsiders have from God, despite the perversion brought about by their idolatries.

The ethical life of the believers, their love, is fully defined by the nature and the vocation of the community of the believers. It is a community of faith, and thus a community which is united by its constant celebration and thanksgiving for the interventions of God. It is a community of hope, which defines itself in terms of this eschatological future that it sees "dimly in a mirror." It is a community of faith, hope, and love which has a vocation toward the outsiders.

### Remain as You Are (1 Cor. 7:1–40)

In 1 Corinthians 7 Paul deals with questions concerning marriage. The question is raised, Should one abstain from sexual intercourse? Paul answers, It is well to do so, as he himself does, but to marry is also good in order to avoid the temptation of immorality. In such a case they should "love" each other ("love does not insist on its own way"), "for the wife does not rule over her own body, but the husband does; likewise the husband does not rule over his own body, but the wife does" (1 Cor. 7:1–9).

Then Paul addresses the question of divorce (1 Cor. 7:10–16). We find in 7:10–11 one of the rare references by Paul to the teaching of Jesus, the Lord (the others are in 1 Cor. 9:14 and possibly 1 Thess. 4:15). At first, Jesus' teaching appears to be presented as an absolute law (the mention of the wife separated from her husband in 1 Cor. 7:10 does not suggest an exception but describes an existing situation), but the following verses (7:12–16) propose Paul's interpretation of this command in the case of marriage to an unbeliever. These verses are difficult to interpret,[15] but they make it clear that while the believer should not initiate divorce, if it is initiated by the unbelieving spouse the believer is "not bound" and thus free to remarry. Again the freedom of the believers is implemented as a valid principle. It should also be noted that Paul carefully states by his argument that for him the sexes are equal (implementing in this way his statement that in Christ "there is neither male nor female" [Gal. 3:28]).

The rest of 1 Corinthians 7 applies the principle "Every one should remain in the state in which he was called" (7:20; this was discussed above, in Chapter 2). In the same way that the Jews should keep their Jewish way of life and the Gentiles their Gentile way of life, so the slave, the unmarried, and the married should remain as they were at the time of their conversion. But once again this is not an absolute law. The slave can remain slave, since "in Christ" "there is neither slave nor free" (Gal. 3:28). Yet the slave should take advantage of any opportunity to become free (1 Cor. 7:21). For the unmarried and the married believers, the argument for remaining as they are is stronger. Two main reasons are given. First, they live in the eschatological time. "The appointed time has grown very short" (7:29a), so even those who are married should behave as if they were not (7:29b). That is, the believers should not make an absolute of any of the situations in which they find themselves. Yes, they should remain as they are, but with the understanding that the state in which they are, whatever it might be, is not an absolute. So Paul writes:

> From now on, let those who have wives live as though they had none, and those who mourn as though they were not mourning, and those who rejoice as though they were not rejoicing, and those who buy as though they had no goods, and those who deal with the world as though they had no dealings with it. For the form of this world is passing away. (1 Cor. 7:29b–31)

Second, Paul emphasizes that it is better for the unmarried to remain as they are, because in this way they are in a better position to fulfill their vocation, to be fully devoted to the "affairs of the Lord" (1 Cor. 7:32). Yet marrying is not a sin, and might even be good so as to avoid the danger of immorality (7:28, 36). As Paul underscores, all this advice, and thus also the principle "remain as you are," is given "to secure your undivided devotion to the Lord" (7:35). In most instances, serving the Lord (i.e., fulfilling one's vocation as Christian, and thus "keeping the commandments of God" [7:19]) is best accomplished by remaining as one is. But certain circumstances make this advice unpractical. Even if one does not commit immoral acts, when one is "aflame with passion" (7:9) one is not free for the service of the Lord. In such a case it is better to marry.

### There Is Neither Male
### nor Female (1 Cor. 11:2–16)

Since we shall not study 1 Corinthians 11–14, it is appropriate to complement what Paul says here about the relation between men and women with a few comments about 1 Cor. 11:2–16. This passage[16] follows an argument in which, as we shall see, Paul explicitly uses the type/ imitator pattern and which he concludes by saying, "Be imitators of me, as I am of Christ" (11:1). Once again in 11:2–16 he uses this pattern for speaking about the status of women, and this in the context of an argument aimed at showing that women should be veiled when participating (praying and prophesying) in the church's worship service. It is clear that Paul's argument is undergirded by his convictional pattern, which he applies to the situation of women as he does to any other issues.

In the Jewish and Hellenistic (idolatrous) systems of convictions,[17] women are viewed as having a subordinate status to men[18] according to which women are inferior and therefore have limited rights. If our discussion of Paul's convictional view of idolatry is correct, we can expect that Paul would have an ambivalent attitude toward these traditions which belong to idolatrous systems of convictions. He would want to affirm a part of these traditions as fundamentally true, but he would want to reject another part of these traditions as resulting from the absolutization of this truth which makes out of it an idolatry with a power of bondage resulting in a perversion of the relationship between men and women.

This is what we find in the present passage. Paul affirms as valid the view which sees women as subordinated to men: "a woman's head is the man" (11:3, au. trans.). But, for Paul, this subordination is to be understood in terms of the relation to God and to Christ.

This issue of the authority of men over women is just another case of authority in the Christian community. We have discussed at length the authority of Paul as apostle (and father), as well as the authority of the other believers (such as the "first fruits" in a region) in the community. Those in authority are due respect as types, and as such they exercise this authority on the one hand, by sharing their own selves with those under their authority (as the crucified Christ, as a nursing mother), and on the other hand, by being among those under their authority as babies, that is, both as children among children (brothers and sisters) and as persons viewing others (those under their authority) as better than themselves because in these others they can discover Christ-like manifestations.

In 1 Cor. 11:2–16 Paul affirms the traditional view of the subordination of women to men. According to the Jewish and possibly Hellenistic traditions, women must be veiled when praying or prophesying (11:4–7, 10, 13–15). This shows that men are first in relation to the divine (as the first converts of a region are). This is also for Paul what nature teaches (since women have long hair and do not cut it, as men do). Men's position of authority over women is further shown by the Genesis creation story (11:8–9, alluding to Genesis 2).

But in 1 Cor. 11:11–12 Paul expresses how this subordination is redefined "in the Lord." Women and men have the same status. "There is neither woman without man nor man without woman" (11:11; Conzelmann's trans.). Indeed, the subordination can be reversed, "For just as woman originated from man, so, too, man exists through woman" (11:12; Conzelmann's trans.). In terms of Paul's structure of authority in the community of believers, men have authority over women in that they are (according to the Jewish and Hellenistic traditions) the first in relation to God ("woman originated from man") and thus a more direct image and reflection of God (11:7). This is also true in Christ. Women have to acknowledge the authority of men who are believers and who themselves acknowledge the authority of Christ ("the head of every man is Christ"; 11:3) and are thus Christ-like (in them, there are Christ-like manifestations of God). But these men who are believers also have to recognize the authority of women by seeing them as preceding them, which is in accord with the Jewish and Hellenistic traditions stating that "man exists through woman." In other words, they should have toward women the attitude they have toward Christ. This is not a paternalistic attitude; indeed, it considers women as better than themselves. In women, men discover Christ-like manifestations of God. And thus women are in turn in a position of authority over men.[19] In Christ "there is neither male nor female" (Gal. 3:28).

## The Weak and the Strong (1 Cor. 8:1—11:1)

Despite the many suggestions that 1 Cor. 8:1—11:1 is not a unity,[20] when this passage is treated as a whole, one can perceive the coherence of the argument.[21] This is especially true when it is read while keeping in mind the provisional results of our study.

In 1 Corinthians 8 Paul argues that as Christians we "know" that idols have no real existence. Thus the believers do have the theoretical freedom to eat meat sacrificed to idols, but for the sake of the weaker believers, they should not do so. The weaker believers are people who have converted from such idolatries (8:7) and have turned away from any idolatrous practices. They have kept other Hellenistic practices, but rejected all that had to do with the cult of idols as sinful before God. Thus the other believers who eat meat sacrificed to idols might be perceived by the weaker believers as an encouragement to do so themselves. The strong believers are even free to eat "at a table in an idol's temple" (a kind of restaurant). But then for the weaker believers it would mean practicing idolatry again and they would "fall." Thus the weaker believers would be destroyed (8:11). This is sinning against these believers (8:12a), "wounding their conscience" (8:12b), and "sinning against Christ" (8:12c).

But being "free" is also knowing that "food will not commend us to God. We are not worse off if we do not eat, and no better off if we do" (1 Cor. 8:8). Yes, we have the right to eat meat sacrificed to idols, but for the sake of other believers it is better not to eat such meat. This is what is demanded by "love in the community." This is how the believers should conform themselves to other believers. This is what builds up the church (8:1), what strengthens the faith of other believers. This is fulfilling one's vocation with respect to other believers by being Christ-like among them, for this vocation necessitates being weak with the weak (9:22), whoever the weak might be (here they are former Hellenistic idolaters, but in Romans 14 they are Jewish Christians).

The strong believers should see their vocation as winning the weak (9:22) to the full freedom of the Gospel. This is helping them grow in the faith not by shocking them and being a stumbling block for them, but by becoming weak with them and "recognizing them as better than oneself," that is, recognizing what they have received from God and helping them to discover it for what it truly is.

The love relationship in the community of believers is the same relationship that the Christians as missionaries have with respect to the outsiders, and thus also that the apostle has with respect to the churches he founded. All these relationships are of the same type as Christ becoming sinful flesh in Judaism so as to save the Jews. And so, Paul introduces the example of his own behavior with respect to the church. Though the topic seems to shift abruptly, Paul is speaking about the same thing.

As an apostle, Paul is free (1 Cor. 9:1–2), and as an apostle he has certain rights. He has the right to be supported financially by the churches he has founded for four reasons. First, he refers to the other apostles and more specifically to "the brothers of the Lord and Cephas" (9:5).

They and their wives are supported financially by the churches. Second, he quotes Scripture, which according to his interpretation clearly shows that the apostles have the right to receive material benefits from their converts (9:8–12). Third, he mentions that the priests in the temple receive material benefits for their service (9:13). Finally, he points out that the Lord (Jesus) himself has "commanded that those who proclaim the gospel should get their living by the gospel" (9:14).

But Paul (and Barnabas) have given up this right and work for a living. "We have not made use of this right, but we endure anything rather than put an obstacle in the way of the gospel of Christ" (1 Cor. 9:12). Yet giving up this right should not be construed as a lack of freedom. On the contrary, it is a manifestation of Paul's freedom (9:15–18). He was not free to choose to announce the Gospel. This mission and responsibility was entrusted to him. He could not but do it. It is a necessity, a constraint laid upon him (9:16). As he says in Gal. 1:12–16, it was a call that he could not refuse; indeed, he was set apart for this mission before he was born. Therefore he cannot claim any reward for being an apostle. By contrast, he can boast of not making use of his right to financial support. This is not something which was imposed upon him, so he can claim a reward for this. "What then is my reward? Just this: that in my preaching I may make the gospel free of charge, not making full use of my right in the gospel" (1 Cor. 9:18).

With this verse Paul concludes the first part of his argument. By taking the example of his own refusal to accept financial support from the churches, he has shown in a preliminary way that the believers' freedom is the freedom to give up one's rights for the sake of the Gospel and thus for the sake of other believers, rather than claiming these rights. Now he carries his argument further by referring to his overall attitude as an apostle. "For though I am free from all men, I have made myself a slave to all, that I might win the more" (9:19). Proclaiming the Gospel, which is the vocation of any Christian, entails using one's freedom to become "slave to all." He then explains this statement by describing several cases.

> To the Jews I became as a Jew, in order to win Jews; to those under the law I became as one under the law—though not being myself under the law—that I might win those under the law. To those outside the law I became as one outside the law—not being without law toward God but under the law of Christ—that I might win those outside the law. (1 Cor. 9:20–21)

We have already discussed this passage (see Chapter 7) to show that this attitude is in effect fulfilling the type "Christ crucified." It is becoming a slave as Christ made himself a slave. It is becoming "sinful flesh." Paul enters the systems of convictions of the Jews (i.e., those who are under the Law) and of the Gentiles (i.e., those who are outside the Law), not meaning that he becomes "under the Law" himself. He does not join the Jews in making out of the Law this absolute which is the power of sin, that is, an idolatry. Similarly, by joining those who are outside the Law, he does not become "lawless," a Hellenistic idolater. He remains "under the law of Christ," Christ-like. But he gives up his rights of not following the Law (and the Jewish customs) as well as his rights of not following Hellenistic customs. This is demanded by his vocation. How could some of the Jews and some of the Gentiles be saved if nobody becomes Christ-like for them?

Paul adopts the same attitude toward the weak believers. "To the weak I became weak, that I might win the weak" (1 Cor. 9:22a). In other words, the case of the weak believers is not different. The attitude toward other believers in the community should be the same as the attitude of the believers toward the outsiders they aim at converting. Indeed, for Paul, it is a general principle, "I have become all things to all men, that I might by all means save some" (9:22b).

It is only by so doing that Paul can hope to share in the Gospel's blessings, that he can truly hope for salvation. In other words, it is only in so doing that one can truly fulfill one's vocation as Christian. It is only in so doing that one fulfills in one's experience the type Christ crucified (by becoming a "slave") and raised (when some are saved). Consequently, it is only in so doing that one's experience is truly the promise of future fulfillments (at the Parousia): the Gospel's blessings.

In the concluding verses of the chapter, 9:24–27, Paul makes it clear that this should not be the attitude of the apostle alone, that the Corinthians should have the same attitude and also "run" in such a way as to obtain the prize.

Paul has made it clear that abstaining from meat sacrificed to idols for the sake of the weaker believers is not giving up one's freedom but making the proper use of one's freedom. It is simply a part of one's vocation as Christian, as "imitator" of Christ. The believers have to "crucify" their rights for the sake of the weaker believers.

So far the argument has been "positive." This attitude is your vocation, and by carrying it you will receive the "prize." Yet there is a
negative side to this argument. If you do not adopt this attitude toward
the weaker believers, you are sinning against them, and in so doing you
are sinning against Christ (1 Cor. 8:12). In other words, the Christians
do not have any alternative. To be a Christian is to carry out this
vocation. It is to be Christ-like for the Jews, the Gentiles, the weak
believers, indeed, for all people by becoming Jewish with the Jews,
Gentile with the Gentiles, weak with the weak. Failing to carry out this
vocation is forsaking one's relationship to Christ. It is sinning against
Christ.

In 1 Cor. 10:1–22 Paul pursues his argument on this negative side.
For this purpose he discusses the place of baptism in the Christian's life.
Paul assumes that the Corinthians would argue that to be a Christian it
is enough to be baptized and to share in the Lord's Supper. Are not the
baptism and the Lord's Supper signs that one is "in Christ"? If it were
so, Paul's preceding argument would be nullified. Being Christian would
be defined as being in a "mystical" union with Christ instead of becoming all things to all people.

As usual, for Paul, baptism and the Lord's Supper are to be understood as the fulfillments of a type: the experience of Israel at the time of
the Exodus. Thus Paul speaks of Israel crossing the Red Sea as their
being "baptized into Moses" (1 Cor. 10:1–2). Then, in the wilderness
they "all ate the same supernatural food and all drank the same supernatural drink. For they drank from the supernatural Rock which followed them, and the Rock was Christ" (10:3–4). In other words, the
manna and the miraculous water from a rock struck by Moses (cf. Exod.
17:6; Num. 20:7–11) are the types of the bread and wine of the Lord's
Supper. Furthermore, the rock is the type of Christ, who was struck so
that the "supernatural drink" (his blood) might flow out of him.[22]

Once these typological relations between Israel in the time of the
Exodus and the sacraments are established, Paul can pursue the typological reasoning. "Now these things are types for us" (1 Cor. 10:6; RSV
translates "types" by "warnings"; in the present case, this typological
relationship is presented by Paul as a warning). Despite the Exodus and
its miracles, Israel was nevertheless punished by God because of their
idolatry and their grumbling against God (10:7–10). Indeed, many of

them were "destroyed," and so will the Christians be punished by God if they become idolaters. Being baptized or partaking in the Lord's Supper will not be a protection against God's punishment. Baptism and the Lord's Supper merely (but it is all that is needed) set the believers in the typological chain: Exodus, Christ, believers.

Paul draws two conclusions from this typological argument. "Therefore let any one who thinks that he stands take heed lest he fall" (1 Cor. 10:12). In other words, beware of becoming inadvertently like the unfaithful Israel. You may think you are behaving as faithful believers by using your Christian freedom. But are you sure? Paul even adds that their temptation is a very common one (10:13a). Indeed, it is the temptation of abandoning the Gospel and returning to an idolatrous system of convictions (centered upon their freedom as an absolute). And Paul comforts them by giving them the assurance that God also gives them the means to overcome this temptation (10:13b).

The second conclusion includes an even stronger warning: "Therefore, my beloved, shun the worship of idols" (1 Cor. 10:14). With this Paul comes back to the issues he had raised about idolatry in 8:4–13. He is now much more negative in his judgment by taking the point of view of the weaker believers.[23] He had mentioned the Corinthians' participation in meals "at table in an idol's temple" (8:10). He needs to elaborate on what is involved when one does so. He had discussed the "reality of the idols" (8:4–6). He needs to explain their power over the weaker believers. His argument against partaking of the table of idols is made by contrast with participation in the Lord's Supper. First, participating in the Lord's Supper is participating in the body of Christ (10:16). "Because there is one bread, we who are many are one body" (10:17). Therefore all the believers are partners in Christ. The interrelation of the believers in Christ's body is therefore a first reason why idolatry should be absolutely avoided. The second argument points out that even though idols have no real existence, they have power, the power of demons. Thus, eating at table in an idol's temple is being partners with demons (10:20).

In the concluding section of our passage (1 Cor. 10:23—11:1), Paul recapitulates the main points of his argument by focusing on still another situation: eating meat sold at the meat market or at the table of an unbeliever. The same principle is restated. The believer is free to eat such meat, whether it was sacrificed to idols or not, but if somebody, pagan or weak believer, points out to you that it was sacrificed to idols, then you should abstain from the meat, for this person's sake (for the sake of this person's conscience; 10:28–29).

Paul can summarize his entire ethical teaching as follows.

So, whether you eat or drink, or whatever you do, do all to the glory of God. Give no offense to Jews or to Greeks or to the church of God, just as I try to please all men in everything I do, not seeking my own advantage, but that of many, that they may be saved. Be imitators of me, as I am of Christ. (1 Cor. 10:31—11:1)

In these verses we recognize many of the characteristics of Paul's system of convictions.

1. The believers' faith is based upon the discovery in their experience of interventions of God which are the fulfillments of the types/promises contained in the experience of Christ and of any other believers (including Paul) who have preceded them in the faith. As such the believers are "imitators" of Paul and of Christ in the sense that God intervenes in their experience in the same way he did in Paul's and Christ's experiences. But in response the believers should also actually imitate Christ and Paul. For this ethical response it is enough for them to imitate Paul, since he himself imitates Christ. Thus this ethical attitude demands (a) a faith which involves trusting in God's promises and types (found in Scripture, in Christ, in previous believers), as well as seeing the interventions of God in the present; and (b) hope which is based upon the believers' experiences as prefigurations of the Parousia experience. Only in this context can true ethical conduct be envisioned.

2. Christians should "try to please" everybody; they should not be "seeking [their] own advantage but that of many, that they might be saved" (1 Cor. 10:33). This statement implies all the convictions of Paul about the process of salvation. Human beings are in bondage under the powers of sin, that is, under idolatrous systems of convictions. In order to be saved, these people need to discover in their experience Christ-like manifestations. Someone should be sent into their experience to proclaim the Gospel and to manifest it among them as the power of God for salvation. The Gospel of Jesus Christ crucified and raised (the kerygma) needs to be proclaimed as the promise that God will intervene and is intervening in the experience of the idolaters, be they Jews or Gentiles. The good news of God's interventions in the

history of Israel (Scripture) and in the experience of the believers after Christ also must be proclaimed as promises of God for the salvation of the idolaters. But it is not enough for the messenger to proclaim this news. For the Jews as well as for the Gentiles, it is foolishness. They hear the message and do not hear it (Rom. 10:14–21). The messenger must also be the manifestation of the power of the Gospel among them. The messenger needs to enter their idolatrous system of convictions ("please them") in such a way as to be recognized both as a manifestation of the divine (of the good) and as a manifestation of "sin." In this way the messenger is Christ-like and thus folly and a sign of contradiction for these idolaters. The messenger is thereby a manifestation of the Gospel as power of God for salvation for these idolaters. The idolaters are thus freed from the bondage of sin and can discover the true nature of the revelation which they had received earlier but which they had perverted and transformed into an idol. Christians should become these Christ-like persons for the outsiders, the Jews and the Gentiles. This is their vocation. For this purpose, in most instances they have to remain as they are. In this way they can be Christ-like figures for those around them who were their partners in idolatry. In fact, they are free to adopt any way of life, since none is absolute; indeed, taking up a specific way of life as an absolute is idolatry. They must use this freedom, however, to fulfill their vocation as messengers and manifestations of the Gospel for others, and as such in most cases they must remain as they are. More positively expressed, it means that they must become as Jews to the Jews, as Gentiles to the Gentiles. Of course, this necessitates "not seeking [their] own advantage." It also means pleasing these (Jew and Gentile) idolaters. Because their idolatries are always based upon true revelation which they have perverted, Christians can truly please the idolaters by affirming, indeed, by receiving from them, the revelation they already had.

Yet it also means giving no offense to them, that is, avoiding being stumbling blocks for the Jews and the Gentiles. Christians should not be stumbling blocks which would prevent Jews and Gentiles from receiving the Gospel as power of salvation. Christians have to be signs of contradiction for the idolaters, and thus a stumbling block upon which their idolatry is broken. This is what happens when they are "sinful flesh according to their idolatry," weak, crucified. At the same time, they must avoid being a stumbling block which would prevent them from reaching faith. They should avoid any attitude which the idolaters identify in their conscience with idolatry. In order to be people in which God can manifest himself to the idolaters, they have to make sure they are clearly perceived as "sinful against idolatry," as rejecting idolatry. But they have to please the idolaters, by affirming and thanking God for the revelations the idolaters have.

3. Believers must have the same attitude toward the church of God, that is, toward other believers. These other believers, because of their own vocations, have different ways of life and different convictions according to the revelations and the gifts of the Spirit that they have received and according to the idolatrous system of convictions from which they converted. Without abandoning their own vocations, which demand that they remain as they are and associate themselves with the idolaters to whom they must proclaim and manifest the Gospel, they should also please these other believers and avoid being a stumbling block for them. In order to please these other believers, Christians should affirm the revelations and gifts that their brothers and sisters have received. They must consider them as better than themselves, for these brothers and sisters are Christ-like manifestations for them. From them they need to receive these revelations and benefit from their gifts. For Christians, other believers are constant reminders that the revelations and gifts they have themselves received are not absolute. They are different members of the same body. But this relationship is reciprocal. Christians must also be Christ-like manifestations for the other Christians. And thus they should not be a stumbling block for the faith of others. Even when carrying out their vocation with respect to outsiders, they must avoid becoming a stumbling block for the other believers. They must remain a clear manifestation of Christ for them.

4. In this way the believers should "do all to the glory of God." The church is indeed glorifying God when it is a community of believers who interact as described above. For the outsiders, the believers are manifestations of the Gospel as power of God for salvation. Furthermore, they are a community of people who give thanks to God for his various interventions and revelations. They give thanks for those revelations that the idolaters have received. They give thanks for those revelations and gifts that other members of the church have received. They give

thanks for God's interventions in the past, and especially in Jesus Christ. But they also give thanks for God's interventions in the present and in others who are part of their experience. They give thanks for the promises contained in these interventions of God. Indeed, they are the eschatological community which will share in the Parousia and will judge the world. Doing all to the glory of God is thus carrying out their vocation as a community of believers, as the body of Christ. It is a vocation which is received through faith when they were and are constantly freed from the powers of sin; which is sustained by their hope which keeps them on the move in a race toward the prize that God's interventions in their experience prefigure; and which is carried out in love through which they discover others inside the community and outside it as better than themselves because they discover Christ in them.

## CONCLUDING REMARKS

Our reading of Paul is not finished. Many passages have not been analyzed; many themes have not been dealt with. We have used only one reading for each text, instead of all those readings presented in this book. So our results are incomplete and tentative. Even though our conclusions regarding the characteristics of Paul's faith need to be refined, the main features of Paul's convictional pattern have been established. I want to summarize by saying that Paul's faith is "a charismatic, eschatological, typological faith in the Gospel as power of God for salvation," a statement in which the term "Gospel" does not refer to the kerygma per se, but to the entire system of convictions proclaimed by Paul.

There is no point in attempting to summarize in a few words these characteristics of Paul's faith. In fact, an abstract formulation would be misleading. In the Index of Subjects these main features are printed in boldface so that the readers will easily identify them and consider how they are discussed in the context of specific readings of various passages of Paul's letters.

These incomplete results call for further readings of Paul's letters which I hope the readers pursue on their own. Yet insofar as this book establishes the main features of Paul's faith, it is also an invitation to compare Paul's faith with other kinds of faith, including various forms of modern Christian faith.

## SUGGESTIONS FOR FURTHER READINGS

Our study of 1 and 2 Corinthians should be complemented by, and compared and contrasted with, two kinds of work: studies entirely focused on the Corinthian correspondence and the situation of the Corinthian church, and studies of Paul's ethics.

The Corinthian correspondence, like Romans, has given rise to numerous and varied studies following different approaches. English commentaries on both 1 and 2 Corinthians are included here: C. K. Barrett, *A Commentary on the First Epistle to the Corinthians*; C. K. Barrett, *A Commentary on the Second Epistle to the Corinthians*; H. Conzelmann, *1 Corinthians*; J. Héring, *The Second Epistle of St. Paul to the Corinthians*; J. Hurd, *The Origin of 1 Corinthians*; W. F. Orr, *1 Corinthians*; A. Plummer, *A Critical and Exegetical Commentary on the Second Epistle of Paul to the Corinthians*; A. Robertson and A. Plummer, *A Critical and Exegetical Commentary on the First Epistle of Paul to the Corinthians*; J. Ruef, *Paul's First Letter to Corinth*; R. H. Strachan, *The Second Epistle of Paul to the Corinthians*; M. Thrall, *First and Second Letters of Paul to the Corinthians*.

For studies on the Corinthian church and Gnostic influences, see W. Baird, *The Corinthian Church*; E. Pagels, *The Gnostic Paul*; W. Schmithals, *Gnosticism in Corinth*; W. Schmithals, *Paul and the Gnostics*.

Reference work and journal articles on various aspects of the Corinthian situation: C. K. Barrett, "Christianity at Corinth," *BJRL* 46 (1964): 269–97; C. K. Barrett, "Paul's Opponents in Second Corinthians," *NTS* 17 (1971): 233–54; D. Georgi, "First Letter to the Corinthians," in *IDBS*, pp. 180–83; D. Georgi, "Second Letter to the Corinthians," in *IDBS*, pp. 183–86; S. M. Gilmour, "First Letter to the Corinthians," in *IDB*, vol. 1, pp. 684–92; S. M. Gilmour, "Second Letter to the Corinthians," in *IDB*, vol. 1, pp. 692–98; R. Kugelman, "The First Letter to the Corinthians," in *JBC*, pp. 254–75; J. J. O'Rourke, "The Second Letter to the Corinthians," in *JBC*, pp. 276–90.

Several works in English have dealt directly with the ethical dimensions of Paul's letters, particularly the Corinthian correspondence. For ethical issues in Paul, see D. Dungan, *The Sayings of Jesus in the Churches of Paul*; M. S. Enslin, *The Ethics of Paul*; V. P. Furnish, *The Moral Teaching of Paul*; V. P. Furnish, *Theology and Ethics in Paul*.

# Appendix: Chronologies of Paul

## by John A. Darr

Our resources for calculating the sequence, time, and date of events in Paul's ministry are essentially restricted to the Pauline letters and to the Acts of the Apostles. Neither of these sources is directly concerned with Pauline chronology, although Acts may provide a rough schema of Paul's later ministry. Since Paul's letters dealt primarily with religious issues and were geared to current circumstances in his churches, there was little opportunity for him to recount his personal history in his writings (with one important exception). The modern historian is therefore forced to reconstruct the chronology of Paul's life from meager and diverse sources which must be constantly evaluated and interpreted. This results in a wide range of scholarly opinions as to the dating of Paul's various activities. Nevertheless, two basic approaches to Pauline chronology may be delineated:

1. *Chronologies based on the sequential outline found in Acts*. In this category, the general procedure has been to fit the various phenomena mentioned or presupposed by the Pauline letters into the narrative framework provided by Acts (the three missionary journeys, Paul's trip to Rome, etc.). This procedure implies a highly positive evaluation of the basic historical trustworthiness of Acts. Dates are supplied by those references which can (to the scholar's satisfaction) be supported by extrabiblical historical evidence, such as ancient inscriptions mentioning Roman officers with whom Paul dealt.

2. *Chronologies based on the Pauline letters*. A number of scholars have been skeptical of the historical narrative found in Acts and have preferred to base their chronologies almost exclusively on evidence gleaned from the Pauline letters, scanty though it may be. The reason-

ing behind this approach is that Paul's own letters constitute primary evidence, while the Acts account can be considered only secondary evidence at best. Acts is not to be trusted, except at those points where it is supported by a specific statement in Paul's letters. Thus, use of the Acts material must be restricted and is advisable only after the essential structure of Pauline chronology has already been developed on the basis of the letters alone. Dating is achieved by reference to certain extrabiblical evidence.

The primary question in a study of Pauline chronology is the placement of the so-called Jerusalem conference in which Paul took part. This incident is crucial in that Paul himself, in one of his few backward glances, recounts all of his previous visits to Jerusalem up to and including the conference visit (Galatians 1 and 2). Acts also knows of Paul's important visit to Jerusalem, but mentions at least one "extra" visit not accounted for by Paul in Galatians. How are we to place the various visits of Paul to Jerusalem? The answer to this question is the basic distinguishing characteristic of all modern reconstructions of Pauline chronology. Historians highly dependent on Acts have identified the conference visit either with the event in Acts 15 or in Acts 11:30. The chronologies based on Paul's writings reject both these options and point instead to Acts 18:22 as an oblique reference to the real conference visit of Paul. For apologetic reasons, the author of Acts inserted two fabricated Jerusalem visits early in Paul's career. The real conference visit took place late in Paul's career and was marked by the instigation of Paul's "collection for the poor in Jerusalem." The progress of this collection process can be traced through almost all of Paul's letters and thus provides a point of reference for Pauline chronology.

The two most significant extrabiblical pieces of evidence used in Pauline chronologies are the following. First, the so-called Gallio Inscription, uncovered at Delphi, from which it has been deduced that Gallio held office at Corinth from the year 51 to 52. Gallio is mentioned in Acts 18:12 in connection with Paul's activities in Corinth. The second piece of evidence is Claudius's edict expelling the Jews from Rome, which is generally assumed to have been issued in the year 49 (based on Orosius) and to have been the reason for Aquila and Priscilla arriving in Corinth from Rome (Acts 18:2). The near coincidence of these dates is taken by many to be a sure sign that Acts' picture of Paul's *first* ministry at Corinth is essentially accurate. Other incidents in Paul's

European ministry are then ordered around this time period. Those who are less accepting of Acts' historical accuracy point out that the Claudius edict may well be dated at 41 rather than 49, and thus a chronology based on Acts 18:2, 12 will begin to unravel. These latter scholars see two widely separated Pauline missions to Corinth, one near the beginning or middle of Paul's career (thus the reference to Aquila and Priscilla) and one at the end (thus the Gallio reference in Acts). The author of Acts simply mixed these two traditions in one narrative about Paul at Corinth.

The evolution of Paul's thinking within his letters has often been used as an *internal* source of evidence for Pauline chronology. Determining the sequence and spacing of Paul's letters through careful comparison of their content could provide a valuable criterion for the chronologist. Toward this end, at least three areas of Pauline thought have been examined:

1. *Ecclesiology* (the doctrine of the church). Can we perceive in Paul's letters a growing awareness of the ongoing institutionalization of the early church (the establishment of specific church offices, a centralization of authority, developed sacramentalism, and so on)? Scholars who feel that Paul wrote the pastoral letters find this criterion especially significant and helpful; others do not.

2. *Christology* (the doctrine of Christ). How is it that in some letters (1 Thessalonians, Philippians) Paul does not speak of Christ's death as an atonement, while in other letters (Romans, 1 Corinthians) Christ's atoning death is a prominent theme? Could this disparity be another indication of long-term development in Paul's thinking?

3. *Eschatology* (the doctrine of the end). In 1 Thessalonians, Paul apparently feels that Christ's Second Coming is imminent and that virtually all Christians will still be alive when Christ returns (cf. 4:13ff.). In 1 Corinthians, however, Paul takes for granted that many Christians will die (indeed, *have* died) before the Second Coming (cf. 6:14; 11:30; 15:6, 18, 51). In the latter case he speaks of a bodily transformation of Christians which will take place at the eschaton (end); yet bodily transformation is not even alluded to in 1 Thessalonians, where one would expect it to be a major motif. Does this indicate a progression in Paul's thought, and if so, how much time would have passed between the writing of 1 Thessalonians and 1 Corinthians? Since answers to these and other such questions are subjective, few concrete results have been obtained, and

no consensus of opinion has been established concerning the sequence or spacing of the letters. There is, however, widespread agreement among scholars that 1 Thessalonians is our earliest authentic letter written by Paul, and that Romans is our latest. Conjectures concerning the sequence of the letters are often used as warranting or supporting arguments for chronological schemas, but rarely form the foundation of such reconstructions.

Some of the basic types of Pauline chronology are schematized below. It should be emphasized that these charts are not comprehensive summaries of the full-scale chronological reconstructions by the scholars in the footnotes. Rather, they are intended to provide elementary conceptualizations of these varying chronologies. The sequence and spacing of events in the charts are much more important than the absolute dates (which, for the most part, are highly conjectural). Note once again the different placements of the "Jerusalem conference" and the varying degrees of reliability accorded the account in Acts.

# I. CHRONOLOGIES DEPENDENT ON THE OUTLINE OF ACTS

## A. *The Jerusalem Conference Visit of Paul (Galatians 2) = Acts 11:30*[1]

| | | |
|---|---|---|
| 33 | Paul's conversion | |
| 35 | Paul's first Jerusalem visit | Acts 9:26 |
| 35–46 | Paul in Syria and Cilicia | |
| 46 | Paul's conference visit to Jerusalem (Galatians 2) | Acts 11:27–30; described as a famine visit |
| 47–48 | Paul and Barnabas in Cyprus and Galatia (first missionary journey) | |
| ?48 | *Letter to the Galatians* | |
| 49 | Council at Jerusalem. Paul's third Jerusalem visit | Acts 15 |
| 49–50 | Paul and Silas travel from Syrian Antioch through Asia Minor to Macedonia and back (second missionary journey) | |
| 50 | *Letters to the Thessalonians* | Claudius's edict (49) = Acts 18:2 |
| 50–52 | Paul in Corinth | Gallio Inscription (51–52) = Acts 18:12 |
| 52 | Paul's fourth Jerusalem visit | Acts 18:22 |
| 52–55 | Paul in Ephesus | |
| 55–56 | *Letters to the Corinthians* | |
| 55–57 | Paul in Macedonia, Illyricum, Achaia | |
| 57 | *Letter to the Romans* | |
| 57 | Last visit to Jerusalem | Acts 21:17 |
| 57–59 | Imprisonment at Caesarea | |
| 60 | Paul's arrival at Rome | |
| 60–62 | Paul under arrest in Rome | |
| | ?Writes the *Captivity Letters* | |
| ?65 | Paul visits Spain | |
| ?65 | Paul dies | |

1. Based on F. F. Bruce, *Paul: Apostle of the Heart Set Free* (Grand Rapids, Mich.: Wm. B. Eerdmans, 1978), p. 475.

## B. The Jerusalem Conference Visit of Paul (Galatians 2) = Acts 15[2]

| | | |
|---|---|---|
| 35 | Paul's conversion | Acts 9 |
| 38 | Paul's first Jerusalem visit | Acts 9:26 |
| 38–47 | Paul in Syria and Cilicia | |
| 46 | Famine relief visit to Jerusalem | Acts 11:30; ?12:25 |
| 47–48 | First missionary journey (Cyprus and Galatia) | Acts 13, 14 |
| 48 | Council at Jerusalem (conference visit) | Gal. 2:1–10 = Acts 15 |
| 49–52 | Second missionary journey (Asia Minor, Macedonia, Caesarea) | Acts 15:36—18:22 |
| 49 | Jews expelled from Rome | Claudius's edict (49); Acts 18:2 |
| 50 | Paul reaches Corinth | |
| 50 | *Letters to the Thessalonians* | |
| 51 | Gallio becomes proconsul of Corinth | Gallio Inscription 51–52 |
| 52 | *Letter to the Galatians* | |
| 52–56 | Third missionary journey (Macedonia and Achaia) | Acts 18:23—21:15 |
| 52–55 | Three years spent at Ephesus | |
| 55 | *Letters to the Corinthians* | |
| 56 | *Epistle to the Romans* | |
| 56 | Arrival at Jerusalem | |
| 56–58 | Imprisonment at Caesarea | Acts 24:27 |
| 59 | Paul reaches Rome | Acts 28:16 |
| 59–61 | Paul at Rome *Philippians, Philemon, Colossians, Ephesians* | |
| 61(64) | Paul's martyrdom | Neronian persecution (64) |

2. Based on B. W. Robinson, *The Life of Paul*, 2d ed. (Chicago: University of Chicago Press, 1928), pp. 240–41.

## C. The Jerusalem Conference Visit
### of Paul (Galatians 2:1–10) = Acts 15 = Acts 11:30[3]

| | | |
|---|---|---|
| 30–32 | Paul's conversion | |
| 32–34 | Paul's first Jerusalem visit | |
| 44/45 | Paul's conference visit to Jerusalem | Gal. 2:1–10/Acts 15/11:30 |
| 46 | Mission to Cyprus and Asia Minor | |
| 46/47 | Quarrel with Barnabas (equated with the disagreement in Gal. 2:13) | |
| 47–51 | Mission to Macedonia and Achaia; *1 Thessalonians* | |
| 52–58 | Mission in Galatia, Phrygia, and Asia; collection journey; *Galatians, 1 and 2 Corinthians, Romans* | |
| 58 | Arrest in Jerusalem and Caesarean imprisonment; *Philemon* | |
| 60 | Journey to Rome | |
| 60— | Roman imprisonment; *Philippians* (?) | |

3. A. J. M. Wedderburn, "Keeping up with Recent Studies, VIII, Some Recent Pauline Chronologies," *ET*, January 1981, p. 107. Notice that the second and third missionary journeys of Acts are inverted and also that the first journey is placed after the conference rather than before it. While maintaining that Acts is basically trustworthy, adherents of this approach feel that the account of the famine visit (Acts 11:30) resulted from a simple historical misinterpretation by the author of Acts and not from any conscious attempt to distort the facts. A famine did take place, and the Antioch church did send aid to Jerusalem. However, it may be that Paul himself never did accompany Barnabas on a trip solely for the purpose of bringing relief to Jerusalem; and/or that Paul took a donation to Jerusalem at the same time he went for the conference visit (Acts 15/Gal. 2:1–10). In either case, the author of Acts (or his sources of information) was not clear in making these historical distinctions. Thus we have two accounts rather than one. Conjectures of this sort are intended to solve (somewhat at the expense of Acts' trustworthiness) the problem of an "extra" Jerusalem visit by Paul in Acts while at the same time preserving the basic integrity of the greater part of Acts.

## II. CHRONOLOGY DERIVED FROM
## PAUL'S LETTERS

### A. The Jerusalem Conference Visit
of Paul (Galatians 2) = Acts 18:22
(J. Knox and G. Lüdemann)[4]

| | | |
|---|---|---|
| 33/34 | Paul's conversion | Gal. 1:15, 16; 2 Cor. 12:2 |
| 36/37 | Paul's first Jerusalem visit | Gal. 1:18 |
| 36/37–38/39 | Mission activity in Syria, Cilicia, and Galatia | Gal. 1:21 |
| 38/39–50/51 | Independent Pauline mission activity in Macedonia, Achaia, and perhaps elsewhere | |
| 41 | Paul in Corinth; *1 Thessalonians* Aquila and Priscilla come to Corinth from Rome | Claudius's edict, (41) = Acts 18:2 |
| 50/51 | Paul's conference visit to Jerusalem (a dramatic and skewed rendering of this is [mis]placed at Acts 15) | Gal. 2:1 = Acts 18:22 |
| 50/51–54/55 | Collection for the Jerusalem church and other mission activity in Asia Minor and Greece | |
| 51 | Paul in Galatia | |
| 51–53 | Paul based in Ephesus | |
| 52 | *1 Corinthians* | |
| 52 | Quick trip to Corinth and back to Ephesus | Gallio Inscription (51–52); Acts 18:12 |
| 53 | Paul travels to Troas and Macedonia; *2 Corinthians and Galatians* | |
| 54 | Paul arrives in Corinth; *Romans* | |
| 54/55 | Final journey to Jerusalem to deliver the collection | |
| | (We have no hard evidence on Paul after this) | |

4. This table is constructed from two slightly varying chronologies which employ the same basic presuppositions and methodology; the spacing and sequence of events is similar despite the difference in the absolute dates (indicated by the diagonals). This display does not represent the entire range of dates proposed by these scholars, but it does accurately represent the sequential aspects of their chronologies of Paul: J. Knox, *Chapters in a Life of Paul* (Nashville: Abingdon Press, 1950), pp. 83–88; G. Lüdemann, *Paulus, der Heidenapostel*, vol. 1, *Studien zur Chronologie* (Göttingen: Vandenhoeck & Ruprecht, 1980), pp. 272–73.

## B. *The Jerusalem Conference Visit*
   *of Paul (Galatians 2:1–10) = Acts 18:22 (R. Jewett)*[5]

| | | |
|---|---|---|
| 34 | Paul's conversion | |
| 35–37 | Activities in Arabia; return to Damascus | |
| 37 | Escape from Aretas IV; first Jerusalem visit | 2 Cor. 11:32–33 Acts 9:23–26 |
| 37–46 | Activities in Syria and Cilicia | |
| 43–45 | First missionary journey: Antioch, Cyprus, Pamphylia, and South Galatia | |
| 46–51 | Second missionary journey: Antioch, North Galatia, Troas, Philippi, Thessalonica, Berea Athens, Corinth; *1 and 2 Thessalonians* | Claudius's edict (49) |
| 51 | Hearing before Gallio at Corinth | Gallio Inscription |
| 51 | Second Jerusalem visit: apostolic conference | Acts 18:22/ Gal. 2:1–10 |
| 52 | Conflict with Peter | Gal. 2:14–17 |
| 52–57 | Third missionary journey North Galatia | |
| 52–54 | Ephesus; *Galatians* | |
| 54/55 | Ephesian imprisonment; *Philippians* | |
| 55 | Visit to Corinth; return to Macedonia and Asia; *1 and 2 Corinthians* | |
| 56/57 | Back to Corinth; *Romans* | |
| 57 | Philippi to Jerusalem; arrest | |
| 57–59 | Imprisonment in Caesarea | |
| 61 | Imprisonment in Rome | |
| 62 | Execution in Rome | |

5. R. Jewett, *A Chronology of Paul's Life* (Philadelphia: Fortress Press, 1979), foldout. This simplified chart can present only a fraction of the information Jewett includes in his complex chronology. Note that although Jewett places the conference visit at Acts 18:22 and opts for only three Jerusalem visits (as per the letters), he is much more dependent on Acts for his chronological framework than Knox (see previous table).

# Notes

CHAPTER 1

1. In the following discussion we allude to an issue which has been the center of attention of critical biblical studies since the beginning of the twentieth century. This question arose over the failure of "scientific" (positivist), objective studies of the Bible attempted at the end of the nineteenth century. See Albert Schweitzer's devastating critique of this type of research on the historical Jesus in his *The Quest of the Historical Jesus* (New York: Macmillan Co., 1968). In view of the conflicting presentations of the historical Jesus, each reflecting the bias of its author, the issue of "pre-understandings" could not be avoided. It is in effect the problem of the role of the interpreters' faith in their interpretation of Scripture. See V. A. Harvey, *The Historian and the Believer* (Philadelphia: Westminster Press, 1981), which discusses how various New Testament scholars dealt with this issue and contains further bibliography on this topic.

2. See, e.g., P. Ramsey, *Basic Christian Ethics* (Chicago: University of Chicago Press, 1980); L. H. Marshall, *The Challenge of New Testament Ethics* (London: Macmillan & Co., 1956); M. S. Enslin, *The Ethics of Paul* (Nashville: Abingdon Press, 1957); V. P. Furnish, *Theology and Ethics in Paul* (Nashville: Abingdon Press, 1968).

3. See *Theological Dictionary of the New Testament,* ed. G. Kittel and G. Friedrich (Grand Rapids: Wm. B. Eerdmans, 1964). The authors have long entries on all the key terms used by Paul showing how these meanings do or do not relate to their meanings in other New Testament texts and in Jewish and Hellenistic literature.

4. See, e.g., B. M. Metzger, *A Textual Commentary on the Greek New Testament* (New York and London: United Bible Societies, 1971).

5. See, e.g., W. G. Doty, *Letters in Primitive Christianity,* GBS (Philadelphia: Fortress Press, 1973).

6. See, e.g., R. Jewett, *A Chronology of Paul's Life* (Philadelphia: Fortress Press, 1979). See also G. Lüdemann, *Paulus, der Heidenapostel,* vol. 1 (Göttingen: Vandenhoeck & Ruprecht, 1980); English translation forthcoming from Fortress Press.

7. See e.g., E. Käsemann, *Perspectives on Paul* (Philadelphia: Fortress Press, 1971); G. Bornkamm, *Paul* (New York: Harper & Row, 1971).

8. The most complete presentation of Greimas's theory can be found in A. J. Greimas and J. Courtés, *Semiotics and Language: An Analytical Dictionary* (Bloomington, Ind.: Indiana University Press, 1982). Our discussion of "faith" in the following pages reexpresses in nontechnical language how this phenomenon can be understood on the basis of Greimas's systematic theory of language and communication. Notes will refer to the elements of this theory that we "translate" in a simpler terminology.

9. The methods we shall use in the present book are based exclusively upon the semiotic theory of A. J. Greimas. Contrary to the appearances, this is not opting for an idiosyncratic method and neglecting the multiplicity of theoretical semiotic proposals. Indeed, when I refer to Greimas's theory I do not want to refer to the partial models and theories about narrative and semantics (such as the actantial schema and the semiotic square) which, for the last fifteen years, have been associated with Greimas's name. Rather, I want to refer to the comprehensive semiotic theory presented in *Semiotics and Language*, in which Greimas and Courtés have brought together the many and disparate proposals concerning the various aspects of the phenomenon of communication and integrated them in an overall semiotic theory which takes into account the insights gained through these various research projects. Consequently the results of these research projects had to be reinterpreted and evaluated. Greimas's former proposals themselves have been submitted to this reevaluation and thus have been revised (for instance, the famous actantial schema had to be abandoned). Even though this theory cannot be viewed as complete, it nevertheless proposes an overall and coherent theoretical framework allowing one to account for the phenomenon "meaningful communication." It is clear that this magistral theoretical synthesis is based upon certain fundamental options (for instance, starting from the question of meaning rather than from the question of the communication process). Yet at present these options are the only ones which allow semioticians to make room for the great variety of semiotic phenomena studied in various fields. Furthermore, for our present purpose we need to underscore that Greimas's theory is the only one which allows us to deal systematically with the phenomenon of faith. For a brief overview of the main elements of Greimas's theory, see D. Patte, "Greimas' Model for the Generative Trajectory of Meaning in Discourses," *AJS* 3 (1982): 59–78.

The methods we shall use have been developed on the basis of Greimas's theory with the specific purpose of studying systematically the characteristics of the faith of an author (the semantic universe of the text). As such they leave aside other dimensions of the meaning of discourses which can be studied with the help of other semiotic or structural methods, which in turn do not take into account textual features that manifest the author's faith. This means that other semiotic/structural studies of Paul's letters are not necessarily pertinent for our own studies. Thus, for instance, both Güttgemanns and the Entrevernes Group have published in their respective journals (*Linguistica Biblica* and *Sémiotique et Bible*) analyses of passages from Paul's letters. But these studies aim at dimensions of the meaning effect of these letters which are quite different from those we need to study in order to elucidate the characteristics of Paul's faith. For a discussion of Güttgemanns's method, see D. Patte, "Universal Narrative Structures and Semantic Frameworks," *Semeia* 10 (1978): 123–35. For a discussion of the Entrevernes Group's method, see D. Patte, "Preface" to Entrevernes Group *Signs and Parables* (Pittsburgh: Pickwick Press, 1978), pp. xv–xx.

I have presented in several publications the methods of structural exegesis which I believe are necessary for the study of an author's faith. An introduction to these methods can be found in D. Patte, *What Is Structural Exegesis?* (Philadelphia: Fortress Press, 1975). Explanations showing why these methods are well equipped to deal with an author's faith and a detailed method are presented in D. Patte and A. Patte, *Structural Exegesis: From Theory to Practice* (Philadelphia: Fortress Press, 1978), and D. Patte, *Aspects of a Semiotics of Didactic Discourse* (Urbino, Italy: Center for Semiotic Studies, 1980). The complementarity of various structural exegetical methods is displayed in *Genesis 2 and 3*, ed. D. Patte, *Semeia* 18 (1980). Further bibliography can be found in these books. Here we shall use simplified forms of these methods which will be presented in the following chapters as we get ready to use them.

10. See "Believing" in Greimas and Courtés, *Semiotics and Language*.

11. C. Loew, *Myth, Sacred History, and Philosophy* (New York: Harcourt Brace Jovanovich, 1967), pp. 3ff.

12. See the discussion of the power of religion over the believers in F. J. Streng, *Understanding Religious Life*, 2d ed. (Encino, Calif.: Dickenson Publishing Co., 1976), pp. 7–9, 86, and passim.

13. See "Wanting" in Greimas and Courtés, *Semiotics and Language*.

14. "Knowing" in ibid.

15. "Axiology" in ibid.

16. For diverse opinions (from the most positive to the most negative) on the historical reliability of Acts, see F. F. Bruce, *The Acts of the Apostles*, 2d ed. (Grand Rapids: Wm. B. Eerdmans, 1952), esp. pp. 1–26; I. H. Marshall, *Luke: Historian and Theologian* (Grand Rapids: Zondervan Publishing House, 1971); C. K. Barrett, *Luke the Historian in Recent Study* (Philadelphia: Fortress Press, Facet Books, 1970); M. Hengel, *Acts and the History of Earliest Christianity* (Philadelphia: Fortress Press, 1980); E. Haenchen, "The Book of Acts as Source Material for the History of Early Christianity," in *Studies in Luke-Acts*, ed. L. Keck and J. L. Martyn (Philadelphia: Fortress Press, 1980), pp. 258–78; M. Dibelius, "The Acts of the Apostles as an Historical Source," in *Studies in the Acts of the Apostles*, ed. H. Greeven (New York: Charles Scribner's Sons, 1956), pp. 102–8; J. Knox, *Chapters in a Life of Paul* (Nashville: Abingdon Press, 1950).

17. See "Desire" and "Value" in Greimas and Courtés, *Semiotics and Language*.

18. See "Having to do or to be" and "Deontic modalities" in ibid.

19. See "Discourse" and "Narrativity" in ibid.

20. See "Veridictory modalities" in ibid.

21. See M. Foucault, *The Birth of the Clinic* (New York: Vintage Books, 1973).

22. See "Universe" in Greimas and Courtés, *Semiotics and Language*.

23. As Lewis Wilkins suggested to me, this discussion of the semantic universe as characterized by a fundamental convictional pattern is closely related to contemporary scientists' assessment of the nature of scientific research and especially to Thomas Kuhn's analysis of scientific revolutions. See T. Kuhn, *The Structure of Scientific Revolutions*, 2d ed. (Chicago: University of Chicago Press, 1970). What I called for the sake of my analogy the "fundamental law," as if it existed in the physical universe, is nothing else than the formulation of what Kuhn calls the "paradigm" which characterizes a given tradition of scientific research. Indeed, for Kuhn, paradigms are the roots from which spring particular coherent traditions of scientific research. A paradigm is what the members of a scientific community share; indeed, such sharing of a paradigm is what constitutes such a group as a scientific community. A particular paradigm, which characterizes the Ptolemaic or Copernican or Newtonian or Einsteinian universe, for example, is a coherent network of commitments to concepts, theories, instruments, and methods from which scientists derive rules or laws, identify puzzles to be solved by their research, and devise methods and tools that will enable them to extract from nature the information they require to understand the world and to order knowledge about it in a systematic fashion. Scientists with different paradigms look at the world, but such is the power of their different ways of looking that they see different things and see them in different relations to each other. To be able to communicate with each other, one or the other must experience the "conversion" which Kuhn calls a "paradigm shift." This conversion is "a transition between incommensurables" and therefore cannot occur a step at a time; "it must occur all at once (though not necessarily in an instant) or not at all" (Kuhn, *Structure of Scientific Revolutions*, p. 150). Paradigms are prior to the formulation of rules or laws that describe a given type of natural phenomena. I call these laws "secondary" because they are nothing else than the manifestations, in specific cases, of the fundamental paradigm from which they are derived. This convergence between the scientists' assessment of scientific research and semiotic and structural views of the semantic organization of discourses is not mere coincidence. In fact, semiotic and structural research is deliberately a "scientific" endeavor in the sense that it shares with the scientific research a hypothetico-deductive approach which involves the construction of models. In fact, the concepts of model, paradigm, and structure are borrowed from scientific research. See "Deduction," "Model," "Paradigm," "Structure," and "Scientificness" in Greimas and Courtés, *Semiotics and Language*.

24. See "Universe," "Universals," and "Category" in ibid.; see also D. Patte, *What Is Structural Exegesis?* chap. 4, and C. Lévi-Strauss, *Structural Anthropology* (New York: Basic Books, 1963), chap. 11 and esp. pp. 222–25. These references deal with both the category "life/death" and the category "nature/culture."

25. For a discussion of the authorship of Ephesians, Colossians, 2 Thessalonians, 1 and 2 Timothy, and Titus, see W. G. Kümmel, *Introduction to the New Testament* (Nashville: Abingdon Press, 1975); W. Marxsen, *Introduction to the New Testament* (Philadelphia: Fortress Press, 1970); and the appropriate articles in the *Interpreter's Dictionary of the Bible*, ed. G. A. Buttrick, 5 vol. (Nashville: Abingdon Press, 1962, 1976).

CHAPTER 2

1. This is a paraphrase of the title of E. Käsemann's *Jesus Means Freedom* (Philadelphia: Fortress Press, 1970).

2. As H. D. Betz argues and shows in his commentary on Galatians, this letter can be viewed as a rhetorical discourse in the strict sense of the term. Despite some modifications demanded by his subject matter, Paul organizes his letter according to the classical rules of rhetoric. Cf. H. D. Betz, *Galatians* (Philadelphia: Fortress Press, 1979), esp. pp. 14–25. While it is quite helpful for other purposes, the analysis of Galatians in terms of its rhetorical organization is not suited for our study. Rhetoric involves the skillful combination of logical arguments (demonstrating the truth of ideas) and of passionate appeals (involving the use of self-evident truths, i.e., of convictions). Since our goal is to study the system of convictions which characterizes Paul's faith and is expressed in this text, we need to consider separately these two components of this rhetorical discourse. In other words, we must study the semantic universe which provides the framework for the rhetorical organization.

3. We shall not attempt to be comprehensive in this historical reading. Besides the mention of specific persons and situations, many statements refer to traditions and doctrines of various origins (Jewish, Hellenistic, and early Christian). A careful study of all these is necessary for a detailed understanding of the *argument* of the letter and can be found in commentaries, monographs, and articles. For all these, see the excellent commentary by H. D. Betz and its bibliography. This commentary presents, among other things, a critical assessment of scholarly research on the referential meaning of the various textual units (i.e., how the reference to something outside the text, such as historical events, situations, and traditions, already defines the meaning of these units). Since our goal is to study the system of convictions manifested by this text, that is, the meaning the textual units have because of their interrelations in the system formed by the text, we do not need to review in detail the referential meaning of each textual unit. As noted in Chapter 1, we need at this point only to understand the overall argument of the letter. For this purpose it is enough to underscore those aspects of the texts which clearly refer to historical situations. We shall rely for this on commentaries such as Betz's to which we shall refer throughout our discussion of the letter.

4. On the question of the location of the churches of Galatia, see Betz, *Galatians*, pp. 1–5, and the bibliography provided in the footnotes.

5. Samples of the Stoics' and Cynics' teaching can be found in C. K. Barrett,

*The New Testament Background* (New York: Harper & Row, Harper Torch-books, 1961), pp. 61–72; 75–79; and H. C. Kee, *The Origins of Christianity* (Englewood Cliffs, N.J.: Prentice-Hall, 1973), pp. 231–78. For the Cynics' reading, see A. J. Malherbe, *The Cynic Epistles* (Chico, Calif.: Scholars Press, 1977).

6. Descriptions of Hellenistic religions can be found in Barrett, *New Testament Background*, pp. 91–104; Kee, *Origins of Christianity*, pp. 74–89, 238–57; R. Bultmann, *Primitive Christianity* (Philadelphia: Fortress Press, 1980), pp. 126–71; and F. C. Grant, *Roman Hellenism and the New Testament* (New York: Charles Scribner's Sons, 1962), pp. 1–98.

7. See Betz, *Galatians*, pp. 1–3. I do not exclude the possibility that some of the Galatians were God-fearers, but I cannot agree with W. D. Davies when he argues that the Galatian churches "were largely made up of proselytes and God-fearers living on the fringe of the synagogue." See W. D. Davies's review of H. D. Betz, *Galatians* in *RSR* 7:4 (1981): 310–18. The features of the letter that he underscores to make this point can be explained in other ways. For instance, one needs to keep in mind that Paul writes to churches which have been under the influence of Judaizers.

8. For the view that Paul's opponents were Jewish-Christian Gnostics, see W. Marxsen, *Introduction to the New Testament* (Philadelphia: Fortress Press, 1970), pp. 52–53, and the bibliography therein. Our analysis of the letter shows that all the passages used to support this thesis are better explained in other ways which support the view that the opponents are Judaizers.

9. On the various proposals concerning the relations of Gal. 2:1–10 and the Book of Acts, see "Appendix: Chronologies of Paul" at the end of this volume.

10. See Betz, *Galatians*, pp. 103–4, 331–32.

11. This is, in brief, Betz's interpretation. See ibid., pp. 9, 273.

12. An example of curses as a ritualistic language can be found in Deut. 27:15–26, which describes the curses solemnly pronounced by the Levitical priests in a ritual setting in which the congregation is expected to respond "Amen" to each curse.

13. What I here call "convictional logic" is nothing else than the mythical logic for which Lévi-Strauss has proposed a first model in C. Lévi-Strauss, *Structural Anthropology* (New York: Basic Books, 1963) and more specifically in the essay (reproduced therein as chap. 11) "The Structural Study of Myth." A discussion of this model and its application to Gal. 1:1–10 can be found in D. Patte, *What Is Structural Exegesis?* (Philadelphia: Fortress Press, 1975), chap. 4. As theoretical research progressed, it appeared that this mythical structure was more precisely described when one made a clear distinction between its syntactic elements (Lévi-Strauss's "functions") and its semantic elements (Lévi-Strauss's "states"). This led to the distinction between the system of pertinent transformations (system of "functions") and the symbolic system (as microsemantic universe) presented in D. and A. Patte, *Structural Exegesis: From Theory to Practice* (Philadelphia: Fortress Press, 1978), chap. 2 and 3. From this it becomes clear that the "convictional logic" (mythical logic) is characterized by the relational

network (the structure) of the symbolic system which Greimas calls in his latest work "narrative semantics" and "fundamental semantics" (which together form the semantic universe). By contrast what I call here the argumentative logic is characterized by another relational network (structure), that of the "fundamental syntax" and of the "surface narrative syntax" (which include what I called the system of pertinent transformations and the system of elementary narratives). For a definition of these technical concepts, see the appropriate entries in A. J. Greimas and J. Courtés, *Semiotics and Language: An Analytical Dictionary* (Bloomington, Ind.: Indiana University Press, 1982). The entry "generative trajectory" includes a graph showing the interrelations of these different structural levels. For a presentation of these interrelations illustrated by an example, see D. Patte, "Greimas' Model for the Generative Trajectory of Meaning in Discourses," *AJS* 3 (1982): 59–78. I have shown in D. Patte, *Aspects of a Semiotics of Didactic Discourse* (Urbino, Italy: Center for Semiotic Studies, 1980), how this model, first established for narratives, also applies to didactic discourses such as Paul's letters. As usual in this book, I "translate" these theoretical models in a simpler and thus less precise language. Our goal in this chapter is to apprehend in a first approximation characteristic relations of the "narrative semantics" (corresponding to Lévi-Strauss's mythical system). For this purpose we look for repetitions, strange reasonings, and metaphoric language, which are, as Lévi-Strauss had already perceived, surface manifestations of the mythical system.

14. I agree with Betz (*Galatians*, p. 25) when he suggests that this letter belongs to the genre "magical letter" (that is, in our terminology, a letter which manifests and transmits the power of a system of convictions).

15. One way of avoiding the question (avoiding puzzlement) and of finding nevertheless a coherence to the argumentative logic is to assume that after the incident at Antioch Paul no longer recognized the validity of the Gospel with the Law for the Jews that he would have equated with the views of the Judaizers. Thus when he wrote the letter (after the incident at Antioch), he could claim, as in 1:7, that there is only one true Gospel, the Gospel without the Law. Such is Betz's argument (*Galatians*, p. 49). But even if it were the case, this would not mean that, at the time he wrote the letter, Paul did not conceive of a Gospel with the Law for the Jews! It would simply mean that Peter (and James), who followed the Gospel with the Law for the Jews, had, in Paul's view, become Judaizers.

16. See Betz's excellent discussion of the Jewish traditions underlying this passage from which Paul draws negative conclusions: the Law is inferior because it does not conform to the principle of the oneness of God. Cf. Betz, *Galatians*, pp. 163–73.

17. Let us note in passing that in Gal. 4:21 the term "law" refers to the story of Abraham and not to commandments. This shows that Paul uses the term "law" as "Torah" is used in Judaism, that is, both to designate the commandments found in Scripture and, at other times, to speak of the entire Scripture as revelation. We shall come back to this.

18. See Lévi-Strauss, *Structural Anthropology*, chap. 11, where he presents what he calls the mythical structure as a series of pairs of opposed mythemes which are homologated, one with the others. See also Patte, *What Is Structural Exegesis?* chap. 4, which includes a discussion of the relations among the pairs of convictions (mythemes) found in Gal. 1:1–10.

19. This last pair of opposed systems of convictions had to be reversed (by comparison to its presentation in Table 1) in order to put the "other gospel" in the column which includes the negative systems of convictions. We shall see that it is indeed homologous with them.

20. This is also suggested by R. W. Funk, "The Apostolic Parousia: Form and Significance," in *Christian History and Interpretation* (Cambridge: At the University Press, 1967), pp. 249–68.

21. See Betz, *Galatians*, pp. 41–43.

22. As Betz emphasizes and discusses at length (ibid., pp. 189–200).

23. The parable in this section attempts to express the role and place of a semantic universe (fundamental semantics and narrative semantics or, in my terminology, symbolic system) in a discourse, be it a written discourse such as a text or a "lived" discourse such as somebody's behavior. I particularly emphasize the "structuring" power of a semantic universe. For a more theoretical presentation, see the works in note 13.

24. Although many commentators have pointed to Gal. 5:1 with its stress on freedom as the basis of Paul's argument, there are various interpretations of the meaning and role of this verse. Martin Luther cautioned against equating this freedom with civil or religious liberty (significant ideals in his and our day). Rather, the freedom of which Paul spoke was to be seen in the liberated human conscience which becomes free and quiet "because it no longer has to fear the wrath of God." Thus Christians are set free not for the sake of freedom but to avoid condemnation and enjoy peace of mind. See M. Luther, "Lectures on Galatians, Chapters 5–6," in *Luther's Works*, vol. 27, ed. J. Pelikan (St. Louis: Concordia Publishing House, 1964), pp. 3–9. E. Burton translates the first part of the verse "With this freedom Christ set us free." Besides being nearly unintelligible, this translation takes the punch out of Paul's argument. Although Burton sees 5:1 as an important transitional verse and "an epitome of the contention of the whole letter," his translation shields him from perceiving its true import. Indeed, he has little to say by way of interpretation of this verse. Cf. E. D. Burton, *A Critical and Exegetical Commentary on the Epistle to the Galatians* (New York: Charles Scribner's Sons, 1920), pp. 269–72. William Neil regards 5:1 as simply a warning against legalism. Christians must resist all attempts to turn Christianity into "a religion of slavish obedience to rules and regulations" (W. Neil, *The Letter of Paul to the Galatians* [Cambridge: At the University Press, 1967], p. 72). Betz (*Galatians*, pp. 255–58) treats Gal. 5:1 in depth. He insists on the translation "for freedom" rather than "with freedom." Freedom is the destiny and purpose of Christ's action for the believer. This verse expresses the logic which ties the argument of the letter (1:6—4:31) to the parenetic section (5:2—6:10). For Paul, freedom "is the central theological concept which sums up the

Christian's situation before God as well as in this world." Paul even goes so far as to equate freedom with the Spirit (2 Cor. 3:17). Betz also seems to link "freedom" and "salvation" in Paul's thought. Paul's uniqueness lies in his contention that Christians have *already* been given salvation (freedom) but now must preserve it. The focus of this understanding of freedom is thus still (as with Luther) directly on the believer's relationship to God rather than on his being free to accept any new revelation which might occur, as will be discussed below.

25. See "Metalanguage" in Greimas and Courtés, *Semiotics and Language*.

26. Our analysis of Gal. 1:1–10, following Lévi-Strauss's model, shows this quite clearly. Cf. Patte, *What Is Structural Exegesis?* chap. 4.

27. In a tradition recorded in the Babylonian Talmud, Shabbat 31a, Hillel is quoted as having said, "Do not do to thy neighbor what is hateful to thee. This is the whole Law. All else is explanation" (quoted in *Theological Dictionary of the New Testament*, ed. G. Kittel and G. Friedrich, vol. 1 [Grand Rapids: Wm. B. Eerdmans, 1964], p. 43).

28. Cf. O. J. F. Seitz, "Lists, Ethical," in *IDB* 3: 137–39; and D. Schroeder, "Lists, Ethical," in *IDBS*, pp. 546–47.

Epictetus *Discourses* 2.16.45b–46: "From just here, from out of your own mind, cast . . . grief, fear, desire, envy, joy at other's ills; cast out greed, effeminacy, incontinency. These things you cannot cast out in any other way than by looking to God alone, being specially devoted to Him only, and consecrated to His commands." (Quoted in *The Discourses as Reported by Arrian, the Manual and Fragments*, vol. 1 [Cambridge, Mass.: Harvard University Press, 1926], pp. 335–37).

Epictetus *Discourses* 4.1.1ff.: "That man is free, who lives as he wishes, who is proof against compulsion and hindrance and violence, whose impulses are untrammelled, who gets what he wills to get and avoids what he wills to avoid. Who then would live in error? No one. Who would live deceived, reckless, unjust, intemperate, querulous, abject? No one. No bad man then lives as he would, and so no bad man is free. Who would live in a state of distress, fear, envy, pity, failing in the will to get and in the will to avoid? No one. Do we then find any bad man without distress or fear, above circumstance, free from failure? None. Then we find none free." (Quoted in Barrett, *New Testament Background*, p. 68.)

Epicurus *Epistle to Menoeceus*: "For it is not continuous drinkings and revellings, nor the satisfaction of lusts, nor the enjoyment of fish and other luxuries of the wealthy table, which produce a pleasant life, but sober reasoning, searching out the motives for all choice and avoidance, and banishing mere opinions, to which are due the greatest disturbance of the spirit." (Quoted in ibid., p. 75).

*Poimandres* 24ff. (describing how a person is to be changed on the ascent to God): "And thus man speeds upward through the framework of the orbits. To the first zone he gives up the power which effects increase and decrease; to the second, evil devices, as guile now inactive; to the third, the lust by which men are deceived, now no longer active; to the fourth, ostentatious authority, no longer greedy of power; to the fifth, unholy audacity and presumptuous temerity; to the sixth, the evil resources, now no longer active, of wealth, and to the seventh zone, the falsehood that ever lies in wait. Then, stripped of those qualities which the spheres have wrought in him, man reaches the ogdoatic nature, having simply his own proper power." (Quoted in ibid., p. 87).

29. This second part of our parable attempts to express some aspects of the phenomenon of "intersemioticity" discussed by Greimas and Courtés, *Semiotics and Language,* in the entry "Semiotics" and other entries mentioned therein. Here I am concerned only with the relation of various semiotic systems at the semantic levels (fundamental, narrative, and discoursive semantics). Cf. also Patte, "Greimas' Model."

## CHAPTER 3

1. At two points in his writings, Josephus includes valuable descriptions of the Essenes: *The Jewish War* 2.8.2–13 and *Antiquities* 18.1.5. On the Essenes, see A. Dupont-Sommer, *The Essene Writings from Qumran* (New York: World Publishing Co., 1962); and G. Vermes, *The Dead Sea Scrolls in English* (New York: Penguin Books, 1962).

2. W. Farmer, "Zealot," in *IDB* 4:936–39. See also S. G. F. Brandon, *Jesus and the Zealots* (New York: Charles Scribner's Sons, 1967).

3. E. R. Goodenough, "Philo Judeus," in *IDB* 3:796–99; E. R. Goodenough, *Introduction to Philo Judeus* (New Haven: Yale University Press, 1940); H. A. Wolfson, *Philo* (Cambridge, Mass.: Harvard University Press, 1947); S. Sandmel, *Philo of Alexandria* (New York: Oxford University Press, 1979).

4. Thus Greimas and his collaborators have established the system of values and the convictional pattern (axiology) presupposed by various contemporary authors by studying a short fragment of their work. The authors who were consulted had to agree that they had such presuppositions. See A. J. Greimas and E. Landowski, eds., *Introduction à l'analyse du discours en sciences sociales* (Paris: Hachette, 1979).

5. Cf. C. Lévi-Strauss, *Structural Anthropology* (New York: Basic Books, 1963), esp. pp. 202–31; and C. Lévi-Strauss, *The Raw and the Cooked: An Introduction to a Science of Mythology* (New York: Harper & Row, 1969). The most striking and clear example of an analysis showing the stability of a mythical structure, in spite of drastic changes of symbols and plots, can be found in L. Brisson, *Le Mythe de Tiresias* (Leiden: Brill, 1976).

6. The famous "Tractate of the Fathers" (in the Mishnah) begins with a description of a continuous succession of prophets and teachers who transmitted "Torah" from one generation to another up to the time of the writing of the Mishnah. This tractate begins: "Moses received the Law from Sinai and committed it to Joshua to the elders, and the elders to the Prophets; and the Prophets committed it to the men of the Great Synagogue. He used to say: . . . Antigonus of Soko received (the Law) from Simeon the Just. He used to say: . . . [etc.]" (*Mishnah,* Aboth [Fathers] [London: Oxford University Press, 1933], p. 446). This clearly expresses that the rabbis saw themselves as heirs of the Pharisees

such as Hillel and Shammai (ca. 30 B.C.–A.D. 10) and their followers, who are mentioned further down in this list.

7. See D. Patte, *Early Jewish Hermeneutic in Palestine* (Chico, Calif.: Scholars Press, 1975). In this book I call this convictional pattern "hermeneutical principles" because most of the fundamental convictions are closely related to the interpretation of Scripture since this convictional pattern governs the interpretation of Scripture.

8. For a more complete description of the content of the Mishnah, see H. L. Strack, *Introduction to the Talmud and Midrash* (New York: Atheneum, 1969), pp. 26–64.

9. E. P. Sanders, *Paul and Palestinian Judaism* (Philadelphia: Fortress Press, 1977), pp. 31–238.

10. Patte, *Early Jewish Hermeneutic*, pp. 11–127.

11. J. Z. Lauterbach, *Rabbinic Essays* (Cincinnati: Hebrew Union College, 1951), pp. 23–159; this book includes three essays dealing with the differences between the Sadducees and the Pharisees: "The Sadducees and Pharisees"; "A Significant Controversy between the Sadducees and the Pharisees"; and "The Pharisees and Their Teachings."

12. Sanders, *Paul and Palestinian Judaism*, p. 235, and passim.

13. Ibid., pp. 84–87.

14. *Mekilta de-Rabbi Ishmael*, vol. 2 (Philadelphia: Jewish Publication Society of America, 1933–35), pp. 229–30, quoted by Sanders, *Paul and Palestinian Judaism*, p. 86.

15. Ibid., pp. 84–101.

16. *Mekilta*, vol. 2, p. 69 in a commentary on Exod. 15:13. Also quoted by Sanders, *Paul and Palestinian Judaism*, p. 86.

17. See Patte, *Early Jewish Hermeneutic*, pp. 105–7, and the works quoted in the footnotes.

18. Ibid., pp. 24–25.

19. Sanders, *Paul and Palestinian Judaism*, pp. 85–86, and passim.

20. As Sanders says quite appropriately (ibid., p. 235; see also pp. 125–47).

21. Ibid., p. 125, and M. Kadushin, *Organic Thinking: A Study in Rabbinic Thought* (New York: Bloch Publishing Co., 1938), pp. 82–94, as quoted by Sanders.

22. Sanders, *Paul and Palestinian Judaism*, p. 179.

23. Ibid., p. 235.

24. Ibid., p. 233.

25. Ibid., p. 180.

26. Ibid., p. 234.

27. *Mishnah*, Aboth, 3:2.

28. *Mishnah*, Aboth, 3:6.

29. Patte, *Early Jewish Hermeneutic*, pp. 11–86.

30. As my eminent colleague L. H. Silberman often says. See his forthcoming book on the Midrash. I am much indebted to him in my understanding of the use of Scripture in the Midrash and the Dead Sea Scrolls. See his "Unriddling

the Riddle: A Study of the Structure and Language of the Habakkuk Pesher,"
*RQ* 11 (1961): 323–64; and "A Midrash on Midrash," mimeographed (paper
circulated at the meeting of Studiorum Novi Testamentum Societas, Amsterdam, 1971).

31. J. Mann, *The Bible as Read and Preached in the Old Synagogue*, vols. 1
and 2 (Cincinnati: Hebrew Union College, 1940, 1966).

32. Patte, *Early Jewish Hermeneutic,* pp. 69–74.

33. The only exceptions are a few interpretations which can be viewed as
having their origin in the Apocalyptic movement. Indeed, in the Apocalyptic
texts and the Dead Sea Scrolls the situation is quite different. According to the
system of convictions of the Apocalyptists, there are present events which can be
viewed as being of the same "type" as the revelatory events of the past sacred
history. This is one of the fundamental differences between the Pharisaic system
of convictions and the Apocalyptic system of convictions. Patte, *Jewish Hermeneutic* includes a comparative discussion of these two systems of convictions regarding the different ways in which they relate Scripture to the present of the
interpreters.

34. Patte, *Early Jewish Hermeneutic,* pp. 78–79.

35. This is true of any religion, as Lévi-Strauss shows in his study of myths.

36. Lauterbach, *Rabbinic Essays,* p. 131.

37. *Sifra* on Lev. 20:26, ed. I. H. Weiss (Vienna, 1862), p. 93d.

38. Patte, *Early Jewish Hermeneutic,* pp. 109–15.

39. *Mishnah,* Hullin, 8:1.

40. J. Stein, *Fiddler on the Roof* (New York: Pocket Books, 1965).

41. The references to the Jewish literature for all these metaphors can be
found in Patte, *Early Jewish Hermeneutic,* pp. 26–27.

42. For other aspects of Pharisaic Judaism, see L. H. Silberman, "Judaism,"
in *Encyclopedia Britannica,* 15th ed. Macropaedia, vol. 10, pp. 284–302; J.
Neusner, *First-Century Judaism in Crisis* (Nashville: Abingdon Press, 1975);
idem, *From Politics to Piety: The Emergence of Pharisaic Judaism* (Englewood
Cliffs, N.J.: Prentice-Hall, 1973). Neusner's thesis that the Pharisees have to be
viewed as sectarians is open to discussion. For the opposite view, see E. Rivkin,
"Defining the Pharisees: The Tannaitic Sources," *Hebrew Union College Annual*
40–41 (1969–70): 205–49.


CHAPTER 4

1. The results of our study should then be compared with the studies devoted
to the phrase "in Christ," esp. M. Bouttier, *Christianity According to Paul* (Naperville, Ill.: Alec R. Allenson, 1966).

2. G. Lüdemann in *Paulus, der Heidenapostel,* vol. 1 (Göttingen: Vandenhoeck & Ruprecht, 1980) reaches similar conclusions about the date of this letter
on the basis of a very different type of research.

3. This view of the purpose and the circumstances of 1 Thessalonians is shared
by most commentators; see esp. E. Best, *A Commentary on the First and*

*Second Epistles to the Thessalonians* (New York: Harper & Row, 1972), pp. 16–22. Others maintain that there were opponents in Thessalonica which Paul had to confront. See, e.g., W. Schmithals, *Paul and the Gnostics* (Nashville: Abingdon Press, 1972), chap. 3, esp. pp. 154–55. But such a theory demands a great deal of speculation and views the letter as written much later, at the time of 1 and 2 Corinthians. This is impossible because of the different view of the Parousia found in these letters, among other reasons. When writing to the Corinthians, Paul does not expect the Parousia to arrive as quickly as he did when he wrote 1 Thessalonians.

4. For a minority point of view, see again Schmithals (*Paul and the Gnostics*, pp. 126–34, 212–14), who feels that 1 and 2 Thessalonians are actually made up of fragments from four different letters. This is a very tenuous thesis. See also B. A. Pearson, "1 Thessalonians 2:13–16: A Deutero-Pauline Interpolation," *HTR* 64 (1971): 79–94. Best (*Commentary on Thessalonians*, pp. 30–35) provides a good discussion of the various theories concerning the question of the unity of 1 Thessalonians; he favors the idea of the letter being a single unit.

5. For the role of warrants in an argument, see S. Toulmin, *The Uses of Argument* (Cambridge: At the University Press, 1958). Yet in what follows we use a model that is more general than the one proposed by Toulmin. We want to refer to a general principle of structural organization which can be found at work in any discourse (narrative as well as any types of didactic discourses). Except in the case of very simple (and very short) discourses, there are several discourse levels. One level is the primary level. A secondary level is based upon the interpretations of the value of the primary level. A tertiary level is based upon the interpretation of the secondary level, and so on. Each level manifests a certain cluster of convictions (a certain part of the semantic universe). This can be understood by noting that, for instance, a secondary level necessarily presupposes values different from those of the primary level, since it interprets (i.e., attributes certain values) to the primary level. According to the type of discourse, the fundamental convictions are found on one or the other level. See D. Patte and A. Patte, *Structural Exegesis: From Theory to Practice* (Philadelphia: Fortress Press, 1978), chaps. 2, 3, 4. In the case of didactic discourses (such as 1 Thessalonians) we have determined that the level formed by the warranting statements is the primary level and manifests the fundamental convictions, while the main argument, which is based upon the interpretation of the values of that primary level, manifests secondary values. See D. Patte, *Aspects of a Semiotics of Didactic Discourse* (Urbino, Italy: Center for Semiotic Studies, 1980). Both these publications propose precise criteria for the identification of these levels. We propose here a simpler approach which produces sound results, even though scholars will want to verify them by using the more sophisticated method. For simplicity's sake we shall speak of only two levels: a warranting level and a dialogic level. In fact, there are three levels in this text. What we call the warranting level actually involves two levels: a primary level found mostly in 1:3—2:16, and a secondary level found mostly in 2:17—3:6. The dialogic level is therefore a tertiary level based upon the interpretation of the value of both the

primary level and the secondary level. Because the fundamental convictions are found on the primary level, we shall study this part of the text in greater detail.

6. Through this example I express the two dimensions of the competence of a subject which Greimas calls "semantic competence" (having the knowledge necessary to perform the action) and "modal competence" (having the will—which can also be an obligation—to perform the action). See "Competence" in A. J. Greimas and J. Courtés, *Semiotics and Language: An Analytical Dictionary* (Bloomington, Ind.: Indiana University Press, 1982). For a discussion of the way in which this twofold competence is established, see A. J. Greimas, "Pour une sémiotique didactique," *Bull*. 7 (January 1979); and Patte, *Aspects of a Semiotics of Didactic Discourse*, pp. 1–20.

7. In interpreting the salutation and closing of the letter, Best (*Commentary on Thessalonians*, pp. 60–64, 242–47) follows the traditional procedure of historical-critical commentators who look for historical and theological "content" in key words or phrases of the text. Thus, such questions as the following are raised: Who was Silvanus? What does the word *ekklēsia* (church) mean for Paul? Do the terms spirit, soul, and body imply a tripartite psychology? Why does Paul speak of "grace and peace"? The latter two terms are unpacked with reference to Paul's theological ideas, that is, salvation, sanctification, wholeness, justification, and so on. The relational network among Paul, the Thessalonians, God, and the Lord Jesus Christ is thus neglected as a meaningful feature.

8. Best (ibid., pp. 112–13) stresses that Paul does not mean the Thessalonians were *conscious* imitators of the Judean churches but rather that they reacted in a similar manner (they endured) to similar pressures (persecution). But as we shall see, such comments do not fully explain the relationship Paul perceives between the Thessalonians and the churches of Judea.

9. According to Best (ibid., pp. 217–18), 5:10 *does* focus attention on the salvific effects of Christ's death in the past: "Though salvation is future it is irrevocably bound to Jesus 'who died for us'; the exalted Lord who achieves salvation for us is the crucified Jesus." Verse 10 is the only place in the letter where Paul gives an explicit interpretation to the death of Jesus. For Best, the phrase used by Paul in this instance "recalls many others," such as Romans 5:6, 8; 14:15; 2 Cor. 5:15. "It implies that through Christ's death we are aided and that in respect of salvation. Its casual introduction without any explanation of how Christ's death does benefit men shows that it was a phrase well known to the Thessalonians." The assumption, then, is that we are to "fill in" the meaning of the phrase here with the content quarried from other Pauline and early Christian texts. But as Best himself notes, "salvation is future" according to 1 Thessalonians. Saying that it is past (achieved on the cross, as Best implies) contradicts Paul's letter. This future salvation is indeed "bound to Jesus who died for us," but it is because Jesus is a type of the believers both in the present and in the future.

10. B. Lindars, *New Testament Apologetic* (London: SCM Press, 1961), pp. 44–51; D. Hay, *Glory at the Right Hand: Psalm 110 in Early Christianity* (Nashville: Abingdon Press, 1973).

11. While admitting that the reading "infants" has better manuscript evidence than the reading "gentle," Best prefers the latter on the grounds (1) that it fits in well with Paul's defense; (2) that "infants" would be an image which Paul elsewhere considers pejorative (1 Cor. 3:1); and (3) that the reading "gentle" does not require a sudden inversion of metaphor as the former does (*Commentary on Thessalonians*, p. 10). However, swift and dramatic changes in metaphor are quite common in Paul's writings. For example, all the following metaphors are used in one short passage (2 Cor. 3:1—5:2): letters written on our hearts, servants of a new covenant, a veil over the old covenant, a treasure in earthen vessels, the earthly tent which is our house, and ambassadors for Christ. We shall see why Paul "mixes" metaphors in our passage.

## CHAPTER 5

1. See, e.g., P. Bonnard, *L'Épître de Saint Paul aux Philippiens* (Neuchâtel and Paris: Delachaux & Niestlé, 1950), p. 60.

2. J. Knox, on the basis of the mention of Onesimus and of Archippus in Col. 4:9 and 17, argues that Archippus is the master of Onesimus and that the letter was addressed to him rather than to Philemon (J. Knox, *Philemon Among the Letters of Paul* [Nashville: Abingdon Press, 1959]). Yet this view is rejected by most scholars. See E. Lohse, *Colossians and Philemon* (Philadelphia: Fortress Press, 1971), esp. pp. 186–208 for a historical reading of this letter and further bibliography.

3. Cf. Lohse, *Colossians and Philemon*, p. 188.

4. For the text of Pliny's letter and a comparison with Paul's see ibid., pp. 196–97.

5. M. Luther, "Preface to the Epistle of Saint Paul to Philemon" (1546), in *Luther's Works*, vol. 35 (Philadelphia: Fortress Press, 1960), p. 390, quoted by Lohse, *Colossians and Philemon*, p. 188.

6. F. W. Beare, *A Commentary on the Epistle to the Philippians* (New York: Harper & Row, 1959). Other scholars view this fragment as also including 4:2–3 and 8–9. Cf. W. Marxsen, *Introduction to the New Testament* (Philadelphia: Fortress Press, 1970), pp. 59–68. For an argument against the composite nature of Philippians (and a review of the main arguments for it), see W. Kümmel, *Introduction to the New Testament* (Nashville: Abingdon Press, 1975), pp. 226–37.

7. On this second interpolation, see the works cited in note 6.

8. "Incision," "circumcision," is the excellent way to render this pun into English proposed by Beare, *Philippians*, p. 104.

9. Cf. ibid., pp. 112–15.

10. Ibid., p. 136.

11. The identification of the passages belonging to the dialogical level has been made by using the same criteria we used for our study of 1 Thessalonians. For a more detailed and rigorous procedure, see D. Patte, *Aspects of a Semiotics of Didactic Discourse* (Urbino, Italy: Center for Semiotic Studies, 1980).

12. This is true even if 3:1 and 4:4 do not contain exhortations to rejoice. These verses have indeed been interpreted by some commentators as farewell greetings, equivalent to our "goodbye," rather than as actual exhortations to rejoice. Cf. Beare, *Philippians*, pp. 145–46. The imperative form "rejoice" was indeed commonly used as parting greetings. Yet in my view the context shows that Paul used this phrase as an exhortation. For instance, what would be the meaning of 4:4 if it was translated "Farewell always in the Lord. I say again farewell"? The repetition and the adverb "always" makes it unlikely that this could be the meaning.

13. At the same time, Christ and Paul (whose experiences are "typical" of what happens to the Philippians) are also models that they need to follow in their lives.

14. As the structure of the sentence shows, this second part of the verse belongs to the warranting level despite the present tense, because it describes an enduring situation and not a situation limited to the dialogic present.

15. For a similar interpretation and a discussion of other opinions, see Bonnard, *Philippiens*, pp. 37–38.

16. The term translated "consolation" and "encouragement" can also mean "exhortation." When such an interpretation is chosen (so Beare, *Philippians*, pp. 70–71), the phrase "in Christ" and the relation with the preceding verses are difficult to understand.

17. Cf. Bonnard, *Philippiens*, p. 38; and Beare, *Philippians*, p. 71.

18. Beare, *Philippians*, p. 71.

19. For a more complete discussion of this hymn, see ibid., pp. 73–88, and the bibliography, pp. 40–42. The question of its authorship is also discussed in this commentary.

20. Ibid., pp. 84–87.

21. Ibid., p. 76; Bonnard, *Philippiens*, pp. 41–42.

22. Ibid., pp. 88–89.


CHAPTER 6

1. The distinction proposed here between "systemic relations" and "relations of process and purposefulness" is my effort to express in nontechnical terminology the distinction between semantic and syntactic relations that one finds in a discourse. The systemic relations are the relations which characterize what Greimas calls "narrative semantics" (see "Semantics [narrative]," in A. J. Greimas and J. Courtés, *Semiotics and Language: An Analytical Dictionary* (Bloomington, Ind.: Indiana University Press, 1982) and what I call "symbolic system" (D. and A. Patte, *Structural Exegesis: From Theory to Practice* [Philadelphia: Fortress Press, 1978], chap. 2), while the convictional pattern is what Greimas calls "fundamental semantics" (see "Semantics [fundamental]," in Greimas and Courtés, *Semiotics and Language*). The relations of process and purposefulness are the relations which characterize the surface narrative syntax and the fundamental syntax (in Greimas and Courtés, see "Syntax [surface narrative]" and

"Syntax [fundamental]"), which approximately correspond to what I call the system of elementary narratives, each of which includes a narrative hierarchy and a system of pertinent transformations (cf. Patte, *Structural Exegesis*, chap. 2). Semantic relations are those which govern a system of convictions. By contrast, syntactic relations are those which interrelate ideas, including theological ideas, in a system of ideas (the fundamental syntax) and in the unfolding of an argument, of a story or history (the narrative syntax). The unfortunate discrepancy in terminology between Greimas's publication and mine comes from the fact that these distinctions were independently reached (the Greimas and Courtés work was published one year after our own work). From now on I will use Greimas's terminology. For a brief but illustrated description of the relations between syntax and semantics, see D. Patte, "Greimas' Model for the Generative Trajectory of Meaning in Discourses," *AJS* 3 (1982): 59–78.

2. These relations can be called "syntagmatic" or "syntactic" in the structuralist/semiotic terminology. They can also be called metonymic relations. Metonymy demands that the various elements be perceived in continuity with each other. In the classical example of metonymy (or more precisely, of this specific type of metonymy which is synecdoche) the sail, which is in continuity with the rest of the boat, can represent the boat as a whole. Similarly, effects are in continuity with causes, and thus an effect can also represent metonymically a cause. Similarly, a container is in continuity with its content and thus a container can also represent metonymically the content. See M. Le Guern, *Sémantique de la métaphore et de la métonymie* (Paris: Larousse, 1973). In saying so, I presuppose that metonymy (syntactic in character) cannot be viewed as a special kind of metaphor (semantic in character). As such I disagree with Greimas and Courtés on "Metonymy," *Semiotics and Language*.

3. We cannot enter in a full discussion of the system of convictions of the various Apocalyptic groups. Let us note simply that, like Paul and unlike the Pharisees, the Apocalyptists had a dynamic system of convictions involving the expectation of new revelations. They also viewed scriptural events, personages, and institutions as types fulfilled in their present or to be fulfilled in the future. But a closer comparison of Paul's and the Apocalyptists' systems of convictions would show significant differences (especially regarding the kind of events in which God is expected to intervene). For an attempt at discerning some of the characteristics of the Apocalyptists' system of convictions, see D. Patte, *Early Jewish Hermeneutic in Palestine* (Chico, Calif.: Scholars Press, 1975), pp. 129–324, and the bibliography therein. See also D. S. Russell, *The Method and Message of Jewish Apocalyptic* (Philadelphia: Westminster Press, 1964); idem, *Apocalyptic: Ancient and Modern* (Philadelphia: Fortress Press, 1978); and P. D. Hanson, *The Dawn of Apocalyptic* (Philadelphia: Fortress Press, 1975).

4. For a translation of the Book of Jubilees, see R. H. Charles, *The Apocrypha and Pseudepigrapha of the Old Testament* (Oxford: At the Clarendon Press, 1913), 2:1–82. For a brief study of the view of sacred history in this book, see Patte, *Early Jewish Hermeneutic*, pp. 145–67.

5. Cf. H. Parzen, "The *Ruah Hakodesh* in Tannaitic Literature," *JQR* 20

(1929): 51–76; and L. Blau, "Holy Spirit," in *Jewish Encyclopedia*, 1st ed. vol. 6 (New York and London: Funk & Wagnalls Co., 1904), pp. 447–50.

6. In a more technical terminology, these explanations are first of all the results of interpretations of the fundamental and narrative semantic systems (the system of convictions). These interpretations by means of the operations of the fundamental syntax include epistemic* judgments, which establish epistemic modal systems (what is judged as having a real existence or not), alethic judgments, which establish alethic* modal systems (what is judged as being necessarily true or not), and deontic* judgments, which establish deontic modal systems (what is judged as good behavior or not). This is the passage from fundamental and narrative semantics* to fundamental syntax* as I see it on the basis of Greimas's discussion of all these elements, although Greimas himself does not spell out these relations between semantics and syntax. Beyond these fundamental interpretations, these systems are narrativized, that is, further interpreted and perceived as providing the basis upon which a story (or history) or an argument can be constructed following the network of relations of the surface narrative syntax*. See the entries corresponding to the terms with asterisks (*) in Greimas and Courtés, *Semiotics and Language*.

7. J. Munck, *Paul and the Salvation of Mankind* (Atlanta: John Knox Press, 1977).

8. O. Cullmann, *Salvation in History* (New York: Harper & Row, 1967).

9. K. Stendahl, "The Apostle Paul and the Introspective Conscience of the West," *HTR* 56 (1963): 199–215; reprinted in *Paul Among Jews and Gentiles* (Philadelphia: Fortress Press, 1976).

10. R. Bultmann, *Theology of the New Testament* (New York: Charles Scribner's Sons, 1955), vol. 1, pp. 185–366.

11. E. Käsemann, *Perspectives on Paul* (Philadelphia: Fortress Press, 1971), pp. 60–78.

12. Note that these "two dimensions of meaning" should not be confused with the discoursive levels (dialogic and warranting levels). One dimension is that of the system of *convictions* and involves a convictional logic (it is a semantic dimension), while the other dimension is that of the system of *ideas* and involves the argumentative logic (it is a syntactic dimension). Each discoursive level includes both these dimensions; the elements of the warranting level includes an argumentative logic and a convictional logic as the elements of the dialogic level also do. The elucidation of the discoursive levels is helpful to identify the parts of an argument which are undergirded by different sets of convictions (the warranting level including in a didactic discourse the parts of the argument undergirding the more fundamental convictions).

13. C. K. Barrett, *A Commentary on the Second Epistle to the Corinthians* (New York: Harper & Row, 1973), p. 173.

14. As E. P. Sanders notes, "reconciliation is only preparatory to being given life"; see his *Paul and Palestinian Judaism* (Philadelphia: Fortress Press, 1977), p. 470.

15. For a similar interpretation of "the righteousness of God," see E. Käse-

mann, *New Testament Questions of Today* (Philadelphia: Fortress Press, 1969), pp. 168–82, and esp. p. 181.

16. This distinction between "justification as reconciliation" and "justification as intervention of God in the believers' experience" is similar to the distinction proposed by Käsemann between "justification as gift" and "justification as power" respectively (although Käsemann does not make his case on the basis of a distinction between dimensions of meaning). Justification as reconciliation (or as gift) can never be separated from justification as intervention of God (or as power). Without the former the latter cannot be understood (i.e., one cannot understand why God intervenes); but without the latter the former is empty (if there is no manifestation of the "power of the cross" in the believers' experience [1 Cor. 1:18], then "Christ died to no purpose" [Gal. 2:21]). Or, in Käsemann's words, "the gift which is being bestowed here is never at any time separable from its Giver. It partakes of the character of power, insofar as God himself enters the arena and remains in the arena with it" (Käsemann, *New Testament Questions*, p. 174, and also the entire essay "The 'Righteousness of God' in Paul," pp. 168–82). For a more complete discussion of this interpretation of righteousness, see also E. Käsemann, *Commentary on Romans* (Grand Rapids: Wm. B. Eerdmans, 1980). Käsemann discusses this concept throughout the commentary, but see esp. pp. 21–32.

17. Sanders, *Paul and Palestinian Judaism*, p. 473.

18. This statement could also be expressed by saying that Christ has the same status as Torah, and thus that he is the New Torah. W. D. Davies has shown, by comparing Paul's texts with early Jewish texts, that this view of Christ as the New Torah can indeed be found throughout Paul's letters; see W. D. Davies, *Paul and Rabbinic Judaism*, 4th ed. (Philadelphia: Fortress Press, 1980), pp. 147–76. Our study of the interrelations of the various components of the warranting level in this chapter of Galatians and then in Romans 4 and 1 Corinthians 15 complements W. D. Davies's conclusions by attempting to show the roles and functions of Torah and the kerygma (the New Torah) in Paul's system of convictions.

19. This passage is not a didactic text (i.e., a discourse which aims at causing the addressees to do something, such as follow certain exhortations). Rather, it aims at communicating convictions, indeed, at changing the convictions of the Corinthians. In such a case it is the dialogic level (the interpretative level) which includes the more fundamental convictions, while the warranting level (the primary level) involves less fundamental convictions. (See Patte, *Structural Exegesis*, pp. 94–112, where I propose to distinguish "sacred" from "profane" texts on this ground, although this vocabulary was poorly chosen). This is further demonstrated by the fact that the convictional logic controls the unfolding of the argument.

20. See B. Lindars, *New Testament Apologetic* (London: SCM Press, 1961), pp. 32–74.

21. See ibid., pp. 60–66.

22. For a complete critical discussion of the various proposals on this issue,

see R. L. Richardson, Jr., "The Function of the Scriptures in the Rise of the Easter Faith" (Ph.D. diss., Vanderbilt University, 1972).

23. See Patte, *Early Jewish Hermeneutic*, pp. 129–314.

24. Our conclusions regarding the function of Christ as the New Torah according to Paul are quite different from those of W. D. Davies (see, e.g., *Paul and Rabbinic Judaism*, pp. 172–76). The differences are the result of (a) the fact that Davies includes in his study Colossians and Ephesians and (b) the methodology that Davies uses. Comparing Paul's letters with the early Jewish literature allows Davies to show what traditional views Paul has made his own (and thus to conclude that Christ is the New Torah/Wisdom). But such a method does not provide any means for determining the function of the kerygma (and of Scripture) in Paul's system of convictions. By contrast, our method does not allow us to say anything about the origin of Paul's views and thus to assess the traditions he uses and the way in which he modified them. Thus the limitations of each method appear clearly, yet their necessary complementarity is also plain.

CHAPTER 7

1. The structural approach is a hypothetico-deductive approach comparable to that of fundamental research in science. It involves constructing a model comparable to the reconstruction of a jigsaw puzzle without the help of the picture of the landscape it represents. After reconstructing the general outline of Paul's system of convictions (the sides of the jigsaw puzzle) in Chapter 2, then several components of this system (putting together pieces of the puzzle which represent parts of the picture even though we do not yet know how they are interrelated among themselves) in Chapters 4, 5, and 6, we reach the point where we can perceive how these components fit together. Thus we can set them in the general framework we had already perceived. Of course, we will have to verify, through the study of Paul's texts, that this organization is indeed valid. But if our hypothesis is correct, we should then be in a position to find out relatively easily where the rest of the pieces of the puzzle fit. On the hypothetico-deductive approach of structural and semiotic research, see "Deduction," in A. J. Greimas and J. Courtés, *Semiotics and Language: An Analytical Dictionary* (Bloomington, Ind.: Indiana University Press, 1982).

2. On "charismatic authority" as defined in a sociological perspective, see B. Holmberg, *Paul and Power* (Philadelphia: Fortress Press, 1980), pp. 137–60.

3. On the limitations of Paul's charismatic authority, see ibid., pp. 183–92. Holmberg's discussion of these limitations in terms of the sociological category "institutionalization of charismatic authority" fails to give a proper explanation of this attitude of Paul. And yet some of his comments point in the right direction. For instance, he writes: "Christians have become fully initiated in the charismatic tradition. . . . His [Paul's] authority is delegated from a higher source of authority to which, in principle, they [his churches] themselves have direct access (cf. 1 Cor. 3:5–9, 21–23)" (p. 185). Holmberg also speaks of Paul's "deep appreciation of the freedom and inherent capacity of local churches to conduct their own lives and attain a state where they will not need apostolic supervision"

(p. 187). But Holmberg fails to recognize the implications of his own statement because the sociological categories he uses lead him to consider and elucidate other issues.

4. Ibid., p. 149.

5. See H. Conzelmann, *1 Corinthians* (Philadelphia: Fortress Press, 1975), pp. 271–72.

6. See K. P. Donfried, ed., *The Romans Debate* (Minneapolis: Augsburg Publishing House, 1977).

7. So N. Perrin, *The New Testament: An Introduction* (New York: Harcourt Brace Jovanovich, 1974), pp. 106–7.

8. Such is the view of, e.g., O. Michel, *Der Brief an die Römer*, 2d ed. (Göttingen: Vandenhoeck & Ruprecht, 1957). For a brief summary of his position, see W. Marxsen, *Introduction to the New Testament* (Philadelphia: Fortress Press, 1970), p. 94.

9. E. Käsemann, *Commentary on Romans* (Grand Rapids: Wm. B. Eerdmans, 1980), pp. 364–87.

10. Marxsen, *Introduction*, pp. 92–109.

11. For a more detailed discussion of the historical situation of the church in Rome, see ibid., pp. 98–104. Here we summarize his argument.

12. T. W. Manson, "St. Paul's Letter to the Romans—And others," *BJRL* 31 (1948): 224–40.

13. In favor of this view, see Käsemann, *Romans*, pp. 409–19; Marxsen, *Introduction*, pp. 107–8; J. Munck, *Paul and the Salvation of Mankind* (Atlanta: John Knox Press, 1977), pp. 197–200. By contrast, chap. 16 is viewed as part of the letter to the Romans by W. G. Kümmel, *Introduction to the New Testament*, rev. ed. (Nashville: Abingdon Press, 1975), pp. 222–26.

14. Cf. F. J. Leenhardt, *The Epistle to the Romans* (London: Lutterworth Press, 1961), pp. 180–86. See also K. Stendahl, *Paul Among Jews and Gentiles* (Philadelphia: Fortress Press, 1976), pp. 78–96.

15. See Käsemann, *Romans*, pp. 105–29; and idem, *Perspectives on Paul* (Philadelphia: Fortress Press, 1971), pp. 79–101.

16. In agreement with Leenhardt, *Romans*, pp. 59–61, but against Käsemann, *Romans*, pp. 35, 38, who assumes, without discussing it further, that it is a revelation to the ungodly and wicked people which he relates primarily to the revelation mentioned in 1:19 (expressed by means of a different verb) rather than the revelation mentioned in 1:17 (expressed by means of the same verb). Yet Käsemann acknowledges that this revelation of the wrath of God is the reverse side of the Gospel.

17. Käsemann, *Romans*, pp. 37–38.

18. See ibid., pp. 39–42.

19. In agreement with Leenhardt, *Romans*, pp. 61–64, and Käsemann, *Romans*, p. 42.

20. According to Paul's system of convictions, this verse and the following verses deal indeed with any human being. Thus this statement is addressed to the Jews as well as to the Gentiles, and indeed also indirectly to the Jewish and Gentile Christians of the church of Rome who are passing judgment upon each

other (14:1). Scholars usually choose as addressees of these exhortations either the pagans (Leenhardt, *Romans*, pp. 71–72) or the Jews (Käsemann, *Romans*, pp. 52–54).

21. This Jewish tradition is found in Philo, in 4 Maccabees, and in *Apocalypse of Moses* as well as in the Talmud. For references to and discussion of this tradition, see Käsemann, *Romans*, p. 194.

22. Cf. P. Berger, *The Sacred Canopy: Elements of a Sociological Theory of Religion* (New York: Doubleday & Co., 1969), pp. 3–28.

23. H. Marcuse, *Eros and Civilization* (New York: Random House, 1962); N. O. Brown, *Love's Body* (New York: Random House, 1966). See also T. Roszack, *The Making of a Counter Culture* (New York: Doubleday & Co., 1969). Once again let me state that I do not intend to present Marcuse's and Brown's theories, as is clear from the fact that I associate Marcuse, Brown, and Sartre despite the fundamental differences of their philosophical views. But each of them perceived the problem of "sin/desire" in a way which can help us understand Paul's view of sin as coveting. One can compare our use of these authors with R. Scroggs, *Paul for a New Day* (Philadelphia: Fortress Press, 1977).

24. J.-P. Sartre, *Being and Nothingness* (New York: Pocket Books, 1956), pp. 474–93, and passim.

25. J.-P. Sartre, *La Putain Respectueuse* (Paris: Nagel, 1946).

26. On this point see Stendahl, *Paul Among Jews and Gentiles*, pp. 78–96; and Käsemann, *Romans*, pp. 201–2.

27. In our interpretation, 7:25b is fully explained as a summary of chap. 7. This, I believe, is a test showing the validity of our interpretation, against those scholars such as Leenhardt, *Romans*, pp. 195–99, and Käsemann, *Romans*, pp. 211–12, who argue that this is a gloss of a later reader, despite the fact that this is "against the whole textual tradition" and that "there is no textual evidence for this."

28. J.-P. Sartre, *No Exit* (New York: Alfred P. Knopf, 1947).

29. There is no reference here to a sacrificial death of Christ (against Käsemann, *Romans*, p. 217; Leenhardt, *Romans*, pp. 202–4). This theological/sacred historical concept involves the expiation of our *sins* (plural) as in 3:25, 1 Cor. 15:3, Gal. 1:4. See E. P. Sanders, *Paul and Palestinian Judaism* (Philadelphia: Fortress Press, 1977), pp. 469–72. Here "sin" is used in the singular to refer to the power of sin. Thus the preposition *peri* should be rendered according to its usual meaning: "with regard to," "in relation to," "with reference to."

30. Cf. P. W. Meyer, "Romans 10:4 and the 'End' of the Law," in *The Divine Helmsman: Studies on God's Control of Human Events*, ed. J. L. Crenshaw and S. Sandmel (New York: Ktav, 1980), pp. 59–78.

## CHAPTER 8

1. Some scholars argue that 1 Corinthians includes parts of this first letter; see W. Schmithals, *Gnosticism in Corinth* (Nashville: Abingdon Press, 1971). I cannot agree with Schmithals on several parts of his argument, as the discussion of

important passages of 1 Corinthians will show, but I do not exclude the possibility that some passages of 1 Corinthians belong to this first letter. A more complete study of 1 Corinthians may lead me to conclude that this is the case. Since our present study will be limited to the exegesis of a number of passages, we do not need to reach a definite conclusion on this issue.

2. One can also argue that chap. 8 is an independent letter of recommendation for Titus. See G. Bornkamm, *Paul* (New York: Harper & Row, 1971), pp. 68–77, 244–46.

3. Cf. W. Marxsen, *Introduction to the New Testament* (Philadelphia: Fortress Press, 1970), pp. 71–91. I am in full agreement with Marxsen's discussion of these points, which I summarized in the preceding pages. See also Schmithals, *Gnosticism in Corinth*. While I am not convinced by Schmithals's discussion of 1 Corinthians, I am in agreement with his discussion of 2 Corinthians. Yet, as will become clear in the following pages, I disagree with Marxsen's and Schmithals's views of the theological positions of Paul's opponents.

4. For a study of the views of Paul's opponents (as distinct from the church's views), see G. Lüdemann, *Paulus, der Heidenapostel*, vol. 2 (Göttingen: Vandenhoeck & Ruprecht, 1982). Yet I cannot agree with Lüdemann when he argues that immorality in the Corinthian church is not linked with the opponents' teaching.

5. In agreement with H. Conzelmann, *1 Corinthians* (Philadelphia: Fortress Press, 1975), pp. 33–34; see also these pages for a discussion of other interpretations proposed by various scholars.

6. Here I follow Schmithals and other scholars who see in this passage the reference to an actual cursing of Jesus rather than to a mere hypothetical situation posited by Paul for the sake of his argument. In the latter case one has to conclude that Paul does not make any clear mention of the Corinthians' question, which would then be only a vague question concerning spiritual gifts. This is unlikely in view of the specificity of the other questions. Furthermore, it becomes difficult to understand 1 Cor. 12:2. For this interpretation, see ibid., pp. 204–6. For the interpretation that we follow, see Schmithals, *Gnosticism in Corinth*, pp. 124–32.

7. The relation between 1 Cor. 12:3 and Gal. 3:13 has already been pointed out by A. Schlatter, *Paulus der Bote Jesu*, 2d ed. (Stuttgart: Calwer Verlag, 1956), p. 333. Yet our argument is quite different.

8. Cf. Schmithals, *Gnosticism in Corinth*, pp. 124–32. I agree with Conzelmann's criticism of this part of Schmithals' argument; see Conzelmann, *1 Corinthians*, p. 205.

9. For a discussion of the various options, see Conzelmann, *1 Corinthians*, pp. 261–63.

10. This is clear even though the interpretation of this verse is difficult. See C. K. Barrett, *A Commentary on the Second Epistle of Saint Paul to the Corinthians* (New York: Harper & Row, 1973), pp. 253–54; and J. Héring's discussion of 2 Cor. 10:3–6 in *The Second Epistle of Saint Paul to the Corinthians* (London: Epworth Press, 1967).

11. The term "conversion" is to be preferred to "repentance" here. The only other place Paul uses this term is in Rom. 2:4, where it refers to turning away from idolatry, that is, once again, to conversion rather than repentance.

12. See Conzelmann, *1 Corinthians*, pp. 97–98.

13. The exact situation cannot be fully reconstructed. Since this immoral behavior is accepted as valid by the Corinthians, we can suppose that the father's wife is the stepmother of the man (and not his mother). See ibid., p. 96.

14. See ibid., p. 98.

15. See ibid., pp. 121–24.

16. We shall not deal with 1 Cor. 14:33–36. The fact that this passage directly contradicts 11:2–16, where Paul presupposes that women participate in worship (praying and prophesying in it), and the fact that it interrupts the flow of the argument show that this passage is an interpolation by a later editor. I thus agree with Conzelmann and other scholars that these verses are not from Paul. See ibid., p. 246.

17. Scholars are divided over the issue of knowing whether Paul alludes to Jewish traditions or to Hellenistic traditions, e.g., Conzelmann (ibid., pp. 184–85 and the footnotes). For our purpose this issue can be left undecided.

18. In agreement with Conzelmann (ibid., p. 184), 11:3 should be interpreted as referring not to the relation of a woman to her husband (so RSV) but to the relation of woman (female) to man (male).

19. Compare our interpretation (in terms of convictional pattern) of Paul's view of the status of women with the scholarly debate between R. Scroggs, "Paul and the Eschatological Woman," *JAAR* 40 (1972): 283–303; "Paul and the Eschatological Woman: Revisited," *JAAR* 42 (1974): 532–37; "Paul: Chauvinist or Liberationist?" *CC* 89 (March 15, 1972): 307–9; *and* E. Pagels, "Paul and Women: A Response to Recent Discussion," *JAAR* 42 (1974): 538–49; *and* W. O. Walker, "1 Corinthians 11:2–16 and Paul's Views Regarding Women," *JBL* 94 (1975): 94–110; *and* J. Murphy-O'Connor, "Non-Pauline Character of 1 Cor. 11:2–16?" *JBL* 95 (1976): 615–21.

The application of Paul's teaching to the contemporary situation would demand that the same convictional pattern be followed: (a) taking note of what the contemporary views of women are (incidentally, these views do not include that women should be veiled); (b) assessing these views so as to recognize what is valid in the structure of authority they represent; (c) reinterpreting this structure of authority to show that, in the Christian community, the opposite structure of authority is also valid, and showing it in terms of other views present in these traditions. Yet it should be noted that for Paul this equal status of women and men can take place only in the context of the freedom of the Gospel and thus in the community of believers. Outside this community, people are necessarily under the power of idols which involve bondage in one sense or another. The performance principle (sin as self-asserting desire) will ensure that women are submitted to men or men to women, and thus that their relationship be perceived as a power play.

20. Cf., e.g., Schmithals, *Gnosticism in Corinth*, pp. 90–96.

21. In agreement with Conzelmann, *1 Corinthians*, pp. 137–80.

22. For the Jewish motifs used by Paul in this passage see ibid., pp. 165–67. Yet note the weakness of Conzelmann's interpretation. Against him, it must be emphasized that there is no concept of the preexistence of Christ here. The phrase "and the Rock was Christ" simply expresses that Christ was the fulfillment of the type "rock," in the same way that Paul can speak of himself as crucified because he sees himself as the fulfillment of the type "Christ crucified." To say that this phrase expresses that Christ was present in the time of the Exodus, and thus was preexistent, one would also need to say that Paul was on the cross of Golgotha with Jesus.

23. For a discussion of the interrelation of 10:14ff. and 8:4–13, see Conzelmann, ibid., pp. 170–71. Yet a better explanation of the situation alluded to in this passage might be the one proposed by Charles A. Kennedy in a paper, presented at the Southeast SBL meeting, March 20, 1982, entitled "The Table of Demons: 1 Corinthians 10:21." In this paper Kennedy argues that Paul refers to a quite different situation in 10:14ff. as compared to the situation in 8:4–13. In 10:14ff. Paul would allude to the cult of the dead (a meaning of the term "demons"). This oral presentation and its argument were quite intriguing. Yet we need to wait for its publication.

# Selected Bibliography

## COMMENTARIES

Barrett, C. K. *A Commentary on the Epistle to the Romans*. HNTC. New York: Harper & Row; BNTC, London: A. & C. Black, 1957.

————. *A Commentary on the First Epistle to the Corinthians*. HNTC. New York: Harper & Row; BNTC, London: A. & C. Black, 1968.

————. *A Commentary on the Second Epistle to the Corinthians*. HNTC. New York: Harper & Row; BNTC, London: A. & C. Black, 1973.

Barth, Karl. *The Epistle to the Romans*. Eng. trans. Edwin C. Hoskyns. New York and London: Oxford University Press, 1933, 1968.

Beare, Francis W. *A Commentary on the Epistle to the Philippians*. HNTC. New York: Harper & Row; BNTC, London: A. & C. Black, 1959.

Best, Ernest. *A Commentary on the First and Second Epistles to the Thessalonians*. HNTC. New York: Harper & Row; BNTC, London: A. & C. Black, 1972.

Betz, Hans Dieter. *Galatians: A Commentary on Paul's Letter to the Churches in Galatia*. Hermeneia. Philadelphia: Fortress Press, 1979.

Bicknell, E. J. *First and Second Epistles to the Thessalonians*. London: Methuen & Co., 1932.

Bonnard, Pierre. *L'Épître de Saint Paul aux Philippiens*. CNT 10a. Neuchâtel and Paris: Delachaux & Niestlé, 1950.

Bruce, F. F. *The Acts of the Apostles: The Greek Text with Introduction and Commentary*. 2d ed. Grand Rapids: Wm. B. Eerdmans; Eastbourne: Kingsway Publications (Tyndale), 1952.

————. *Epistle of Paul to the Romans*. Grand Rapids: Wm. B. Eerdmans, 1963; Eastbourne: Kingsway Publications (Tyndale), 1971.

Burton, E. DeWitt. *A Critical and Exegetical Commentary on the Epistle to the Galatians*. ICC. New York: Charles Scribner's Sons; London: T. & T. Clark, 1920.

Collange, J. F. *The Epistle of St. Paul to the Philippians*. Eng. trans. A. W. Heathcote. London: Epworth Press, 1979.

Conzelmann, Hans. *1 Corinthians: A Commentary on the First Epistle to the*

*Corinthians*. Hermeneia. Eng. trans. James W. Leitch. Philadelphia: Fortress Press, 1975.

Cranfield, C. E. B. *A Critical and Exegetical Commentary on the Epistle to the Romans*. Edinburgh: T. & T. Clark, 1975.

Dodd, C. H. *The Epistle of Paul to the Romans*. New York: Long & Smith; London: Hodder & Stoughton, 1932.

Frame, J. E. *A Critical and Exegetical Commentary on the Epistles of St. Paul to the Thessalonians*. ICC. New York: Charles Scribner's Sons; London: T. & T. Clark, 1912.

Guthrie, Donald. *Galatians*. NCBC. Grand Rapids: Wm. B. Eerdmans, 1981; London: Marshall, Morgan & Scott, 1973.

Héring, Jean. *The Second Epistle of Saint Paul to the Corinthians*. London: Epworth Press, 1967.

Jackson, Foakes J., and Lake, Kirsopp. *The Acts of the Apostles: The Beginnings of Christianity*. 5 vols. Grand Rapids: Baker Book House, 1979; London: Macmillan & Co., 1920.

Käsemann, Ernst. *Commentary on Romans*. Eng. trans. Geoffrey W. Bromiley. Grand Rapids: Wm. B. Eerdmans; London: SCM Press, 1980.

Leenhardt, Franz J. *The Epistle to the Romans: A Commentary*. Eng. trans. Harold Knight. London: Lutterworth Press, 1961.

Lightfoot, J. B. *The Epistle of St. Paul to the Galatians*. 3d ed. Grand Rapids: Zondervan Publishing House, 1962.

———. *St. Paul's Epistle to the Philippians*. Lynn, Mass.: Hendrickson Publishers, 1981.

Lohse, Eduard. *Colossians and Philemon*. Hermeneia. Eng. trans. William R. Poehlmann and Robert J. Karris. Philadelphia: Fortress Press, 1971.

Martin, Ralph. *Philippians*. NCBC. Grand Rapids: Wm. B. Eerdmans, 1980; London: Marshall, Morgan & Scott, 1976.

Metzger, Bruce M. *A Textual Commentary on the Greek New Testament*. New York and London: United Bible Societies, 1971.

Michael, J. H. *Epistle of Paul to the Philippians*. New York: Doubleday & Co., 1929.

Michel, Otto. *Der Brief an die Römer*. Meyers kritisch-exegetischer Kommentar über das Neue Testament 4. 2d ed. Göttingen: Vandenhoeck & Ruprecht, 1957.

Morris, Leon. *The Epistles of St. Paul to the Thessalonians*. NICNT. Grand Rapids: Eerdmans, 1957; Eastbourne: Kingsway Publications (Tyndale), 1971.

Müller, Jacobus J. *The Epistles of Paul to the Philippians and to Philemon*. NICNT. Grand Rapids: Wm. B. Eerdmans, 1955.

Neil, William. *The Epistles of Paul to the Thessalonians*. New York: Harper & Row, 1950.

———. *The Letter of Paul to the Galatians*. Cambridge: At the University Press, 1967.

Nygren, Anders. *Commentary on Romans*. Eng. trans. Carl C. Rasmussen. Philadelphia: Fortress Press, 1949.

Orr, William F. *1 Corinthians*. AB. New York: Doubleday & Co., 1976.

Plummer, Alfred. *A Critical and Exegetical Commentary on the Second Epistle of Paul to the Corinthians*. ICC. New York: Charles Scribner's Sons; London: T. & T. Clark, 1915.

Ramsay, William M. *A Historical Commentary on St. Paul's Epistle to the Galatians*. Grand Rapids: Baker Book House, 1979.

Robertson, Archibald, and Plummer, Alfred. *A Critical and Exegetical Commentary on the First Epistle of Paul to the Corinthians*. ICC. New York: Charles Scribner's Sons; London: T. & T. Clark, 1911.

Ruef, John. *Paul's First Letter to Corinth*. Philadelphia: Westminster Press; London: SCM Press, 1977.

Strachan, R. H. *The Second Epistle of Paul to the Corinthians*. London: Hodder & Stoughton, 1935.

Taylor, Vincent. *The Epistle to the Romans*. London: Epworth Press, 1955.

Thrall, Margaret E., ed. *First and Second Letters of Paul to the Corinthians*. Cambridge: At the University Press, 1965.

Vincent, M. R. *A Critical and Exegetical Commentary on the Philippians and to Philemon*. ICC. New York: Charles Scribner's Sons; London: T. & T. Clark, 1897.

## GENERAL STUDIES

Baird, William. *The Corinthian Church: A Biblical Approach to Urban Culture*. Nashville: Abingdon Press, 1964.

Barrett, C. K. "Christianity at Corinth." *BJRL* 46 (1964): 269–97.

———. *Luke the Historian in Recent Study*. Philadelphia: Fortress Press, Facet Books, 1970; London: Epworth Press, 1961.

———, ed. *The New Testament Background: Selected Documents*. New York: Harper & Row, Harper Torchbooks, 1961.

———. "Paul's Opponents in Second Corinthians." *NTS* 17 (1971): 233–54.

Beare, Francis W. "First Letter to the Thessalonians." In *IDB*, vol. 4, pp. 621–25. Nashville: Abingdon Press, 1962.

———. "Letter to the Romans." In *IDB*, vol. 4, pp. 112–22. Nashville: Abingdon Press, 1962.

Berger, Peter. *The Sacred Canopy: Elements of a Sociological Theory of Religion*. New York: Doubleday & Co., 1969.

Betz, Hans Dieter. "Galatians." In *IDBS*, pp. 252–53. Nashville: Abingdon Press, 1976.

Bickerman, Elias. *From Ezra to the Last of the Maccabees: Foundations of Post-Biblical Judaism*. New York: Schocken Books, 1978.

Blau, L. "Holy Spirit." In *Jewish Encyclopedia*, 1st ed., vol. 6, edited by Isidore Singer, pp. 47–50. New York and London: Funk and Wagnalls Co., 1904.

Boomershine, Thomas E. "The Structure of Narrative Rhetoric in Genesis 2–3." *Semeia* 18 (1980): 113–29.

Bornkamm, Gunther. *Paul*. Eng. trans. D. M. G. Stalker. New York: Harper & Row; London: Hodder & Stoughton, 1971.

Bouttier, Michel. *Christianity According to Paul*. Eng. trans. Frank Clarke. SBT 49. Naperville, Ill.: Alec R. Allenson; London: SCM Press, 1966.

Brandon, S. G. F. *Jesus and the Zealots: A Study of the Political Factor in Primitive Christianity*. New York: Charles Scribner's Sons; Manchester: University of Manchester Press, 1967.

Bremond, Claude. "The Narrative Message." *Semeia* 10 (1978): 5–55.

Brisson, Luc. *Le Mythe de Tiresias*. Leiden: E. J. Brill, 1976.

Brown, Norman O. *Love's Body*. New York: Random House, 1966.

Bruce, F. F. *Paul: Apostle of the Heart Set Free*. Grand Rapids: Wm. B. Eerdmans, 1978.

Bultmann, Rudolf. *Primitive Christianity: In Its Contemporary Setting*. Eng. trans. Reginald H. Fuller. New York: Meridian Books, 1956; Philadelphia: Fortress Press, 1980.

———. *Theology of the New Testament*. 2 vols. Eng. trans. K. Groebel. New York: Charles Scribner's Sons, 1951.

Calloud, Jean. *Structural Analysis of the Narrative*. Semeia Studies. Philadelphia: Fortress Press; Chico, Calif.: Scholars Press, 1976.

Charles, R. H. *The Apocrypha and Pseudepigrapha of the Old Testament*. 2 vols. Oxford: At the Clarendon Press, 1913.

Cook, Michael J. "Early Rabbinic Judaism." In *IDBS*, pp. 499–505. Nashville: Abingdon Press, 1976.

———. "Hellenistic Judaism." In *IDBS*, pp. 505–9. Nashville: Abingdon Press, 1976.

Corti, Maria. *An Introduction to Literary Semiotics*. Eng. trans. Margherita Bogat and Alan Mandelbaum. Bloomington, Ind.: Indiana University Press, 1978.

Crespy, Georges. "The Parable of the Good Samaritan: An Essay in Structural Research." *Semeia* 2 (1974): 27–50.

Crossan, John D. "The Good Samaritan: Towards a Generic Definition of Parable." *Semeia* 2 (1974): 82–112.

Culley, Robert C. "Action Sequences in Genesis 2–3." *Semeia* 18 (1980): 25–33.

Cullmann, Oscar. *Salvation in History*. Eng. trans. Sidney G. Sowers. New York: Harper & Row; London: SCM Press, 1967.

Davies, W. D. *Paul and Rabbinic Judaism: Some Rabbinic Elements in Pauline Theology*. 4th ed. Philadelphia: Fortress Press; London: SPCK, 1980.

———. "Presidential Address: Paul and the People of Israel." *NTS* 24 (1977): 4–39.

Detweiler, R. "Generative Poetics as Science and Fiction." *Semeia* 10 (1978): 137–50.

Dibelius, Martin. "The Acts of the Apostles as an Historical Source." In *Studies in the Acts of the Apostles*. Edited by Heinrich Greeven. Eng. trans. Mary Ling. New York: Charles Scribner's Sons; London: SCM Press, 1956.

Donfried, Karl P., ed. *The Romans Debate: Essays on the Origins and Purpose of the Epistle*. Minneapolis: Augsburg Publishing House, 1977.

Doty, William G. *Letters in Primitive Christianity*. GBS. Philadelphia: Fortress Press, 1973.

———. "The Parables of Jesus, Kafka, Borges, and Others, with Structural Observations," *Semeia* 2 (1974): 152–93.

Duncan, George S. "Letter to the Philippians." In *IDB*, vol. 3, pp. 787–91. Nashville: Abingdon Press, 1962.

Dungan, David. *The Sayings of Jesus in the Churches of Paul*. Philadelphia: Fortress Press, 1971.

Dupont-Sommer, A. *The Essene Writings from Qumran*. Eng. trans. Geza Vermes. New York: World Publishing Co., 1962.

Eco, Umberto. *A Theory of Semiotics*. Bloomington, Ind.: Indiana University Press, 1976.

Ellis, E. Earle. *Paul's Use of the Old Testament*. Grand Rapids: Baker Book House, 1981; Edinburgh: Oliver & Boyd, 1957.

Enslin, Morton Scott. *The Ethics of Paul*. Nashville: Abingdon Press, 1957.

The Entrevernes Group. *Signs and Parables: Semiotics and Gospel Texts*. PTMS 23. Eng. trans. Gary Phillips. Pittsburgh: Pickwick Press, 1978.

Epictetus. *The Discourses as Reported by Arrian, the Manual and Fragments*, 2 vols. Eng. trans. W. A. Oldfather. Cambridge, Mass.: Harvard University Press; London: W. Heinemann, 1926.

Farmer, William. "Zealot." In *IDB*, vol. 4, pp. 936–39. Nashville: Abingdon Press, 1962.

Fitzmyer, Joseph, "The Letter to Philemon." In *JBC*, pp. 332–33. Englewood Cliffs, N.J.: Prentice-Hall, 1968.

———. "The Letter to the Galatians." In *JBC*, pp. 236–46. Englewood Cliffs, N.J.: Prentice-Hall, 1968.

———. "The Letter to the Philippians." In *JBC*, pp. 247–53. Englewood Cliffs, N.J.: Prentice-Hall, 1968.

———. "The Letter to the Romans." In *JBC*, pp. 291–331. Englewood Cliffs, N.J.: Prentice-Hall, 1968.

Forstell, J. T. "The Letters to the Thessalonians." In *JBC*, pp. 227–33. Englewood Cliffs, N.J.: Prentice-Hall, 1968.

Foucault, Michel. *The Birth of the Clinic: An Archaeology of Medical Perception*. New York: Vintage Books, 1973; London: Tavistock Publications, 1976.

Funk, Robert W. "The Apostolic Parousia: Form and Significance." In *Christian History and Interpretation: Studies Presented to John Knox*. Edited by William R. Farmer et al. Cambridge: At the University Press, 1967.

———. "The Good Samaritan as Metaphor." *Semeia* 2 (1974): 74–81.

———. "Structure in the Narrative Parables of Jesus." *Semeia* 2 (1974): 57–73.

Furnish, Victor P. *The Moral Teaching of Paul*. Nashville: Abingdon Press, 1979.

———. *Theology and Ethics in Paul*. Nashville: Abingdon Press, 1968.

Georgi, Dieter. "First Letter to the Corinthians." In *IDBS*, pp. 180–83. Nashville: Abingdon Press, 1976.

———. "Second Letter to the Corinthians." In *IDBS*, pp. 183–86. Nashville: Abingdon Press, 1976.

Gilmour, S. MacLean. "First Letter to the Corinthians." In *IDB*, vol. 1, pp. 684–92. Nashville: Abingdon Press, 1962.

———. "Second Letter to the Corinthians." In *IDB*, vol. 1, pp. 692–98. Nashville: Abingdon Press, 1962.

Goodenough, Erwin R. *Introduction to Philo Judaeus*. New Haven: Yale University Press, 1940; London: Oxford University Press, 1940. (2d rev. ed. New York: Barnes & Noble, 1963; Oxford: Basil Blackwell, 1962.)

———. "Philo Judeus." In *IDB*, vol. 3, pp. 796–99. Nashville: Abingdon Press, 1962.

Grant, Frederick C. *Roman Hellenism and the New Testament*. New York: Charles Scribner's Sons, 1962.

Greimas, A. J. "Pour une sémiotique didactique," *Bull*. 7 (January 1979).

Greimas, A. J., and Courtés, J. *Semiotics and Language: An Analytical Dictionary*. Eng. trans. L. Crist, Daniel Patte, et al. Bloomington, Ind.: Indiana University Press, 1982.

Greimas, A. J., and Landowski, E., eds. *Introduction à l'analyse du discours en sciences sociales*. Paris: Hachette, 1979.

Guern, Michel Le. *Sémantique de la métaphore et de la métonymie*. Paris: Larousse, 1973.

Güttgemanns, Erhardt. "Introductory Remarks Concerning the Structural Study of Narrative." Eng. trans. William G. Doty. *Semeia* 6 (1976): 23–125.

———. "Linguistic Literary Critical Foundation of a New Testament Theology." Eng. trans. William G. Doty. *Semeia* 6 (1976): 181–220.

———. "Narrative Analysis of Synoptic Texts." Eng. trans. William G. Doty. *Semeia* 6 (1976): 127–79.

———. "What Is 'Generative Poetics'? Theses and Reflections Concerning a New Exegetical Method." Eng. trans. William G. Doty. *Semeia* 6 (1976): 1–21.

Haenchen, Ernst. "The Book of Acts as Source Material for the History of Early Christianity." In *Studies in Luke-Acts*, edited by Leander E. Keck and G. Louis Martyn. Philadelphia: Fortress Press, 1980.

Hanson, Paul D. *The Dawn of Apocalyptic: The Historical and Sociological Roots of Jewish Apocalyptic Eschatology*. Philadelphia: Fortress Press, 1975.

Harvey, Van A. *The Historian and the Believer: The Morality of Historical Knowledge and Christian Beliefs*. Philadelphia: Westminster Press, 1981.

Hawkes, Terence. *Structuralism and Semiotics*. Berkeley and Los Angeles: University of California Press; London: Methuen & Co., 1977.

Hay, David. *Glory at the Right Hand: Psalm 110 in Early Christianity*. Nashville: Abingdon Press, 1973.

Hengel, Martin. *Acts and the History of Earliest Christianity*. Eng. trans. John Bowden. Philadelphia: Fortress Press, 1980; London: SCM Press, 1979.

Herford, R. Travers. *Pharisaism: Its Aims and Its Methods*. New York: G. P. Putnam's Sons, 1912.

Holmberg, Bengt. *Paul and Power: The Structure of Authority in the Primi-*

*tive Church as Reflected in the Pauline Epistles*. Philadelphia: Fortress Press, 1980.

Hurd, John C. "First Letter to the Thessalonians." In *IDBS*, p. 900. Nashville: Abingdon Press, 1976.

———. *The Origin of 1 Corinthians*. London: S.P.C.K., 1965.

Jewett, Robert. *A Chronology of Paul's Life*. Philadelphia: Fortress Press; London: SCM Press, 1979.

Jobling, David, "The Myth Semantics of Genesis 2:4b—3:24." *Semeia* 18 (1980): 41–49.

Kadushin, Max. *Organic Thinking: A Study in Rabbinic Thought*. New York: Bloch Publishing Co., 1938, 1976.

Käsemann, Ernst. *Jesus Means Freedom*. Eng. trans. Frank Clarke. Philadelphia: Fortress Press, 1970; London: SCM Press, 1969.

———. *New Testament Questions of Today*. Eng. trans. W. J. Montague. Philadelphia: Fortress Press; London: SCM Press, 1969.

———. *Perspectives on Paul*. Eng. trans. Margaret Kohl. Philadelphia: Fortress Press; London: SCM Press, 1971.

Keck, Leander E. *Paul and His Letters*. Philadelphia: Fortress Press, 1979.

Kee, Howard C. *The Origins of Christianity: Sources and Documents*. Englewood Cliffs, N.J.: Prentice-Hall, 1973.

Kittel, Gerhard, and Friedrich, Gerhard, eds. *Theological Dictionary of the New Testament*. 10 vols. Eng. trans. Geoffrey W. Bromiley. Grand Rapids: Wm. B. Eerdmans, 1964–76; London: SCM Press, 1964–77.

Klausner, Joseph. *From Jesus to Paul*. Eng. trans. William F. Stinespring. Boston: Beacon Press, 1961.

Klein, Günter. "Letter to the Romans." In *IDBS*, pp. 752–54. Nashville: Abingdon Press, 1976.

Knox, John. *Chapters in a Life of Paul*. Nashville: Abingdon Press, 1950.

———. "Galatians." In *IDB*, vol. 2, pp. 338–43. Nashville: Abingdon Press, 1962.

———. *Philemon among the Letters of Paul: A New View of Its Place and Importance*. Nashville: Abingdon Press, 1959.

Koester, Helmut. "Letter to the Philippians." In *IDBS*, pp. 665–66. Nashville: Abingdon Press, 1976.

Kovacs, Brian W. "Philosophical Foundations for Structuralism." *Semeia* 10 (1978): 85–105.

Kugelman, Richard. "The First Letter to the Corinthians." In *JBC*, pp. 254–75. Englewood Cliffs, N.J.: Prentice-Hall, 1968.

Kuhn, Thomas. *The Structure of Scientific Revolutions*. 2d ed. Chicago: University of Chicago Press, 1970.

Kümmel, Werner G. *Introduction to the New Testament*. Rev. ed. Nashville: Abingdon Press, 1975.

Lauterbach, Jacob Z. *Rabbinic Essays*. Cincinnati: Hebrew Union College, 1951.

Lévi-Strauss, Claude. *The Raw and the Cooked: An Introduction to the Science of Mythology*. New York: Harper & Row, 1969.

————. *Structural Anthropology*. Eng. trans. C. Jacobson and B. Schoepf. New York: Basic Books, 1963.

Lindars, Barnabas. *New Testament Apologetic*. London: SCM Press, 1961.

Loew, C. *Myth, Sacred History, and Philosophy*. New York: Harcourt Brace Jovanovich, 1967.

Lüdemann, Gerd. *Paulus, der Heidenapostel*. Vol. 1: *Studien zur Chronologie*. Göttingen: Vandenhoeck & Ruprecht, 1980. English translation forthcoming from Fortress Press.

————. *Paulus, der Heidenapostel*. Vol. 2: *Antipaulinismus im frühen Christentum*. Göttingen: Vandenhoeck & Ruprecht, 1982. English translation forthcoming from Fortress Press.

Luther, Martin. "Lectures on Galatians." In *Luther's Works*, vols. 26 and 27, edited by Jaroslav Pelikan. St. Louis: Concordia Publishing House, 1964.

————. "Preface to the Epistle of Saint Paul to Philemon" (1546). In *Luther's Works*, vol. 35, edited by E. Theodore Bachmann. Philadelphia: Fortress Press, 1960.

Lyman, Mary Ely. "Letter to Philemon." In *IDB*, vol. 3, pp. 782–84. Nashville: Abingdon Press, 1962.

Malherbe, Abraham J. *The Cynic Epistles*. SBLSBT 12. Chico, Calif.: Scholars Press, 1977.

Manson, T. W. "St. Paul's Letter to the Romans—And Others." *BJRL* 31 (1948): 224–40.

Marcuse, Herbert. *Eros and Civilization*. New York: Random House, 1962.

Marshall, I. Howard. *Luke: Historian and Theologian*. Grand Rapids: Zondervan Publishing House, 1971; Exeter: Paternoster Press, 1979.

Marshall, L. H. *The Challenge of New Testament Ethics*. London: Macmillan & Co., 1956.

Marxsen, Willi. *Introduction to the New Testament: An Approach to its Problems*. Eng. trans. Geoffrey Buswell. Philadelphia: Fortress Press, 1970; Oxford: Basil Blackwell, 1968.

McKnight, Edgar V. "Generative Poetics as New Testament Hermeneutics." *Semeia* 10 (1978): 107–21.

*Mekilta de-Rabbi Ishmael*. 3 vols. Edited and translated by Jacob Z. Lauterbach. Philadelphia: Jewish Publication Society of America, 1933–35.

Meyer, Paul W. "Romans 10:4 and the 'End' of the Law." In *The Divine Helmsman: Studies on God's Control of Human Events*, edited by James L. Crenshaw and Samuel Sandmel, pp. 59–78. New York: Ktav, 1980.

Minear, Paul. *The Obedience of Faith: The Purpose of Paul in the Epistle to the Romans*. Naperville, Ill.: Alec R. Allenson, 1971.

*Mishnah*. Eng. trans. Herbert Danby. New York and London: Oxford University Press, 1933.

Moody-Smith, D. "The Use of the Old Testament in the New." In *The Use of the Old Testament in the New*, Festschrift for William F. Stinespring, edited by James M. Efrid, pp. 3–65. Durham, N.C.: Duke University Press, 1972.

Moore, George Foote. *Judaism in the First Centuries of the Christian Era*. 3 vols. Cambridge, Mass.: Harvard University Press, 1927–30.

Munck, Johannes. *Paul and the Salvation of Mankind*. Eng. trans. Frank Clarke. Atlanta: John Knox Press, 1977; London: SCM Press, 1959.

Murphy-O'Connor, Jerome. "Non-Pauline Character of 1 Cor. 11:2–16?" *JBL* 95 (1976): 615–21.

Neusner, Jacob. *Between Time and Eternity: The Essentials of Judaism*. Belmont, Calif.: Dickenson Publishing Co., 1975.

———. *First-Century Judaism in Crisis: Yohanan Ben Zakkai and the Renaissance of Torah*. Nashville: Abingdon Press, 1975.

———. *From Politics to Piety: The Emergence of Pharisaic Judaism*. Englewood Cliffs, N.J.: Prentice-Hall, 1973.

———. *Method and Meaning in Ancient Judaism*. Brown Judaic Series. Missoula, Mont.: Scholars Press, 1979.

O'Rourke, John J. "The Second Letter to the Corinthians." In *JBC*, pp. 276–90. Englewood Cliffs, N.J.: Prentice-Hall, 1968.

Pagels, Elaine. *The Gnostic Paul: Gnostic Exegesis of the Pauline Letters*. Philadelphia: Fortress Press, 1975.

———. "Paul and Women: A Response to a Recent Discussion." *JAAR* 42 (1974): 538–49.

Parzen, H. "The *Ruah Hakodesh* in Tannaitic Literature." *JQR* 20 (1929): 51–76.

Patte, Daniel. "An Analysis of Narrative Structure and the Good Samaritan." *Semeia* 2 (1974): 1–26.

———. *Aspects of a Semiotics of Didactic Discourse: Analysis of 1 Thessalonians*. Urbino, Italy: Center for Semiotic Studies, 1980.

———. *Early Jewish Hermeneutic in Palestine*. SBLDS 22. Chico, Calif.: Scholars Press, 1975.

———. "Greimas' Model for the Generative Trajectory of Meaning in Discourses." *AJS* 3 (1982):59–78.

———. "One Text: Several Structures." *Semeia* 18 (1980): 3–22.

———. "Preface." In *Signs and Parables: Semiotics and Gospel Texts*, edited by the Entrevernes Group. PTMS 23. Eng. trans. Gary Phillips, pp. xv–xx. Pittsburgh: Pickwick Press, 1978.

———. "Universal Narrative Structures and Semantic Frameworks." *Semeia* 10 (1978): 123–35.

———. *What Is Structural Exegesis?* GBS. Philadelphia: Fortress Press, 1976.

———, ed. *Genesis 2 and 3: Kaleidoscopic Structural Readings*. *Semeia* 18 (1980).

Patte, Daniel, and Parker, Judson F. "A Structural Exegesis of Genesis 2–3." *Semeia* 18 (1980): 55–75.

Patte, Daniel, and Patte, Aline. *Structural Exegesis: From Theory to Practice*. Philadelphia: Fortress Press, 1978.

Pearson, Birger A. "1 Thessalonians 2:13–16: A Deutero-Pauline Interpolation." *HTR* 64 (1971): 79–94.

Perrin, Norman. *The New Testament: An Introduction*. New York: Harcourt Brace Jovanovich, 1974.

Propp, Vladimir. "Structure and History in the Study of the Fairy Tale." *Semeia* 10 (1978): 57–83.

Ramsey, Paul. *Basic Christian Ethics*. Chicago: University of Chicago Press, 1980.

Richardson, R. L., Jr. "The Function of the Scriptures in the Rise of the Easter Faith." Ph.D. dissertation, Vanderbilt University, 1972.

Rivkin, Ellis. "Defining the Pharisees: The Tannaitic Sources." *Hebrew Union College Annual* 40–41 (1969–70): 205–49.

Robinson, Benjamin W. *The Life of Paul*. 2d ed. Chicago: University of Chicago Press, 1928.

Ropes, James H. *The Singular Problem of the Epistle to the Galatians*. Cambridge, Mass.: Harvard University Press, 1929.

Roszack, Theodore. *The Making of a Counter Culture*. New York: Doubleday & Co., 1969; London: Faber & Faber, 1970.

Russell, D. S. *Apocalyptic: Ancient and Modern*. Philadelphia: Fortress Press; London: SCM Press, 1978.

———. *The Method and Message of Jewish Apocalyptic*. Philadelphia: Westminster Press; London: SCM Press, 1964.

Sanders, E. P. *Paul and Palestinian Judaism: A Comparison of Patterns of Religion*. Philadelphia: Fortress Press; London: SCM Press, 1977.

Sanders, Jack T. *The New Testament Christological Hymns*. SNTSMS 15. Cambridge: At the University Press, 1971.

Sandmel, Samuel. *The Genius of Paul: A Study in History*. Philadelphia: Fortress Press, 1979.

———. *Philo of Alexandria*. New York: Oxford University Press, 1979.

Sartre, Jean-Paul. *Being and Nothingness*. Eng. trans. H. Barnes. New York: Pocket Books, 1956; London: Methuen & Co., 1969.

———. *La Putain Respectueuse*. Paris: Nagel, 1946.

Schlatter, Adolph. *Paulus der Bote Jesu*. 2d ed. Stuttgart: Calwer Verlag, 1956.

Schmithals, Walter. *Gnosticism in Corinth: An Investigation of the Letters to the Corinthians*. Eng. trans. John E. Steely. Nashville: Abingdon Press, 1971.

———. *Paul and the Gnostics*. Eng. trans. John E. Steely. Nashville: Abingdon Press, 1972.

Schoeps, Hans J. *Paul: The Theology of the Apostle in the Light of Jewish Religious History*. Eng. trans. Harold Knight. Philadelphia: Westminster Press, 1961.

Scholes, Robert. *Structuralism in Literature: An Introduction*. New Haven: Yale University Press, 1974.

Schroeder, David. "Lists, Ethical." In *IDBS*, pp. 546–47. Nashville: Abingdon Press, 1976.

Schütz, J. H. *Paul and the Anatomy of Apostolic Authority*. SNTSMS 26. Cambridge: At the University Press, 1975.

Schweitzer, Albert. *The Quest of the Historical Jesus: A Critical Study of Its Progress from Reimarus to Wrede*. Eng. trans. W. Montgomery. New York:

Macmillan Co., 1968.

Scroggs, Robin. "Paul and the Eschatological Woman." *JAAR* 40 (1972): 283–303.

———. "Paul and the Eschatological Woman: Revisited." *JAAR* 42 (1974): 532–37.

———. "Paul: Chauvinist or Liberationist?" *CC* 89 (March 15, 1972): 307–9.

———. *Paul for a New Day*. Philadelphia: Fortress Press, 1977.

Seitz, Oscar J. F. "Lists, Ethical." In *IDB*, vol. 3, pp. 137–39. Nashville: Abingdon Press, 1962.

Silberman, Lou H. "Judaism." In *Encyclopedia Britannica*, 15th ed., Maropaedia, vol. 10, pp. 284–302. Chicago: University of Chicago Press, 1974.

———. "A Midrash on Midrash." Paper circulated at the meeting of Studiorum Novi Testamentum Societas, Amsterdam, 1971. Mimeographed.

———. "Unriddling the Riddle: A Study of the Structure and Language of the Habakkuk Pesher." *RQ* 11 (1961): 323–64.

Stein, Joseph. *Fiddler on the Roof*. New York: Pocket Books, 1965.

Stendahl, Krister. "The Apostle Paul and the Introspective Conscience of the West." In *Paul Among Jews and Gentiles*. Philadelphia: Fortress Press, 1976; London: SCM Press, 1977. Also in *HTR* 56 (1963): 199–215.

Strack, Hermann L. *Introduction to the Talmud and Mishnah*. New York: Atheneum, 1969.

Streng, Frederick J. *Understanding Religious Life*. 2d ed. Encino, Calif.: Dickenson Publishing Co., 1976.

Toulmin, Stephen. *The Uses of Argument*. Cambridge: At the University Press, 1958.

Vermes, Geza. *The Dead Sea Scrolls in English*. New York: Penguin Books, 1962.

Walker, William O. "1 Corinthians 11:2–16 and Paul's Views Regarding Women." *JBL* 94 (1975): 94–110.

Wedderburn, A. J. M. "Keeping up with Recent Studies, VIII, Some Recent Pauline Chronologies." *ET*, January 1981.

White, Hugh. "Direct and Third Person Discourse in the Narrative of the 'Fall.'" *Semeia* 18 (1980): 91–106.

Whiteley, D. E. H. *The Theology of Paul*. Philadelphia: Fortress Press; Oxford: Basil Blackwell, 1964.

Wilder, Amos N. "The Parable of the Sower: Naiveté and Method in Interpretation." *Semeia* 2 (1974): 134–51.

Wolfson, Harry A. *Philo: Foundations of Religious Philosophy in Judaism, Christianity, and Islam*. Cambridge, Mass.: Harvard University Press, 1947.

# Indexes

## INDEX OF SUBJECTS

## INDEX OF BIBLICAL PASSAGES